Readings in Social Psychology

Harry Kaufmann
Hunter College, City University of New York

Linda Zener Solomon
Baruch College, City University of New York.

HOLT, RINEHART AND WINSTON, INC.
New York   Chicago   San Francisco   Atlanta
Dallas   Montreal   Toronto   London   Sydney

Introduction

A book of readings can serve several purposes:
1. It is a useful complement to a formal text;
2. It can serve as an adjunct to the instructor's lectures without a basic text;
3. It may serve as a sample display, from which instructor and students may select, cafeteria style, only those articles which are of interest to them. These would be, one hopes, points of departure for further study.
4. Finally, a book of readings can be a showcase: It can present some typical areas of a discipline by means of "classical" articles, that is, those articles which by consensus have contributed strongly to further research in the area, and which can be considered to be substantial contributions to knowledge even if they are dated.

This book tries to fit all of these uses, even though the authors recognize that they cannot hope to succeed at any single endeavor as well as if it had been their only one.

Most articles in this book should fit in well with most of the major texts, but are also illustrative and wide-ranging enough to stand side by side with an instructor's lectures without a formal text. The articles are, of course, *samples* of a wide-ranging discipline not even a five-volume handbook (Lindzey and Aronson, 1968–1969) can hope to fully illumine; if they serve to whet the appetite and induce the reader to further research, their purpose is well served. Such a reader will unavoidably feel disappointed because certain important articles are not included here, but even such disappointment can serve as a motivator for further study.

Finally, a considerable proportion of the articles are what many psychologists would consider to be "classics." Sometimes such classic studies have been superseded by more recent work which either replicates the earlier study with more precise controls, or casts strong doubts upon the generalizability of the earlier findings. In those cases, the more recent studies have been substituted. But the emphasis of the book is on "milestones."

There is one further desirable purpose to a book of readings: that of presenting the very latest findings in one or more areas. As a glance at the table of contents will show, we have not ignored the present in favor of the past. But we have not made it our primary purpose to compete with the latest issue of a professional journal. To have done so would, first of all, have been an effort doomed to failure from the start, for such a book would have to have several new editions each year. Besides, an excessive concern with the latest work can, for the student, lead easily to the neglect, even ignorance of the indispensable body of work that has led up to it. A discipline is not a fad or a fashion.

The readings are organized into a number of parts. This division is partly one of logic, partly one of convenience: It reflects some of the major areas in social psychology. It should be kept in mind, however, that most of the articles could easily fit under diverse supraheadings.

Part 1 is a very brief look at the rationale of conducting an experiment and drawing conclusions therefrom. It lays claim to little more than answering the question: "Does it really make any sense at all to do 'an experiment' and if so, why?"

Part 2 deals with the topic of socialization, an area which overlaps into the discipline of developmental psychology. But the emphasis here is on the socialization of black children, not because the authors wished to be condescending, ingratiating, or "with it," but because these studies are particularly effective in illustrating how not only parents, but society in general, shape and influence the growing individual.

Part 3 concerns the formation and organization of attitudes. In our daily conversation we use the term "attitude" in many ways, and psychologists too have differed in their definitions. For the present, it suffices to assume that an attitude contains an element of liking or disliking toward its object, a belief about it, and at least a latent readiness to "do something about" translating these feelings and beliefs into some kind of action.

Part 4 deals with another major topic: How do people perceive one another and what makes them like or dislike one another? This definition illustrates what has been said above: Topics are not necessarily clearly separable. Is there a clear difference between how we *perceive* our friends and what makes us *like* or *dislike* them on the one hand, and our attitude toward them? Probably not. Yet, there is usefulness in the separation of the two topics. Perception and attitude often go together, but not always. We do have attitudes toward such concepts as "punctuality" or "general disarmament," which are obviously not amenable to perception. Conversely, it is important to find out the determinants that make us perceive another person as possessing certain attributes, even though this *perception* in turn leads to *attitudes* toward that person or what he represents. (As we shall see, the obverse also happens: Existing attitudes influence the attributes we perceive in another person.)

Part 5 deals with man's behavior—frequently, alas, man's inhumanity —to man. Fortunately, man can also be altruistic, though not as often as we would hope.

Part 6 examines the topic often thought to be the sole one with which social psychology is concerned, that of interactions between the individual and the groups to which he belongs, and interactions among groups. How do such groups function? What are some of the determinants that make a person submit to group pressure, direct or covert? And last but not least, what are the incentives for submerging one's individuality in a crowd or mob?

Most articles are discussed and amplified at some length. It is the primary purpose of these commentaries to enable the student to read an article written by a professional for his colleagues without a bowdlerization which is self-defeating in that the student is never challenged to increase his ability to read the professional literature. The commentaries precede their respective articles, but it will usually be desirable to read the commentary before and after reading the article, in order to benefit fully from both. Usually, the formal journal article is arranged under the following headings:

Introduction. This is the first section of the report and is given no heading. In the introduction, the author poses the problem, sketches any relevant previous research, and describes relevant theory. He discusses why he did the study, and what problem he hoped to solve. Finally, he describes his hunches, hypotheses, and predictions.

Method. Here the author describes what he did in his study. The method is divided into some or all of these sections: subjects, instruments or materials, procedure. The author describes in detail the composition of his sample, his experimental setting, the instructions given to subjects, and the tasks performed by the subjects.

Results. Here the author gives an objective, detailed report of the results of his study. Both descriptive and inferential statistics may be reported, the first being a summary of the data (e.g. means, medians, variances), the second, a means of determining the statistical significance of results.

Discussion. In the discussion, the author interprets the data and draws conclusions from them. He refers his results to the introduction section, and discusses the extent to which he has fulfilled his objectives or supported the theory cited. He also compares his results to those of previous studies, and tries to account for differences and contradictions. If relevant, he may discuss his method, its adequacies or inadequacies, and any particular features of it which may have accounted for his results. The discussion is an open-ended section. The author may use it for almost any purpose, including conjectures on future research.

In reading the articles and notes, try to develop a "set" of what to look for in a journal article; you will want to be aware of the different ways in which research expands and proceeds, of the various possible procedures used in human research, both laboratory and field, and of the experiment as a social situation. You will want to have some basis for evaluation of later articles, using criteria such as: significance of the topic, relevance of the procedures to the purpose, extent of generalizability of the results, justifiability of the conclusions drawn from the results, and unintended factors affecting the results.

Before beginning the articles, you should be aware of the format that is often used for a journal article. This has been described for you above. In addition, you might need to have some understanding of statistical techniques in order to be able to understand and evaluate research results. With this in mind, the editors have included some discussion of the uses of descriptive and inferential statistics in the succeeding section. It is hoped that the brief discussion will jog your statistical memory sufficiently to enable you to cope with the results sections of the articles. Should you feel that a book on experimental design and analysis would be helpful, Winer's *Statistical Principles in Experimental Design* (1962) or Edwards' *Experimental Design in Psychological Research* (1969) are recommended. For an abbreviated treatment, you might look at Sarbin and Coe's *The Student Psychologist's Handbook* (1969).

As a final introductory note, you should be aware that, when you find a special interest in an area, it is always possible for you to trace the work done on a particular topic, or by a particular author, using the *Psychological Abstracts*. As part of your journal-reading experience, you might become familiar with this periodical source of information. The abstracts generally are found in the reference or periodicals section of the school library. The index is divided in two ways: subject, and author, and will lead you to a summary of almost any article published in a psychological journal (with the exception of doctoral theses published only in the *Dissertation Abstracts,* a publication also available in most reference or periodical rooms). Other sources of information are the *Handbook of Social Psychology* (Lindzey and Aronson, 1969), and the *Advances in Experimental Social Psychology* (Berkowitz, continuing series). Also, several paperback series provide short works on a number of social psychological topics.

References

Berkowitz, L. (Ed.) *Advances in experimental social psychology.* 5 vols. New York: Academic Press.

Edwards, A. L. *Experimental design in psychological research* (3d ed.). New York: Holt, Rinehart and Winston, 1969.

Lindzey, G. & Aronson, E. (Eds.) *Handbook of social psychology.* (2d ed., 5 vols.) Reading, Mass.: Addison-Wesley, 1969.

Sarbin, T. R. & Coe, W. C. *The student psychologist's handbook.* Cambridge, Mass.: Schenkman Publishing Co., 1969.

Winer, B. J. *Statistical principles in experimental design.* New York: McGraw-Hill, 1962.

Contents

PART 1

A Much Abbreviated Guide to Research and Statistical Vocabulary

RESEARCH DESIGN

Experiments versus "Uncontrolled" Studies

There is one great advantage to the experiment which cannot be emphasized too strongly: Only a procedure in which the independent variables are fully known can generate laws of causal, as opposed to correlational, relationships. For, no matter how frequently we observe x and y occurring together, we can never know whether

(a) x causes y;
(b) y causes x;
(c) z causes x and z causes y,

i.e., both x and y are caused by a third variable.

How does a science grow in terms of the precision of its statements? Initially, the observer (who is as yet only a proto-scientist) is content to observe events in nature, as they occur. Soon, he may, on the basis of his cumulative observations, formulate partially defined theories. But because he has as yet no sufficiently precise formulations to warrant minute and carefully controlled experimentation, or because technology has not yet devised appropriate equipment, he may choose to let Nature carry out his experiment. (In some instances, Nature will always have to remain the "Experimenter," as when we wish to study the effects of galactic movements upon a light spectrum.)

At a third stage the scientist should have tested and refined his theories to the point where he is in a position to make fairly precise predictions. At that stage it is then also usually the case that the presumed independent variables have to be administered with meticulous care, in order to avoid undesirable influences by unsuspected extraneous factors.

Finally, however, a fourth stage in the scientist's inquiry is reached: He has now discovered some of the basic laws with great precision. But life involves a good deal more than basic laws: usually a great many variables act together, producing the very complex state of affairs in which organisms normally exist. It is necessary, therefore, to observe the objects of study in a natural setting; but it is important to keep in mind that, at this stage, such natural "observation" takes place with a great deal more information than at Stage Two: Now the scientist has available some well verified laws relating some of the more important variables which he is now observing in a more complex setting, and can utilize this knowledge to formulate complex hypotheses suitable for the complex, natural situation he is observing.

A simple and plausible instance is afforded by scholastic achievement. At the first stage, we send our children to school. They learn, but we do not really know whether they could learn more efficiently, or with less resentment, and whether what they learn contributes to the goals established for them.

This lingering sense of uncertainty may induce us to observe our children's learning experiences more carefully. At this second stage we may notice that certain teachers "do better than others." But why is it so? Is the teacher friendlier, better informed, does he speak more (or less), is he older, is "he" conceivably a "she," that is does the sex of the teacher make a difference? Or is it possible that the "better" teacher is more successful because he has better equipment or a more evenly heated classroom? How can we be sure that he did not start out with better prepared students?

This is Stage Three. Whether we design classroom situations to suit our purposes precisely or utilize minimal learning situations in a "pure" laboratory setting is of only peripheral importance. What matters is that if we think that a teacher's friendliness (defined, say, by the amount of his smiling) affects learning, regardless of his other characteristics, or those which may differentiate the environment or the students themselves, we have a situation in which that aspect of the teacher's performance is systematically varied, and all other possible "confounding" factors are carefully controlled. An experiment is usually necessary to answer a question of this sort.

Finally, at the fourth stage, there is little doubt that we should wish to check out—and eventually to apply—our experimental findings on academic learning in real-life classrooms. We now look for generalizability, ecological validity, and practicality.

The following example is both more complex and more closely related to social psychological issues:

The reactions of people to situations of stress have long intrigued historians, philosophers, theologians, and, of course, social scientists. At the first stage of naive observation, we encounter writings of early historians recounting the behavior of men under tyranny, and how a people fearful of its leader would act in a number of "unusual" ways.

At the second stage, men like Machiavelli would formulate some general ideas as to what acts of a political leader might lead to contentment, fear, or rebellion on the part of his followers.

Stage Three belongs to social psychology. Here, we wish to know precisely what aspect of a leader's role, such as his warmth, his knowledgeability, or his "legitimacy" (that is, whether he has attained power by due process or through usurpation), etc., elicits certain responses from his subjects. This means that these separate attributes of a leader have to be assessable separately while keeping constant, or controlling for, yet other attributes in which we may not be interested at the time, such as the subjects' age or education. Thus, the social psychologist designs experiments in which he "controls for" all variables varying only, say, the leader's legitimacy and his ostensible knowledgeability, or how good he seems to be at his job.

The effect of these two variables upon, say, "liking for the leader," might be examined by means of the following experimental design:

	Leader's know-how	
	High	Low
Leader's ⎰ High	Group 1	Group 2
legitimacy ⎱ Low	Group 3	Group 4

in which only the two variables are varied (over two levels), and where all other variables are controlled for, through careful "matching" of incidental conditions (such as locale, temperature, etc.) and subjects (to make sure that the subjects in one group do not differ systematically from the others in their response to the leader). In addition, there is one type of control which is particularly difficult to attain: If we use four different leaders for the four conditions, how can we be sure that it is indeed the know-how and the legitimacy of the leader of Group I which affects his subjects in a given manner? It is surely conceivable that he, but not the other leaders, possesses a characteristic which is not related to the two variables under study, but nevertheless affects the dependent variable of "liking" very strongly. Perhaps he speaks too loudly, or wears a spotty tie, or (worst of all) exudes a cadaverous smell from his mouth.

What is the answer to this seemingly unsolvable drawback? Using the *same* leader enacting all four roles (or a number of leaders, each of whom assumes all of the roles at different times) provides a better approximation to an ideal answer than could be obtained in any "natural" situation.

But suppose that we now have a fairly good idea of the effects of some of the major attributes of a leader upon "liking" by his followers. The acid test (Stage Four) is still whether our hypotheses work not only in the laboratory, but in the real world, too.

DESCRIPTION AND ANALYSIS OF RESULTS

The mean. The mean is used to describe the central point, average, or "typical" score of a group of scores. It is obtained by summing all of the scores and dividing that sum by the number of scores.

The variance. The variance is used to describe the homogeneity or heterogeneity of a group of scores. Two groups with the same mean might differ in variance as for instance,

Group 1	Group 2
2	1
3	3
4	5

A graphic illustration of two groups with the same mean and unequal variances is as follows:

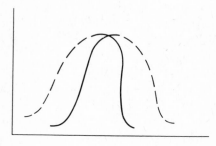

The standard deviation is the square root of the variance and has certain special properties which we will not go into here.

t test and analysis of variance.[1] The test most commonly used to assess the significance of a difference between two means is known as a t test. Using a statistical formula, the researcher finds the numerical value of "t" for his data; he then checks his t value in a table provided in most statistical texts to find the probability that his result was obtained by chance. (The importance of this was discussed above.)

A second technique for assessing differences between means is known as the analysis of variance. Results of the analysis of variance are circulated by means of formulae involving values of F's rather than t's. However, in

---

[1] The t test, analysis of variance, and product moment correlation are based upon certain statistical assumptions concerning the data which are beyond the scope of this briefest of overviews.

both cases, the researcher obtains the probability that the differences between the means are due to chance.

The advantage of the analysis of variance over the t test is that it can be used when either more than two means or more than one variable are involved. In cases of more than one variable, the analysis of variance allows computation, not only of a probability (p) value for each variable, but also a p value for each of the possible combinations or interactions of variables.

The correlation coefficients. A correlation refers to an association or relationship between two or more variables or measures. We have already noted that such an association tells us nothing about whether one variable *causes* the other. Most correlation measures are defined in such a manner that +1 represents a perfect positive relationship and −1 a perfect negative one. For a perfect positive relationship it is necessary that one variable increases as the other increases, regularly and at the same rate. Numerically, this might look as follows:

	Measure X	Measure Y
Person A	2	3
B	5	6
C	6	7
D	9	10

Graphically, the relationship would look like this:

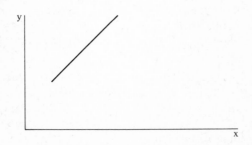

For the perfect negative correlation, it is necessary that the variables be related in the opposite, rather than the same, direction. As one variable decreases, the other must increase, with no deviations or exceptions. Numerically, an example would be:

	Measure 1	Measure 2
Person A	2	5
B	3	4
C	4	3
D	5	2

Graphically, this would appear as follows:

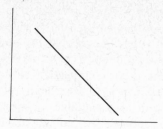

When a correlation is perfect, knowing a person's rank on one measure enables us to predict his rank on the other (since they must be the same). However, in real and in experimental life, it is just about impossible to find a perfect correlation (unless the two variables are really the same thing). Thus, most correlations are (positive or negative) decimal numbers smaller than ± 1; the closer the number is to ± 1, the stronger the relationship.

The Meaning of "Significance" in Statistical Inference

Usually, an experimental report will state that a certain finding was "significant at the .05 (or the .01) level." This means that if the conditions that are being compared "really" do not differ, that is, if they are drawn from the same population, then the obtained difference between the samples would occur no more than five times (or once) in 100 times on the average. Therefore, we conclude (at some risk of being wrong) that there exists a "true" difference, and that the two samples represent two different populations.

Also, we can easily see why it makes no sense to reduce too much the probability of making this type of error: Suppose we decide that we wish to be so certain of our findings that we will accept as indicating a "true" difference between populations only those differences between samples that are large enough to occur by chance but once in 1,000,000 times. We have now made it highly unlikely that we shall allow ourselves to be persuaded that a "true" difference indeed exists. But in doing so we have enormously increased the likelihood of overlooking a "true" difference, simply because our criterion may have become so stringent that the sample difference was not large enough to reach it.

The following simple example will illustrate this point: Suppose we want to know whether adult American males are, on the average, taller than adult American females of comparable socioeconomic and ethnic background.

We select random samples of 100 males and 100 females. (The randomness of selection, of course, must occur *within* the specifications stated above.) We obtain a mean height of 5′9″ for males and of 5′4″ for females (these are arbitrary, not census figures). Moreover, we know, by a simple statistical calculation, that such a difference between two means would occur only, say, once in 10,000 times *if* males and females in truth did not differ, and if, therefore, the present difference were a highly unlikely accident.

Now, we could declare that we have found reasons to believe that males are indeed taller than females. By doing so, we do run a small risk of being wrong. On the other hand, we can continue to believe that the height of males and females does not "truly" differ, because we have decided beforehand that the only evidence to the contrary that we will accept is a difference in sample means large enough to occur only once in 1,000,000 times by chance. Clearly, we do now run a considerable risk of ignoring some fairly persuasive evidence about differences in stature between males and females.

It is also clear that the two types of errors (called, respectively, type I error, or alpha, and type II error, or beta) are inextricably interdependent: Other things (such as sample size) being equal, a reduction of one automatically increases the other.

THE USES OF SIMULATION

A rather novel way of studying human behavior is by means of simulation. The term does not, as many think, imply deception or trickery. It simply means "to act as if." Actually, simulation is used in many situations where we do not even think about it. A little girl playing "house" is engaged in simulating the behavior of a housewife, however imperfectly. Thor Heyerdahl, in his famous books *Kon-Tiki* (1950) and *Aku-Aku* (1958), in his attempt to recreate the putative voyages of early South American peoples by using rafts similar to those they would have used, was engaged in simulation. Psychodrama, the enacting by emotionally disturbed people of their problems, is simulation.[2]

Now, suppose we wish to study a situation in which two individuals, groups, or nations, are in conflict, or perhaps have to find an optimal strategy for attaining a mutually beneficial goal which neither could attain singly.

---

[2] I would not classify true stage acting as simulation, since the attempt is to go beyond life. True art, as any aesthetician will avow, must go beyond simulation, precisely in order to qualify as art.

We might want to know just how two or more participants in a fully defined situation behave. Do they proceed rationally, selfishly, vindictively, or, perhaps, even altruistically? How long till they reach an agreement? If they are engaged in a common problem, are they more efficient when working together, or individually? A good example, used by Deutsch and Krauss (1960) illustrates a situation of this sort very well.

Two players are asked to assume the roles of two truck drivers, representing different companies, starting at opposite points, and travelling over a common road which has only one lane for a certain distance. Obviously, one or the other has to backtrack, unless the two trucks are to remain facing each other till the end of time. There is an alternate route, but it is so much longer that even after backtracking, the contested route is still preferable. In the sense that a simple strategy would assure both players of the best possible outcome, there is no optimal "solution."

Since we are discussing methods of simulation, we shall not here dwell upon the specific variants introduced, and their results, but we can surmise how nonrational practices, such as threat or cajoling, might alter the fortunes of one player or the other.

More frequently, such "two-person strategy games" are conducted using the so-called "prisoner's dilemma" game. This game gets its name from the old police trick of separating two suspects, and telling each of them that the other has blabbed, and that there is therefore no point in being obstinate, and increasing the severity of the penalty. Cooperation with the law will ensure some degree of leniency. Each suspect is now in a dilemma. If the policeman is telling the truth and his companion has confessed, then it would indeed be a mistake to remain silent, since to do so would surely intensify the judge's wrath, while a double confession would result in a moderate sentence. But suppose the policeman is lying, and the other has not confessed at all! Then our suspect has everything to gain by remaining silent (we assume that there is no other evidence), while confession would make him subject to some penalty, even though that penalty would be less than if both had confessed.

We might diagram the situation as follows, and attach values to the outcomes as seen by one of the two suspects. These values are somewhat arbitrary, though they have certain restrictions which can be simply paraphrased:

1. The situation is such that, if I think the other chose behavior A (talked) I am better off choosing A too.
2. If I think he chose B (did not talk) I am better off choosing B.
3. If I choose A and he chooses B, I am better, and he is worse off, than if we both choose A.
4. We would both be best off if both of us choose B.

The dilemma is insoluble on purely rational grounds, if we assume that our protagonist does not know what the other person has done (or will do).

Using monetary payoffs instead of jail terms, this situation has produced a great many enlightening studies (see for example Rapoport and Chammah, 1965). Guetzkow (1962) and Raser (1969) have written fine

OTHER

	A (talked)	B (did not talk)
A (talk)	We both get two years. But, seeing that he talked (I think), I had to do likewise: −20 for me −20 for him	At least, I did get off with one year. Too bad about poor Muggsy. One year for me: −10 Four years for him: −40
B (do not talk)	He got off with one year, the rat. At my expense! Four years for me: −40 One year for him: −10	Hurrah, we pulled it off! Both of us go free. +100 for me +100 for him

descriptions of some of these methods. Siegel and Fouraker (1960) present a fascinating series of two-person bargaining games in which a buyer and a seller arrive at a mutually agreeable purchase price for imaginary goods, under various conditions of salability or monopoly. Studies of this sort are of as much interest to economists as to psychologists.

We can also see that here we have excellent instances of the great advantage of controlled experiments; for not only can we reproduce such a variable as "gain" with considerable precision, but we can systematically vary the amount of damage threatened.

Sometimes we are confronted with a real-life situation such as an international conflict, which does not permit of trial and error. Still, by "playing out" such a situation in microcosm we might discover aspects that had not even occurred to us. For instance, we might find that one player, insulted beyond endurance, will seek to destroy his opponent even if such an act means his own ruin. It is not necessary to assume that the "mini-situation" is equivalent to two super-nations threatening each other—and the rest of the world—with annihilation in order to gain some useful insights. Also, by introducing additional variables, we may be able to anticipate contingencies that might happen. Suppose two nations hold unquestioned power over the rest of the world, and are reasonably well matched. What if a third power, friendly to one of the two and hostile to the other, appears to become equally powerful? Guetzkow, Alger, Grody, Noel, and Snyder (1963) dedicate a volume solely to the simulation of international conflicts.

References

Deutsch, M., and Krauss, R. M. The effect of threat upon interpersonal bargaining, *Journal of Abnormal and Social Psychology,* 1960, *61,* 181–189.

Guetzkow, H. Simulation in social science: Readings. Englewood Cliffs: Prentice-Hall, 1962.

Guetzkow, H., Alger, C. F., Brody, R. A., Noel, R. C., Snyder, R. C., Simulation in international relations: Developments for research and teaching. Englewood Cliffs: Prentice-Hall, 1963.

Heyerdahl, T. Kon-Tiki. Chicago: Rand McNally, 1950.

Heyerdahl, T. Aku-Aku, Chicago: Rand McNally, 1958.

Rapoport, A., and Chammah, A. M. Prisoner's dilemma—a study in conflict and cooperation. Ann Arbor: University of Michigan Press, 1965.

Raser, J. R. Simulation and society: An exploration of scientific gaming. Boston: Allyn and Bacon, 1969.

Siegel, S., and Fouraker, L. E. Bargaining and group decision making: Experiments in bilateral monopoly. New York, McGraw-Hill, 1960.

PART 2
Socialization

One of the nicest things about social psychology is that you can learn about it by "people-watching," a very enjoyable occupation. Now suppose that you try som people-watching for several days. You will probably notice (among many other observations) that there are certain similarities among the behaviors of your subjects. These behaviors may be specific to situations. For instance, people in our society tend to wear shoes when walking; they say hello on meeting; they cross the road when the traffic light is green; they push when trying to get on the subway train, and so on. Presumably people have been "socialized" or trained to behave in these ways that are appropriate to our particular society, and to their age, sex, and status in it.

Socialization begins the minute a person is born into a society. The training is accomplished in a number of ways. For instance, he is rewarded for behaving in one way, and punished for behaving in another. The person also has an opportunity to observe the behavior of others and its consequences, and then to imitate the behavior or to avoid it. He is presented either verbally or implicitly with values, ideas and concepts that he may or may not be encouraged to make his own. Socialization is carried out not only by parents and by teachers, but also by textbooks, television, and the other media. This whole notion of socialization and the influence of our culture on us is vital to social psychology. After all, in a different culture any of the research reported in this volume might have had very diverse results.

The articles in this section deal with three disparate issues relevant to the effects and process of socialization. The Hraba and Grant (1970) and Rosenhan (1966) articles discuss the effect of being Black and lower-class in our society, with Hraba and Grant finding that this effect may have changed in the past 30 years. Goldberg and Lewis (1969) are concerned with the sex differences in our society, and they suggest that mothers are implanting these differences in their children as early as six months of age.

Grusec (1972) investigated the effect of both altruistic and aggressive models on the behavior of elementary-school children and found that with aggression (but not necessarily with altruism), children are more likely to do what you *do* than what you *say*.

One rationale for the choice of these particular articles is that they all imply some ways to prevent what one might consider to be problems in our society. Behaviors related to altruism, aggression, independence, and achievement are presented as learned in and related to the environment of the child. Thus, a change in the environment might well change the behaviors observed. Unfortunately, one problem in the field of psychology is that, while solutions appear to be emerging, parents and educators are often unaware of the possibilities and alternatives.

On the other hand, it should be noted that not all psychologists share the idea that learning and environment are the most important variables in the determination of child development. For instance in one view, development proceeds largely through a series of stages. Freud described personality development in this way; Piaget has suggested a series of stages in cognitive development; and Kohlberg has advanced a similar set of stages in the development of moral thought.

In these theories, as compared to the learning notion described earlier, the stages of development are "universal" and all children go through the same stages in the same order. Individual differences occur only if some children stop at a lower stage and never reach the most advanced stage.

The stage theory point of view is favored by some psychologists; it provides an alternative to the socialization point of view favored by the authors of the reprinted papers. The reader should be aware of this differing emphasis. For a better understanding of the "stage" point of view and its relationship to socialization, the reader might look at one of the recent child psychology tests, for example Mussen, et al. (1969).

References

Goldberg, S., & Lewis, M. Play behavior in the year-old infant: early sex differences. *Child Development*, 1969, *40*, 21–31.

Grusec, J. E., Demand characteristics of the modeling experiment: altruism as a function of age and aggression. *Journal of Personality and Social Psychology*, 1972, *22*, 139–148.

Hraba, J., & Grant, G., Black is beautiful: a reexamination of racial preference and identification. *Journal of Personality and Social Psychology*, 1970, *16*, 398–402.

Kohlberg, L. Stage and Sequence: the cognitive-developmental approach to socialization. In D. A. Goslin (Ed.), *Handbook of socialization theory and research*. Chicago: Rand-McNally, 1969. Pp. 347–480.

Mussen, P. H., Conger, J. J., & Kagan, J. *Child development and personality.* 3d ed. New York: Harper & Row, 1969.

Rosenhan, D. L. Effects of social class and race on responsiveness to approval and disapproval. *Journal of Personality and Social Psychology,* 1966, *4,* 253–259.

INTRODUCTION

There is no doubt that minority group persons are often seen in terms of a negative stereotype. A more surprising consideration is that the minority group persons may come to view themselves in the same negative light. For example, Jewish anti-Semitism has been discussed by several authors, including Lewin, 1948, and it has recently been shown that women show some prejudice against others of their sex, evaluating work supposedly done by a man more highly than identical work attributed to a woman (Pheterson, Kiesler, and Goldberg, 1971.) In 1947, Clark and Clark presented data indicating that the majority of black children (ages 3 to 7), even when aware of their racial identity, preferred "white" dolls to dark brown dolls. Some conflicting evidence exists. For instance, Gregor and McPherson (1966) found that black children preferred "black" dolls when only a dark brown and a "white" doll were shown. But the great majority of studies have corroborated the original Clark and Clark findings. For example, in 1968, Greenwald and Oppenheim replicated that study, adding a white control group and a "mulatto" doll, lighter in color than the dark brown one. These authors again found that the black children tended to reject the "colored" dolls, as did the white children. However, presumably due to the added doll, 13 percent of the black children (as compared to 39 percent in the Clarks' northern sample) identified themselves with a "white" rather than a "black" doll. On the other hand, oddly enough, 44 percent of the *white* children identified themselves with the improper doll. Apparently, the grayish-beige color of the "mulatto" doll caused some confusion.

A tendency of black children to reject their own group has important implications for education and development. One of the assumptions of North American society is that high self-esteem is conductive to mental health, as well as achievement. In fact, some preschool enrichment programs for disadvantaged children make a point of building self-identity and esteem through such techniques as individual attention and the use of cameras and mirrors.

The study reprinted here was an attempt to see if the Clark and Clark result would remain true for contemporary black children in an interracial setting.

METHOD

Hraba and Grant used much the same procedure as Clark and Clark, with the addition of a white as well as a black experimenter. The doll technique, by the way, is rather like a "projective" test. It is assumed that the child projects his feelings about people onto the dolls.

RESULTS

The data for the racial preference items are presented in Table 1. As you can see, racial preference in this study is very different from that in the Clarks' study. The data for the other points of comparison are not presented. However, the authors summarize the results. The most notable point may be the lack of correspondence between doll preference and race of friends. Even some of those children who answered in favor of their own race on all of the preference questions felt that they had friends of the opposite race.

DISCUSSION

Hraba and Grant offer alternate explanations of the two results above. They suggest that the race preferences may have been due to the changes between 1947 (the Clarks' study) and 1969, or something unique to Lincoln, Nebraska, or recent black pride campaigns, or acceptance by white friends. (The reader might consider how one would design research to indicate the relative validity of the suggestions.) With regard to the discrepancy between doll choice and friendship, the authors suggest that the explanation may be availability of white friends, or the age of the children. The authors give the impression that only children are subject to conceptual inconsistencies. However, this is far from being the case; many studies with adults indicate a discrepancy between attitudes and behavior. For example, LaPiere (1934) found that restaurant owners answered an inquiry by saying that they would not allow an Oriental couple to dine in their establishment. However, when visited by an Oriental couple, these same owners were perfectly polite. In fact, the combination of black pride and interracial friendship indicated by this study, would seem to demonstrate, not a research problem, but an encouraging trend for the future.

References

Clark, K. B., and Clark, M. K. Racial identification and preference in Negro children. In T. Newcomb, and E. Hartley (Eds.), *Readings in social psychology*. New York: Holt, Rinehart and Winston, 1947.

Greenwald, H. J., and Oppenheim, D. B. Reported magnitude of self-misidentification among Negro children—artifact? *Journal of Personality and Social Psychology*, 1968, *8*, 49–52.

Gregor, A. J., and McPherson, D. A. Racial attitudes among White and Negro children in a deep south standard metropolitan area. *Journal of Social Psychology*, 1966, *68*, 95–106.

LaPiere, R. T. Attitudes versus actions. *Social Forces*, 1934, *13*, 230–237.

Lewin, K. *Resolving social conflicts*. New York: Harper & Row, 1948.

Pheterson, G. I., Kiesler, S. G., & Goldberg, P. A. Evaluation of the performance of women as a function of their sex, achievement, and personal history. *Journal of Personality and Social Psychology*, 1971, *19*, 114–118.

2.1 Black Is Beautiful: A Reexamination of Racial Preference and Identification

Joseph Hraba
Geoffrey Grant

This study examined the racial preferences of black children in an interracial setting. The Clark and Clark doll study was duplicated in Lincoln, Nebraska, during May 1969. Unlike the Clarks, the present authors found that the majority of the black children preferred the black dolls. Like the blacks, the majority of the white children preferred the doll of their own race. The racial identifications of both black and white children are reported. Furthermore, the effects of age and skin color upon racial preference and identification are compared with those reported by Clark and Clark. A control for the race of interviewers showed that this variable did not have a significant effect upon the dependent variable. The correspondence between doll choice and friendship was ambiguous. Interpretations of all the results are given.

Clark and Clark (1947) found that black children preferred white dolls and rejected black dolls when asked to choose which were nice, which looked bad, which they would like to play with, and which were a nice color. This implies that black is not beautiful.

This observation has been repeated, using a variety of methods and in a variety of settings (Asher & Allen, 1969; Frenkel-Brunswik, 1948; Goodman, 1952; Greenwald & Oppenheim, 1968; Landreth & Johnson, 1953; Morland, 1958, 1966; Radke, Sutherland, & Rosenberg, 1950; Radke, Trager, & Davis, 1949; Trager & Yarrow, 1952).

However, Gregor and McPherson (1966) found that Southern, urban black children, 6 and 7 years old, generally preferred a black doll. Their procedures were identical to Clark and Clark's, except only two dolls were presented. They proposed that black children's preference for white stems from their contact with whites; ". . . Negro children tend to be more outgroup oriented the more systematically they are exposed to white contact [p. 103]." Clark and Clark did find that black children in interracial nursery schools were more pronounced in their preference for white dolls than those in segregated nursery schools. However, Morland (1966), using a picture technique, found just the opposite.

Reprinted from the *Journal of Personality and Social Psychology,* 1970, *16,* 398–402. Copyright 1970 by the American Psychological Association and reproduced by permission.

Still, Clark and Clark and Goodman (1952), when using similar techniques, found that black children in interracial settings preferred objects representing whites. However, Johnson (1966) found 18 black youths (mean age of 12) in a Harlem freedom school rated black equal to white. He concluded that his "study presents evidence that not all Negroes have negative self-attitudes . . . [p. 273]." Perhaps, but the techniques used by Johnson and Clark and Clark differ. Johnson had groups of respondents rate black and white on four semantic differential scales. Furthermore, the samples are not comparable on age and social setting. Possibly techniques, sampling, and attitudes are confounded in a comparison of these two studies.

The thesis that for black children interracial contact engenders preference for white cannot be overlooked in this literature. Some have advocated this interpretation (Gregor, 1963; Armstrong & Gregor, 1964; Gregor & McPherson, 1966). Unfortunately, any comparison of the evidence confounds time, techniques, sampling, and setting with the dependent variable. The present study will test this thesis in an interracial setting by duplicating the Clark and Clark doll study.

METHOD

Procedure

The procedures used by Clark and Clark were followed as closely as possible. The respondents were interviewed individually using a set of four dolls, two black and two white, identical in all other respects. The same questions used by the Clarks were asked. They are as follows:

1. Give me the doll that you want to play with.
2. Give me the doll that is a nice doll.
3. Give me the doll that looks bad.
4. Give me the doll that is a nice color.
5. Give me the doll that looks like a white child.
6. Give me the doll that looks like a colored child.
7. Give me the doll that looks like a Negro child.
8. Give me the doll that looks like you.

Clark and Clark contended that Items 1–4 measure racial preference, Items 5–7 measure racial awareness or knowledge, and Item 8 measures racial self-identification.

In an attempt to identify the behavioral consequences of racial preference and identification, we asked the children to name and indicate the race of their best friends. We also asked the teachers for the same information.

Sample

For our sample, respondents had to be 4–8 years of age. Five public schools provided a sampling frame containing 73% of the correct age black children in the public school system of Lincoln, Nebraska. The total sample consisted of 160 children, 89 blacks, or 60% of the eligible blacks attending Lincoln public schools. The 71 white children were drawn at random from the classrooms containing black respondents. The interviews were completed at the five schools during May 1969.

The respondents were assigned to both black and white interviewers. Previous research has controlled for race of interviewer (Asher & Allen, 1969; Morland, 1966). Morland reported that race of interviewer does not significantly affect respondents' choices. Nevertheless, we controlled for race of interviewer.

Setting

Blacks comprise approximately 1.4% of the total population of Lincoln. The five public schools reflected this fact. Blacks accounted for 3% of the enrollment of three schools, and 7% and 18% of the other two schools. Furthermore, 70% of the black sample reported they had white friends.

RESULTS

Racial Preference

The Clarks' finding that the majority of the black children preferred a white doll has been interpreted that they would rather be white. This was one of the Clarks' important findings and is the focus of this paper.

Table 1 provides two comparisons. First, the differences in racial preference of the Clark and Clark (1939) sample and the Lincoln sample of 1969 are striking. On all the items the difference reaches statistical significance using chi-square.

Secondly, the sample of white children was collected to provide a bench mark against which to compare the racial preferences of black children. Gregor and McPherson (1966) and Morland (1966) have found that white children are more likely to prefer their own race than are black children. Table 1 shows that black and white children preferred the doll of their own race. The white children were significantly more ethnocentric on Items 1 and 2, there was no significant difference on Item 3, and the black children were significantly more ethnocentric on Item 4 using chi-square.

Age.   The Clarks found that black children preferred white dolls at all ages (3–7), although this decreased with age. We found that a majority of the black children at all ages (3–8) preferred a black doll, and this preference increased with age. With white children there was a similar age trend except on Item 4.

Skin color.   The Clarks classified their subjects by skin color into three categories: light (practically white), medium (light brown to dark brown), and dark (dark brown to black). The interviewers in our study

TABLE 1 *A Comparison of the Present Results with the Clark and Clark (1939) Data*

ITEM	CLARK & CLARK [a] (1939) BLACKS	LINCOLN SAMPLE (1969) BLACKS	χ^2 (1939–1969) BLACKS	LINCOLN SAMPLE (1969) WHITES
1. (Play with)				
White doll	67 (169)	30 (27)	36.2**	83 (59)
Black doll	32 (83)	70 (62)		16 (11)
Don't know or no response				1 (1)
2. (Nice doll)				
White doll	59 (150)	46 (41)	5.7*	70 (50)
Black doll	38 (97)	54 (48)		30 (21)
3. (Looks bad)				
White doll	17 (42)	61 (54)	43.5**	34 (24)
Black doll	59 (149)	36 (32)		63 (45)
Don't know or no response		3 (3)		3 (2)
4. (Nice color)				
White doll	60 (151)	31 (28)	23.1**	48 (34)
Black doll	38 (96)	69 (61)		49 (35)
Don't know or no response				3 (2)

Note.—Data in percentages. Ns in parentheses.

a Individuals failing to make either choice not included, hence some percentages add to less than 100.

* $p < .02$.

** $p < .001$.

used the same criteria. The Clarks found that the children of light skin color showed the greatest preference for the white doll and the dark children the least. We did not find this trend. The children of light skin color were at least as strong in their preference for a black doll as the others.

Racial Identification

Items 5, 6, and 7 were to measure knowledge of racial differences, while Item 8 was to measure racial self-identification. On Items 5 and 6 the Clarks found that a majority of their respondents correctly identified white and "colored" dolls (94% and 93%, respectively). Our black sample was comparable. Ninety percent correctly identified a white doll and 94% correctly identified a colored doll. In regard to Item 7 (doll that looks like a Negro child), we found that more of our respondents made the correct identification (86% as compared to 72%).

Age. Like the Clarks, we found an inverse relationship between misidentification (Items 5–8) and age. This relationship held for whites as well.

Skin color. Like the Clarks, we found insignificant differences in misidentification (Items 5–7) among black children by skin color. However, on Item 8 the Clarks had found that more black children with light skin color misidentified themselves (80%). Adding a mulatto doll, Greenwald and Oppenheim (1968) reduced the misidentification for these respondents to 11%. Fifteen percent of our black respondents with light skin color misidentified themselves. However, there was no significant difference in misidentification on Item 8 by skin color.

Race of interviewer. Race of interviewer was not related to choice of doll on any of the items for both black and white children.

Race of respondents' friends. For both black and white children there was no apparent relationship between doll preference and race of friends. The sociometric information agreed and were combined. If a relationship were to be found, it would be most pronounced for those who preferred dolls of their own race without exception. Furthermore, only these respondents demonstrated reliability in their doll preferences. Twenty-three black and 20 white children made the choices favorable to their own race on all four items measuring racial preference.

Even for these children there appears to be no relationship between doll preference and race of friends. Twenty, or 87%, of the 23 black children had white friends. Twelve, or 60%, of the 20 white children had all white friends. However, 41% of all white children had all white friends.

DISCUSSION

Doll Preference

These results indicate that black children in interracial settings are not necessarily white oriented. We will offer possible interpretations. First, times may be changing. That is, Negroes are becoming Blacks proud of their race. If change is occurring, previous research indicates that it is not at a universal rate across the country (Asher & Allen, 1969; Gregor & McPherson, 1966).

A second interpretation is that even 30 years ago black children in Lincoln, unlike those in other cities, would have chosen black dolls. This interpretation cannot be examined. A third and more reasonable interpretation is that conditions indigenous to Lincoln have mediated the impact of the "Black Movement." Johnson (1966) suggested that local organizations in black communities disseminate black pride. We note that during the past

2 years a black pride campaign, sponsored by organizations which are black conscious, has been directed at adolescents and young adults in Lincoln. Black children through interaction with kin and friends may be modeling these attitudes.

The fourth interpretation is that interracial contact may engender black pride. Pettigrew (1967) proposed that interracial acceptance mediated the effect of interracial contact on the academic performance of blacks. Perhaps it influences black pride. The fact that 70% of the black sample had white friends and 59% of the white sample had black friends, given the racial composition of the schools, suggests this interpretation.

Doll Preference and Friendship

The above interpretations have assumed that doll choice corresponds with interpersonal behavior. Our findings suggest that such correspondence cannot be presumed. Three explanations of the lack of relationship between doll choice and friendship will be offered. These explanations are predicated on two assumptions, one about the doll technique and the other about the meaning of "Black is beautiful."

The first explanation assumes that children will use the same criteria in friendship and doll choice. "Black is beautiful" is assumed to mean a rejection of whites. Combining these two assumptions, we expected those black children who without exception preferred black dolls to have all black friends. This expectation was not realized. However, being pupils of predominately white schools, these respondents may have found it impractical to have all black friends in spite of their preferences.[1]

The second explanation makes the same assumption about the doll technique. But it assumes that "Black is beautiful" translates into an acceptance of and by whites. Combining these we expected black children who without exception preferred black dolls to have both black and white friends. This expectation was nearly realized. More black children who had friends of both races preferred black dolls (except on Item 4) than those who had all black friends. This relationship approached statistical confirmation.

The third explanation does not assume doll choice corresponds with interpersonal behavior. First, in the experimental setting, four dolls, which were identical except for race, were presented to the respondents. Although black children may prefer a doll of their own race when race is the only cue that differentiates it from other dolls, they may consider other criteria more important in friendship. Perhaps race is not salient in friendship at this age

[1] The restricted racial composition previously noted and sample size prevented a test of this possibility.

(Criswell, 1937; Moreno, 1934). Secondly, Piaget has observed that children before 11 or 12 years of age cannot detect conceptual self-contradictions (Hunt, 1961; Maier, 1969). The fact that a majority of the respondents who were consistent in answering the four preference questions did not clearly reflect the bases for their doll preferences in their friendships suggests this possibility. Furthermore, the fact that a majority (73%) of all the respondents were inconsistent in answering the four preference questions supports this suggestion.

References

Armstrong, C. P., & Gregor, A. J. Integrated schools and Negro character development. *Psychiatry*, 1964, *27*, 69–72.

Asher, S. R., & Allen, V. L. Racial preference and social comparison processes. *Journal of Social Issues*, 1969, *25*, 157–165.

Clark, K. B., & Clark, M. K. The development of consciousness of self in the emergence of racial identification in Negro pre-school children. *Journal of Social Psychology*, 1939, *10*, 591–597.

Clark, K. B., & Clark, M. K. Racial identification and preference in Negro children. In T. Newcomb & E. Hartley (Eds.), *Readings in social psychology*. New York: Holt, Rinehart and Winston, 1947.

Criswell, J. H. Racial cleavage in Negro-white groups. *Sociometry*, 1937, *1*, 81–89.

Frenkel-Brunswik, E. A study of prejudice in children. *Human Relations*, 1948, *1*, 295–306.

Greenwald, H. J., & Oppenheim, D. B. Reported magnitude of self-misidentification among Negro children—artifact?" *Journal of Personality and Social Psychology*, 1968, *8*, 49–52.

Goodman, M. E. *Racial awareness in young children*. Cambridge, Mass.: Addison-Wesley.

Gregor, A. J. Science and social change: A review of K. B. Clark's "Prejudice and your child." *Mankind Quarterly*, 1963, *3*, 229–237.

Gregor, A. J., & McPherson, D. A. Racial attitudes among white and Negro children in a deep south standard metropolitan area. *Journal of Social Psychology*, 1966, *68*, 95–106.

Hunt, J. McV. *Intelligence and experience*. New York: Ronald Press, 1961.

Johnson, D. W. Racial attitudes of Negro freedom school participants and Negro and white civil rights participants. *Social Forces*, 1966, *45*, 266–272.

Landreth, C., & Johnson, B. C. Young children's responses to a picture and inset test designed to reveal reactions to persons of different skin color. *Child Development*, 1953, *24*, 63–80.

Maier, H. W. *Three theories of child development*. New York: Harper & Row, 1969.

Moreno, J. L. *Who shall survive?* (Monograph No. 58) Washington, D.C.: Nervous and Mental Disease, 1934.

Morland, K. J. A comparison of race awareness in northern and southern children. *American Journal of Orthopsychiatry*, 1966, *36*, 22–31.

Morland, K. J. Racial recognition by nursery school children in Lynchburg, Virginia. *Social Forces*, 1958, *37*, 132–137.

Pettigrew, T. F. Social evaluation theory: Convergences and applications. *Nebraska Symposium on Motivation*, 1967, *15*, 241–319.

Radke, M. J., Sutherland, J., & Rosenberg, P. Racial attitudes of children. *Sociometry*, 1950, *13*, 151–171.

Radke, M. J., Trager, H., & Davis, H. Social perception and attitudes of children. *Genetic Psychology Monographs*, 1949, *10*, 327–447.

Trager, H., & Yarrow, M. *They live what they learn.* New York: Harper & Row, 1952.

Foreword to Reading 2.2

INTRODUCTION

Rosenhan is concerned with the academic failure of the culturally deprived, most of whom are lower-class and nonwhite. In order to assess the importance of the problem, we might first review some evidence on the extent of such failure. Unfortunately, many such instances can be cited. Numerous studies have indicated that there are pronounced reading disabilities among children from disadvantaged backgrounds (e.g., Deutsch, 1965). Furthermore, these children are more likely than others to fail in school and to leave at an early stage (Harlem Youth Opportunities Unlimited, 1964). Somewhat dated information on academic failure and the conditions of ghetto life can be obtained from Kenneth Clark's *Dark Ghetto* (1966). For information on poverty in general, you might look at Michael Harrington's *The Other America* (1963).

As mentioned by Rosenhan, a number of factors have been advanced as potential causes of the academic failure of the lower class. However, in general, the search for explanations and solutions has changed somewhat over the last ten years. One decade ago, it was assumed that middle-class children are not deprived, whereas lower-class children (particularly black) are deprived. This point of view has been critical in determining the form of some head start programs in which enrichment and stimulation are provided for the children (e.g., Klaus and Gray, 1968). On the other hand, presently there is greater emphasis on the notion that the lower-class environment is different, not necessarily deprived. For instance, some writers (e.g., McCandless, 1970) have suggested that black children speak a dialect different from that of white children, rather than showing a less sophisticated use of language. This point of view has led to rather different preschool programs, including one that teaches the English language to lower-class children much as if they were foreigners (Bereiter and Engelmann, 1966).

Rosenhan's thesis is that the lower-class child finds himself in a middle-class environment when he goes to school. Feeling uncomfortable and alienated in that environment, he is exceptionally sensitive to the way that the people around him react to him (just as most of us are in strange situations). Rosenhan suggests that if his hypothesis is correct, lower-class children would be expected to react more positively to approval and more negatively to disapproval from a middle-class adult than would middle-class children. He also suggests that since lower-class black children have both an alienation problem and a problem of low self-esteem (see Hraba and Grant, 1970, in this volume for a discussion of this issue), they would be expected to react more positively to approval and more negatively to disapproval from a middle-class white adult than would lower-class white children.

METHOD

In order to test his hypothesis, Rosenhan carried out a study in which the first-grade subjects were either given approval for correct responses or disapproval for incorrect responses.

In evaluating this type of study, it is particularly important to note the characteristics of the experimenter and the subjects, since these could influence the results. The subjects here were drawn from the Trenton School System (Trenton is a small city); their public schools were mixed in terms of socioeconomic class, and also, perhaps, in terms of race (color). The experimenter was white, middle-class, and male. One wonders why a male experimenter was used, since Rosenhan was interested in the school environment (where the teachers are usually female in the early grades).

RESULTS

Rosenhan's description of his results is clear; only the hypothesis comparing lower-class and middle-class boys was confirmed; however, one misprint appears in the tables of analysis of variance. If the MS and F columns relating to the "between subjects" factors are moved down one line, then the figures correspond both to the written text and to the data in Table 1 (e.g., the line beginning "Groups (A)" should continue as follows:

df	MS	F	MS	F	etc.)
1	1.5052	.06	16.9216	1.27	

In making interpretations from these and other group data, one should remember that a significant difference between groups means only that they are not the same, *on the average.* This is a particularly important qualification when one is considering research which could lead to social change. In this study, it is likely that there was overlap of scores from group to group, and that, for instance, every lower-class child in the approval condition did not perform at a higher level than every middle-class child in the approval condition. Thus, this experiment cannot be taken to mean that approval by a white adult would facilitate the performance of every Negro child on simple tasks, even if all of these children were from the Trenton School System.

DISCUSSION

In his discussion section, Rosenhan gives a clear and detailed account of the difficulties and alternate explanations of his procedure. By providing an objective evaluation of his own research, Rosenhan has acted to prevent rash generalizations and applications of his findings.

Thoughts for the reader: Does Rosenhan's research lead you to think of new possibilities and variations? For instance, what effect would an age variable have on the results? Would alienation increase or decrease with age? What effect would changing the sex of either experimenter or child or both have on the results? Finally, how would the race of the experimenter influence behavior?

Katz, Henchy, and Allen (1968) investigated this last question as part of a test of the alienation hypothesis. Using lower-class Negro children approximately two years older than those used by Rosenhan, and more personal expressions of approval and disapproval ("I'm very disappointed . . ."), Katz, et al. found that their subjects performed better with Negro male testers than with white testers, and under conditions of approval rather than disapproval. This result is interesting, not only from the point of view of educational implications, but also with reference to all the research on intellectual ability in which impersonal white testers have administered IQ tests to black children.

References

Bereiter, C., & Engelmann, S. *Teaching disadvantaged children in the pre-school.* Englewood Cliffs, N.J.: Prentice-Hall, 1966.

Clark, K. B. *Dark ghetto.* New York: Harper & Row, 1965.

Deutsch, M. The role of social class in language development and cognition. *American Journal of Orthopsychiatry,* 1965, *35,* 78–88.

Harlem Youth Opportunities Unlimited, Inc. Youth in the ghetto: a study of the consequences of powerlessness and a blueprint for change. New York: Haryou, Inc., 1964.

Harrington, M. *The other America.* Baltimore: Penguin Books, 1963.

Katz, I., Henchy, T., & Allen, H. Effects of race of tester, approval–disapproval, and need on Negro children's learning. *Journal of Personality and Social Psychology,* 1968, *8,* Part 1, 38–42.

Klaus, R. A., & Gray, S. W. The early training project for disadvantaged children: a report after 5 years. *Monographs of the Society for Research in Child Development,* 1968, *33,* 1–66.

McCandless, B. *Adolescents.* Hinsdale, Illinois: Dryden Press, 1970.

2.2 Effects of Social Class and Race on Responsiveness to Approval and Disapproval[1]

David L. Rosenhan

An interaction theory of social class behavior was proposed in which young lower-class children were presumed to be more alienated and uncomfortable than middle-class children with middle-class people and institutions. As a consequence of alienation it was deduced that relative to middle-class children, approval should facilitate the performance of lower-class children while disapproval should retard it. The hypothesis was substantiated. Within the lower class, there were no performance differences between Negro and white Ss, indicating that for young children social class differences are more potent determiners of behavior than are racial differences. The potential implications of the data for longer term performance are noted.

Recent concern with the academic failure of the culturally deprived or the culturally different has yielded a number of hypotheses regarding the potential sources of this failure (cf. Passow, 1963; Riessman, 1962). Since the term culturally deprived implies primarily lower-class children, and particularly those who are nonwhite, these hypotheses have sought to explain the failures of these children in terms of characteristics that are presumed to be possessed primarily by the lower class. Thus, their relatively impoverished status is seen as relevant to their academic failure. So, too, their transient status in the community, their unstable parental identifications, their negative self-images, the degree to which they are encouraged to achieve—all these and others are seen as potential sources for the academic performance discrepancies between young children from the lower and middle classes (cf. Passow, 1963, for a discussion of these issues).

Empirical research in this area has been meager and, to a large extent, inconclusive. Douvan (1956) has reported that lower-class children are less responsive to the idea of being correct than middle-class children. Zigler and Kanzer (1962) demonstrated further that middle-class children were

Reprinted from the *Journal of Personality and Social Psychology,* 1966, *4,* 253–259. Copyright 1966 by the American Psychological Association and reproduced by permission.

[1] This research was supported in part by Grant HD-01762-01 from the National Institute of Child Health and Human Development, United States Public Health Service. Gratitude is expressed to Arthur Kender who collected the data, to Albert Beaton and Henrietta Gallagher who performed the analyses, and to Anthony Greenwald, Paul Jacobs, and Nathan Kogan who commented on the manuscript.

more responsive to abstract reinforcers, that is, reinforcers directed at performance, while lower-class children responded more to concrete reinforcers, or those reinforcers that generally connoted praise. However, a replication of this study by Rosenhan and Greenwald (1965) did not bear out the findings. No differences were found between middle- and lower-class children in their tendency to respond to performance (i.e., abstract) or person (i.e., concrete) reinforcers.

The present study takes a social class interaction position (cf. Clark, 1963; Rosenhan, 1965) and examines the notion that the lower-class child may be more alienated than the middle-class child in a middle-class school system. Taking alienation to mean a lack of relationship with one's environment (English & English, 1958) and particularly an inability to comprehend environmental expectancies, the argument runs as follows: For the middle-class child, the middle-class school may be seen as an extension of his middle-class home. Often, long before he has entered first grade, he anticipates going to school and has learned something about school from his parents. Commonly enough, he has been introduced to some of the materials that he will subsequently encounter in school. Moreover, he is reasonably familiar with middle-class institutions and is comfortable with middle-class people. Thus, for this child, the school is a comfortable situation with which he often has prior familiarity. For the lower-class child, however, the situation may be quite different. In his environment, attending school may not be an especially high-status activity. He has probably received little if any of the vicarious and anticipatory reinforcement that the middle-class child receives prior to going to school. Indeed, what with the larger family that he tends to come from and the greater need for both of his parents to be employed, the school may have subtly acquired negative reinforcing properties in the sense that it may be viewed as a repository in order to permit the parents greater freedom. From whatever source, then, it is conceivable that the lower-class child experiences greater alienation in middle-class institutions and with middle-class people than does the middle-class child.

In the present study we examine one hypothesis derivable from the above proposition: If lower-class children are more alienated in a middle-class institution, they should be more responsive to praise than middle-class children would be. By the same token, the performance of lower-class children should be more disrupted by disapproval than that of their middle-class peers. In general, the relationship of a lower-class child to middle-class institutions can be viewed in much the same way that a Westerner might experience, say, an Oriental wedding. Feeling quite unfamiliar with the rites and rituals, he would be more delighted than an Oriental would be by a remark that approved of his behavior. On the other hand, having done something that evoked disapproval, he would be more disturbed by the criticism than would one who was relatively more at home at such ceremonies.

In order to test the hypothesis, a middle-class male experimenter verbally reinforced the performance of first-grade lower- and middle-class subjects in a binary-choice game. Half of the subjects were given positive reinforcement when they made the correct response. No reinforcement was offered for incorrect responses. The remaining subjects were given negative reinforcement for incorrect responses, with no reinforcement given for correct responses.

It has been suggested (Riessman, 1962) that the Negro lower-class child suffers an especial handicap in that his color leads him to acquire a negative-identity image more rapidly and more deeply than the white child. We examine this hypothesis in this experiment by considering separately the effects of disapproval and approval on white and Negro lower-class children. (Negro middle-class children were not available for this study.) If both the alienation and the negative-identity hypotheses are correct, then Negro children should be more positively affected by approval than white children and more negatively affected by disapproval.

METHOD

Subjects

Subjects were 72 first-grade boys who were drawn from two public schools of mixed socioeconomic class.[2] Socioeconomic class was determined on the basis of parental occupation (Warner, Meeker, & Eells, 1949, p. 140). Subjects were randomly assigned to the approval and disapproval conditions. Twenty-four subjects were middle- and 48 were lower-class children. Of the lower-class children, half were Negro and half were white. A comparable Negro middle-class sample could not be obtained. Table 1 describes the composition of the groups.

A middle-class white male experimenter conducted the study. He was told that the experiment dealt with the effects of approval and disapproval on probability learning, but was not aware of the social class hypotheses. Nor did he realize that the subjects had been presorted on the basis of social class and race.

Apparatus

A black metal box, measuring $7 \times 12 \times 7$ inches, served as the binary-choice apparatus. Mounted on the lower right and left corners of the panel was a toggle-type automatic-return switch which the subject manipulated.

[2] The assistance of the Trenton School System, and particularly of Olive Brown, director of instruction, Lester Blinn, and Merle Lloyd, principals, is gratefully acknowledged.

The subject's responses activated either of two lights on the experimenter's clipboard indicating which lever the subject had depressed. The experimenter then responded accordingly. The apparatus is described fully in Rosenhan (in press).

Procedure

The experimenter met the subject outside of his classroom and chatted with him on the way to the experimental room. Once inside, the subject was seated before a low table on which was the binary-choice game. The experimenter instructed the child in the use of the switches and, for the ap-

TABLE 1 *Composition of the Sample and Performance of the Subjects (N = 12 in Each Group)*

SUBJECT GROUP	CA[a]		SOCIOECONOMIC CLASS		RESPONSES TO LEFT LEVER (PERCENTAGE OF 160 TRIALS)	
	M	Range	M	Range	M	Range
Middle-class white						
Approval	6:1	5:10–6:6	1.4	1–3	60	04
Disapproval	6:2	5:11–6:4	1.4	1–3	62	03
Lower-class white						
Approval	6:2	5:10–6:7	5.8	5–7	64	06
Disapproval	6:3	5:9–6:8	6.0	5–7	55	04
Lower-class Negro						
Approval	6:3	5:11–6:10	6.4	6–7	63	09
Disapproval	6:1	5:9–6:11	6.0	5–7	55	04

[a] At time of testing.

proval condition, told him that "each time you press the right button, I will say 'right.'" For the disapproval condition, the instructions were reversed, namely, "each time you press the wrong button, I will say 'wrong.'" The instructions were repeated several times.

Prior to the training trials, the subject was administered four practice trials, for which the first and last trials were correct (i.e., they were reinforced for the approval condition; for the disapproval condition the second and third practice trials were negatively reinforced).

When it was clear that the subject understood the instructions, he was administered 160 training trials. A reinforcement ratio of 70 : 30 to the left and right levers, respectively, was employed. That is, for the approval condition the left lever was positively reinforced 70% of the time, and the right lever 30% of the time. For the disapproval condition the reinforcement ratio was reversed—70% of the right and 30% of the left lever presses were negatively reinforced. Reinforcements were randomized in blocks of 20 trials. Thus, the response behavior demanded—pressing the left lever—was the same for both the approval and disapproval conditions and constituted the dependent variable for this study.

RESULTS

Three analyses of variance were applied to the mean performance data shown in Table 1. The first analysis considered the effects of approval and disapproval on lower-class children. It examined whether Negro and white boys responded differentially to these reinforcers. As will be seen in Table 2, no race differences emerged either as main effects or in interaction with other variables. The effects of reinforcers were such that lower-class children were much more responsive to approval than to disapproval.

The trials' main effect in this as in the subsequent analysis indicates that the tendency to respond to the left lever increased over the four blocks of trials. The subject's performance began at or near the 50% level and

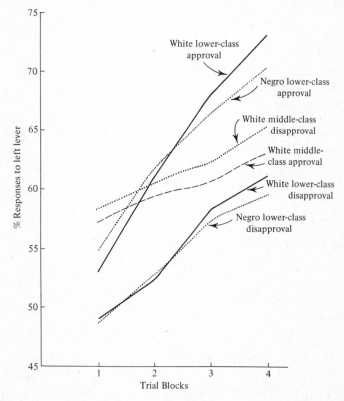

FIG. 1. Mean performance of subjects by experimental group and blocks of 40 trials.

increased as he gained more experience with the reinforcement contingencies. The interaction between trials and the reinforcer valence demonstrated that the subject's tendency to respond to the left lever rose under approval conditions but remained relatively stable (and low) under conditions of disapproval. Figure 1 presents the data across trials for these lower-class subjects and for the middle-class subjects.

The second analysis of variance (Table 2) examined the responsiveness of lower- and middle-class white children to approval and disapproval. Again, the main effects of the reinforcement dimension were significant. However, they interacted with social class such that compared to middle-class boys, the performance of lower-class boys was facilitated by approval and retarded by disapproval.

Looking now to the between-blocks-of-trials analysis, we find that the main effects of trials are marked: The subjects' performances improve over trials. The Trials × Social Class interaction is seen in Figure 1, where the early performance of lower-class subjects in the approval condition is below that of middle-class subjects in either condition. Terminal performance of lower-class subjects under approval is, however, higher than that of any other group.

Approximately similar results obtained from the third analysis which considered the effects of approval and disapproval on lower-class Negroes and middle-class whites (Table 2). While the overall effect of approval was greater than that of disapproval, lower-class Negroes performed better with approval and worse with disapproval than did middle-class whites. And while the performance of all groups improved over the four blocks of trials, the amount of improvement for Negroes in the approval condition (whose initial performance was below that of the middle-class boys in either condition) was substantially greater than it was for middle-class whites.

DISCUSSION

It is clear from these data that identical reinforcers—approval or disapproval—have differential effects according to the social class of the subject. Taking performance to mean the number of times the subjects pressed the left lever, the performance of lower-class subjects was substantially improved under conditions of approval relative to middle-class subjects. Under conditions of disapproval, however, lower-class boys performed more poorly than their middle-class peers.

The data are consistent with the view that lower-class children, at least on entry into middle-class institutions and with middle-class people, are unfamiliar with their surroundings and therefore experience a greater sense of alienation than do middle-class boys. This presumed sense of alienation

TABLE 2 Summary of the Analyses of Variance for the Color and Class Comparisons

SOURCE	df	I LOWER CLASS: WHITE VERSUS NEGRO SUBJECTS		II WHITE SUBJECTS: LOWER VERSUS MIDDLE CLASS		III LOWER-CLASS NEGRO VERSUS MIDDLE-CLASS WHITE	
		MS	F	MS	F	MS	F
Between subjects							
Groups (A)	1	1.5052	.06	16.9216	1.27	28.5208	1.30
Reinforcers (B)	1	577.5469	22.05*	97.7552	7.32*	102.0833	4.65**
A × B	1	.0469	.00	194.0052	14.53*	200.0833	9.12*
Error (b)	44	26.1928		13.3509		21.9461	
Within subjects							
Trials (C)	3	313.4219	125.39	179.8108	158.26*	133.1875	71.94*
A × C	3	3.8108	1.52	38.6302	34.00*	19.4097	10.48*
B × C	3	13.3524	5.34*	4.5469	4.00*	1.3889	.75
A × B × C	3	1.0191	.41	6.4358	5.66*	2.3889	1.29
Error (w)	132	2.4995		1.1362		1.8513	

* $p < .05$.
** $p < .01$.

leaves them especially sensitive to external social reinforcers that convey approval or disapproval of their behavior. Unable, as it were, to assure themselves that they are legitimate members of the environment in which they find themselves, they rely more heavily than middle-class children on external indexes of the quality of their performance.

At the same time we have an instance where alienation is not necessarily deleterious to performance. If learning is viewed as the tendency to respond to the more reinforced lever, then for lower-class children, approval facilitated learning. And while the paradigm is limited to a brief experimental event and to a small sample of performance, the data are sufficiently encouraging to speculate that the longer term effects of middle-class approval might produce a generally elevated performance in lower-class children. Long-term disapproval, on the other hand, might have relatively enduring opposite effects, reducing the performance of lower-class children far below what it might be under other conditions.

It is also possible and consistent with the above interpretation that lower- and middle-class children differ in their approaches to a positively reinforced binary-choice game. While children of both classes may recognize that the left lever is correct more often than the right one, middle-class children employ a problem-solving approach, attempting to get each item correct. Lower-class children, on the other hand, may tend to employ the more conservative strategy of maximizing their correct responses. Such differences in strategy are consistent with the relative incentive value of praise for lower- and middle-class children, since, in general, the greater the value of the reward the more the subject will tend to maximize (cf. Tune, 1964; Weir, 1964).

Under conditions of negative reinforcement, a problem-solving approach might similarly hold for middle-class children, the problem in this instance being the avoidance of wrong responses. Maximizing, on the other hand, makes little psychological sense where negative reinforcement is concerned, since locating rewards may be more important for the subject than avoiding punishment.

A problem-solving versus maximizing interpretation of these data, however, is limited by the fact that the children apparently did not achieve asymptotic performance (see Figure 1). Clearly, additional trials would have been necessary in order to reach asymptote, yet it is doubtful that such young children could have handled more trials. Moreover, an internal analysis of responses, such as the number of consecutive times the subject depressed the left lever (cf. Rosenhan, 1966) was not possible in this study because the responses to the levers were summarized on counters, rather than individually recorded. Nevertheless, a strategy interpretation remains a distinct possibility for these data.

Alternative Interpretations of These Findings

Differential child-rearing practices in lower- and middle-class homes: The effect of reinforcer adaptation and variability. Sears, Maccoby, and Levin (1957) have shown that social classes differ in their methods of child rearing. Specifically, lower-class parents are more prone to employ physical punishment with their children while middle-class parents use verbal persuasions and penalties. It is conceivable that by the time the middle-class child is 6 years old, he has become relatively adapted to (satiated on?) verbal reinforcers such that neither approval nor disapproval affect him deeply or differentially. For lower-class children, however, who are relatively less adapted to verbal methods of behavior control, approval and disapproval have more potent effects.

There is in fact some experimental evidence that can be interpreted to support the notion that middle-class children are to some extent satiated on verbal reinforcers. Gewirtz and Baer (1958) compared the responses to approval of children who had been experimentally satiated with or deprived of approval for a brief period of time. They found that compared to a matched untreated control group, deprived children were more responsive to approval. Subsequent evidence (Rosenhan, in press) demonstrated that deprived subjects were more responsive to both approval and disapproval than were satiated subjects. The combined data would be consistent with the view that young middle-class children are relatively adapted to verbal reinforcement regardless of valence, that their responsiveness to such reinforcers increases only after periods of deprivation. While comparable data are not available for lower-class children, they might conceivably be more "deprived of sociality" than their middle-class peers and hence more responsive to it (cf. Zigler, 1961; Zigler & Williams, 1963).

If there is some difficulty with this interpretation, it rests with the strong effects of disapproval on lower-class children. For while lower-class parents tend to utilize physical means of punishment, they do not use such means exclusively. Presumably it is combined with verbal disapproval such that lower-class children ought to have become adapted to both kinds of disapproval, or perhaps to disapproval in general. Their performance in the disapproval condition, relative to middle-class children, indicates clearly that this is not the case, weakening thereby a child-rearing interpretation of these data or requiring a more complex model.

Anxiety. The data are clearly interpretable within an anxiety framework; namely, lower-class children are more anxious in a middle-class setting than are middle-class children. Thus, for lower-class children, approval reduces anxiety while disapproval heightens it. Since middle-class children, on the other hand, are presumed to be quite secure in this setting, neither approval nor disapproval affects them strongly.

Such an interpretation is not inconsistent with an alienation view of lower-class children's behavior in that these children may be anxious because they are alienated. Offered by itself, of course, an anxiety interpretation gives no clue as to why lower-class children should be more anxious. And since no independent measures of anxiety were obtained it was felt that the alienation interpretation offered was the more appropriate one at this time.

Intelligence. Probability learning has been conceptualized as a problem-solving task in which the subject devises strategies to maximize his gain (i.e., to get the most correct answers). As such, one might expect intelligence to play something of a role. Numerous studies have shown that relative to the lower class, middle-class children possess superior IQs (cf. Deutsch & Brown, 1964), and one would therefore have expected such children to have performed better under all conditions. Since this did not in fact occur, an interpretation that rests on social class differences in intelligence is not appropriate to these data.

Class versus Color

While there is considerable evidence that young children are perceptive of and sensitive to racial differences, these differences do not appear to affect their responsiveness to verbal reinforcement. Ordinarily, one might have expected Negro lower-class children to experience most alienation with a middle-class white experimenter, by virtue of the combined effects of both class and color differences. Thus, their responsiveness to both approval and disapproval should have been heightened relative to lower-class white children. Since this did not occur it can be argued that, at least for very young boys, social class differences rather than color differences are the critical variables that determine responsiveness in reinforcement situations. It should be noted that a similar failure to obtain differences between Negro and white lower-class children, this time in a simple conditioning task, occurred previously (Rosenhan & Greenwald, 1965).

Clearly, the failure to obtain race differences in performance in two studies may simply reflect the restricted range of the experimental paradigms employed. Perhaps different experimental tasks or conditions might have elicited the presumed racial differences. At the same time, we note that this experiment *was* sufficiently sensitive to distinctions of social class which were presumably based on the same dynamics of alienation that should argument that the experiment considers a restricted range of behavior is only partially compelling.

It is also possible that the tendency to be sensitive to racial differences reflects primarily the tendency to distinguish people and behaviors that are within one's social class from those that are outside of it. In other words, racial differences may be one aspect of social class differences, particularly insofar as relatively few Negroes are in the middle class. In any event, it seems clear that as far as the performance of young children is concerned (as distinguished from perceptions and attitudes), class is far more significant than color.

References

Clark, K. B. Educational stimulation of racially disadvantaged children. In A. H. Passow (Ed.), *Education in depressed areas.* New York: Teachers College, Columbia University, Bureau of Publications, 1963. Pp. 142–162.

Deutsch, M., & Brown, B. Social influences in Negro-white intelligence differences. *Journal of Social Issues,* 1964, *20,* 24–35.

Douvan, E. Social status and success striving. *Journal of Abnormal and Social Psychology,* 1956, *52,* 219–233.

English, H. B., & English, A. C. *A comprehensive dictionary of psychological and psychoanalytical terms.* New York: Longmans, Green, 1958.

Gewirtz, J. L., & Baer, D. M. The effect of brief social deprivation on behaviors for a social reinforcer. *Journal of Abnormal and Social Psychology,* 1958, *56,* 49–56.

Passow, A. H. *Education in depressed areas.* New York: Teachers College, Columbia University, Bureau of Publications, 1963.

Riessman, F. *The culturally deprived child.* New York: Harper & Row, 1962.

Rosenhan, D. *Cultural deprivation and learning: An examination of method and theory.* (Res. Memo. 65–4) Princeton, N. J.: Educational Testing Service, 1965.

Rosenhan, D. Double alternation in children's binary-choice responses: A dilemma for theories of learning and arousal. *Psychonomic Science,* 1966, *4,* 431–432.

Rosenhan, D. Aloneness and togetherness as drive conditions in children. *Journal of Experimental Research in Personality,* in press.

Rosenhan, D., & Greenwald, J. A. The effects of age, sex, and socioeconomic class on responsiveness to two classes of verbal reinforcement. *Journal of Personality,* 1965, *33,* 108–121.

Sears, R. R., Maccoby, E. E., & Levin, H. *Patterns of child rearing.* Evanston, Ill.: Row, Peterson, 1957.

Tune, G. S. Response preferences: A review of some recent literature. *Psychological Bulletin,* 1964, *61,* 286–302.

Warner, W. L., Meeker, M., & Eells, K. *Social class in America.* Chicago: Science Research Associates, 1949.

Weir, M. W. Developmental changes in problem-solving strategies. *Psychological Review,* 1964, *71,* 473–490.

Zigler, E. Social deprivation and rigidity in the performance of feebleminded children. *Journal of Abnormal and Social Psychology,* 1961, *62,* 413–421.

Zigler, E., & Kanzer, P. The effectiveness of two classes of verbal reinforcers on the performance of middle- and lower-class children. *Journal of Personality,* 1962, *30,* 157–163.

Zigler, E., & Williams, J. Institutionalization and the effectiveness of social reinforcement: A three-year follow-up study. *Journal of Abnormal and Social Psychology,* 1963, *66,* 197–205.

Foreword to Reading 2.3

INTRODUCTION

In our society, there are a number of differences between the behavior of
men and of women. For instance, it is generally accepted that men tend
to be more aggressive than women (physically aggressive at least), and less
dependent than women. They also seem to place more stress on achievement than women, and less stress on social relationships. In the past few
years, these differences have become a popular subject due to the upswing
of the women's liberation movement, and the academic world has reacted
by instituting courses in the psychology of women. The student who is
interested in this topic might want to look at such recent books as *Sex
and Identity* by Rosenberg and Sutton-Smith (1972) and *Psychology of
Women* by Bardwick (1971).

The question of how women come to act in a "feminine" way and
men in a "masculine" way, is an unsettled one at the present time. There
are a number of theories available, but very little in the way of hard data.
The classic theory in the area is that of Freud, who proposed that boys and
girls between about 3 and 5 years of age undergo different experiences in
the "phallic" stage. Little boys at this stage presumably desire sexual contact
with their mothers, and resent their fathers for having this privilege.
However, they also fear that their fathers will castrate them for having
these feelings, and so they eventually change their feelings into an identification with their fathers. By feeling themselves to be like their fathers, they
achieve both vicarious possession of their mothers, and some assurance of
good treatment from their fathers. Little girls, on the other hand, channel
their sexual feelings into a desire for contact with their fathers and a
resentment of their mothers. However, they never totally resolve the conflicts of this stage, because they have no fear of castration, feeling instead
that they have already been castrated. Freud felt that it is through resolution
of the Oedipal complex that little boys develop a superego or conscience,

41

since in identifying with the father, the little boy also accepts for himself
the father's moral point of view. Since little girls can never resolve their
Oedipal complex, Freud felt that they can never have as strong a superego
as little boys. As a result, he suggested that women "show less sense of
justice than men . . . they are less ready to submit to the great necessities
of life . . . (and) they are more often influenced in their judgments by
feelings of affection or hostility. . . . (Schaeffer, 1971, p. 20)

Freud is not the only theorist to have emphasized possible physiological
determinants of sex differences. Bardwick (in Bardwick et al., 1970)
suggests that since little girls are not only less active than little boys, but
also tend to masturbate less (presumably because of having a less visible
genital organ), they encounter less discipline from their parents. Thus,
they are not forced to develop an internal sense of who they are, but depend
on others to provide them with praise and a feeling of worth.

There are, of course, theorists who take the opposite tack, ignore the
biological aspects of sex differences and concentrate on the possibility that
the behavioral differences can be attributed to the environment. One such
theorist is David Lynn (1966) who has suggested that the little girl finds
it simpler to find an appropriate model for identification than the little boy
since the average mother is at home much of the day, and her activities can
be viewed by the child. Lynn feels that both boys and girls initially identify
with the mother, since the mother is a rewarding and familiar figure. The
little girl can continue to desire similarity with her mother, but the little
boy is not rewarded for feeling this way. Moreover, he is often told by
others that "little boys don't act in that way"; he is defined by others as a
male and is faced with the problem of figuring out how a male should act.
Since his father's activities are not always visible, he has to base his behavior
on inferences from conversation, rewards for behavior, and the mass
media. Thus, Lynn feels that the early social learning to be a boy or a
girl in our society encourages the boy to be an active problem-solver and
analytical thinker, and the girl to be an other-directed and socially sensitive
person.

Then, as a related theory, we might cite that of Kohlberg (1966),
mentioned in the discussion section of this article. Kohlberg also stresses
the importance of being labeled by others as a girl or a boy. He feels that
by the time the child is 6 or so, he can label himself as either a boy or a
girl, can label objects and activities as being either appropriate to masculinity
or to feminity, and is motivated to adopt the values and behaviors that are
appropriate to his own self-identification. As part of this process, he is
also motivated to identify with and imitate the same-sex parent. The source
of this motivation, according to Kohlberg, is the general human tendency
to maintain a cognitive consistency or balance. The reader will notice that

this notion of consistency is found in several sections of this volume. It is clearly an influential one in social psychology. Briefly stated, the idea is that people prefer that their ideas, behaviors and so on fit together in some reasonable way. They feel some discomfort if, say, they label themselves as men, and yet are aware of acting as women are supposed to in our society. It is not clear if this tendency to prefer balance to imbalance (which is not always the case, by the way) derives from the structure of the human brain, or from a learned tendency to prefer simpler units of thought to more complex ones.

Gewirtz (also mentioned in the discussion section of this article) has raised several possibilities for the development of sex-appropriate and other behaviors (see Mussen, 1970). In earlier formulations, Gewirtz concentrated on the notion that children learn a "drive" for social reinforcement, such as approval. He found that children who had not received social approval for some length of time were more eager to receive it than children who had not been deprived of this reward. Presumably, children might acquire such a drive because approval from a parent is associated with the physical contact that is thought to be innately pleasurable to infants. This drive would motivate the child to behave in ways that gain approval from adults. In later formulations of his ideas, Gewirtz abandoned the drive notion, and concentrated on the idea that, through reward and punishment, children learn when and whom to imitate. This notion is not specific to that of sex-appropriate behavior, but it is applicable to it.

Leaving the theories for the moment, Goldberg and Lewis point out that there has been little empirical work on infancy in any area (no doubt because infant subjects are not readily available). The area of sex differences is no exception. The authors do cite some studies by Kagan and Lewis (1965), which indicated that sex differences appear at an early age. Kagan and Lewis observed that infant girls display more sustained attention to visual stimulation, and prefer more novel auditory patterns than infant boys at both 6 and 13 months of age.

METHOD

In the study reported here, Goldberg and Lewis were concerned with sex differences in personality, and the cause of these differences. They were able to obtain data on the interaction of mothers and children when the children were 6 months old, and again when the children were 13 months old. They regard their study as unusual in that the situation used at 13 months of age was one of choice and free play, rather than a response to a specific experimental stimulus.

RESULTS

The observations of the free play situation indicated that, statistically speaking, there are highly significant differences between the play and social behavior of 13-month-old infant boys and infant girls. The infant girls played less vigorously than the infant boys; the infant girls touched their mothers more and spent more time close to them; and the infant girls displayed less independence and perseverance in their attempts to circumvent a barrier placed between themselves and their toys and mothers.

The authors relate these findings to the six-month data indicating that the mothers of girls of this age touch their infants more than the mothers of boys. While one cannot know from this which came first, the touching or the dependence, the authors feel that it is the behavior of the mothers that created the dependence and quiet style of the girls, and the independence and activity of the boys.

They also note (and this seems to be a contradiction) that the *female* children of highly rejecting mothers (as well as highly nurturant mothers) are highly dependent. It is not clear from this article why this relationship between rejection and dependence should not occur for male infants as well; perhaps male infants are less likely to be rejected, or perhaps they have less of a biological need to be touched.

DISCUSSION

Goldberg and Lewis analyze their results by suggesting that in the first several years of life, children learn sex-appropriate behavior because it is rewarded. (As mentioned above, however, this does not account for the behavior of the female children of rejecting mothers. Perhaps the behavior of the fathers, which was not tested, would provide some explanation.) The authors also feel that the reinforcement notion does not account for the behavior of older children and suggest that at a later age Kohlberg's cognitive theory would provide a better explanation.

In comparing the results here with the theories described in the introduction, it would seem that there is little evidence against any of the theories; however, the early appearance of the sex differences is not necessarily predicted by them. In any case, this is a "hot" issue in psychology today, and the reader can expect new theories and data in the near future.

References

Bardwick, J. M. *Psychology of women.* New York: Harper & Row, 1971.
Bardwick, J. M., Douvan, E., Horner, M. S., & Gutmann, D. *Feminine personality and conflict.* Belmont, California: Brooks/Cole, 1970.

Kagan, J., & Lewis, M. Studies of attention in the human infant. *Merrill-Palmer Quarterly,* 1965, *11,* 95–127.

Kohlberg, L. A cognitive-developmental analysis of children's sex-role concepts and attitudes. In E. E. Maccoby (Ed.), *The development of sex differences.* Stanford: Stanford University Press, 1966.

Lynn, D. B. The process of learning parental and sex-role identification. *Journal of Marriage and the Family,* 1966, *28,* 466–470.

Mussen, P. H. (Ed.), *Carmichael's manual of child psychology.* Third Edition. New York: Wiley, 1970.

Rosenberg, B. G., & Sutton-Smith, B. *Sex and identity.* New York: Holt, Rinehart and Winston, 1972.

Schaeffer, D. L. (Ed.), *Sex differences in personality: readings.* Belmont, California: Brooks/Cole, 1971.

2.3 Play Behavior in the Year-Old Infant: Early Sex Differences

Susan Goldberg
Michael Lewis

32 boys and 32 girls, 13 months old, were observed with their mothers in a standardized free play situation. There were striking sex differences in the infants' behavior toward their mothers and in their play. Earlier observation of the mothers' behavior toward the infants at 6 months indicates that some of these sex differences were related to the mothers' behavior toward the infants. It was suggested that parents behave differently toward girls and boys, even as infants, reinforcing sex-appropriate behavior. This study emphasizes the importance of observing the freely emitted behavior of the very young child.

Until recently, the largest proportion of studies in child development gave attention to nursery and early grade school children. The literature on sex differences is no exception. A recent book on development of sex differences which includes an annotated bibliography (Maccoby, 1966) lists fewer than 10 studies using infants, in spite of the fact that theoretical discussions (e.g., Freud, 1938 [originally published in 1905]; Piaget, 1951) emphasize the importance of early experience. Theoretical work predicts and experimental work confirms the existence of sex differences in behavior by age 3. There has been little evidence to demonstrate earlier differentiation of sex-appropriate behavior, although it would not be unreasonable to assume this occurs.

Recently, there has been increased interest in infancy, including some work which has shown early sex differences in attentive behavior (Kagan & Lewis, 1965; Lewis, in press). The bulk of this work has been primarily experimental, studying specific responses to specific stimuli or experimental

Child Development, 1969, *40*, 21–31. © 1969 by the Society for Research in Child Development, Inc. All rights reserved.

This research was conducted at the Fels Research Institute and was supported in part by grants HD-00868, FR-00222, and FR-05537 from the National Institute of Mental Health, U. S. Public Health Service. Editorial assistance was supported by research grant 1 PO1 HD01762 from the National Institute of Child Health and Human Development. Portions of this paper were presented at the 1967 meeting of the Society for Research in Child Development, New York. We would like to thank Lynn Godfrey, Cornelia Dodd, and Helen Campbell for their aid in data analysis. Author Lewis' address: Center for Psychological Studies, Educational Testing Service, Princeton, New Jersey 08540.

conditions. Moreover, it has dealt with perceptual-cognitive differences rather than personality variables. There has been little observation of freely emitted behavior. Such observations are of importance in supplying researchers with the classes of naturally occurring behaviors, the conditions under which responses normally occur, and the natural preference ordering of behaviors. Knowledge of this repertoire of behaviors provides a background against which behavior under experimental conditions can be evaluated.

The present study utilized a free play situation to observe sex differences in children's behavior toward mother, toys, and a frustration situation at 13 months of age. Because the Ss were participants in a longitudinal study, information on the mother-child relationship at 6 months was also available. This made it possible to assess possible relations between behavior patterns at 6 months and at 13 months.

METHOD

Subjects

Two samples of 16 girls and 16 boys each, or a total of 64 infants, were seen at 6 and 13 months of age (±6 days). All Ss were born to families residing in southwestern Ohio at the time of the study. All were Caucasian. The mothers had an average of 13.5 years of schooling (range of 10–18 years) and the fathers had an average of 14.5 years of schooling (range of 8–20 years). The occupations of the fathers ranged from laborer to scientist. Of the 64 infants, 9 girls and 10 boys were first-born and the remaining infants had from 1 to 6 siblings.

The 6-Month Visit

The procedure of the 6-month visit, presented in detail in Kagan and Lewis (1965), included two visual episodes and an auditory episode where a variety of behavioral responses were recorded. The infant's mother was present during these procedures. At the end of the experimental procedure, the mother was interviewed by one of the experimenters, who had been able to observe both mother and infant for the duration of the session. The interviewer also rated both mother and infant on a rating scale. The items rated for the infant included: amount of activity, irritability, response to mother's behavior, and amount of affect. For the mother, the observer rated such factors as nature of handling, amount of playing with the baby, type of comforting behavior, and amount of vocalization to the baby. Each item was rated on a 7-point scale, with 1 indicating the most activity and 7 the least. For the purpose of this study, it was necessary to obtain a measure of the amount of physical contact the mother initiated with the child. Since scores on the individual scales did not result in sufficient variance in the population, a composite score was obtained by taking the mean score for each mother over all three of the touching-the-infant scales. These included:

amount of touching, amount of comforting, and amount of play. The composite touch scores (now called the amount of physical contact) resulted in a sufficiently variable distribution to be used for comparison with the 13-month touch data.

The 13-Month Visit

Kagan and Lewis (1965), who employed the same 64 infants for their study, described the procedures used at 6 months, which were similar to those of the present (13-month) study. The only addition was a free play procedure, which will be discussed in detail below.

The playroom, 9 by 12 feet, contained nine simple toys: a set of blocks, a pail, a "lawnmower," a stuffed dog, an inflated plastic cat, a set of quoits (graduated plastic doughnuts stacked on a wooden rod), a wooden mallet, a pegboard, and a wooden bug (a pull toy). Also included as toys were any permanent objects in the room, such as the doorknob, latch on the wall, tape on the electrical outlets, and so forth. The mother's chair was located in one corner of the room.

Procedure

Each S, accompanied by his mother, was placed in the observation room. The mother was instructed to watch his play and respond in any way she desired. Most mothers simply watched and responded only when asked for something. The mother was also told that we would be observing from the next room. She held the child on her lap, the door to the playroom was closed, and observation began. At the beginning of the 15 minutes of play, the mother was instructed to place the child on the floor.

Measurement

Two observers recorded the S's behavior. One dictated a continuous behavioral account into a tape recorder. The second operated an event recorder, which recorded the location of the child in the room and the duration of each contact with the mother.

Dictated recording. During the initial dictation, a buzzer sounded at regular time intervals, automatically placing a marker on the dictated tape. The dictated behavioral account was typed and each minute divided into 15-second units, each including about three typewritten lines. The typed material was further divided into three 5-second units, each unit being one typed line. Independent experimenters analyzed this typed material. For each minute, the number of toys played with and amount of time spent with each toy was recorded.

Event recorder. To facilitate recording the activity and location of the child, the floor of the room was divided into 12 squares. For each square, the observer depressed a key on the event recorder for the duration of time the child occupied that square. From this record it was possible to obtain such measures as the amount of time spent in each square and the number of squares traversed. A thirteenth key was depressed each time the child touched the mother. From this record, measures of (*a*) initial latency in leaving the mother, (*b*) total amount of time touching the mother, (*c*) number of times touching the mother, and (*d*) longest period touching the mother were obtained.

The data analysis presented in this report provides information only on sex differences (*a*) in response to the mother and (*b*) in choice and style of play with toys. Other data from this situation are presented elsewhere (Lewis, 1967).

RESULTS

Response to Mother (13 Months)

Open field.   Boys and girls showed striking differences in their behavior toward their mothers (see Table 1). First, upon being removed from

TABLE 1 *Summary of Infant Behavior to Mother in Free Play Session*

BEHAVIOR	GIRLS	BOYS	*p*
Touching mother:			
$\bar{x}$ latency in seconds to return to mother ...	273.5	519.5	<.002
$\bar{x}$ number of returns	8.4	3.9	<.001
$\bar{x}$ number of seconds touching mother	84.6	58.8	<.03
Vocalization to mother:			
$\bar{x}$ number of seconds vocalizing to mother ..	169.8	106.9	<.04
Looking at mother:			
$\bar{x}$ number of seconds looking at mother	57.3	47.0	<.09
$\bar{x}$ number of times looking at mother	10.8	9.2	NS
Proximity to mother:			
$\bar{x}$ time in squares closest to mother	464.1	351.4	<.05
$\bar{x}$ time in squares farthest from mother	43.8	44.3	NS

their mothers' laps, girls were reluctant to leave their mothers. When *Ss* were placed on the floor by their mothers, significantly more girls than boys returned immediately—in less than 5 seconds (*p* < .05 for both samples by Fisher Exact Probability Test). This reluctance to leave their mothers is further indicated by the time it took the children to first return to their mothers. Girls, in both samples, showed significantly shorter latencies than boys. Out of a possible 900 seconds (15 minutes), girls returned after an average of 273.5 seconds, while boys' average latency was nearly twice as long, 519.5 seconds. This difference was highly significant (*p* < .002, Mann-Whitney *U* test). All significance tests are two-tailed unless otherwise specified.

Once the children left their mothers, girls made significantly more returns, both physical and visual. Girls touched their mothers for an average of 84.6 seconds, while boys touched their mothers for only 58.8 seconds (*p* < .03, Mann-Whitney *U* test). Girls returned to touch their mothers on an average of 8.4 times, and boys 3.9 times ($p < .001$, Mann-Whitney U test). For the visual returns, the number of times the child looked at the mother and the total amount of time spent looking at the mother were obtained from the dictated material. The mean number of times girls looked at the mother was 10.8 (as compared with 9.2 for boys), a difference which was not significant. The total amount of time looking at the mother was 57.3 seconds for girls and 47.0 seconds for boys ($p < .09$, Mann-Whitney U test).

Finally, vocalization data were also available from the dictated material. The mean time vocalizing to the mother was 169.8 seconds for girls and 106.9 seconds for boys ($p < .04$, Mann-Whitney U test).

Another measure of the child's response to his mother was the amount of physical distance the child allowed between himself and his mother. Because the observers recorded which squares the child played in, it was possible to obtain the amount of time Ss spent in the four squares closest to the mother. The mean time in these squares for girls was 464.1 seconds; for boys, it was 351.4 seconds ($p < .05$, Mann-Whitney U test). Moreover, boys spent more time in the square farthest from the mother, although the differences were not significant.

Barrier frustration. At the end of the 15 minutes of free play, a barrier of mesh on a wood frame was placed in such a way as to divide the room in half. The mother placed the child on one side and remained on the opposite side along with the toys. Thus, the child's response to stress was observed.

Sex differences were again prominent, with girls crying and motioning for help consistently more than boys (see Table 2). For both samples,

TABLE 2 *Summary of Infant Behavior during Barrier Frustration*

BEHAVIOR	GIRLS	BOYS	p
$\bar{x}$ number of seconds crying	123.5	76.7	$<.05$
$\bar{x}$ number of seconds at ends of barrier	106.1	171.0	$<.001$
$\bar{x}$ number of seconds at center	157.7	95.1	$<.01$

amount of time crying was available from the dictated record. Girls' mean time crying was 123.5 seconds, compared with 76.7 seconds for boys ($p < .05$, Mann-Whitney U test). Boys, on the other hand, appeared to make a more active attempt to get around the barrier. That is, they spent significantly more time at the ends of the barrier than girls, while girls spent significantly more time in the center of the barrier—near the position where they were placed ($p < .01$, Mann-Whitney U test).

Toy Preference (13 Months)

A second area of experimental interest was toy preference. When the nine toys were ranked in order of the total amount of time they were played with, girls and boys showed similar patterns of preference.

Table 3 presents each toy and the amount of time it was played with. Play with the dog and cat were combined into one category. The toys which were used most were the lawnmower, blocks, and quoits, and those that were used least were the stuffed dog and cat. On a *post hoc* basis, it seems as if the toys which received the most attention were those that offered the most varied possibilities for manipulation.

TABLE 3 *Mean Time Playing with Toys, by Sex*

	GIRLS	BOYS	p
Total time with:			
Mallet	51.7	60.8	...
Bug	50.2	45.3	...
Pail	34.6	22.9	...
Blocks	126.5	77.5	<.03
Lawnmower	220.3	235.6	...
Cat plus dog (combined)	31.0	9.1	<.01
Quoits	122.7	130.3	...
Pegboard	37.2	28.7	<.05
Nontoys	6.9	31.0	<.005
Putting toys in pail	28.2	43.0	...
Banging toys	19.7	34.8	<.05
Lawnmowing on other toys	2.8	9.8	...
Other manipulation of two toys	28.2	10.3	<.05

FIG. 1. These two pictures illustrate typical sex differences in children reacting to a frustration situation. The girl, at the left, is standing at the middle of the barrier and crying helplessly, while the boy, at the right, though showing signs of distress, is making an active attempt to get around the barrier.

Although there were no sex differences in overall toy preference, there were significant sex differences in the amount of time spent with individual toys and in the ways toys were used. Girls played with blocks, pegboard, and with the dog and cat (the only toys with faces) more than boys did ($p < .03$, $p < .03$, $p < .01$, respectively, Mann-Whitney U test).

In terms of style of play, there were also sex differences. Observation of girls' play indicates that girls chose toys which involved more fine than gross muscle coordination, while for boys, the reverse was true—building blocks and playing with dog and cat versus playing with mallet and rolling the lawnmower over other toys. Moreover, boys spent more time playing with the nontoys (doorknob, covered outlets, lights, etc.; $p < .005$, Mann-Whitney U test).

In terms of overall activity level, boys were more active than girls. Girls tended to sit and play with combinations of toys ($p < .05$, Mann-Whitney U test), while boys tended to be more active and bang the toys significantly more than girls ($p < .05$, Mann-Whitney U test). In addition, the children were rated by two observers on the vigor of their play behavior; a rating of 1 was given for high vigor, 2 was given for medium vigor, and 3 for low vigor. These ratings were made from the dictated material for each minute, so that the final score for each S represented a mean of 15 vigor ratings. The interobserver reliability was $p = 0.78$. The boys played

FIG. 2. These pictures illustrate some of the sex differences observed in play behavior. The little girl, at the left, is squatting in one place, cuddling a soft animal. In contrast, the little boy, right, is actively swinging and banging the lawnmower over other toys.

significantly more vigorously than girls (mean for boys was 2.45, varying from 1.2 to 3.0; for girls, the mean was 2.65, varying from 1.9 to 3.0 [$p <$ .05, Mann-Whitney U test]). This vigor difference was also seen in the style of boys' play; for example, boys banged with the mallet and mowed over other toys. Thus, there were not only significant differences in the choice of toys, but also in the way the toys were manipulated. The data indicate that there are important and significant sex differences in very young children's response to their mothers, to frustration, and in play behavior.

Mother-infant touch (6 months). One possible determinant of the child's behavior toward the mother in the playroom is the mother's behavior toward the child at an earlier age. The 6-month data indicated that mothers of girls touched their infants more than mothers of boys. On the composite score, where 1 indicated most touching and 7 least, there were twice as many girls as boys whose mothers were rated 1–3 and twice as many boys as girls whose mothers were rated 5–7 ($p <$ .05, χ^2 test). Moreover, Mothers vocalized to girls significantly more than to boys ($p <$ .001, Mann-Whitney U test), and significantly more girls than boys were breast-fed rather than bottle-fed ($p <$ .02, Mann-Whitney U test). Thus, when the children were 6 months old, mothers touched, talked to, and handled their daughters more than their sons, and when they were 13 months old, girls touched and talked to their mothers more than boys did. To explore this relationship further, mothers were divided into high, medium, and low mother-touch-infant groups (at 6 months), with the extreme groups consisting of the upper and lower 25 per cent of the sample. For the boys at 13 months, the mean number of seconds of physical contact with the mother indicated a linear relation to amount of mother touching (14, 37, and 47 seconds for the low, medium, and high mother-touch groups, respectively; Kruskal-Wallis, $p <$ .10). Thus, the more physical contact the mother made with a boy at 6 months, the more he touched the mother at 13 months. For the girls, the relation appeared to be curvilinear. The mean number of seconds of touching the mother for the low, medium, and high mother-touch groups was 101, 55, and 88 seconds, respectively (Kruskal-Wallis, $p <$ .10). The comparable distribution for number of seconds close to the mother was 589, 397, and 475 seconds (Kruskal-Wallis, $p <$ .03). A girl whose mother initiated very much or very little contact with her at 6 months was more likely to seek a great deal of physical contact with the mother in the playroom than one whose mother was in the medium-touch infant group.

Observation of the mothers' behavior when their infants were 6 months old revealed that five of the seven mothers of girls who showed little physical contact were considered by the staff to be severely rejecting mothers. The data suggest that the child of a rejecting mother continues to seek contact despite the mother's behavior. This result is consistent with Harlow's work with rejected monkeys (Seay, Alexander, & Harlow, 1964) and Provence's work with institutionalized children (Provence, 1965; Provence & Lipton, 1962) and suggests that the child's need for contact with his mother is a powerful motive.

DISCUSSION

Observation of the children's behavior indicated that girls were more dependent, showed less exploratory behavior, and their play behavior reflected

a more quiet style. Boys were independent, showed more exploratory behavior, played with toys requiring gross motor activity, were more vigorous,
and tended to run and bang in their play. Obviously, these behavior differences approximate those usually found between the sexes at later ages.
The data demonstrate that these behavior patterns are already present in
the first year of life and that some of them suggest a relation to the mother's
response to the infant in the first 6 months. It is possible that at 6 months,
differential behavior on the part of the mother is already a response to
differential behavior on the part of the infant. Moss (1967) has found behavioral sex differences as early as 3 weeks. In interpreting mother-infant
interaction data, Moss suggests that maternal behavior is initially a response
to the infant's behavior. As the infant becomes older, if the mother responds
contingently to his signals, her behavior acquires reinforcement value which
enables her to influence and regulate the infant's behavior. Thus, parents
can be active promulgators of sex-role behavior through reinforcement of
sex-role-appropriate responses within the first year of life.

The following is offered as a hypothesis concerning sex-role learning.
In the first year or two, the parents reinforce those behaviors they consider
sex-role appropriate and the child learns these sex-role behaviors independent of any internal motive, that is, in the same way he learns any appropriate response rewarded by his parents. The young child has little idea as
to the rules governing this reinforcement. It is suggested, however, that as
the child becomes older (above age 3), the rules for this class of reinforced
behavior become clearer and he develops internal guides to follow these
earlier reinforced rules. In the past, these internalized rules, motivating without apparent reinforcement, have been called modeling behavior. Thus,
modeling behavior might be considered an extension or internalization of
the earlier reinforced sex-role behavior. However, it is clear that the young
child, before seeking to model his behavior, is already knowledgeable in
some appropriate sex-role behavior. In that the hypothesis utilizes both early
reinforcement as well as subsequent cognitive elaboration, it would seem to
bridge the reinforcement notion of Gewirtz (1967) and Kohlberg's cognitive theory (1966) of identification.

The fact that parents are concerned with early display of sex-role-
appropriate behavior is reflected in an interesting clinical observation. On
some occasions, staff members have incorrectly identified the sex of an
infant. Mothers are often clearly irritated by this error. Since the sex of a
fully clothed infant is difficult to determine, the mistake seems understandable and the mother's displeasure uncalled for. If, however, she views the
infant and behaves toward him in a sex-appropriate way, our mistake is
more serious. That is, the magnitude of her displeasure reveals to us the
magnitude of her cognitive commitment to this infant as a child of given
sex.

Regardless of the interpretation of the observed sex differences, the free play procedure provides a standardized situation in which young children can be observed without interference from experimental manipulation. While behavior under these conditions may be somewhat different from the young child's typical daily behavior, our data indicate that behavior in the play situation is related to other variables, that behavior can be predicted from earlier events, and that it is indicative of later sex-role behavior. The results of the present investigation as well as the work of Bell and Costello (1964), Kagan and Lewis (1965), and Lewis (in press) indicate sex differences within the first year over a wide variety of infant behaviors. The fact that sex differences do appear in the first year has important methodological implications for infant research. These findings emphasize the importance of checking sex differences before pooling data and, most important, of considering sex as a variable in any infant study.

References

Bell, R. Q., & Costello, N. S. Three tests for sex differences in tactile sensitivity in the newborn. *Biologia Neonatorum,* 1964, *1,* 335–347.

Freud, S. Three contributions to the theory of sex. Reprinted in *The basic writings of Sigmund Freud.* New York: Random House, 1938.

Gewirtz, J. The learning of generalized imitation and its implications for identification. Paper presented at the Society for Research in Child Development Meeting, New York, March, 1967.

Kagan, J., & Lewis, M. Studies of attention in the human infant. *Merrill-Palmer Quarterly,* 1965, *11,* 95–127.

Kohlberg, L. A cognitive-developmental analysis of children's sex role concepts and attitudes. In E. Maccoby (Ed.), *The development of sex differences.* Stanford, Calif.: Stanford University Press, 1966.

Lewis, M. Infant attention: response decrement as a measure of cognitive processes, or what's new, Baby Jane? Paper presented at the Society for Research in Child Development Meeting, symposium on "The Role of Attention in Cognitive Development," New York, March, 1967.

Lewis, M. Infants' responses to facial stimuli during the first year of life. *Developmental Psychology.*

Maccoby, E. (Ed.) *The development of sex differences.* Stanford, Calif.: Stanford University Press, 1966.

Moss, H. Sex, age and state as determinants of mother-infant interaction. *Merrill-Palmer Quarterly,* 1967, *13*(1), 19–36.

Piaget, J. *Play, dreams and imitation in childhood.* New York: Norton, 1951.

Provence, S. Disturbed personality development in infancy: a comparison of two inadequately nurtured infants. *Merrill-Palmer Quarterly,* 1965, *2,* 149–170.

Provence, S., & Lipton, R. C. *Infants in institutions.* New York: International University Press, 1962.

Seay, B., Alexander, B. K., & Harlow, H. F. Maternal behavior of socially deprived rhesus monkeys. *Journal of Abnormal and Social Psychology,* 1964, *69*(4), 345–354.

Foreword to Reading 2.4

INTRODUCTION

The socialization of aggression and of altruism are topics of great concern to a parent in our society, a society that is sometimes accused of being both cold and violent. To date, a small amount of research has indicated the effectiveness of reward on the production of these behaviors, and a much larger body of research has focused on the effect of real-life models of both pro- and antisocial behavior. (For the interested reader, Kaufmann, 1970, outlines this research.) Another research effort has been directed at the effect of violent (but not altruistic) models in the mass media. Goranson (1970) and Weiss (1969) provide reviews of this literature, and the reader might be interested in looking at Feshbach and Singer (1971), a longitudinal field study, or Turner and Berkowitz (1972) and Meyer (1972), laboratory studies in this area.

The studies reported in this article are unique in that the effects of altruistic and aggressive adult models were compared. Grusec introduces the research by outlining some of the theories that have been invoked to explain why children will often imitate such models. The reader might refer back to the commentary on the Goldberg and Lewis (1968) article in this volume for a further explanation of some of these theories.

Grusec also suggests that children in experimental situations may imitate adults, not because of any complicated reason, but simply because of "demand characteristics." The concept of "demand characteristics" was first suggested by Orne (1962) who raised the possibility that subjects in experiments want to play their role well and to contribute to science. Orne feels that there may be cues in the experimental situation that reveal the experimenter's hypothesis, and that the subjects may feel that it is part of their role to validate this hypothesis. He refers to these cues that indicate a hypothesis to the subjects (even if it is a wrong one) as "demand characteristics," presumably because the subjects feel a "demand" to act

in response to these cues. Orne's original discussion of "demand characteristics" seemed to suggest that they are a "nuisance" factor in laboratory
studies. However, to put it into a more general framework, in any situation,
people may try to act as they are "supposed" to be acting. It certainly
seems reasonable that children would react in this way, and would feel
that an adult model should be a good source of information as to the
appropriate action in a strange situation.

In order to test this hypothesis, Grusec and Skubiski (1970) investigated the effect of a model who spoke about the appropriate altruistic
behavior but never carried it out. They found that this "verbalization"
model was much less effective in producing imitation than the "performance" model who actually carried out the altruistic action. In other words,
the "demand characteristics" hypothesis was not confirmed for 8- and
10-year-old subjects, with the exception of girls in the condition in which
the model was particularly warm and friendly ("nurturant") to the subjects.

In order to further investigate this hypothesis, in the study reprinted
here the effect of "verbalization" and "performance" models on the
altruistic behavior of 7- and 11-year-old children was examined (experiment 1). Also, the effect of "verbalization" and "performance" models
on the *aggressive* behavior of 8- and 9-year-old children was studied
(experiment 2). Finally, experiments 1, 2, and 3 compared the extent to
which the children *remembered* the actions of the two models. The author
hypothesized that the performance and verbalization models would be
equally effective in eliciting altruism in older subjects (since these subjects
would be aware of the desirability of generous behavior), and in eliciting
aggression in subjects of all ages (since aggression would seem to be more
pleasurable than altruism, and thus more readily called forth).

METHOD

Experiments 1 and 2: In experiment 1, both the models (who were adult
and the same sex as the children) and the children were given rewards for
supposed high performance in a bowling game. The adult models, who
played the game before the children, either *donated* half of their winnings
to a charity for "poor children," or *stated*, before being called away to a
telephone call, that this was probably what "they" expected "us" to do.

In experiment 2, both the models and the children were exposed to
potentially aggressive and nonaggressive toys and allowed to play with the
toys. The adult models either *demonstrated* an aggressive sequence of
actions with the toys, or *described* (again before being called away) that
sequence of actions as the way that "one ought" to play.

RESULTS (Experiments 1, 2)

In general, the results did not support the predictions. In the case of the altruistic models, only the 7-year-old boys reacted differentially to the performance and verbalization models. In the case of the aggressive models, both the 8- and 9-year-old boys and the 8- and 9-year-old girls matched more of the performance model's behaviors than the verbalization model's behaviors (although even those children exposed to the verbalization model matched more behaviors than did a no-model control group).

DISCUSSION

As the reader will see, Grusec interprets her results in terms of the differences in our society between males and females. Much of this analysis is congruent with information discussed in the Goldberg and Lewis (1968) article in this volume. For instance, Grusec refers to the greater desire of females to win social approval as an explanation of some of the altruism data, and to the lesser tendency of females to be aggressive as an explanation of some of the aggression data. These explanations are plausible and fit the data well and the reader will want to consider them in conjunction with the results. However, the reader should also, as with any research, reanalyze the procedure in the light of the results. Here one might take a critical look at the procedures of experiments 1 and 2 to determine any important differences between them. For instance, in experiment 1, the subject was told by the verbalization model that "they expected" the players to share, whereas in experiment 2, the subject was told that "one ought" to be aggressive. It is conceivable that the first type of exhortation has a stronger effect on children concerned with pleasing adults than the second, although it is also possible that the differences between experiment 1 and experiment 2 were not crucial in determining the results. This kind of question can be answered by further research.

References

Feshbach, S., & Singer, R. D. *Television and aggression.* San Francisco: Jossey-Bass, 1971.

Goldberg, S., & Lewis, M. Play behavior in the year-old infant: early sex differences. *Child Development,* 1969, *40,* 21–31.

Goranson, R. E. Media violence and aggressive behavior: a review of experimental research. In Berkowitz, L. (Ed.), *Advances in experimental social psychology.* Vol. 5. New York: Academic Press, 1970.

Grusec, J. E., & Skubiski, L. Model nurturance, demand characteristics of the modeling experiment, and altruism. *Journal of Personality and Social Psychology*, 1970, *14*, 352–359.

Kaufmann, H. *Aggression and altruism*. New York: Holt, Rinehart and Winston, 1970.

Meyer, T. P. Effect of viewing justified and unjustified real film violence on aggressive behavior. *Journal of Personality and Social Psychology*, 1972, *23*, 21–29.

Orne, M. On the social psychology of the psychological experiment: with particular reference to demand characteristics and their implications. *American Psychologist*, 1962, *17*, 776–783.

Turner, C. W., & Berkowitz, L. Identification with film aggressor (covert role taking) and reactions to film violence. *Journal of Personality and Social Psychology*, 1972, *21*, 256–264.

Weiss, W. Effects of the mass media of communication. In Lindzey, G., & Aronson, E. (Eds.), *The handbook of social psychology*. 2d ed. Vol. 5. Reading, Mass: Addison-Wesley, 1969.

2.4 Demand Characteristics of the Modeling Experiment: Altruism as a Function of Age and Aggression[1]

Joan E. Grusec

The effects on subsequent imitation of observing a model perform a particular behavior or merely say that he thought it was the appropriate thing to do were compared for sharing (which involves self-sacrifice) and aggression (which may be pleasurable). Eleven-year-old boys and girls and 7-year-old girls shared under both performance and verbalization conditions. Seven-year-old boys shared in a performance but not in a verbalization condition, although they were equally aware of the model's behavior in the two conditions. Eight- and 9-year-old boys and girls tended to display more imitative aggression in a performance than a verbalization condition. Those in the latter condition, however, were more aggressive than children who did not observe any model. Performance-verbalization differences in boys appeared to be mediated by learning differences. This explanation could not account for the behavior of girls, however, who learned performed and verbalized behaviors equally well. The implications of these findings for the role of the model in imitation studies are discussed.

Explanations of the phenomena of imitation and identification have been abundant. Freud (1925) proposed that the young boy identifies with his father in order to reduce anxiety over anticipated punishment for his incestuous wishes toward his mother and, at the same time, to vicariously gain her affection. Mowrer (1950) and Sears (1957) suggested that children imitate their caretakers because this matching of behavior has intrinsic reinforcement value. Maccoby (1959) hypothesized that children attend more closely to the behavior of powerful models in order to maximize their own rewards, thus learning more about that behavior and hence reproducing more of it in an appropriate stimulus situation. Lately, Gewirtz and Stingle (1968) have proposed that observers imitate because they have previously

Journal of Personality and Social Psychology, 1972, Vol. 22, No. 2, 139–148. Copyright 1972 by the American Psychological Association, and reproduced by permission.

1 This investigation was supported by Grant 116 from the Ontario Mental Health Foundation. The author wishes to thank officials of the North York Parks and Recreation Department, their playground supervisors, and the principal and teachers of Transfiguration School, Toronto, and of the Institute of Child Study at the University of Toronto for their generous cooperation. Appreciation is due to Valerie Hunt, who acted as the experimenter, and to Nancy Satterberg, Karen Seabrook, William Glover, and Norman Greenberg who acted as models.

been reinforced for matching their behavior to that of a model. Many of the innumerable laboratory demonstrations during the last decade that individuals will, in fact, fashion their behavior after that of someone they have observed have been explained by these theories, or variants thereof. Lately, however, it has been suggested that subjects in many studies of imitation may be imitating observed behaviors not for any of these relatively complex reasons, but simply in response to the demand characteristics of the experimental situation. Thus, for the child placed in an unusual situation, the model's behavior may provide information about the appropriateness of a given act (Aronfreed, 1968; Flanders, 1968; Krebs, 1970). This information need not be mediated by actual performance of the behavior, but presumably could just as easily be provided by nonsocial cues or verbal instruction. Thus, a subject in a modeling study need not actually observe someone perform the behavior of interest; a statement about what ought to be done in the situation should be sufficient.

A test of this hypothesis was undertaken by Grusec and Skubiski (1970). They exposed 8- and 10-year-old subjects to an adult who either performed the behavior of interest—in this case giving half of his winnings from a game to poor children—or who merely verbalized what he thought the appropriate behavior was—to donate half of what he won to charity. An attempt was made to keep the amount of information conveyed to the subjects in each condition constant. In the performance condition the model shared five times, while in the verbalization condition, he stated, in five various ways, that one ought to share. Grusec and Skubiski found that the subjects in the performance condition shared, while those in the verbalization condition, with the exception of girls to whom the model had previously been warm and friendly, shared virtually not at all. Similarly, Bryan and Walbek (1970), using 8- to 10-year-olds, found that moral exhortations about the general desirability of sharing were ineffective in producing that behavior. It seems evident, then, that at least with regard to the behavior of sharing by children aged 8–10, and with the exception of nurtured girls, actual demonstration of that behavior by a model, rather than just verbal references to it, is necessary for it to be displayed. The reason for this is not obvious. Performance may produce sharing, while verbalization or moral exhortation do not since only in the former situation do subjects see that people who give up rewards do not necessarily feel unhappy and uncomfortable afterwards. Perhaps performance leads to disinhibition of the tendency not to engage in novel behaviors in a strange situation, while verbalization still necessitates too much initiative on an observer's part in translating words into actions. Again, subjects who observe a model share would have to label themselves as selfish by comparison with a generous model if they did not also share. In a verbalization condition the model would not have established himself as generous, and so nonsharers would suffer much less in comparison with him. These are probably only a few of the possible explanations.

In order to gain some idea of why performance and verbalization were not equally effective, and thereby just what function a model does serve in imitation, the present studies were devised to, hopefully, illustrate conditions under which performance and verbalization *would* be equally effective. The first study compares the effects of performance and verbalization in a sharing situation in which subjects of different ages were employed. Numerous studies have shown that sharing increases with age (Handlon & Gross, 1959; Ugurel-Semin, 1952). If a belief about the virtue of sharing, or a "norm of social responsibility" (Berkowitz & Daniels, 1963) has been well-learned, we might expect that simple statements about appropriate behavior should suffice to remind the subjects of that norm and induce them to share. On the other hand, for subjects for whom the norm is not well-established, verbalization, for the kinds of reasons offered above, might not be sufficient to produce sharing. Thus, young subjects might not realize that self-sacrifice is virtuous and approved of, and that one is supposed to feel good after he has engaged in it, even if he is not discovered in the act.

In an initial experiment, then, to compare the relative effectiveness of performance and verbalization with younger and older children, 7- and 11-year-old boys and girls[2] saw a model either share some of his winnings from a game with poor children or merely verbalize his expectations that it was appropriate to share in that situation. Then, the subjects played the game alone, and the amount of sharing they did was observed through a one-way mirror. Subjects were also asked to recall as much as they could of the model's behavior in the two conditions in order to see if the model's behavior might be better remembered in the performance than the verbalization condition and thus if differences in acquisition might account for any observed differences in sharing. In addition to the performance and verbalization groups, a control group of 11-year-olds was run to see how much sharing they would do in the absence of a model. Previous data from the Grusec and Skubiski (1970) study indicated that younger children would not share at all under these conditions. It seemed possible, however, that an experimenter's permissive reference to sharing might elicit that behavior in older subjects.

Sharing is a behavior whose performance has no attraction in and of itself. Giving up to others material rewards that one might have kept for oneself necessitates self-denial, especially when no external reinforcement

---

[2] Seven-year-olds were chosen because they were the youngest subjects who could reliably understand the rules of the game employed by Grusec and Skubiski (1970), and 11-year-olds were chosen because they were the oldest subjects available—and older than Grusec and Skubiski's subjects.

for this is offered. Not only does altruistic behavior appear unnatural in the sense that it runs counter to learning theory principles, but it also is dissonant with psychoanalytic theory, which maintains that children are basically selfish and id driven. It is not too surprising, then, that something more than a verbal indication of its appropriateness would be necessary to induce some subjects, at least, to share.

But what of a behavior whose performance is not aversive, and may even be attractive? If subjects actually enjoy doing something, then verbalization of its appropriateness might be sufficient to ensure its occurrence. This hypothesis was tested in a second study, with aggression chosen as the relevant behavior. Certainly aggression involves no self-denial, and something about its production—perhaps the strong proprioceptive feedback it provides—may be pleasurable. Psychoanalytic theory suggests that aggression is one of man's basic drives, and Lorenz (1963) talks of man's instinctive aggressiveness. Even research inspired by social learning theory may be interpreted to suggest that aggressiveness has some intrinsic attractiveness. Bandura and Huston (1961) found that aggressive responses were readily imitated by young children regardless of a model's social characteristics, while the reproduction of neutral behaviors depended more greatly upon those characteristics.

In an experiment to test this second hypothesis that performance and verbalization would be equally effective in producing aggression, children either observed a model who engaged in a series of aggressive behaviors or one who stated that it was appropriate to perform these same behaviors. A third group of children did not see or hear a model, but were placed in a situation with the same physical materials as the first two groups in order to control for the amount of aggression these materials themselves might elicit.

EXPERIMENT I

Method

SUBJECTS

The subjects were 20 boys and 20 girls aged 7 years, and 30 boys and 30 girls aged 11 years. Twelve boys and 12 girls from the 7-year-old group and 18 boys and 18 girls from the 11-year-old group were attending summer playgrounds run by the North York Recreation Department, while the rest of the subjects came from a Metropolitan Toronto separate school and participated in the experiment approximately 3 months later.

DESIGN

A $2 \times 2 \times 2$ factorial design was employed, with the model's method of presentation—performance or verbalization—of sharing behavior, age of subjects, and sex of subjects being the factors of interest. Forty 7-year-old and forty 11-year-old boys and girls were randomly assigned to either a performance or verbalization group, and twenty 11-year-olds were assigned to a control group which did not observe a model. The same proportion of boys and girls from the playground and from the separate school were in each group. A male and female adult served as models, with each child seeing a same-sexed model. The same female experimenter was used with all subjects, with a different set of models being employed during the summer and the fall.

PROCEDURE

Performance and verbalization manipulations.   Children were brought individually by the experimenter to a mobile laboratory parked in the school yard, supposedly to test a bowling game designed for use by both children and adults. As they entered the trailer, the experimenter introduced the child to an adult who, she said, was also going to play the game. The game apparatus was a miniature bowling alley, bounded at the far end by a vertical shield. Eight jewel lights, labeled with numbers ranging from 10 to 80, were mounted in three staggered rows on the front of the shield. The model and subjects were told that the game involved skill and that when a ball was rolled into one of the holes (which they could not see) behind the shield, the corresponding light would come on. In fact, scores were preset from a control panel located in the adjoining observation room. Thus, the model and child could receive predetermined scores in all conditions. The players were told that when they bowled winning scores of 70 or 80, they would receive two marbles from a dispenser attached to the game. These marbles could be traded for prizes, and the more marbles they won, the better the prize they would get. Players were told to knock on the door at the end of their game so that the experimenter could then give them a prize in exchange for their marbles. The model was instructed to play first.

Just as she was leaving, the experimenter informed the players, almost as an afterthought, that marbles were being collected for toys for poor children. She indicated a red bowl which held a large number of marbles on a table across the room from the game and behind which was a picture of a child clothed in rags. The experimenter stated that, if they wanted, players could give some of the marbles they won to the poor children, but that they did not have to if they did not want to.

1. Performance: As soon as the experimenter left, the model played his game. He bowled 20 trials, winning on 5 of these trials and donating one of every two marbles he won to the poor children. On winning trials the model would gather his two marbles from the dispenser, cross in front of the subject to the poor children's bowl, deposit a marble in it, and say, "One for the poor children." The other marble he put in a blue bowl provided for players beside the game, saying, "And one for me." When he had finished playing, the model knocked on the door and was taken by the experimenter to another room to get his prize.

2. Verbalization: When the experimenter left, the model stood before the game, musing slowly to himself and taking care not to look at the child. He said:

Well, I guess they expect us to share our marbles with those poor children. Probably that's what one had better do. I guess if I gave one out of every two marbles I win to the poor children, that would be fair. So that means whenever I get a score of 70 or 80, I would get two marbles. I'd put one in the red dish for the poor children [the model looked at the bowl] and one in the blue dish for me. If I got any other score, I wouldn't win anything, so I really ought to hope I get a lot of 70s and 80s. Then there would be a chance to share some of the marbles with the poor children.

As in the Grusec and Skubiski (1970) study, an attempt was made in this speech to equate the amount of information that the subjects received about sharing with the information they received in the performance condition. In the performance condition the subjects saw the model share five times, while in the verbalization condition that number of references were made to sharing.

Immediately after this speech, before the model had a chance to begin his game, the experimenter returned to explain that the model's boss had called on the phone and would like to talk to him. The model left the room, followed by the experimenter who had instructed the child to go ahead and play.

Measurement of internalization and acquisition. The subject was left alone to bowl 40 trials, during which he won 20 marbles. The number of marbles he donated to the poor children's bowl was observed through a one-way mirror by the experimenter and recorded. A check on the number of marbles donated was also made at the end of the experiment, after the subject had left, by counting the number of marbles in the poor children's bowl and subtracting from this the number in it before the child began to play. In every case, there was complete agreement between these two numbers. When the child had finished bowling, the experimenter returned and announced that the model had had to go back to work and so would not be seeing the child again. He also stated that it would be possible for the subject to win more marbles, and hence an even better prize, if he could remember everything the model had done when he bowled (performance condition) or had said just before he was going to bowl (verbalization condition). The subject was then given a marble for every item of behavior correctly recalled. Finally, the child was given a prize in exchange for his marbles and was asked not to discuss the events in the trailer with any other children. Prizes were not distributed until all children at a given playground or from a given class in the school had been to the trailer.

Control groups. Children in the control groups were treated identically to those in the experimental groups except that they were not exposed to a model. They were brought to the trailer, were instructed about the game and the poor children's bowl, and were then left alone to bowl 40 trials. Only 11-year-olds were run in a control condition.

Results

The mean number of marbles given to the poor children in each performance and verbalization condition is presented in Table 1. Analysis of variance of these data yielded a significant main effect of method of presentation ($F = 5.38$, $df = 1/72$, $p < .05$) and an interaction between method of presentation, age, and sex ($F = 4.13$, $p < .05$). All other F values were less than 1. Further analysis of the terms involved in the three-way interaction showed that younger boys shared more in the performance than in the verbalization condition ($t = 2.51$, $df = 18$, $p < .02$, one-tailed). None

TABLE 1 *Mean Number of Marbles Shared in Each Condition*

CONDITION	BOYS		GIRLS	
	7 yr.	*11 yr.*	*7 yr.*	*11 yr.*
Performance	7.4	6.6	6.0	7.7
Verbalization	3.0	6.4	5.7	4.5
Control	—	1.0	—	2.2

of the other comparisons between performance and verbalization reached statistical significance ($t < 1$ for older boys and younger girls, and $t = 1.83$ for older girls). There were no differences between performance groups ($t < 1$ in every case). Younger boys shared less in the verbalization condition than did older boys ($t = 1.94$, $p < .05$, one-tailed), while there was no difference between younger and older girls ($t < 1$). It appears, then, that observation of an altruistic model was necessary to produce sharing in younger boys. The amount of sharing they did in the verbalization condition did not differ significantly from zero ($t = 1.96$, $df = 9$, $p < .10$, two-tailed; a two-tailed test was used here since no difference was predicted). Younger girls and all older children were equally affected by modeled behavior and verbal description of appropriate behavior.

Finally, the mean number of marbles shared by 11-year-olds in the control groups is also reported in Table 1. The amount of sharing in the control groups did not differ significantly from zero ($t = 1.25$ for boys, and $t = 1.10$ for girls).

The number of children in the performance condition who were able to recall that the model had shared half of the marbles he had won were: younger boys, 7; younger girls, 9; older boys, 9; older girls, 10. In the verbalization condition these acquisition scores were: younger boys, 6; younger girls, 9; older boys, 10; older girls, 10. The acquisition scores of interest in light of differences in sharing—the recall scores of younger boys in the performance and verbalization conditions—clearly did not differ from each other. Thus, although 7-year-old boys in the performance condition shared more than did 7-year-old boys in the verbalization condition, they did not recall the model's sharing behavior any better.

Discussion

These data do not completely support the hypothesis the study was designed to test. In accord with prediction, performance and verbalization were equally effective in producing sharing in older children. They were, contrary to prediction, also equally effective in producing sharing in 7-year-old girls. Verbalization did not, however, lead to any significant amount of sharing in 7-year-old boys.

Recall the findings of the Grusec and Skubiski (1970) study. Again, girls exposed to an adult who verbalized appropriate behavior shared as much as children in a performance condition, provided that the adult was warm and rewarding. Extrapolating from the findings of the present study, then, it would appear that the model's nonnurturance in the Grusec and Skubiski experiment may have served to suppress the effectiveness of verbalization rather than nurturance facilitating it.

The results of the present study might be explained in terms of 11-year-old boys and girls and 7-year-old girls having better internalized a norm of social responsibility than 7-year-old boys. There is, however, no evidence for sex differences in the speed with which the norm of sharing is acquired. Thus, the following speculations about the data are offered. The first is that young girls are more concerned with behaving in ways that would be approved of by adults than are young boys. Although boys may respond to deeds, as they did in the performance condition, they may feel less pressure to conform to mere words, as appeared to be the case in the verbalization condition. Adult females do show greater concern with displaying socially desirable behavior and are more conforming in their behavior (Crutchfield, 1955). Presumably, this is motivated in part, at least, by the importance of social approval—real or inferred—for them. If this differential importance of social approval for males and females has already developed by the age of 7, then we might expect that girls in the verbalization condition who had been told that sharing is appropriate behavior might have been more highly motivated to do the socially acceptable thing than were boys. In the Grusec and Skubiski (1970) study, nonnurtured girls may not have felt inclined to share when reminders came from someone who was cool and aloof, and who might therefore be considered a less credible source of information about the kind of behavior that people generally like. It is also possible that for individuals who desire social approval, more pleasure is derived from conforming to the suggestions of someone who is liked, and whose approval thereby has value, than of someone who is not particularly liked. This explanation, of course, does not account for the sharing of both sexes in the 11-year-old groups. Here, one might resort to the original hypothesis that the norm of social responsibility has been fairly well internalized by the age of 11, that verbalization of appropriate behavior makes that norm more salient, and that such additional motivators as a desire for inferred social approval are no longer necessary for the production of altruistic behavior.

Another explanation of the present findings[3] may lie in the fact that girls seem, until about the age of 10, to be more verbally fluent than boys (Maccoby, 1966). If this means that 7-year-old girls are also more capable of comprehending the meaning of speeches and translating these speeches

---

[3] The author is indebted to Gordon Finley for suggesting this explanation.

into action than are 7-year-old boys, this would account for the differences in effectiveness of verbalization. By the age of 11, boys have caught up to girls in verbal skills, and thus no differences in the effectiveness of verbalization should be apparent, as indeed they were not. This explanation is incomplete when the Grusec and Skubiski (1970) data are considered. Staub (1971) recently suggested that adult nurturance may decrease tension and fear of punishment for initiating novel action. Perhaps nonnurtured girls felt ill at ease and were therefore reluctant to translate the model's words into action, even though they had the cognitive ability to do so.

One additional finding of this first experiment should be noted. Even by the age of 11, an experimenter's permissive reference to sharing did not produce altruistic behavior since older children in the control group did not share at all. Apparently, even at this age, sharing has to be made more salient at least by verbal reminder.

EXPERIMENT II

Method

SUBJECTS

Subjects were 27 boys and 27 girls, aged 8 and 9 years. Fifteen boys and 15 girls were attending playgrounds organized by the North York Recreation Department and participated in this second experiment during the same period of time as Experiment I was being run. The rest of the subjects came from the Institute of Child Study at the University of Toronto and were run approximately 2½ months later.

DESIGN

A 3 × 2 factorial design was employed. Boys and girls either saw a model perform a series of aggressive responses, state that these were appropriate responses to perform, or were not exposed to a model. Five subjects in each group were from the summer playground, and four were from the Institute of Child Study. The same models and experimenter served in the study as had been employed in Experiment I, with the same change in models between summer and fall.

PROCEDURE

Performance, verbalization, and control group manipulations. Children from the playground were brought individually by the experimenter to the mobile laboratory in the school yard. Those at the Institute were run in a research room in the school itself. This room was approximately the same size as the experimental room in the trailer and was also equipped with a one-way mirror. Subjects were told that the experimenter was from a toy company and wanted to find out about the kinds of toys with which children and adults prefer to play. As they entered the experimental room, the experimenter introduced the child to an adult who was also going to take part in the study. Located in the room were the following items: a panda bear, a mallet, five balloons, two safety pins, a book, a small doll, a bow and several arrows, a plastic boat, a plastic bottle, and a rope. In addition to these items, which were used as props in the display of aggression, a coloring book, crayons, and a puzzle were included so as not to make the experimental situation entirely demanding of aggression. After the introductions, the experimenter excused herself, saying she had a few things to do in the other room, and instructed the model to play first since he had been waiting the longest. The subject was told to play when the model had finished.

1. Performance: As soon as the experimenter left the room, the model proceeded to play. He punched the doll and then kicked it across the room, shot arrows at the panda, whipped it with the rope, and stabbed it in the stomach with the mallet. Then he pounded the bottle on the table, jumped on the boat, ripped a page from the book, and broke two balloons. At this point the experimenter knocked on the door, entered the room, and instructed the model to come into the next room. The subject was told he could now play with the toys.

2. Verbalization: When the experimenter left, the model, musing slowly to himself and taking care not to look at the child, said:

> If one were to make up games with these toys, one ought to punch the baby doll and kick it across the room. Then one ought to shoot arrows at the panda and whip it with that rope and stab it in the stomach with the mallet. Then one ought to pound the bottle on the table, stomp on the boat, rip a page from the book, and break a couple of those balloons.

Immediately after the speech, before the model had a chance to begin playing with the toys, the experimenter knocked and entered the room, explaining that the model's boss had called on the phone and would like to talk to him. The model left the room, and the experimenter then told the child to go ahead and play with the toys. At this point, the experimenter, too, left the room.

3. Control: Each subject in this condition was brought to the experimental room, was told the experimenter wanted to find out what kinds of toys children prefer to play with, and was instructed to play with the toys. No model was present. The subject was then left alone by the experimenter.

Measurement of internalization and acquisition.   The child was observed through a one-way mirror for 10 minutes, and a complete written description was made of his activities by both models. Analysis of these descriptions later revealed that the recorders were in agreement 98% of the time. At the end of 10 minutes, the experimenter returned, announcing that the model had had to return to work and so would not be seeing the child again. She also stated that it would be possible for the child to win a prize if he could remember everything that the model had done when he had played with the toys (performance condition) or had said before he started to play with the toys (verbalization condition). Approval and encouragement were given for every item correctly recalled, and the child was occasionally reminded of the prize that could be his. Subjects in the control condition, of course, could not be tested for acquisition. Finally, all subjects were given a prize and asked not to discuss events that had just taken place with any other children. Again, as in the first experiment, prizes were not distributed until children from a given playground or class had taken part in the study.

When the subject left, any props that showed signs of wear were replaced before the next subject was run.

Results

The mean number of aggressive responses similar to those displayed by the model that were exhibited by children in the various conditions is presented in Table 2. Analysis of variance of these data yielded a main effect of method of presentation ($F = 11.01$, $df = 2/48$, $p < .01$). The effect of sex approached significance ($F = 3.65$, $p < .10$), with boys tending to display more aggression than girls. The interaction between method of presentation and sex was not significant ($F = 1.88$). Further analysis of the significant main effect yielded a t of 2.00 ($df = 34$, $p < .06$, two-tailed) for the comparison between performance and verbalization groups and a t of 2.66 ($p < .02$) for that between verbalization and control groups. Thus, children in the performance conditions were more aggressive than those in the verbalization conditions, with this difference falling *just* short of an accepted level of statistical significance. Subjects in the verbalization conditions clearly displayed more aggression than those in the control conditions.

Additional aggressive responses performed by subjects beyond those displayed by the model are also reported in Table 2. Analysis of variance of these data revealed no main effects of either method of presentation ($F = 2.00$) or sex ($F < 1$), nor was there a significant interaction between the two ($F = 1.48$). Thus, the experimental variables did not appear to have any effect on the subjects' willingness to display novel aggression.

Finally, the number of aggressive responses similar to the model's that were made by subjects in the control condition did not differ from zero ($t < 1$ for both boys and girls). Novel aggressive responses did differ from zero for boys ($t = 2.39$, $df = 8$, $p < .05$) but not for girls ($t = 1.05$).

The mean number of the model's behaviors recalled in the performance and verbalization conditions is also reported in Table 2. Analysis of variance of these data produced a significant main effect of method of presentation ($F = 15.32$, $df = 1/32$, $p < .001$). The effect of sex was not statistically significant ($F = 3.03$), nor was the interaction between method of presentation and sex ($F = 1.18$). Thus, children in the performance condition were able to recall more of the model's behavior than were children in the verbalization condition.

The reason for this difference in recall cannot, of course, be clear from the present study. The actual performance of aggression may have been more salient than a verbal description of the same behaviors. If this were

TABLE 2 *Mean Number of Behaviors Displayed and Recalled by Subjects in All Conditions*

VARIABLE	BOYS			GIRLS		
	Perfor-mance	*Verbal-ization*	*Control*	*Perfor-mance*	*Verbal-ization*	*Control*
Model's behaviors displayed	3.33	2.22	.11	1.89	1.00	.44
Novel aggressive behaviors displayed	4.44	5.56	1.22	5.11	1.56	1.89
Model's behaviors recalled	7.00	5.56	—	6.67	4.11	—

so, then the marginally significant difference in display of aggressive behaviors between the performance and verbalization groups might have resulted from the fact that subjects in the performance group knew more possible behaviors that they might exhibit. On the other hand, if performance subjects were more aggressive than verbalization subjects for some other reason, acquisition differences might have occurred because performance subjects had had more practice at recalling the model's behaviors. In order to assess these possibilities, an additional study was carried out in which subjects were asked to recall the model's acts or words immediately after he left the experimental room.

EXPERIMENT III

Method

SUBJECTS

Subjects were 10 boys and 10 girls, aged 8 and 9 years, from the same Metropolitan Toronto separate school as those children employed in Experiment I. This study was run immediately upon completion of Experiment I.

DESIGN

A 2 × 2 factorial design was employed. Boys and girls either saw a model perform aggressive responses or state that it was appropriate to do so. The models who had served in Experiment II with the Institute children also were employed in this study. The same female was the experimenter again, and all subjects were run in the mobile laboratory.

PROCEDURE

The procedure was identical to that for the performance and verbalization groups of Experiment II except that subjects were not allowed to play with the toys. As soon as the model left the room, the experimenter returned and asked them to recall all the model had done or said. Again, material and social incentives were offered for all accurate recall.

Results

The mean number of items of the model's behavior recalled by boys were: performance, 7.00; verbalization, 5.00. For girls they were: performance, 6.60; verbalization, 6.20. Analysis of variance of these data yielded an F of 7.20 for method of presentation ($df = 1/16$, $p < .05$), an F of < 1 for sex, and an F of 3.20 for the interaction between method of presentation and sex ($p < .10$). It is evident, then, that more of the aggressive behaviors were recalled by subjects in the performance condition than by those in the verbalization condition.

DISCUSSION

From these last two experiments, it appears that when 8- and 9-year-old children observe an adult actually perform a series of aggressive behaviors, they show a decided tendency ($p < .06$) to reproduce more of these behaviors than when they merely hear the adult state that one ought to be aggressive in a particular way. This latter condition, however, clearly did facilitate the display of aggression, for it led to greater production of the adult's behaviors than when no performing or verbalizing model was present. In this latter way, sharing and aggression are certainly different, at least for boys. While verbalization elicited a fair amount of aggression from 8- and 9-year-old boys, relative to a control group, it elicited no sharing at all in the same age group (Grusec & Skubiski, 1970).

The effects of performing or verbalizing aggressive behaviors seemed to be quite specific to the model's behaviors. There was no difference between the two experimental groups and the control group in their display of novel aggression. Thus, the presence of a performing or verbalizing model apparently did not convey to the subjects that they were freer to aggress in any way than if they had not seen or heard the model but only in the ways indicated by the model.

The difference between the effects of performance and verbalization seems at first inspection accountable for by differences in the amount learned by the two groups. Watching the performance of a relatively complex set of aggressive behaviors apparently produced better learning than just hearing them described. This difference presumably was translated into the observer's behavior. Children in the verbalization condition simply could not remember as many things to do as could the children in the performance condition. (It will be recalled, of course, that acquisition differences could not account for the obtained results of Experiment I—here the behaviors displayed by the model were fewer and less complex.) Thus, one could suggest that if modeled aggressive behaviors were simple, and therefore easily learned, performance and verbalization would be equally effective. One finding, however, that was nearly statistically significant, casts some doubt on this as a complete explanation. This was the Method of Presentation × Sex interaction of Experiment III, which yielded an F with an associated p value of less than .10. If one were to compare the mean recall scores for performance and verbalization, the difference for boys is quite significant ($t = 3.17$, $df = 8$, $p < .01$), while the comparison for girls is not ($t < 1$). Boys remembered more performed than verbalized material, while girls tended to remember both equally well. For boys, then, differences in acquisition do seem to account for the differential effectiveness of performance and verbalization. For girls, the picture is less clear.

Repeatedly, it has been found that girls display less aggressive behavior than boys (e.g., Bandura, 1965; Sears, 1951; Terman & Miles, 1936). Presumably, this is at least partly because our society discourages physical aggression in girls while encouraging it, to a degree, in boys (Kagan, 1964; Mischel, 1966). If girls with their greater verbal facility (Maccoby, 1966) were able to learn verbalized material as well as performed material, their greater willingness to display aggression in performance conditions may have reflected a fear of the consequences of aggression. Seeing a model perform aggression unpunished certainly would be more indicative to a female subject that she could be aggressive with impunity. A model who merely verbalized aggression could in no way give her this assurance. (Note that the model was always a female. Had it been a male, of course, girls might have decided the behavior was appropriate for him but not for them.) The fact that aggression was greater in the verbalization than control condition, with no tendency toward an interaction between sex and method of presentation, does indicate, of course, that verbalization had some effect on the display of aggression for girls. At any rate, the behavior of girls in this situation—as it was also in the sharing situation—seems somewhat more ambiguous than that of boys and must be the object of further inquiry.

References

Aronfreed, J. The concept of internalization. In D. A. Goslin & D. C. Glass (Eds.), *The handbook of socialization theory*. New York: Rand McNally, 1968.

Bandura, A. Influence of models' reinforcement contingencies on the acquisition of imitative responses. *Journal of Personality and Social Psychology*, 1965, *1*, 589–595.

Bandura, A., & Huston, A. C. Identification as a process of incidental learning. *Journal of Abnormal and Social Psychology*, 1961, *63*, 311–318.

Berkowitz, L., & Daniels, L. Responsibility and dependency. *Journal of Abnormal and Social Psychology*, 1963, *66*, 429–436.

Bryan, J. H., & Walbek, N. Preaching and practicing generosity: Children's actions and reactions. *Child Development*, 1970, *41*, 329–354.

Crutchfield, R. S. Conformity and character. *American Psychologist*, 1955, *10*, 191–198.

Flanders, J. P. A review of research on imitative behavior. *Psychological Bulletin*, 1968, *69*, 316–337.

Freud, S. Mourning and melancholia. In E. Jones (Ed.), *Collected papers*. Vol. 4. London: Hogarth, 1925.

Gewirtz, J. L., & Stingle, K. G. Learning of generalized imitation as the basis for identification. *Psychological Review*, 1968, *75*, 374–397.

Grusec, J. E., & Skubiski, L. Model nurturance, demand characteristics of the modeling experiment, and altruism. *Journal of Personality and Social Psychology*, 1970, *14*, 352–359.

Handlon, B. J., & Gross, P. The development of sharing behavior. *Journal of Abnormal and Social Psychology,* 1959, *59,* 425–428.

Kagan, J. Acquisition and significance of sex typing and sex role identity. In M. L. Hoffman & L. W. Hoffman (Eds.), *Review of child development research.* Vol. 1. New York: Russell Sage Foundation, 1964.

Krebs, D. L. Altruism—An examination of the concept and a review of the literature. *Psychological Bulletin,* 1970, *73,* 258–302.

Lorenz, K. *On aggression.* New York: Harcourt, Brace & World, 1963.

Maccoby, E. E. Role-taking in childhood and its consequences for social learning. *Child Development,* 1959, *30,* 239–252.

Maccoby, E. E. Sex differences in intellectual functioning. In E. E. Maccoby (Ed.), *The development of sex differences.* Stanford: Stanford University Press, 1966.

Mischel, W. A social-learning view of sex differences in behavior. In E. E. Maccoby (Ed.), *The development of sex differences.* Stanford: Stanford University Press, 1966.

Mowrer, O. H. *Learning theory and personality dynamics.* New York: Ronald Press, 1950.

Sears, P. S. Doll play aggression in normal young children: Influence of sex, age, sibling status, father's absence. *Psychological Monographs,* 1951, *65*(6, Whole No. 323).

Sears, R. R. Identification as a form of behavioral development. In D. B. Harris (Ed.), *The concept of development.* Minneapolis: University of Minnesota Press, 1957.

Staub, E. A child in distress: The influence of nurturance and modeling on children's attempts to help. *Developmental Psychology,* 1971, *5,* 124–132.

Terman, L. M., & Miles, C. C. *Sex and personality studies in masculinity and femininity.* New York: McGraw-Hill, 1936.

Ugurel-Semin, R. Moral behavior and moral judgment of children. *Journal of Abnormal and Social Psychology,* 1952, *47,* 463–474.

PART 3

Attitude Formation and Attitude Change

In this section of the reader, the research dealing with attitudes and attitude change is presented. The aim of the research is to determine the conditions under which a person can be persuaded to "change his mind" about an issue. Research on attitude change generally falls into two broad categories. First, there is the research that attempts to prove any of the theories dealing with attitude change. Two of the most influential theories are that of *"social judgment,"* which is a cognitive process described by Sherif and Hovland (1961), and "cognitive dissonance," which was first proposed by Festinger in 1957. In the reprints here, research dealing with the first theory is described in the Hovland, Harvey, and Sherif (1957) article, and research dealing with the second theory in the Janis and Rausch (1970) article. The first article was chosen because it is considered to be a classic in the field, and the second because it illustrates a recent trend in social psychology to determine the applicability of laboratory findings to real life situations. Since the theories are described in the commentaries on the articles, or in the articles themselves, they will not be outlined here. However, it should be mentioned that they are having a continuing influence on social psychological research, as a glance through the recent social psychology journals will verify. To give just one example, a number of recent articles in the *Journal of Personality and Social Psychology* dealt with the effect on attitudes of "counter attitudinal" behavior. In other words, suppose that a person is asked to go in front of an audience and say that he thinks that people should not brush their teeth (even though he believes exactly the opposite). What will happen to that person's attitudes on tooth brushing? Dissonance theory would say that a person prefers as consistent a world as possible, and that the person would try to increase the correspondence between his behavior and attitude by changing his attitude toward tooth brushing. A 1972 study by Hoyt, Henley, and Collins indicated that this effect does occur, but only when the person feels that he *chose* to make the anti-tooth brushing speech, and that the speech will have important consequences (in this instance, convince impressionable youngsters not to brush their teeth).

The "social judgment" line of research in the attitude-change field has not been limited to any one theoretical line (in fact it often has been totally free of theory). Rather, the emphasis has been on tight empirical studies to determine the conditions under which one person can change the opinion of another. The research is often summarized under the topic heads of "who" says "what" to "whom." In other words, the characteristics of the communicator, his speech, and his audience have all been found to have an effect on attitude change. This type of research is represented here in the article by Mills and Harvey (1972) which is chiefly concerned with the different effects of expert versus attractive communicators. Again, it should be noted that other articles dealing with similar topics can be found in the current literature. For example, in a somewhat new direction, an attempt is being made to assess the conditions producing not only attitude change, but also behavior change. Mazen and Leventhal (1972) investigated the effect of communicator-audience similarity on the behavior and attitudes of pregnant women. They found that similarity of pregnancy and "color" had a positive effect on adoption of the behaviors advocated (rooming-in and breast-feeding), but little positive effect on attitude change. Since attempts to change attitudes are often begun with the eventual goal of changing behavior, such a discrepancy presents a problem of practical importance and continuing interest.

References

Festinger, L. *A theory of cognitive dissonance.* Stanford: Stanford University Press, 1957.

Hovland, C. I., Harvey, O. J., & Sherif, M. Assimilation and contrast effects in reactions to communication and attitude change. *Journal of Abnormal and Social Psychology,* 1957, *55,* 242–252.

Hoyt, M. F., Henley, M. D., & Collins, B. E. Studies in forced compliance: confluence of choice and consequence on attitude change. *Journal of Personality and Social Psychology,* 1972, *23,* 205–210.

Janis, I. L., & Rausch, C. N. Selective interest in communications that should arouse decisional conflict: a field study of participants in the draft-resistance movement. *Journal of Personality and Social Psychology,* 1970, *14,* 46–54.

Mazen, R. & Leventhal, H. The influence of communicator-recipient similarity upon the beliefs and behavior of pregnant women. *Journal of Experimental Social Psychology,* 1972, *8,* 289–302.

Mills, J., & Harvey, J. Opinion change as a function of when information about the communicator is received and whether he is attractive or expert. *Journal of Personality and Social Psychology,* 1972, *21,* 52–55.

Sherif, M., & Hovland, C. I. *Social judgment.* New Haven, Conn.: Yale University Press, 1961.

Foreword to Reading 3.1

INTRODUCTION

The broad hypothesis of this study is based on results obtained in studies of object perception. In these psychophysical studies, it has been found that one's perception of an object can serve as an "anchor" or standard against which other objects are judged. The authors here suggest that one's own attitude on an issue can serve as an anchor, with other positions on the issue being evaluated in the light of this anchor. They predict that, when ego-involving issues (i.e., issues about which the individual has attitudes) are being used, a communication close to a subject's own position will be "assimilated." The individual will consider the communication to be close to his own position (possibly closer than it really is), will judge it favorably, and may change his attitude toward that advocated by the communicator (i.e., the author of the communication). A communication far removed from a subject's own position will have a "contrast" effect. The individual will consider the communication to be far from his own position (possibly farther than it really is), will judge it unfavorably, and as a result, will be unlikely to change his attitude toward that advocated by the communicator. (In fact, his attitude may change away from that advocated by the communicator, a boomerang effect.)

METHOD

In order to test their hypothesis, Hovland et al. presented three communications with three different stands on the value of "Prohibition" to three groups of subjects. Their procedure incorporated some of the features of good experimental design. For instance, all of the communications were presented by tape recording with the same voice being used. Thus, there was no danger that an experimenter might present a communication more or less persuasively on separate occasions.

RESULTS

In looking at the results of the experiment, you will find it helpful to be familiar with the skill of reading a graph. For instance, figure 1 illustrates the percent of subjects favorable to each communication. As is customary, the independent variable (here, recipient's position) is marked on the horizontal axis (the abscissa), the dependent variable on the vertical axis (the ordinate). To find the percent of subjects with position C who reacted favorably to the wet communication (the first graph), you would mark a straight vertical line from the C on the abscissa to the point marked, and then a horizontal line to the ordinate, to find that approximately 55 percent of those with position C reacted favorably to the wet communication. Generally, figure 1 shows that subjects tended to be more favorable to the communication, the more they were of the same opinion as the communication.

The next item in the results, the placement of the communicator's position, represents the "assimilation-contrast" test crucial to the psychophysical model, and the notion of anchoring. Although there is no statistical test cited here to ascertain the degree of fit between the theoretical and actual curves, the authors conclude that their prediction was confirmed. "Dry" subjects judged the communication as being "wetter" than it was, while "wet" subjects displaced the communication in the direction of "dryness." The authors do note that the small number of subjects with intermediate positions makes it difficult to determine the correct shape of the graph at these points. One might wonder whether this same objection could be applied to the graphs of figure 1 as well.

The third results section relates to the authors' theory of "thresholds of acceptance and rejection." The notion of threshold, like that of anchor, originates in the psychology of perception. The theoretical definition of threshold is the minimum physical energy necessary for perception or for activating a sensory system (e.g., the minimum volume necessary for an individual to "hear" a sound). The authors here are discussing a threshold for accepting or rejecting positions on an issue. (The threshold, then, represents the point on a position scale at which the individual is able to accept, rather than reject, the opinion.) In general, the authors again obtained the pattern of results that they expected; as compared to more moderate subjects, subjects with extreme views on this issue had wider "regions of rejection."

The final results section deals with the measure of "influence" or opinion change. Again, predictions were confirmed. People who held extreme positions were less influenced than moderates. This section includes an interesting description of the advantages and disadvantages of the method of subject selection used for the experiment. As Hovland et al. admit, subjects with different initial positions might well have differed in other characteristics as well. For instance, persons holding the less socially acceptable position (the "wet" stand) might have been persons who generally were nonconformists. On the other hand, persons selected for their extreme positions were unlikely to change their responses over time, or to exhibit random fluctuations around a mean response. A standard procedure used to control for or assess such instability of response is a control group given only the before and after attitude measures, without an intervening communication.

DISCUSSION

The authors present a model of latitude (range) of acceptance and rejection. This model is derived from the results of the study, and therefore, of course, corresponds closely to them. The model, however, is useful for more than merely re-stating data; it may predict the points of assimilation-contrast, judgments of fairness of communication, and susceptibility to opinion change on the issue for any subject, once his initial position is known. In addition, the model provides us with increased understanding of why a person with an extreme initial position on an issue often proves to be strongly resistant to persuasion.

3.1 Assimilation and Contrast Effects in Reactions to Communication and Attitude Change

Carl I. Hovland
O. J. Harvey
Muzafer Sherif

This paper presents an experiment on reactions to communication and on attitude changes by individuals whose initial stands on a controversial social issue diverged in varying degrees from positions advocated in communication. Study of the relationship between subject's (*S*'s) attitude and the position advocated in communication may help resolve some apparently contradictory effects of communication aimed at changing attitudes.

Attempts to change attitudes in the direction advocated by communication on a social issue at times produce shifts in the direction opposite to that intended—the "boomerang effect." While numerous investigators have reported shifts of average test scores in the direction of communication (Hovland, 1954), a fairly common finding, even in these studies, is that some individuals shift their stand *away* from that presented in communication. Several studies reporting both positive and negative shifts in attitudes toward out-groups following communication are summarized by Williams (1947).

Thus, at times, persuasive communication produces a bi-modal distribution of attitude scores (Murphy, Murphy, and Newcomb, 1937, pp. 874–875). For example, Remmers (1938) obtained positive shifts on average scores following communications on conservation, social insurance, and labor unions, but the latter communication "sharply divided the group into two opposing tents" (Remmers, 1938, p. 201). In Knower's study prior to repeal of prohibition, "wet" communication to generally "dry" *S*s

This investigation was conducted as part of the Yale Communication Research Program. This series of studies, devoted to an analysis of factors related to attitude and opinion formation, is financed by a grant to Carl I. Hovland from the Rockefeller Foundation, whose support is gratefully acknowledged. Thanks are extended to Dr. Charles Shedd, now of Berea College, Mr. William Smith, and Mr. Richard Disney who participated in developing the procedures and in writing the communications used. We are also grateful to Dr. Laurence H. Snyder, Dean of the Graduate College, University of Oklahoma, for necessary administrative arrangements, and to Drs. Irving L. Janis, Robert P. Abelson, and Jack W. Brehm for suggestions made in the course of reading the manuscript.

and "dry" communication to generally "wet" Ss resulted in shifts in both positive and negative directions in each group (Knower, 1935). A rather striking instance of such opposing effects was reported by Wilke (1934), whose antiwar communication was presented at a time when the student population from which Ss were drawn was divided in controversy over this very issue.

A few studies, such as those by Manske (1937) and Russell and Robertson (1947), have found group shifts in the direction opposite to the stand presented in communication. A related finding reported by Williams and Remmers (1939) following communication on a rural issue was reduced variability and a comparatively less favorable stand by a group of rural youth in contrast to the increased variability in an urban group. Some authors who have obtained results in the direction away from communication insert the suggestion that too great divergence between S's stand on the issue and the stand presented in communication may have been responsible.

On the other hand, data from several recent studies suggest that the extent of influence increases as a function of the distance between position of communication and position of the recipient. Goldberg (1954) reports that the greater the discrepancy between an announced group norm and the S's own judgment the greater the change produced. In a still unpublished paper, French and Gyr (summarized in French, 1956) found a positive correlation between the degree of deviation between inducer and inductee and the amount of change. In a perceptual task, Lubin and Fisher (1956) obtained an increase in conformity to a partner's judgment as the distance increased up to a point where with great distance the proportion of movement declined. Hovland and Pritzker (1957) have shown that the larger the change in opinion advocated the greater the amount of change produced. The issues that were employed did not pertain to strongly rooted attitudes, but represented opinions on rather factual topics. The communicators used were authorities respected by the recipients.

A comprehensive analysis may be necessary to handle the above findings as well as results of studies employing communication on controversial social issues which suggest that too great a distance between S's attitude and the position advocated in communication produces "boomerang effects." One possible approach is through analysis of processes underlying judgments of motivationally neutral material, exemplified by psycho-physical stimuli, as well as ego-involving verbal material, exemplified by controversial social issues. Investigations of judgmental processes and their theoretical relevance for the study of reaction to communication and attitude change will be presented in a forthcoming volume.

One set of findings suggests that S's position shifts toward the stand advocated in communication when the topic is not highly ego-involving and S's position does not diverge in the extreme from the stand advocated. This result seems akin to extension of an established reference scale in judgment of weights or inclinations following introduction of anchoring stimuli near the end stimulus of the series, as reported by Rogers (1941), Heintz (1950), and others. Sherif, Taub, and Hovland (Mimeo. Rep.) demonstrated this extension toward the anchor ("assimilation effect") as well as the effect of more remote anchors beyond either end of the stimulus series in constricting the reference scale of judgment and displacing judgment away from the anchor ("contrast effect"). Contrast phenomena may also appear in reaction to communication on an issue which is not highly involving for S if the position advocated is removed sufficiently from S's position, as the Lubin and Fisher results seem to indicate.

The above analysis based on findings from judgment studies suggested the further possibility that when Ss have established attitudes and are personally involved in a controversial social issue, their "own stand" functions as the major anchorage affecting reaction to and evaluation of communication. In this case, communication near S's stand would be assimilated to it, while communication at variance with S's own stand would be displaced still further away ("contrast effect"). Whether assimilation or contrast effects appear would be a function of the relative distance between S's own stand and the position of communication.

Accordingly, in the present experiment communications representing two opposite extremes and one moderate position on an ego-involving issue were presented to Ss whose initial stands on the issue ranged from one extreme to the other. The following hypotheses were formulated in terms of the effect of the relative distance between S's own stand and the position advocated upon evaluation and placement of communication as well as acceptance-rejection of that position:

1. Reactions to a communication will decrease in favorableness as the distance between S's own stand and the position advocated in the communication increases.
2. In evaluations by S of what position is advocated by a communication, the greater the distance between S's own stand and the position advocated in the communication, the greater the displacement *away* from S's position ("contrast effect"). When only a small discrepancy in position exists there will be a tendency for displacement *toward* S's stand ("assimilation effect").
3. With small distances between the position of the communication and that of the S, changes in S's opinion in the direction advocated by the communication will occur. With large distances between the stands taken by communication and by S, opinion changes in the direction advocated will be infrequent.

METHOD

Issue and Communications

The problem required that a controversial issue be selected, that Ss' stands on the controversy be ascertained, and that communications advocating various positions be presented to Ss with differing stands on the issue.

The issue chosen was the controversy over prohibition and repeal in a "dry" state. Shortly before the study began, a referendum was held to determine the fate of existing prohibition laws. The vote favored prohibition by a narrow margin.

In order to differentiate existing stands on the issue, representative statements made during the referendum campaign were collected from leading newspapers in two large cities. In addition, statements were obtained from 500 people in several localities on a random basis. These statements from public and private sources were sorted by 20 judges to secure clearly differentiated stands actually taken in the state. As a result, eight statements were chosen representing prevailing stands ranging from strong advocacy of prohibition to strong advocacy of repeal. One additional "wet" statement was added as a logical counterpart of the most extreme "dry" stand, giving a total of nine statements. These statements are as follows, (I) being the additional item:

(A) Since alcohol is the curse of mankind, the sale and use of alcohol, including light beer, should be completely abolished.

(B) Since alcohol is the main cause of corruption in public life, lawlessness, and immoral acts, its sale and use should be prohibited.

(C) Since it is hard to stop at a reasonable moderation point in the use of alcohol, it is safer to discourage its use.

(D) Alcohol should not be sold or used except as a remedy for snake bites, cramps, colds, fainting, and other aches and pains.

(E) The arguments in favor and against the sale and use of alcohol are nearly equal.

(F) The sale of alcohol should be so regulated that it is available in limited quantities for special occasions.

(G) The sale and use of alcohol should be permitted with proper state controls, so that the revenue from taxation may be used for the betterment of schools, highways, and other state institutions.

(H) Since prohibition is a major cause of corruption in public life, lawlessness, immoral acts, and juvenile delinquency, the sale and use of alcohol should be legalized.

(I) It has become evident that man cannot get along without alcohol; therefore, there should be no restriction whatsoever on its sale and use.

Three communications of equal length were prepared, each requiring approximately 15 minutes for delivery. Arguments were those actually made by prohibition and repeal advocates during the referendum campaign. Arguments in the three communications were arranged in the same order, but from the viewpoint of the different parties to the controversy. One communication presented an extreme "dry" stand; one an extreme "wet" stand; and one a moderately wet stand, as typified in statement (F) above. All communications were presented by tape recording. The same voice was used in recording wet and dry communications.

Procedure

In the first session, data on Ss' attitudes were obtained. At the time, Ss were not told that an additional session would be held. A schedule on "public issues" was presented with assurance of anonymity to Ss. Following a "dummy" issue (college football) Ss responded to the nine representative statements on prohibition. The following instructions were printed on the schedule and read aloud by the experimenter (E):

Below are some statements recently made concerning the wet-dry issue in this region.
Please read *all* of the statements carefully first before making any marks on this page.
Now that you have carefully read all the statements, *underline* the *one* statement that comes closest to your own point of view on the topic.
There may be other statement or statements which you find not objectionable from your point of view. Put a circle around the letter in front of such a statement or statements which are *not objectionable* to you.
Now cross out that one statement which is *most objectionable* from your point of view.
There may be other statement or statements which you find *objectionable* from your point of view. Cross out the letter in front of such a statement or statements which are *objectionable* to you.

These procedures yielded data on S's stand and also on the range of his tolerance for other stands in the series (*latitude of acceptance*), the range of stands he rejected (*latitude of rejection*) and those stands which he did not consider either acceptable or unacceptable. Thus the procedures gave S an opportunity not to take a stand in relation to items which he did not include in his latitude of acceptance or latitude of rejection, rather than requiring artificial "indifference" or "neutral" checkings.

From 1–3 weeks after the first session, a communication was presented by tape recording. Arrangements for its presentation were made through a member of the group being exposed and it was introduced as a talk actually made by a proponent of the stand advocated. The wet (repeal) communication was presented to extreme dry *S*s and unselected *S*s. The dry (prohibition) communication was presented to extreme wet and unselected *S*s. The moderate communication was presented to wet, dry, and unselected *S*s. The *S*s participated in both "before" and "after" sessions in small groups of 10–30 under close supervision.

Following the communication, the same questionnaire for securing *S*'s stand, latitudes of acceptance and rejection was filled in a second time. Reactions to the communication presented were obtained through ratings on like-dislike, reasonable-unreasonable, biased-unbiased, propaganda-fact dimensions. The *S*s in the moderate communication groups also checked on a graphic rating scale ranging from extreme dry (A) to extreme wet (I) positions what they thought to be the stand taken in the communication itself.

Subjects

Since the objective was to secure *S*s who were definitely ego-involved, a special point was made of obtaining *S*s with established and publicly committed dry or wet stands as a validity check of the paper-and-pencil checkings. It was not difficult to select *S*s in the dry groups on the basis of known information concerning their stand. Two small samples from Women's Christian Temperance Union groups were obtained and a group of Salvation Army workers. The four remaining dry groups were students in preparation for the ministry or in strict denominational colleges. A total of 183 dry *S*s participated in both sessions. It was much more difficult to obtain *S*s whose position was known to be wet. However, on the basis of cases personally known to the *E*s or their assistants, 25 wet *S*s were secured. For comparison, 290 additional *S*s were obtained representing more moderate positions on the issue. These were college students secured from classes in journalism, speech, education, chemistry, etc. All *S*s were residents of the dry state where prohibition was a lively topic of controversy at the time of the study. For the reason indicated, it was not possible to match the age levels of *S*s in the three categories.

RESULTS

Evaluation of the Communication

A five-item scale was used to measure the audience's evaluation of the fairness and impartiality of the communication. In Figure 1, the percentages of *S*s in each group whose reactions were favorable are graphed for the three communications. On the abscissa the stands of the recipient (mean of state-

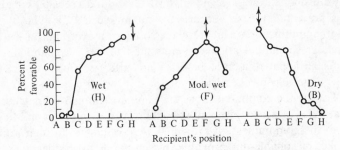

FIG. 1. Percentage of favorable evaluations of wet (H), moderately wet (F), and dry (B) communications for Ss holding various positions on prohibition (based on mean acceptable statement). (Positions of communications indicated by arrow.)

ments checked acceptable) are presented and on the ordinate the percentage of favorable evaluations. It will be observed that there is an extremely close relationship between the individual's own stand on the issue and his evaluation of communication. The two communications advocating extreme positions have their peak of favorable responses among those holding corresponding extreme positions. The maximum favorable reaction for the moderate communication is found among those holding a moderate position. The data provide quantitative information to support the expectation from earlier studies (Hovland, Janis, and Kelley, 1953; Weiss and Fine, 1955) that individuals who are in favor of the opinion advocated will consider the communication fair and unbiased, but that those with an opposed stand will regard an identical communication as propagandistic and unfair.

Placement of the Position of the Communication

The principal results of the experiment are those pertaining to the recipient's perception of the stand advocated in the communication. We asked S to indicate on a graphic scale, ranging from extreme dry position to extreme wet position, what he thought to be the position of the moderately wet communication (at F). From our previous study on assimilation-contrast effects with psychophysical data we predicted that positions differing only slightly from one's own would be "assimilated," while larger differences between one's own position and that of the communication would be exaggerated, showing a "contrast" effect. In Figure 2, results concerning this prediction are presented. The S's own position is indicated on the abscissa and along the ordinate the average rating of the position of the communication is given for the speech in which a moderately wet position (about F) was advocated. The dots indicate the mean placement of the position of the communication for Ss who indicate each particular position as their own stand. The squares

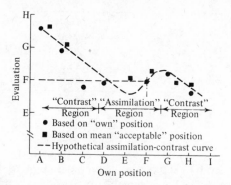

Fig. 2. Average placements of position of moderately wet communication (F) by Ss holding various positions on the issue, plotted against hypothetical assimilation-contrast curve.

represent the mean placement of the position advocated when S's position is estimated from the mean of the acceptable positions checked. The dotted line indicates a hypothetical relationship in which Ss holding the same position as the communication report its position accurately (at F), those a small distance removed assimilate it to their own position, and those still further removed exaggerate the position revealing a contrast effect.

The expectation is fulfilled that those at the wet end judge that the communication advocated a drier position than it did and those at the dry end judge that it was advocating a wetter position than it did. Those nearer the position of the communication reported it more objectively. The evidence concerning assimilation deviates somewhat from the theoretical curve. There were too few Ss with intermediate positions to enable us to determine these positions adequately.

Acceptance-Rejection of Stands

Each S was asked to indicate not only the stand which best represented his, but also other stands which were more or less acceptable (i.e., his latitude of acceptance), the stand most clearly opposed to his position, and others not acceptable (i.e., his latitude of rejection). From these data, we find that Ss with more extreme positions tend to reject more frequently positions not within their latitude of acceptance. The Ss with middle positions are more apt to rate positions removed from their own as indifferent. In Table 1, data are presented showing the mean number of items rated "also acceptable," "unacceptable" and "neither acceptable nor unacceptable" by Ss with strong positions (A, B, G, H, I) as compared with those by Ss with more moderate

TABLE 1 *Acceptability of Statements in Relation to Extremity of Subjects' Position on Issue*

S's Positions	N	MEAN NUMBER OF ITEMS ACCEPTABLE	MEAN NUMBER OF ITEMS NOT CHECKED	MEAN NUMBER OF ITEMS REJECTED
1. Extreme (A, B, G, H, I)	193	2.81	1.48	4.71
2. Intermediate (C, D, E, F)	37	3.05	2.24	3.70
p				<.03

positions (C, D, E, F). It will be observed that a significantly greater number of items are judged unacceptable by Ss with extreme stands. Smaller differences between the groups exist in the number rated acceptable. These results tie in with our earlier studies (Hovland and Sherif, 1952; Sherif and Hovland, 1953) in which we found that Ss with extreme positions and considerable ego-involvement in an issue have raised thresholds of acceptance and lowered thresholds of rejection in placing items concerning that issue, resulting in smaller latitudes of acceptance and greater latitudes of rejection than for Ss with moderate positions. These findings can be used in constructing the expected latitudes of acceptance and rejection of the individual for an ego-involving issue once his own position is ascertained and possibly in predicting evaluation of communication which stands at a given distance from his own position. An attempt in this direction is presented in the discussion.

Changes in Opinion for Groups with Different Stands on the Issue

Finally, it would be expected on the basis of the considerations previously discussed that those holding a position at great variance with that being presented in the communication would be relatively little modified in their opinion. The index of opinion change was based on the mean position of the statements checked by Ss as being "acceptable" to them. A value of 1 indicates the extreme dry end in which only statement A was checked. Correspondingly, a value of 9 is at the wet end with only statement I checked. The positions of the three speeches at B, F, and H would thus be represented by values of 2, 6, and 8, respectively.

Table 2 gives the mean position for five criterion groups before and after the communication, together with the average amount of change. Only the unselected group exposed to the wet communication should be expected to show sizeable change. The four other groups all have initial positions

TABLE 2 *Opinion Change—Changes in Mean Acceptable Statement for Ss with Differing Initial Stands*

GROUP	N	BEFORE COMM.	AFTER COMM.	CHANGE IN DIRECTION OF COMM.
Wet Communication (H)				
Drys	69	2.39	2.34	—.05*
Unselected	92	5.10	5.65	+.55*
Dry Communication (B)				
Wets	25	6.70	6.74	—.04
Unselected	87	5.90	5.78	+.14
Moderately Wet Communication (F)				
Drys	114	2.17	2.26	+.09

* Difference between changes: $p = <.03$ (one tail).

quite removed from the position being advocated. While the dry and unselected groups exposed to the wet communication do differ substantially in their initial positions, the positions of the wet and unselected groups are similar, since the unselected group (college students) initially holds a rather wet position.

As predicted, there is a significantly greater change for the unselected group given the wet communication than for the dry group ($p = < .03$). As in all studies in which the variable with which we are concerned cannot be directly manipulated, the possibility must be considered that there are factors other than position on the issue which are correlated with it and provide the basis for the relationship obtained.

In Table 3, results are presented for the same groups in terms of the percentage of Ss who are influenced either in the direction advocated by the communication or in the direction opposed to it. The net change column represents the differences between those changed in the direction advocated and those changed in the opposite direction. The net change is greater among the unselected group than among the drys when a wet communication is presented ($p = < .04$). Twenty-eight per cent of the former and only four per cent of the latter changed in the direction advocated. It will also be seen that the amount of change produced among the drys by a moderately wet communication (at F) is greater than that produced by the more extreme wet communication (at H). The net proportion changed by the former is 12 per cent, while it is only 4 per cent for the latter. This difference, however, is not statistically significant and, in any case, it is difficult to establish that the two different communications were inherently equivalent in persuasiveness.

TABLE 3 *Opinion Change—Percentage of Ss Changing in Direction of Communication or in Opposed Direction*

Group	N	Change in Direction of Comm.	No Change	Change in Direction Opposed to Comm.	Net Change
		Wet Communication (H)			
		%	%	%	%
Drys	69	27.5	49.3	23.2	+4.5*
Unselected	92	52.2	23.9	23.9	+28.3*
		Dry Communication (B)			
Wets	25	24.0	56.0	20.0	+4.0
Unselected	87	40.2	33.4	26.4	+13.8
		Moderately Wet Communication (F)			
Drys	114	31.6	49.1	19.3	+12.3

* Difference between changes: $p = <.04$ (one tail).

It will be noted that by confining our comparisons to groups who were initially selected as having known differences in their stand on the issue (either wet or dry) we were able to avoid the regression effects often found in studies where amounts of change are compared for groups differentiated solely on the basis of initial scores on the attitude measure. Under the latter conditions, those with more extreme scores often regress toward the mean and this can either obscure the effect or produce a relationship artifactually.

Finally, it will be noted from Table 3 that the predominant response among Ss holding extreme positions is to remain uninfluenced by the communication. Even where Ss in these groups were influenced, changes were seldom found in the item they checked as best representing their own position. Instead, there was typically only an increase in the number of other statements intermediate between their own position and that of the communication which they would check as "also acceptable."

DISCUSSION

The results presented lend support to the three hypotheses pertaining to evaluation and placement of communication and attitude change as a function of the relative distance between S's stand and the position of communication on an ego-involving issue. Our findings suggest that the relative distance between S's attitudes and position of communication may be useful in explaining apparently contradictory effects of communication in producing attitude change in the intended direction, no change, and change in the opposite direction. This approach seems to have predictive value for S's reactions to other positions on an issue and susceptibility to change once his own stand is ascertained.

On the basis of results in Table 1 and evidence from previous studies (Hovland and Sherif, 1952; Sherif and Hovland, 1953), we can formalize the pattern of acceptance and rejection for various positions by Ss holding each initial position. In Table 4, the expected response to each opinion item

TABLE 4 *Hypothetical Latitudes of Acceptance and Rejection of Ss Holding Each Position*

(Columns show latitude of acceptance (strongly accept plus accept), latitude of rejection (strongly reject plus reject) and positions neither acceptable nor unacceptable to Ss holding given positions.)

RATING POSITIONS	OWN POSITION								
	A	B	C	D	E	F	G	H	I
A	√√	√	0	✕	✕	✕✕	✕✕	✕✕	✕✕
B	√	√√	√	0	✕	✕	✕	✕	✕
C	0	√	√√	√	0	✕	✕	✕	✕
D	✕	0	√	√√	√	0	✕	✕	✕
E	✕	✕	0	√	√√	√	0	✕	✕
F	✕	✕	✕	0	√	√√	√	0	✕
G	✕	✕	✕	✕	0	√	√√	√	0
H	✕	✕	✕	✕	✕	0	√	√√	√
I	✕✕	✕✕	✕✕	✕✕	✕	✕	0	√	√√

Code: √√ = strongly accept; √ = accept; 0 = neither accept nor reject; ✕ = reject; ✕✕ = strongly reject.

Mean frequencies in above table:

	A,B,G,H,I	C,D,E,F
√ and √√	2.7	3.0
0	1.3	2.0
✕ and ✕✕	5.0	4.0

is given for Ss checking positions from A to I as their most acceptable stand. The S's own stand is indicated by √ √, "also acceptable" with √, completely unacceptable with ✕✕, other stands unacceptable with ✕, and not clearly acceptable or unacceptable with 0. Thus, the table presents a hypothetical pattern for the "latitude of acceptance" (consisting of S's own position and other acceptable positions) and "latitude of rejection" (consisting of all unacceptable positions) for Ss holding each position. Where sufficient numbers of Ss are available for a given stand, the empirical distributions of responses show a close correspondence to these hypothetical patterns.

This model for latitudes of acceptance and rejection can be used to explicate results on reaction to communication. By comparison with Figure 2, showing placement of the position advocated in the moderate communication, it can be seen that "contrast effects" begin to appear when the position advocated falls within S's latitude of rejection, an area far removed from his own stand. If the position advocated in communication falls at the limits or slightly beyond the latitude of acceptance, it would be more likely to be assimilated to the latitude of acceptance, although this trend is less clear in the present study.

If we assume that evaluation of communication on an issue in which S is personally involved depends on two factors: (a) what the position of communications is perceived to be and (b) what segment of the acceptance-rejection range is associated with the perceived position, we can predict from Fig. 2 and Table 4 the degree of favorableness of evaluations of the communication (Fig. 1). When the communication falls within the latitude of acceptance ($\sqrt{}$ or $\sqrt{}$ $\sqrt{}$), it is judged fair and unbiased. As the perceived position of communication moves outside the latitude of acceptance into the latitude of rejection ($\times$), it is increasingly considered unfair and propagandistic. For example, an individual checking B as his most acceptable stand displaces the F communication to G ("contrast effect") which, according to Table 4, is clearly in his latitude of rejection; an S checking A as his own stand places the F communication between G-H, still further toward the extreme end of the latitude of rejection, and the percentage of favorable evaluations of the communication declines still further (cf. Fig. 1).

Two general problems are suggested by the present analysis. Since S's stands on an issue of personal concern produce variation in reaction to communication and attitude change, the effect of the degree of ego-involvement in issues needs exploration. It is expected that latitudes of acceptance and rejection will vary as a function of the degree of ego-involvement, and these variations may affect the ranges in which assimilation and contrast effects in judging communication occur. A person strongly committed on an issue will be more discriminating in accepting stands (raised threshold of acceptance) while one who is less committed will be willing to consider a larger number of alternative positions (lowered threshold of acceptance). Corresponding effects on extent of opinion change with different distances between S and communication are to be expected. With low involvement issues one would anticipate increase in opinion change with increased separation over a considerable range, whereas with high involvement issues one would expect opinion change over only a narrow range of separation, with resistance to acceptance of the communication for the remaining distances.

Finally, an interesting problem remains as to the role of the communicator in influencing the range of assimilation. In the Hovland-Pritzker study (1957) the communicator was an authority respected by Ss on the issue presented. There the greater the distance between communicator position and that of S, the greater the opinion change. In the present study, on the other hand, the communicator was an anonymous individual whose acceptability might be determined by the stand taken by him on the issue under discussion. If he differed in position only slightly from S he would be regarded as fair and authoritative and bring about a shift in opinion, but if he differed greatly he would be regarded as incompetent and biased and fail to influence S's opinion. To explore this factor and the one of involvement mentioned in the preceding paragraph, a factorially designed experiment will be required in which type of communicator (positive, negative, and neutral), type of issue (high involvement and low involvement), and distance between the communicator's stand and S's own stand are all systematically varied to permit analysis not only of the main effects but also of the more interesting interaction effects.

SUMMARY

The relationship between the attitude of the recipient and the position advocated in a communication was studied under conditions where a communicator not known to S presents a point of view on a controversial issue which differs from that of S by varying amounts.

The topic discussed was prohibition of alcohol. The Ss came from a dry state where this was a lively issue. Each S indicated for a series of nine statements ranging from extreme dry to extreme wet: (a) the position most acceptable to him, (b) other acceptable positions, (c) the position most objectionable to him, and (d) other objectionable positions. Groups of Ss were selected whose stands on the issue were known (e.g., WCTU members) for comparison with unselected groups of college students. In all, 514 Ss were used. In a subsequent session "wet" groups received a "dry" or "moderately wet" communication; "dry" groups received a "wet" or "moderately wet" communication; unselected groups received a "dry," "wet," or "moderately wet" communication. After the communication, opinion measurements and reactions to communication were obtained. The findings were as follows:

1. When the distance between S's own stand and the position advocated in communication is small, the communication is judged favorably, as fair and factual. With increasing distance, the favorable reaction is sharply reduced and the communication perceived as propagandistic and unfair.
2. The Ss whose own stands diverge widely from the position advocated per-

ceive the communication as further removed from their own stand than it is ("contrast effect"). The present results indicate, though less clearly, that *S*s whose own stands are close to the position advocated perceive the communication as closer to their own stand than is the case ("assimilation effect").
3. The most frequent result for *S*s whose own stand diverges widely from that advocated in communication is to remain unchanged in their initial attitudes. More *S*s with moderate positions closer to the stand in communication changed in the direction advocated.

It is suggested that the relative distance between *S*'s own attitude and communication along with *S*'s latitudes of acceptance and rejection for various stands on the issue may provide a basis for predicting reactions to communication and susceptibility to change. Further research varying degree of ego-involvement in issues and attitudes toward the communicator is suggested.

References

French, J. R. P., Jr. A formal theory of social power. *Psychological Review,* 1956, *63,* 181–194.

Goldberg, S. C. Three situational determinants of conformity to social norms. *Journal of Abnormal Social Psychology,* 1954, *49,* 325–329.

Heintz, R. The effect of remote anchoring points upon judgments of lifted weights. *Journal of Experimental Psychology,* 1950, *40,* 584–591.

Hovland, C. I. Effects of mass media of communication. In G. Lindzey (Ed.), *Handbook of social psychology,* Vol. 2. Reading, Mass.: Addison-Wesley, 1954.

Hovland, C. I., Janis, I. L., and Kelley, H. H. *Communication and persuasion.* New Haven: Yale Univer. Press, 1953.

Hovland, C. I., and Pritzker, H. Extent of opinion change as a function of amount of change advocated. *Journal of Abnormal Social Psychology,* 1957, *54,* 257–261.

Hovland, C. I., and Sherif, M. Judgmental phenomena and scales of attitude measurement: item displacement in Thurstone scales. *Journal of Abnormal Social Psychology,* 1952, *47,* 822–833.

Knower, F. H. Experimental studies of changes in attitudes: I. A study of the effect of oral argument on change of attitude. *Journal of Social Psychology,* 1935, *6,* 315–347.

Lubin, A., and Fisher, S. Distance as a determinant of influence in a two-person continuous interaction situation. E.P.A. Talk. Title in *American Psychologist,* 1956, *11,* 491.

Manske, A. J. The reflection of teachers' attitudes in the attitudes of their pupils. In G. Murphy, L. B. Murphy, and T. M. Newcomb (Eds.), *Experimental social psychology.* New York: Harper & Row, 1937.

Murphy, G., Murphy, L. B., and Newcomb, T. M. *Experimental social psychology.* New York: Harper & Row, 1937.

Remmers, H. H. Propaganda in the schools: do the effects last? *Public Opinion Quarterly*, 1938, *2*, 197–210.

Rogers, S. The anchoring of absolute judgments. *Archives Psychologiques*, 1941, No. 261.

Russell, D. H., and Robertson, I. V. Influencing attitudes toward minority groups in a junior high school. *School Review*, 1947, *55*, 205–213.

Sherif, M., and Hovland, C. I. Judgmental phenomena and scales of attitude measurement: placement of items with individual choice of number of categories. *Journal of Abnormal Social Psychology*, 1953, *48*, 135–141.

Sherif, M., Taub, D., and Hovland, C. I. Assimilation and contrast effects of anchoring stimuli on judgments. (Mimeo. Rep.)

Weiss, W., and Fine, B. J. Opinion change as a function of some intrapersonal attributes of the communicatees. *Journal of Abnormal Social Psychology*, 1955, *51*, 246–253.

Wilke, W. H. An experimental comparison of the speech, the radio, and the printed page as propaganda devices. *Archives Psychologiques*, 1934, No. 169.

Williams, A. C., and Remmers, H. H. Persistence of attitudes concerning conservation issues. *Journal of Experimental Education*, 1939, 40, 354–361.

Williams, R. M., Jr. *The reduction of intergroup tensions*. New York: Soc. Sci. Res. Council, Bull. 57, 1947.

INTRODUCTION

This article is concerned with the notion of "selective exposure," the theory that, given a choice, people prefer to expose themselves to information which agrees with their opinions or decisions. This is a rational-sounding proposition. It is pleasant to be told that you are right. Antiprejudice mass media campaigns are commonly expected to "fail" for this reason; it is assumed that they will be unable to attract many of the people for whom they are intended.

One of the theories that predicts selective exposure was formulated by Festinger in 1957. Dissonance theory is one of several psychological theories based on the notion that people prefer consistency to inconsistency. Specifically, dissonance theory deals with inconsistency between cognitions (ideas or information). The term "dissonance" is usually used to refer to both the inconsistency and the resulting feeling. Thus, when cognitions are dissonant, the person experiences dissonance, or psychological tension, and is motivated to reduce the dissonance. This does not mean that dissonance for me is necessarily dissonance for you. Suppose that I have recently studied extremely hard for an examination and received a B. I am very pleased with myself, because I have learned that, for me, studying hard and grades of B "should" go together. Now, for you, studying hard may "deserve" grades of A, not B; this same experience might arouse dissonance for you. How could you reduce your dissonance? It is too late to change your behavior (studying hard), but you might try to argue the grade with your professor; you might "rationalize" by denying your effort in studying ("I didn't really study as hard as usual"); you might collect additional information (e.g., determine that no A's were given this term); or you might even lower your sights regarding marks for the future.

One of the editors of this reader (LZS) is rather fond of dissonance theory because the notion of dissonance seems to describe a gut feeling that she gets when her experience does not meet her expectations. However, as a scientific theory, dissonance theory has not escaped criticism. The reader is referred to Chapanis and Chapanis (1964) and Brehm and Cohen (1962) for samples.

Now back to selective exposure. For most people, it may be dissonant to hear good arguments that go against a choice that they have made. Having decided to buy a 3-speed bicycle, one could experience discomfort on reading that 10-speed bicycles are infinitely better. The possession of the bicycle and the new information are inconsistent.

In the Janis et al. research, the authors expected that students committed to a "We Won't Go" (to Vietnam) policy would avoid information on the other side of the issue.

RESULTS

(a)   As expected, the closer the subjects were to being "We Won't Go" signers, the more willing they were to engage in war-protest actions. The term "linear trend" means that if you drew a graph of the relationship, it would be a straight line, rather than a curve.

(b)   The curious finding for the second measure was that men committed to signing the pledge indicated the most interest in reading the *anti*pledge articles. In other words, they appeared to be increasing, not reducing their dissonance.

DISCUSSION

Janis and Rausch indicate the utility, for the pledge signers, of awareness of antipledge arguments. Although they felt committed to a position against the war, these men could still expect to have to support this position in the face of dissenting others; also, they were not yet fully aware of the consequences of their decision or of the steps that they would have to take to implement it.

There does seem to be a difference between this kind of commitment and the one that involves the purchase of a 3-speed bicycle. The bicycle is not only less controversial, it is also more final, more complete; it involves fewer future unknowns. Perhaps the selective exposure hypothesis holds only when one is committed to a position that one does not expect to have to defend, or even to give much thought to in the future.

Of course, there is always the possibility that the result was due to the nature of the people involved. It may be that men are more tolerant of dissonance than women (the subjects were all male), or that college students are more "open-minded" than the rest of the population; or perhaps just more *committed* to being open-minded. It is also possible that "We Won't Go" petition signers represent a particular type of person and personality.

The most important point is that the selective exposure hypothesis does not always work. Some important variables other than dissonance often enter into the situation.

References

Brehm, J. W., & Cohen, A. R. *Explorations in cognitive dissonance.* New York: Wiley, 1962.

Chapanis, N. P., & Chapanis, A. Cognitive dissonance: 5 years later. *Psychological Bulletin,* 1964, *61*, 1–22.

Festinger, L. *A theory of cognitive dissonance.* Stanford, Calif.: Stanford University Press, 1957.

3.2 Selective Interest in Communications That Could Arouse Decisional Conflict: A Field Study of Participants in the Draft-Resistance Movement[1]

Irving L. Janis
Curt N. Rausch

This study was carried out during a period when large numbers of draft-age students were undergoing a decisional conflict about whether or not to sign a pledge to refuse to be drafted. On the basis of a standardized interview, 62 Yale undergraduates were sorted into those favoring and those opposing this pledge by classifying them into four groups: (*a*) signers of the "We-Won't-Go" pledge; (*b*) potential signers who were still undecided; (*c*) formerly conflicted refusers; and (*d*) prompt (unconflicted) refusers. After exposing the subjects to persuasive articles, significant differences were found indicating the expected relation between initial position and acceptance. But the reverse outcome was found for interest ratings of four antipledge communications that were presented in summary form just before the men were asked to read the articles: the men who refused to sign the We-Won't-Go pledge expressed less interest in reading articles that supported their position than did the men who were in favor of signing. This outcome is the opposite of what is predicted by the selective exposure hypothesis. Several pertinent factors are suggested that might help explain the conditions under which the selective counteravoidance tendency observed will be most likely to occur.

During the spring of 1968, there was a growing movement among students throughout the United States to oppose being drafted to fight the war in Vietnam. At Yale University, an antidraft petition—known as the "We-Won't-Go" pledge—had been circulating for many months and was signed by hundreds of students. The present study involved showing persuasive messages on both sides of the draft resistance issue to men who favored signing the pledge and comparing their interest ratings and acceptance reactions with those who were opposed to signing the pledge.

Reprinted from the *Journal of Personality and Social Psychology*, 1970, *14*, 46–54. Copyright 1970 by the American Psychological Association and reproduced by permission.

[1] This study was facilitated by Grant MH-08564 to the senior author from the National Institute of Mental Health, United States Public Health Service.

FIELD SETTING

Within the university community the issue of whether or not to sign the We-Won't-Go pledge was widely discussed and received a great deal of publicity in the college newspaper. During the 7 months preceding our study, the *Yale Daily News* carried over 30 news stories or editorials devoted to this topic, most of which were favorable toward the draft-resistance movement.

During the month when the interviews were being conducted, the local press, radio, and television newscasts gave daily reports about Senator Eugene McCarthy's campaign, which was devoted mainly to attacking the Johnson administration on moral grounds for their failure to end the war in Vietnam and which was receiving strong student support. Moreover, just before our study began, another antiwar campaign was also receiving considerable publicity. The Yale chaplain, Reverend William Coffin, had been indicted, along with Dr. Benjamin Spock and other leaders of a draft resistance movement. Coffin and the others were repeatedly appealing to Yale students to examine their own consciences on the morality of refusing to participate in an immoral war. Thus the draft resistance movement was constantly in the focus of attention of the Yale community.

The antidraft pledge, which was circulated in all the residential colleges, declared:

> We are men of draft age who believe that the United States is waging an unjust war in Vietnam. We cannot, in conscience, participate in this war. We therefore declare our determination to refuse induction as long as the United States is fighting in Vietnam.

The signers realized that they were making a very strong personal commitment to resist being drafted, especially since all their names, along with the text of the pledge, were regularly published in local newspapers.

While there was a great deal of controversy about the legal and moral status of the pledge and about its probable effectiveness as a political tactic, there was general agreement that adhering to it could have serious personal consequences. The students knew that the legal penalty for refusing induction was 5 years in prison and a $10,000 fine. Moreover, many draft resisters expected their careers to be seriously disrupted, particularly if they were planning to obtain a United States Government fellowship, to enter the legal profession, or to work on any project or in any agency financed by government funds.

PURPOSE OF THE FIELD INVESTIGATION

The main purpose in comparing men who took varying stands on the antidraft pledge was to investigate a theoretical issue bearing on selective responsiveness to opposing communication that could arouse decisional conflict.

There is fairly general agreement among social psychologists that people who favor a given course of action will show more resistance than others whenever they are exposed to any persuasive communication that opposes their position (see Festinger, 1964; Janis & Mann, 1968; Jones & Gerard, 1967; Kiesler, 1968; McGuire, 1968a). There is, however, considerable controversy about how a person's initial position on the issue will affect his *interest* in being exposed to opposing communications. Until a few years ago, it was taken for granted by social scientists that people have little interest in exposing themselves to any message that challenges their existing beliefs and attitudes, particularly if they have already committed themselves on the issue (see Klapper, 1949). But the early opinion surveys on which this conclusion was based provide at best highly equivocal evidence and the results of subsequent experiments leave us with a mixed picture (see Freedman & Sears, 1965). Recently, McGuire (1968b) pointed out that although a few experiments provide supporting evidence, a larger number of others fail to confirm the selective exposure hypothesis, even though some of the authors had expected a positive outcome on the basis of one or another theory of cognitive consistency.

Even before consistency theories became popular a great deal of research had been done on the selective exposure hypothesis, and in recent years the amount of this work has been increasing steadily. In spite of all this research, or perhaps because of it, one can hardly claim that nature has spoken out univocally regarding the validity of this prediction. Still, frequent disconfirmations and even apparent reversals of the prediction have not discouraged its proponents, perhaps because the assumption is central to the consistency theories and a number of other theories as well and because somehow the hypothesis seems to deserve to be true [McGuire, 1968c, p. 769].

Recent discussions have repeatedly suggested that a number of additional factors may enter into one's willingness to be exposed to supporting or opposing communications, including expected utility of the information and expected social rewards for acquiring information about what one's opponents are saying (Freedman & Sears, 1965; Katz, 1968; McGuire, 1968b; Mills, 1968; Sears, 1968). The view that is beginning to emerge is that no single generalization can be expected because people have strong tendencies to satisfy curiosity and to obtain information about potential setbacks as well as strong tendencies to avoid the tensions generated by information that is inconsistent with existing expectations and preferences (Katz, 1968; McGuire, 1968b; Sears, 1968). With these considerations in mind, we have tried in the present field study to learn something about how and why interest in opposing communications varies as a function of the person's stand on an issue that requires making a vital decision that could have serious consequences.

Katz (1968) pointed out that it is not easy to determine whether people are selectively interested in messages that will support their current policies and whether they selectively avoid messages that challenge them. He mentioned four essential requirements that a field investigation must meet in order to provide dependable data on these selective tendencies: (a) Subjects must be available for study who take a stand on opposing sides of a controversial issue; (b) a time sequence must be established to ascertain that the subjects' partisan stand on the issue was there first, before exposure to the persuasive messages under investigation; (c) communications on both sides of the issue must be equally accessible to all subjects; and (d) the subjects must have a chance to scan informative headlines or have some other way of knowing in advance, before actually exposing themselves to the communications, whether the contents will support or oppose their position.

In the field study of supporters and opponents of the antidraft movement, the authors were able to meet all four of these requirements. Preliminary opinion surveys of several hundred Yale students showed us that we could easily meet the first requirement by obtaining subjects on both sides of the issue, and that we could also satisfy our own additional requirement of having some subjects in intermediate stages of the decision-making process. The other three requirements were met by using a quasi-experimental design, whereby every subject was asked to report his interest in reading various pro and anti articles, summaries of which were presented after his stand on the issue had been ascertained.

METHOD

Subjects

Since the vast majority of Yale students had not, in fact, signed the We-Won't-Go pledge, we took special steps in order to have a sizable subgroup of men who had overtly committed themselves by signing it. Campus polls showed that in the spring of 1968 the vast majority of undergraduate students at Yale felt that the United States should not continue the war in Vietnam, but only a small minority favored open resistance to the draft. Our own preliminary survey of about 200 students in undergraduate social sciences classes indicated that 25% of the men in the sample were considering the possibility of signing the We-Won't-Go pledge but only 2% had already signed it. Accordingly, we decided to work from the published lists of signers of the We-Won't-Go pledge, which had appeared in the local newspapers and which was part of the signers' act of overt commitment. After selecting a sample of the names on a random basis, we sought out the men in their residential colleges. A total of 23 signers were interviewed. Several men on the list could not be located, but there were no refusals. Each of the signers readily acknowledged, in response to the opening question, that he had signed the pledge.

The sample of 40 nonsigners was obtained on a stratified random basis by knocking at doors in the same residential colleges, in the same way the signers were approached. Again, there were no refusals, but one subject had to be eliminated from the sample because an unavoidable interruption may have affected the interview.

Standard Interview

All 62 subjects, whether signers or nonsigners, were interviewed privately and were given exactly the same explanation for conducting the interview, namely that this was a preliminary study designed to gather some information about the ways in which people go about making an important decision. They were told that the particular example of a decision selected for study involved the We-Won't-Go pledge. Each interviewee was also informed that the interviewer was himself a Yale student and was assured that there were no hidden purposes in conducting these interviews. The standard interview was designed to provide information on three main types of variables:

Partisan stand on the issue.   The study began with questions designed to ascertain each subject's current position with respect to his personal decision about signing the We-Won't-Go pledge. For this purpose, a set of categories was devised that was based on an analysis of the stages in the decision-making process, which provides a more differentiated classification scheme than the usual dichotomy that merely sorts people into the pro or anti category. The following five main stages have been differentiated on the basis of observations of the changes people undergo when they relinquish their initial position and end up committing themselves to a new policy (Janis, 1968): (*a*) *appraisal of a challenge* that makes the person begin to doubt the desirability of the policy to which he had been adhering; (*b*) *generating and appraising feasible alternatives* for meeting the challenge; (*c*) making a *tentative decision* about the best available policy; (*d*) *committing* oneself to the chosen policy by revealing one's decision to others; (*e*) *adhering* to the new policy despite negative feedback and persuasive messages that challenge it. For assessing a person's initial position on a given new policy, such as committing oneself to the We-Won't-Go pledge, a sixth category must be added: unchallenged adherence to the original policy. This category can be regarded as Prestage 1 for any new policy; it of course is equivalent to Stage 5 for the original one.

Each subject was asked to look over a set of six categories (corresponding to the above stated stages) and to select the one showing his own personal stand on the issue of whether or not to sign the We-Won't-Go pledge. When we examined their answers, we found that all the subjects fell into the following four categories:

1. Prompt refusers, consisting of 12 subjects who had immediately ruled themselves out as possible signers without giving the pledge much thought. These men evidently had never been seriously challenged by any persuasive communications or by any encounters with advocates of the draft-resistance movement and hence never reached Stage 1 with respect to signing the pledge.

2. Refusers after deliberation, consisting of 16 subjects who had ruled themselves out as possible signers of the pledge after considering the possibility of signing. These men evidently had passed through at least the first

stage (successful challenge) of making a decision to oppose the draft, and had been in some conflict about what to do, but had ended up by rejecting the alternative of signing the "We-Won't-Go" pledge. Although opposed to the pledge, they would presumably be in more conflict about it than those refusers who had never been challenged.

3. Potential signers, consisting of 11 subjects who thought that they might possibly sign the pledge, but had not yet made up their minds. These men were currently in a state of predecisional conflict about whether or not to sign the pledge. They could be classified as being in the second or possibly the third stage of the decision-making process—having appraised the recommended course of action as an acceptable candidate for meeting the challenge and perhaps regarding it as the best available policy, without yet having decided to take any action.

4. Committed signers, consisting of 23 men who had already signed the pledge. These men had obviously passed the fourth stage since they had publicly committed themselves to the decision, and were now in the fifth stage of adhering to the decision despite whatever negative feedback they were encountering.

In order to check further on the subjects' partisan stand concerning the draft-resistance movement, we included a series of questions about their willingness to engage in other protest actions: the subject was handed a sheet on which were listed the following six forms of protest in which a student might participate to show his opposition to continuing the war in Vietnam: (a) signing propeace petitions that urge the Government to stop the war in Vietnam; (b) writing letters to Congressmen expressing disagreement with current policies regarding the war in Vietnam; (c) marching or demonstrating for propeace purposes; (d) making monetary contributions to a propeace organization; (e) sitting in (to protest military recruiting, to oppose Dow Chemical Company, etc.); (f) doing clerical work (e.g., mailing out leaflets) for a propeace organization or committee. The subject was asked to indicate his willingness to perform each of these actions, with choices ranging from "Would not consider" at one extreme to "Will definitely do" or "Have done" at the other.

Interest in being exposed to pro and anti articles. Each subject was shown a summary of eight magazine articles, consisting of the title and a sentence or two that summed up the article in about 50 words, making it clear whether it would present arguments that were for or against the draft-resistance movement. Four of the articles supported the We-Won't-Go pledge and the other four opposed it. Although the experimenter did not explicitly tell the subjects that their choices would determine which articles they would be given to read, he implied that their interest ratings would be used for this purpose. This was done by telling the subject that

a little later I'll be asking you to read a few articles in their entirety and comment on them; but for now you'll be dealing with summaries of several articles that I'm going to ask you to rate in terms of how interested you would be in reading them.

The articles were presented in a fixed but randomized order and the subject was asked to rate each of them in terms of "how interested would you be in actually reading this article?" He was asked to check one choice on the following rating scale:

————Great interest—definitely would read this article
————Some interest—probably would read this article
————Undecided—might read this article, might not
————Little interest—probably would *not* read this article
————No interest—definitely would *not* read this article

Acceptance ratings. In the last part of the interview, each subject was asked to read two articles on the issue of draft resistance, one pro and the other anti. Each article consisted of five paragraphs and contained a total of almost 600 words. One article, which was entitled "The Case *For* The Draft Dissenters," consistently supported the We-Won't-Go pledge and related acts of resistance to the draft. The second article, entitled "The Case *Against* The Draft Dissenters," consistently argued against the pledge and emphasized the unfavorable consequences of violating our constitutional draft laws.

After reading both articles in a standard (pro followed by anti) order, the subject was asked to what extent he agreed with the opinions expressed in each of the two articles. He indicated his degree of acceptance on a 5-point scale ranging from "Strongly agree with the opinions expressed" to "Strongly disagree with the opinions expressed." Then the subject was asked to recall the major points of each article. First, he was asked to summarize the main points of the two articles—the points that he recalled as being of particular interest. After that he was asked to try to remember any other arguments, ideas, or statements that he had not yet mentioned, in order to show how much detail from each article he was able to recall.

RESULTS

Differences in Partisan Stand Concerning Resistance to the Draft

The four categories pertaining to the subjects' stand on the We-Won't-Go pledge constitute the independent (predispositional) variable against which each dependent-variable measure was run. In order to draw any valid inferences from group differences in reactions to the communications we showed to the subjects, it is essential to check first on background factors that might be correlated with differences in their initial position on this issue. Since all subjects were undergraduates at the same university, it seems safe to assume that there would be no significant group differences in either IQ or general educational level. As to the students' personal draft status, relevant data were obtained from a question asked at the end of the interview. The results showed that the four groups were well equated in that approximately the same high percentage of men (about 90%) expected to be deferred (in Selective Service Category 2S) up to the time of their graduation. But only a very small percentage in each group felt secure about being exempt from the draft *after* graduation, by obtaining a 4F deferment, by going into medical school, or by entering some other exempt category. On all of these categories concerning expected draft status, the differences among the groups were small and nonsignificant.

When age and class year (proximity to graduation) were checked there was a somewhat unequal proportion of younger men among the signers. (Of the 5 freshmen in the total sample of 62, 4 turned out to be signers.) Further checks, however, showed that neither age nor class year had any significant correlation with any of the dependent measures used in this study and hence the slight differences on these two attributes could not account for any of the significant differences reported below. Nevertheless, as an added precaution, all the findings were recomputed with the five freshmen eliminated, and exactly the same outcomes were found: every significant difference obtained from using the total sample (shown in the tables below) also emerged as significant when differences in proximity to graduation were reduced by eliminating the freshmen.

Evidence of consistent differences in initial position concerning the draft-resistance movement was obtained by comparing scores for the four groups on willingness to engage in six types of protest action. Each subject's score on willingness to engage in a given type of action ranged from 0 (for being unwilling to consider doing it) to 3 (for being definitely willing to do it or for having already done it). (A score of 1 was given if the subject said he "might consider it" and a score of 2 if he said he was "seriously considering it.") A total score was obtained for each man by adding up the scores on all six items and dividing by six. The mean total scores for the four groups were as follows: (a) prompt refusers, .76; (b) refusers after deliberation, 1.05; (c) potential signers, 1.73; and (d) committed signers, 2.26. As expected, the total scores show a consistent and highly significant linear trend, indicating a strong positive relation between the subjects' stand on the We-Won't-Go pledge and their willingness to engage in alternative types of protest actions ($F = 17.58$, $df = 3/58$, $p < .01$).[2]

Interest in Being Exposed to Pro and Anti Articles

The interest ratings of the four pro articles and the four anti articles are shown in Table 1. Each rating, obtained on a 5-point scale accompanying

---

[2] The same linear trend appears for each of the six types of protest action and is statistically significant ($p < .01$) for five of them. (The only nonsignificant result was for writing letters to congressmen, which probably involves a somewhat different type of predisposition: we found that correlations between this type of action and the other five types of action were relatively low, ranging from .29 to .43; whereas, the correlations among the other five types of action were significantly higher, ranging from .53 to .71.)

TABLE 1 *Comparison of Men Who Oppose the "We-Won't-Go" Pledge with Men Who Favor the Pledge: Mean Scores on Interest in Being Exposed to Pro and Anti Articles*

ARTICLES	OPPOSED TO PLEDGE		IN FAVOR OF PLEDGE		OVERALL M
	Promptly refused to sign (n = 12)	*Refused after deliberation (n = 16)*	*Might sign (n = 11)*	*Have already signed (n = 23)*	
Propledge	9.83	11.81	11.09	10.83	10.94
	⎰ 10.96 ⎱		⎰ 10.91 ⎱		
Antipledge	7.50	9.38	10.09	11.31	9.84
	⎰ 8.64 ⎱		⎰ 10.82 ⎱		

the description of each article, was given a score ranging from 0 for "no interest" to 4 for "great interest."[3]

For the pro articles, there are no significant differences among the four groups ($F = 1.06$, $df = 3/58$, $p > .25$). For the anti articles, however, there are large and significant differences in interest scores among the four groups ($F = 3.18$, $df = 3/58$, $p < .05$). It will be noted that the linear trend for the antipledge articles is the reverse of what would be expected on the basis of an inconsistency-avoidance hypothesis; that is, it is in the opposite direction from the attitude trend found for willingness to participate in acts of resistance to the draft. The same outcome is obtained when the combined mean for the two groups who were opposed to signing the pledge are compared with that of the two groups who were in favor of signing it. The results of a 2 × 2 analysis of variance, summarized in Table 2,

TABLE 2 *Analysis of Variance: Interest Ratings by Subject's Initial Position (Dichotomized) and Type of Article Rated (Pro versus Anti Draft Resistance)*

SOURCE	df	MS	F
Between Ss	62		
Initial position (A)	1	35.02	2.59
Ss within groups	60	13.52	
Within Ss	62		
Pro versus anti articles (B)	1	44.55	7.35**
A × B	1	38.10	6.28*
B × Ss within groups	60	6.06	

* $p < .05$.
** $p < .01$.

show: (*a*) a significant main effect for type of article, indicating that for all subjects the mean interest ratings were significantly higher for the propledge articles (10.94) than for the antipledge articles (9.84); and (*b*) a significant interaction effect, again indicating that the outcome was not the same for the two types of articles, that is, when asked about the *anti*pledge articles, the men opposed to signing the pledge expressed less interest than did

[3] Another type of exposure-preference question was also presented just before the subjects were asked to give their interest ratings. Each subject was shown the four pairs of article summaries, one pair at a time, and was asked to select the article in each pair that he would prefer to read. No significant difference was found when the four groups were compared on article preferences. The absence of group differences implies that there was no differential tendency toward selective preference among the four groups. But since the preference score based on the four pairs is a relatively insensitive measure, we give more weight to the evidence based on the interest ratings obtained for each of the eight articles.

the men who favored signing the pledge; whereas when asked about the *pro*pledge articles, the two groups did not differ in their interest ratings.

Our finding for the antipledge articles is the reverse of what is predicted by a selective avoidance hypothesis, since the men who initially disagreed with the position taken by these articles expressed more interest in reading them than did the men who initially agreed with the articles. A detailed comparison of the four groups on each of the four antipledge articles shows that this reversed trend arises primarily from the ratings on two of the four articles, one of which argued that refusing to be drafted is illegal and immoral, while the other claimed that angry Congressmen threaten reprisals against draft resisters. A third article, which predicted that the government will prosecute draft resisters, contributes slightly but yields differences of only borderline significance. The only anti article on which the four groups hardly differ at all dealt with the alleged ineffectiveness of petitions. In contrast to the latter article, the other three referred directly to *unfavorable personal consequences* that might ensue from carrying out the We-Won't-Go pledge.

Additional Findings

Agreement scores were obtained on a 5-point scale immediately after the subject had finished reading two articles, one pro and the other anti. These scores ranged from 5 for "Strongly agree with the opinions expressed" to 1 for "Strongly disagree with the opinions expressed." In the ratings obtained for both articles, large and significant differences were found in the direction expected on the basis of the subjects' initial stand on the We-Won't-Go pledge: the more opposed the men were to signing the pledge, the more likely they were to express disagreement with the propledge article and to express agreement with the antipledge article.[4]

Although agreement or acceptance ratings are generally assumed to be positively correlated with interest ratings, these findings do not support any such assumption. In fact, low negative correlations were found between the two types of ratings: the Pearsonian correlation coefficient between agreement scores and interest scores was $-.06$ ($p > .25$) for antipledge articles and $-.22$ ($p < .05$) for propledge articles.

Another dependent variable investigated was recall of pro and anti arguments. At the end of the session, when asked to try to recall as much

---

[4] For the article entitled, "The Case *For* the Draft Dissenters," the mean ratings were as follows: (*a*) prompt refusers, 3.42; (*b*) refusers after deliberation, 3.62; (*c*) potential signers, 4.36; and (*d*) committed signers, 4.35 ($F = 4.39$, $df = 3/58$, $p < .01$). For the article entitled, "The Case *Against* The Draft Dissenters," the corresponding mean ratings were as follows: 2.67, 2.06, 1.82, and 1.59 ($F = 3.39$, $df = 3/58$, $p < .05$).

as they could of each of the two persuasive communications, the subjects in each of the four groups reproduced accurately about one-half of the main points in each article (i.e., an average of about three out of six arguments). There were no significant differences in recall scores among the four groups ($F = .4$ for the prodraft resistance article and $F = 1.4$ for the antidraft resistance article). Nor were there any significant differences in the number of minor details reproduced. Thus, so far as the learning and immediate retention of persuasive arguments are concerned, our findings show no differential selective tendencies whatsoever, for any of the groups investigated in this study.

DISCUSSION

The main finding bearing on selective exposure indicates that men who opposed signing the We-Won't-Go pledge were less interested in reading antipledge articles (which would support their own initial position) than were men who favored signing the pledge. When we examine the pertinent data in Table 1, it looks like this outcome is mainly attributable to the low mean score (8.64) for the men opposed to signing the pledge. In view of their low interest ratings, one might surmise that these men may have been uninterested in reading anything more on their own side of the issue because they were already over-familiar with the supporting arguments.

Other plausible factors that might account for the observed outcome are suggested when we take note of the obvious fact that the men who favor signing the pledge deviate as much above the overall mean score of 9.84 for the antipledge articles as the men who oppose signing differ in the opposite direction. Perhaps there were some special reasons why the prosigners were more strongly interested than the others in being exposed to statements by their opponents concerning the allegedly bad consequences that might be in store for them if they were to live up to the We-Won't-Go pledge. Some clues along these lines were obtained from a separate series of intensive interviews of 28 Yale men, which focused on attitudes and plans concerning resistance to the draft and was carried out as a pilot study to supplement the data from the present study. Almost all of the men described themselves as strongly opposed to continuing the war in Vietnam and hoped that they would not be drafted, although only 12 of the 28 expected to refuse induction if drafted, in accordance with the We-Won't-Go pledge. Every one of the 12 resisters acknowledged that his refusal to be inducted would be a legally punishable offense and stated that if necessary he would leave the country or go to jail. When queried about the considerations that entered into their decision, the 12 resisters admitted feeling considerable conflict, anxiety, and uncertainty about their decision. Their comments suggested two specific sources of vigilance that would incline them to pay attention to counterarguments: (a) vigilant interest in information about the type of objections to the draft resistance movement that they were likely to encounter, so as to deal effectively with their parents or others in their personal social network who do not share their views, and (b) vigilant interest in information about the probable unfavorable consequences of adopting one or another specific course of action as a means for implementing the general policy stated in the pledge (e.g., to apply for conscientious objector status, Project Vista, the Peace Corps, or a draft-deferred teaching job, or to escape the draft by leaving the United States).

Obviously, there are other motivations that might also enter into the decision to read a communication that goes counter to one's own stand. For example, a desire to be regarded as a fair and judicious person might incline a man to express a strong interest in being exposed to the opposing communications. These and related tendencies, which have been repeatedly mentioned in publications on selective exposure, could be operating among the college students in the field study. Furthermore, since the data are correlational, one must also consider the possibility that some important predispositional attribute—such as a personality or ideological variable that makes for marked differences in open-mindedness—might be the underlying determinant both of attitudes toward the We-Won't-Go pledge and readiness to expose oneself to the pro or anti communications.

Although there is no basis for selecting among the alternative mediating factors that could account for the differences in interest ratings shown in Table 1, the data, nevertheless, bear directly on the status of the selective exposure hypothesis, which predicts the opposite outcome from what we found. Our data on recall of pro and anti arguments also indicate that the reality-testing orientation of the college students in our study remained unaffected by whatever motivation they may have had to avoid decisional conflict. The findings show that the men's initial position had no relation to the number of pro or anti arguments they were able to recall after reading two persuasive communications.

Our findings are consistent with Sears' (1968) conclusions in his recent critique of the selective exposure hypothesis. He pointed out that although several communication experiments show a selective exposure tendency, at least seven other pertinent studies fail to yield any significant differences that would show the predicted preference for supportive communications or avoidance of nonsupportive communications. He also cited findings from experiments by Walys and Cook (1966) and Greenwald and Sakurmura (1967), showing that nonsupportive arguments are learned as readily as supportive ones. Sears concluded that the available evidence calls into question the earlier reports of selective exposure and selective learning since it implies that in everyday life people do *not* generally resort to information-avoidance techniques to soften the impact of unpleasant information, even though such avoidance may be displayed in extreme situations of psychological stress involving the threat of bodily injury, death, or the loss of a loved person.

The results from our field study not only fail to support the selective exposure hypothesis but indicate that at least under certain conditions we should expect the reverse tendency to be dominant. We have suggested several factors that might prove to be the determining conditions—such as overfamiliarity with supporting arguments and vigilant concern about unfavorable consequences to be averted when one is facing the dilemma of selecting the most appropriate means for implementing a policy to which one has already committed himself (or is about to do so). Such factors will require systematic investigation as potentially interacting variables in subsequent studies of selective exposure.

References

Festinger, L. *Conflict, decision, and dissonance.* Stanford, Calif.: Stanford University Press, 1964.

Freedman, J. L., & Sears, D. O. Selective exposure. In L. Berkowitz (Ed.), *Advances in experimental social psychology.* Vol. 2. New York: Academic Press, 1965.

Greenwald, A. G., & Sakurmura, J. S. Attitude and selective learning: Where are the phenomena of yesteryear? *Journal of Personality and Social Psychology,* 1967, *1,* 387–397.

Janis, I. L. Stages in the decision-making process. In R. P. Abelson et al. (Eds.), *Theories of cognitive consistency: A sourcebook.* New York: Rand McNally, 1968.

Janis, I. L., & Mann, L. A conflict-theory approach to attitude change and decision making. In A. Greenwald, T. Brock, & T. Ostrom (Eds.), *Psychological foundations of attitudes.* New York: Academic Press, 1968.

Jones, E. J., & Gerard, H. B. *Foundations of social psychology.* New York: Wiley, 1967.

Katz, E. On reopening the question of selectivity in exposure to mass communications. In R. P. Abelson et al. (Eds.), *Theories of cognitive consistency: A sourcebook.* New York: Rand McNally, 1968.

Kiesler, C. A. Commitment. In R. P. Abelson et al. (Eds.), *Theories of cognitive consistency: A sourcebook.* New York: Rand McNally, 1968.

Klapper, J. T. *The effects of the mass media.* New York: Columbia University Bureau of Applied Science Research, 1949.

McGuire, W. J. The nature of attitudes and attitude change. In G. Lindzey & E. Aronson (Eds.), *Handbook of social psychology.* Reading, Mass.: Addison-Wesley, 1968. (a)

McGuire, W. J. Selective exposure: A summing up. In R. P. Abelson et al. (Eds.), *Theories of cognitive consistency: A sourcebook.* New York: Rand McNally, 1968. (b)

McGuire, W. J. Selective exposure to information: Editor's introduction. In R. P. Abelson et al. (Eds.), *Theories of cognitive consistency: A sourcebook.* New York: Rand McNally, 1968. (c)

Mills, J. Interest in supporting discrepant information. In R. P. Abelson et al. (Eds.), *Theories of cognitive consistency: A sourcebook.* New York: Rand McNally, 1968.

Sears, D. O. The paradox of *de facto* selective exposure without preferences for supportive information. In R. P. Abelson et al. (Eds.), *Theories of cognitive consistency: A sourcebook.* New York: Rand McNally, 1968.

Walys, P., & Cook, S. W. Attitude as a determinant of learning and memory: A failure to confirm. *Journal of Personality and Social Psychology,* 1966, *4,* 280–288.

Foreword to Reading 3.3

INTRODUCTION

This article by Mills and Harvey has a long tradition of research behind it. It is now possible to list a number of the conditions under which one might expect a communicator to be able to change the attitude of his audience. For the reader who wishes to know more, Karlins and Abelson (1970) provide a good summary of these conclusions, and Zimbardo and Ebbesen (1970) have written a small, readable book that is an effort to "turn the reader on" to the area of attitude change.

To give the reader some idea of the research to date, several of the conclusions cited in Zimbardo and Ebbesen (pp. 20–23) are listed below:

1. There will be more opinion change in the desired direction if the communicator has high credibility (meaning that he is expert and trustworthy) than if he has low credibility.
2. Communicator characteristics irrelevant to the topic of his message can influence acceptance of his conclusion.
3. A communicator's effectiveness is increased if he initially expresses some views that are also held by his audience.
4. It is most effective to present one side of the argument (rather than both sides) when the audience is generally friendly, or when your position is the only one that will be presented, or when you want immediate, though temporary, opinion change.
5. The individual's personality traits affect his susceptibility to persuasion; he is more easily influenced when his self-esteem is low.
6. Audience participation (group discussion and decision-making) helps to overcome resistance.

This article by Mills and Harvey is concerned with the effect of communicator characteristics. The predictions are derived from a description by Kelman (1961) of the different types of opinion change. Kelman suggests that what appears to be attitude change can really be either compliance, identification, or internalization. Compliance occurs when the individual accepts influence because he hopes to achieve a favorable reaction from the person who is attempting to influence him. This type of attitude change tends to disappear as soon as the influencing person does. Identification occurs when the individual is influenced by a person or group because he considers them to be attractive and finds it satisfying to be like them. Internalization occurs when the individual accepts influence because the new attitude or behavior fits in with his existing values and seems to him to be a true representation of reality. Kelman's notions are interesting in that they pinpoint accurately the various kinds of social influence that are often brought to bear.

Although Mills and Harvey use Kelman as a framework for their predictions, it seems to these editors that the framework is not an essential one. Moreover Kelman and Harvey make no attempt to *prove* the existence of either internalization or identification. Rather, without theory, what they have is a reasonable-sounding notion that an attractive communicator may have an influence regardless of what he says, whereas the expert communicator has to buttress his advantage with his arguments. (One might suppose that the audience might change their views of the communicator's expertness if his arguments are poor; whereas the communicator's attractiveness is irrelevant to the arguments and so is not affected by them.)

METHOD

The experiment included four conditions: In two of these, the communicator was described before the communication; in the other two, the communicator was described after the communication. Moreover, in one of the "before" groups and in one of the "after" groups, the communicator was presented as both similar to the subjects and physically attractive; in the other "before" and "after" groups, the communicator was presented as an "expert" in the area, but older than the subjects and physically unattractive.

The procedure contained several features which might limit the generality of conclusions to be drawn from the study. First, the subjects were all women. Second, the subjects completed the attitude change measure only *after* they had attempted to perform what was said to be a "difficult" test of memory for the communication. Third, the experimenter informed the subjects several times that there was more to the experiment than he had originally admitted. These last two aspects are somewhat unrealistic and may have caused the subjects to be self-conscious in their behavior.

In this experiment, as in many others in this area, it is said that attitude "change" has been measured, when in fact no measure of "change" has been included. The assumption is that, on the average, the groups in each condition of the experiment started out feeling the same about the issue, and that differences in attitude between the groups at the end of the experiment represent attitude "change." The measure of attitude here consisted of ten "Likert-type" items. An item is designated as Likert-type when the subject is given a statement or item and asked to indicate the extent of his agreement or disagreement with it using the scale provided. The scale is generally marked at several points with notations ranging from "strongly agree" to "strongly disagree."

RESULTS AND DISCUSSION

Mills and Harvey predicted that hearing about the expertness of a communicator after rather than before his communication would impair his ability to produce attitude change, while the before-after variable would not affect the persuasiveness of an attractive communicator. (Presumably, as discussed above, being attractive is irrelevant to one's arguments, but still leads others to change their opinions for you.) This prediction was supported. The practical implication is that when the expert hopes to influence his audience, he cannot afford to be modest. He must state the grounds for his competence before he states his arguments. Otherwise, he takes the chance that some charismatic communicator will sway his audience away from him.

References

Karlins, M., & Abelson, H. I. *Persuasion,* 2d ed. New York: Springer, 1970.
Kelman, H. C. Processes of opinion change. *Public Opinion Quarterly,* 1961, 25, 57–78.
Zimbardo, P., & Ebbesen, E. B. *Influencing attitudes and changing behavior.* Revised printing. Reading, Mass.: Addison-Wesley, 1970.

3.3 Opinion Change as a Function of When Information About the Communicator is Received and Whether he is Attractive or Expert[1]

Judson Mills
John Harvey

An experiment tested the hypothesis that whether the audience receives information about the communicator before or after the communication will have less effect on its persuasiveness when the communicator is attractive than when he is expert. College women read the same communication under four conditions; information indicating that the communicator was either attractive or expert was presented either at the beginning or at the end. In confirmation of the hypothesis, it was found that agreement with the expert communicator was lower when the information about him was given after the communication than when it was given before, but agreement with the attractive communicator was just as great when the information about him was given after as when it was given before.

Kelman (1961) has made a distinction between opinion change based on identification and on internalization. According to Kelman,

Identification can be said to occur when an individual adopts behavior derived from another person or a group because this behavior is associated with a satisfying self-defining relationship to this person or group. . . . Identification is similar to compliance in that the individual does not adopt the induced behavior because its content per se is intrinsically satisfying. Identification differs from compliance, however, in that the individual actually believes in the opinions and actions he adopts. . . . Finally, *internalization* can be said to occur when an individual accepts influence because the induced behavior is congruent with his value system. It is the content of the induced behavior that is intrinsically rewarding here [pp. 63–65].

Kelman (1961) proposed that:

To the extent that the agent's power is based on his *attractiveness,* influence will tend to take the form of identification. . . . To the extent that the agent's power is based on his *credibility,* influence will tend to take the form of internalization. An agent possesses credibility if his statements are considered truthful and valid, and hence worthy of serious consideration [p. 68].

Journal of Personality and Social Psychology, 1972, Vol. 21, No. 1, 52–55. Copyright 1972 by the American Psychological Association and reproduced by permission.

[1] This study was supported by a grant from the National Science Foundation. It was conducted while the second author held a National Defense Education Act predoctoral fellowship.

From these conceptions it might be expected that if the communicator is very attractive, when the audience receives information about him may not make as much difference as it would if the communicator were considered an expert on the topic. If agreement with the attractive communicator is based on identification, then it may be relatively unimportant whether or not the audience has accepted the specific arguments of the communication. However, if agreement with an expert communicator is based on internalization, the reduction in acceptance of the content of the communication that may occur if the audience is not informed about the communicator beforehand may materially decrease his effectiveness.

An experiment was designed to test the hypothesis that whether the audience receives information about the communicator before or after receiving the communication will have less effect on the communication's persuasiveness when the communicator is attractive than when he is expert.

METHOD

Female college students read a speech favoring general education under four experimental conditions: attractive before, attractive after, expert before, and expert after. In the before conditions, a description and photograph of the communicator were presented at the beginning of the speech. In the after conditions, the description and photograph were presented at the end of the speech. In the attractive conditions, the communicator was described as a college sophomore majoring in education who had been elected vice president of his freshman class, and the accompanying photograph showed him as rather attractive. In the expert conditions, the communicator was described as a professor of education who was one of the country's leading experts on problems of higher education, and the accompanying photograph showed him as rather unattractive. Agreement with the communicator's position was measured after the subjects had rated his personality characteristics and completed a test of memory for what they had read.

The subjects were 72 college women who participated in order to earn extra credit toward their course grade in general psychology. They were run during three sessions. Within each session, the subjects were randomly assigned to the experimental conditions with as near an equal number as possible in each condition. There were 18 subjects in each of the four conditions.

At the beginning of each session, the experimenter told the subjects that the study concerned impression formation. Each of them would read a speech and then rate the personality characteristics of the person who delivered it. Booklets were distributed containing a fictitious speech arguing that every college student should receive a broad, general education.

In the before conditions, a page containing a description and photograph of the communicator was placed before the text of the speech. In the after conditions, the page containing the description and photograph of the communicator was placed after the text of the speech.

In the attractive conditions, the material describing the communicator was as follows:

This speech was given by a sophomore majoring in education at a large Midwestern state university. He was elected vice president of his freshman class by popular vote. A photograph of him appears below.

Printed on the page was a 1 × 2 inch photograph of an attractive, smiling, young man.

In the expert conditions, the material describing the communicator was as follows:

This speech was given by a professor of education at a large Midwestern state university. He is one of the country's leading experts on the problems of higher education. A photograph of him appears below.

Printed on the page was a 1 × 2 inch photograph of an unattractive, frowning, middle-aged man.

When the subjects had finished reading the speech, the speech booklets were collected, and each subject was given a rating form with the same code number as their speech booklet. The subjects were asked to indicate how well various characteristics applied to the communicator by circling a number on a scale from 0 (extremely inappropriate) to 20 (extremely appropriate) for each characteristic. The characteristics were attractive, competent, cold, earnest, expert, friendly, frank, knowledgeable, likable, sincere, and unpleasant. The subjects were told that their ratings would be kept completely confidential and were not asked to put their names on the rating forms.

After the subjects had completed the rating forms, the experimenter told them that there was more to the study than he had mentioned at the beginning. He said that another purpose was to study the relationship between impressions of a person and memory for what the person had said. He was now going to pass out a memory questionnaire to determine how well they could recall exactly what the communicator said in the speech. He explained that he could not reveal this earlier because, if he had, they might have made a special effort to memorize the speech. The subjects were warned that the memory test was difficult.

The rating forms were collected, and each subject was given a booklet for the memory test with the same code number as their speech booklet and rating form. The subjects were not asked to put their names on the memory test booklet. The first section of the booklet contained 20 multiple-choice questions with three alternatives each. The subjects were instructed to choose the word or phrase that completed each statement in the way which was closest to what was said in the speech.

After all of the memory test booklets were distributed, the experimenter interrupted the subjects and said he should have mentioned that the last page of the booklet was included to get their personal reactions to some statements in order to see if there was a relationship between personal reactions and memory. Some of the subjects invariably turned to the last page, and the experimenter immediately cautioned everyone not to look at the last page until they had answered all of the memory items, and not to return to the memory items once they had begun to give their personal reactions. The last page contained 10 Likert-type items concerning general versus specialized education, with seven alternatives from "strongly agree" to "strongly disagree." Six of the items were in favor of general education, and the other four were opposed to general education. A measure of favorability to general education was calculated by assigning scores from +3 to −3 to the alternatives for each item and then summing over the 10 items; the more positive the score, the greater the favorability to general education.

After the subjects had answered all of the items in the booklet, the experimenter asked them to write a few sentences on the back describing their reactions to the study. He told them that they could say anything they wanted about the study. None of the subjects made comments indicating suspicion about the procedure. Finally, before dismissing the subjects, the experimenter explained the necessity of their not discussing the experiment with anyone.

RESULTS AND DISCUSSION

It was assumed that the communicator would be perceived as more attractive in the attractive conditions than in the expert conditions. The means for the ratings for the adjective "attractive" for the four experimental conditions are presented in Table 1. It can be seen from Table 1 that ratings of

TABLE 1 *Means for the Ratings for Attractive*

COMMUNICATOR	WHEN INFORMATION ABOUT COMMUNICATOR WAS RECEIVED	
	Before	After
Attractive	15.2	15.7
Expert	8.9	8.1

Note.—N = 18 for each cell.

the communicator's attractiveness were higher in the attractive conditions than in the expert conditions. An analysis of variance showed that the main effect for the attractive–expert variable was highly significant ($F = 48.32$, $df = 1/68$, $p < .001$). The main effects for the before–after variable and the interaction were not significant.

It was also assumed that the communicator would be perceived as more expert in the expert conditions than in the attractive conditions. The means for the ratings for the adjective "expert" for the four experimental conditions appear in Table 2. As can be seen from Table 2, ratings of the communicator's expertness were higher in the expert conditions than in the attractive conditions. An analysis of variance showed that the main effect for the attractive–expert variable was highly significant ($F = 19.84$, $df = 1/68$, $p < .001$). The main effect for the before–after variable was not significant. The interaction between the attractive–expert variable and the

TABLE 2 *Means for the Ratings for Expert*

COMMUNICATOR	WHEN INFORMATION ABOUT COMMUNICATOR WAS RECEIVED	
	Before	*After*
Attractive	11.5	9.0
Expert	14.0	15.8

Note.—$N = 18$ for each cell.

before–after variable was significant ($F = 6.60$, $df = 1/68$, $p < .025$). The difference in the ratings for "expert" between the attractive and expert conditions was greater for the after conditions than for the before conditions. Although this interaction was not predicted, it is easily understandable in terms of better recall of the information about the communicator in the after conditions. When it was received closer in time to the ratings, the information about the communicator had more effect on the ratings of his expertness.

Further evidence that the communicator was perceived as more expert in the expert conditions than in the attractive conditions is provided by the subjects' ratings for the adjective "knowledgeable." The ratings for knowledgeable were significantly higher for the expert conditions than for the attractive conditions ($F = 4.93$, $df = 1/68$, $p < .05$). The only other significant effects for the ratings for the adjectives were a significant interaction for the ratings for "competent" and a significant main effect of the before–after variable for the ratings for "frank." For the ratings for competent, the difference between the attractive and expert conditions was greater for the after conditions than for the before conditions ($F = 4.46$, $df = 1/68$, $p < .05$). This interaction is similar to the interaction for the ratings for expert and can be understood in the same way. The ratings for frank were higher for the before conditions than for the after conditions ($F = 4.60$, $df = 1/68$, $p < .05$). The subjects may have felt that the communicator's identity should have been revealed before the communication. When it was not, they may have held the communicator responsible, and consequently perceived him as being less frank.

Before presenting the results for the measure of agreement with the communicator's position, it should be mentioned that there were no differences between the conditions in the number of correct answers on the memory test. An analysis of variance of the scores on the memory test did not yield any significant effects. The subjects averaged approximately 14 correct answers on the 20 memory items.

It was hypothesized that whether the audience receives information about the communicator before or after receiving the communication will have less effect on the communication's persuasiveness when the communicator is attractive than when he is expert. From this hypothesis it would be expected that the difference in favorability to the communicator's position between the attractive-before condition and the attractive-after condition would be less than the difference between the expert-before condition and the expert-after condition. The means for the measure of favorability to general education for the four experimental conditions are presented in Table 3. It can be seen from Table 3 that while the mean for the expert-after condition was considerably lower than the mean for the expert-before condition, the mean for the attractive-after condition was actually slightly higher than the mean for the attractive-before condition. An analysis of variance showed that the interaction between the attractive-expert variable and the before-after variable was significant beyond the .05 level ($F = 4.20$, $df = 1/68$). Neither of the main effects approached significance.

In designing the study, an attempt was made to describe the attractive and expert communicators so that they would be about equally persuasive. As can be seen from Table 3, this attempt was successful. The mean for the

TABLE 3 *Means for the Measure of Agreement with the Communicator's Position*

COMMUNICATOR	WHEN INFORMATION ABOUT COMMUNICATOR WAS RECEIVED	
	Before	After
Attractive	8.2	9.3
Expert	9.5	1.9

Note.—The higher the scores, the greater the agreement with the communicator's position. $N = 18$ for each cell.

attractive-before condition was very similar to the mean for the expert-before condition; the difference did not approach significance. However, the difference between the mean for the attractive-after condition and the mean for the expert-after condition was significant ($t = 2.67$, $df = 1/34$, $p < .02$).[2] Looking at the results from a different angle, the difference between the expert-before condition and expert-after condition was significant ($t = 2.60$, $df = 1/34$, $p < .02$), while the difference between the attractive-before condition and the attractive-after condition was not.

The results provide good support for the hypothesis, based on Kelman's (1961) distinction between identification and internalization, that whether the audience receives information about the communicator before or after the communication will have less effect on the communication's

[2] All significance tests are two-tailed.

persuasiveness when the communicator is attractive than when he is expert. They demonstrate that the processes which produce agreement with an attractive communicator are not identical to the processes which produce agreement with an expert communicator.

Reference

Kelman, H. C. Processes of opinion change. *Public Opinion Quarterly,* 1961, *25,* 57–78.

PART 4

Social Perception
and Attraction

The topic of "social perception" includes all of the determinants of our perception of other people as well as the conditions that determine our perception of ourselves.

To put this topic into historical perspective, the early research concerned itself with the picture or impression one formed of a person when presented with adjectives describing that person. For instance, Asch (1946) found that certain traits in the stimulus list tended to dominate the impression. When the word "warm" was included in the list: "intelligent, skillful, industrious, determined, practical, cautious," 91 percent of the subjects saw the person as generous; when the word "cold" was included in the *same* list, 8 percent of the subjects saw the person as generous. Asch concluded that "warm" and "cold" are "central traits," in that they affect the total evaluation of a person. Other "peripheral" traits, "polite" and "blunt" for instance, did not produce the same polarizing effect. Moreover, even the effect of warm and cold depended on context. In other lists of adjectives, they were less central or dominating.

While Asch's approach affected research for the next 15 years (e.g., Kelley, 1950; Wishner, 1960), current emphasis in this area is on the notion that people may either "average" or "add" information from favorable or unfavorable adjectives. Since most textbooks summarize this research, and some of it is quite technical, we have not provided an example here.

Instead, six articles, all with practical applications and dealing with questions that might be of interest to students today, were chosen to represent this area. Two of the articles deal with the issue of moral judgment. The selection by Kaufmann (1970) asks: Under what conditions do we consider a person to have committed an immoral act after he has failed to prevent a disaster? The other article (Vidmar, 1972) examines a similar question in a different context and theoretical framework. How would a jury judge a defendant who has committed a crime? Under what circumstances would they consider him responsible for what he has done and issue

127

a guilty verdict? These two articles have implications for the workings of law and justice in our society.

Three of the articles are concerned with the variables that determine the attraction of one person for another. Ellsworth and Carlsmith (1968) look at a subtle aspect of interaction, that of eye contact, indicating that eye contact can make you dislike as well as like a person, information of importance to both dating couples and traffic cops, as you will see. Berscheid, Boye, and Walster (1968) have investigated the tendency of persons who have harmed another to derogate that person as well. They show that when the victim is expected to do some harm in return, then he is not disliked for having suffered (which might break a vicious circle of discrimination, dislike, and prejudice). Byrne, Ervin, and Lamberth (1970) took a reliable laboratory finding that people like those who are like them, and retested it in a timely field study involving computer dating.

Finally, one of the articles is concerned with the question of how people perceive themselves, specifically, how do they decide what emotion they are experiencing. The Nisbett and Schachter (1966) selection indicates that by changing a person's perception of the *cause* of his pain, we can change his perception of the amount of pain he is experiencing.

The reader will find variety in these articles in that they have several theoretical bases (consistency theory and attribution theory) and demonstrate several procedural techniques including simulation (pretend that you are a jury), deception (we say that we are studying one thing, but we are really studying another), and the field study (study outside of a laboratory).

References

Asch, S. E. Forming impressions of personality. *Journal of Abnormal and Social Psychology,* 1946, *41,* 258–290.

Berscheid, E., Boye, D., & Walster, E. Retaliation as a means of restoring equity. *Journal of Personality and Social Psychology,* 1968, *10,* 370–376.

Byrne, D., Ervin, C. R., & Lamberth, J. Continuity between the experimental study of attraction and real-life computer dating. *Journal of Personality and Social Psychology,* 1970, *16,* 157–165.

Ellsworth, P. C., and Carlsmith, J. M. Effects of eye contact and verbal content on affective response to a dyadic interaction. *Journal of Personality and Social Psychology,* 1968, *10,* 15–20.

Kaufmann, H. Legality and harmfulness of a bystander's failure to intervene as determinants of moral judgment. In J. Macaulay and L. Berkowitz (eds.), *Altruism and helping behavior.* New York: Academic Press, 1970.

Kelley, H. H. The warm-cold variable in first impressions of persons. *Journal of Personality,* 1950, *18,* 431–439.

Nisbett, R. E., and Schachter, S. Cognitive manipulation of pain. *Journal of Experimental Social Psychology,* 1966, *2,* 227–236.

Wishner, J. Reanalysis of "impressions of personality." *Psychological Review,* 1960, *67,* 96–112.

Vidmar, N. Effects of decision alternatives on the verdicts and social perceptions of simulated jurors. *Journal of Personality and Social Psychology,* 1972, *22,* 211–218.

Foreword to Reading 4.1

INTRODUCTION AND METHOD

If you read the newspapers these days, you know that even a crowd of people is no guarantee of help in an emergency. Kaufmann (1968) began his study of bystander help or intervention (for a related study, see Latané and Darley, 1968, in this volume) using a procedure in which the subject observed a confederate giving electric shocks to another confederate. As in the Milgram study (1963, in this volume), the rationale for the shocks was that the investigators were concerned with the effect of punishment on learning. Despite a number of experimental variations and protests from the victim, few of the bystander subjects protested or managed to stop the experiment.

In the present study, Kaufmann looked at moral judgment instead of intervention. Subjects were asked to indicate the morality of a failure to intervene in an emergency, and each subject participated in all of the experimental conditions. There were four of these conditions, representing all of the possible combinations of two variables: (a) failure to intervene: legal or illegal; (b) outcome after failure to intervene: harmful for victim or not harmul for victim.

The reader who is confused about the control exercised over stories and the order of stories should put himself in the role of experimenter. First, he would have to make up eight case histories of failure to intervene. Now he would have to divide the eight case histories into four pairs (in any way). Next he would have to write, for each of the four pairs of stories, four endings representing the four experimental conditions. Then, he would have to assign case histories to subjects so that each subject would read four pairs of stories, each pair representing a different experimental condition, and so that over all the subjects the possible combinations of pairs of stories, and experimental conditions (and condition appearing first) would be given to an equal number of subjects. The reader can, no doubt, see that this careful control was necessary to ensure that only the independent variables affected the results.

RESULTS

The major finding for all four dependent variables was that both the illegal nature and the harmful outcome of failure to intervene acted to increase the perceived immorality of the lack of action. The main effect and inter-actions of the "subjects" variable, by the way, indicate that on questions A and D, there were also large individual differences in response (i.e., the subjects differed from each other, apart from the differences caused by the independent variables).

DISCUSSION

It is interesting that an illegal failure to intervene was judged more harshly than one not punishable by law. This indicates that the passing of appro-priate laws may be one way in which to promote socially responsible behaviors.

With regard to the "outcome" variable, Kaufmann compares his results to those of Piaget (1948). When Piaget asked children "Which boy was more naughty—a boy who unintentionally broke five glasses, or one who unintentionally broke ten glasses?", the younger children chose the latter boy (the ten-glass breaker), basing their judgment on the outcome of the crime; the older children thought them equally naughty, basing their judgment on intention, rather than outcome.

However, the college students here did use outcome as a factor in consideration of moral judgment and perceived pleasantness. As mentioned by the author, perhaps the explanation lies in the salience of legal con-siderations (since the law does consider outcome when determining punishment). As another explanation, the outcomes here (e.g., drowning in the sample story) were much more serious than those described by Piaget.

Landy and Aronson (1969) carried out a study which seems to demonstrate the same sort of phenomenon. In that study, the accidental killing (through a traffic accident) of an unattractive victim was judged *less* harshly than the accidental killing of an attractive victim. Again, the person and his act were evaluated in the context of the result of the act.

References

Kaufmann, H. The unconcerned bystander. In Proceedings of the Annual Convention of the American Psychological Association, 1968.

Landy, D., and Aronson, E. The influence of the character of the criminal and his victim on the decisions of simulated jurors. *Journal of Experimental Social Psychology*, 1969, *5*, 141–52.

Latané, B., and Darley, J. Group inhibition of bystander intervention in emergencies. *Journal of Personality and Social Psychology*, 1968, *10*, 215–221.

Milgram, S. Behavioral study of obedience. *Journal of Abnormal and Social Psychology*, 1963, *67*, 371–378.

Piaget, J. *The moral judgment of the child.* New York: Free Press, 1948.

4.1 Legality and Harmfulness of a Bystander's Failure to Intervene as Determinants of Moral Judgment

Harry Kaufmann[1]

Recent incidents in a number of metropolitan centers have focused attention on the passivity of witnesses to crimes of various sorts. Not only has this extreme noninvolvement been documented by a number of newspaper articles, but, in a laboratory test of intervention, Kaufmann[2] found that only 19 out of 186 subjects who had been given an accessory task protested when a "teacher" ostensibly gave increasingly severe shocks to a stooge as punishment for learning errors. Of these 19, only ten refused to complete the experiment. Moreover, the willingness to intervene did not appear to be affected by such variables as respective status of the teacher and the subject, the authority for the choice of shock level expectation for future participation, or the moral deservingness of the "learner."

It might be supposed that legal prohibitions would operate as codified "norms" or as influential statements of presumed majority opinion. However, recent studies (Walker & Argyle, 1964; Berkowitz & Walker, 1967) have shown that, in fact, knowledge of "peer" opinion has a greater effect on moral judgment than knowledge of legal prohibition. Psychologically, then, morality and legality are not equivalent. Harmfulness might conceivably be seen as irrelevant to the morality of the bystander's behavior since he was not aware of the eventual outcome when he failed to act. However, Piaget (1948) has shown that children under seven judge "naughtiness" only in terms of "damage," while older children are more apt to consider "intentions." On the other hand, common as well as criminal law considers both intention and outcome.

The present study was conducted to assess evaluative attitudes toward noninvolvement of a bystander, where such noninvolvement is either legal or illegal, and does or does not result in harm. Intention was not explicitly stated, and might have been assumed to be the same regardless of legality or outcome.

---

[1] The present study was conducted while the author held a S.P.S.S.I. Grant-in-Aid.

[2] From an article of the same name by Harry Kaufmann in J. Macaulay and L. Berkowitz (Eds.), *Altruism and Helping Behavior*. Copyright © 1970 by Academic Press.

METHOD

Subjects

One hundred and fifty-four male and female students between the ages of 18 and 27 were used as subjects. The students were taking an introductory course in psychology and were given the questionnaire as a group.

Procedure

Subjects were told that the investigator was interested in assessing student attitudes. All students filled out a questionnaire which presented eight situations. In each situation, a potentially harmful event was taking place, and a Mr. X (who was given a different initial for each of the eight situations) failed to attempt to prevent this harm. The situations were ambiguous enough so that failure to intervene could be said to be either legal or illegal. The potential harm either occurred or was prevented by a change in the situation which came about after the bystander had failed to intervene. A sample situation follows.

> A man drowned when he fell through the ice on a frozen lake, 10 feet from shore. Mr. A, who observed the event, did nothing to help. The law does not require a person to render assistance in such a situation. Therefore, Mr. A is not liable to criminal prosecution. (legal-harm condition)

There were four experimental conditions, and each subject was asked to judge two situations for each of these four conditions. The eight situations were arbitrarily divided into four pairs. In each questionnaire, the paired situations were put in the same condition, and an approximately equal number of subjects was given each combination of paired situations and experimental condition. Each pair of situations, therefore, occurred in each of the four conditions an equal number of times. In each questionnaire, the paired situations followed each other, but the order of conditions was varied so that each condition appeared first in an equal number of questionnaires.

After reading about each situation, the subjects answered four questions evaluating either Mr. X or his actions. These four questions and the scales following them are shown in Table 1.

RESULTS

Table 2 shows mean responses for the four questions and the four experimental conditions. Analysis of variance of responses to question A, judging the morality of Mr. X's lack of action, yielded three significant main effects, legality ($p < .001$), harmfulness ($p < .001$), and subjects ($p < .01$), and one significant interaction, legality by subjects ($p < .01$). Regarding the two manipulated variables, illegal failure to intervene was considered significantly less moral than legal failure to intervene, and harmful outcomes rendered these failures significantly less moral than nonharmful outcomes.

TABLE 1 *Questionnaire*

A. As a question not of law but of morality, is Mr. X's action:

wrong as possible	very wrong	wrong	slightly wrong	not wrong	very right

B. Quite apart from legal aspects, Mr. X:

	did not do anything wrong	did slightly wrong	did wrong	did very wrong

C. Leaving legal aspects aside, Mr. X:

should not be censured or punished in any way	should be reprimanded	should be punished slightly	should be punished moderately	should be punished severely	should be punished very severely

D. Although I know very little of Mr. X, my guess is that, as a person, he might be:

very unpleasant	moderately unpleasant	slightly unpleasant	neither pleasant nor unpleasant	slightly pleasant	moderately pleasant	very pleasant

TABLE 2 *Mean Response to Questionnaire as a Function of Experimental Condition[a]*

		LEGALLY REQUIRED TO INTERVENE		NOT LEGALLY REQUIRED TO INTERVENE	
	QUESTION	*Harm*	*No Harm*	*Harm*	*No Harm*
A:	Morality	4.70	4.44	4.46	4.18
B:	Morality	3.12	3.00	2.98	2.74
C:	Deserved punishment	2.82	2.58	2.48	2.14
D:	Pleasantness	5.12	4.79	4.92	4.72

[a] A higher mean indicates a less moral act, an act more deserving of punishment, and a less pleasant Mr. X.

Question B, which raised much the same issue as A, but phrased it differently and provided different responses, yielded the same three main effects ($p < .01$), but no interactions.

For question C, concerning recommended punishment, there were again three significant main effects ($p < .01$, $< .01$, $< .05$, respectively), and no significant interactions.

Finally, for question D, concerning the perceived pleasantness of Mr. X, there were three significant main effects, as well as three significant interactions (legality × harmfulness, legality × subjects, harmfulness × subjects). The legality × harmfulness ($p < .05$) interaction reflects the finding that the difference between the judgments in legal and illegal situations was greater when harm was involved than when no harm was involved. The other interactions, both significant at the .01 level, indicate that subjects were differentially affected by the legality or harmfulness variables.

DISCUSSION

In this study, an illegal failure to intervene was seen as more reprehensible (morally wrong and deserving of punishment) than such an act when it is legal. Berkowitz and Walker (1967) suggest that this effect stems from at least two sources: *(1)* the implication of majority opinion, and *(2)* the support of "legitimate authority."

It also appeared in this study that failure to intervene was viewed as more reprehensible when harm occurred, even though the prevention or lack of it could in no way be attributed to the bystander. This result appears to be at variance with Piaget's description of mature moral judgments which take intention into account. However, it should be noted that each case history mentioned both legality and "legal prosecution." Since the law does, in fact, consider outcome as well as intention when determining punishment, the mention of "legal prosecution" may have increased the salience of outcome.

Not surprisingly, subjects differed in the severity of their judgments. However, as was shown by the interaction effects for the "pleasantness" question, they were also differentially susceptible to the experimental manipulations.

Mr. X's personality (his pleasantness) was judged in the context of the situation in which it appeared. He was thought to be most pleasant when involved in a nonharmful and legal nonintervention situation, and least pleasant when involved in a harmful and illegal nonintervention situation. People, it thus appears, are judged by the manner in which their actions and intentions turn out, even if these outcomes are fortuitous.

References

Berkowitz, L., & Walker, N. Laws and moral judgments. *Sociometry*, 1967, *30*, 410–422.

Kaufmann, H. The unconcerned bystander. *Proceedings of the American Psychological Association*, 1968.

Piaget, J. *The moral judgment of the child*. New York: Free Press, 1948.

Walker, N., & Argyle, M. Does the law affect moral judgments? *British Journal of Criminology*, 1964, October, 570–581.

Foreword to Reading 4.2

INTRODUCTION

This paper deals with a psychological process known as "attribution," in other words, a process by which causes are assigned. Heider (1944) first drew attention to this process, calling his theory a "naive" one because it relied heavily on "common-sense." Heider suggested that people want to predict and control their environment so that they can obtain good outcomes from it. In order to be able to predict and control, they act as observers and try to determine the causes of an action or of an event. When a person has been observed to act in a particular way, the observer is interested in knowing whether or not that action can be attributed to external causes (the pressure of the environment) or to internal causes (the person's abilities or motivations) or to some combination of the two. DeCharms (1968) speaks of this as the distinction between the person as a "pawn" or as an "origin." If we know that the person has been an origin rather than a pawn in a particular act, then we have increased our probability (or at least we think we have) of predicting his behavior in the future. If a student is doing well in one of his classes because he is working hard (rather than because he is afraid of the teacher), then we can predict that he may do well in his other classes as well.

Jones and Davis (1965) extended and systematized Heider's theory, concentrating on the conditions under which the observer would infer the personality or "dispositions" of the actor from his actions. If the observer has reason to assume that the actor was aware that his action would have the effects that it did, and that the actor had the ability to carry out the action as he did, then the observer tends to conclude that the act was intentional and to make a "correspondent inference" about the actor. A correspondent inference is one in which the action, intention, and disposition are said to correspond or are described in the same terms. As an example, "He was helpful to me in slipping answers to me on the last test; he intended to be helpful, and his character is that of a kind person." The observer is more likely to make a correspondent inference in certain kinds of situations rather than others. For instance, a correspondent inference is unlikely when we observe someone doing something that is expected or socially desirable in our society. We learn little about a person's character when we observe him saying "thank you" for a favor, or stopping his car at a red light.

Bem (1970) has also extended the attribution notion, applying it to the situation in which the individual observes his own behavior, and having no clear "internal" cause for it, tries to find the cause in the behavior. For instance, suppose that the conforming teenager begins to smoke pot on his friend's recommendation. Not knowing himself to have any terrible desire to sample this new form of experience, he may come to the conclusion that his behavior indicates that he has a favorable attitude toward the issue of whether or not the individual should smoke pot.

A person on trial, whether he knows it or not, is vitally concerned with the process of attribution. It is most important to him whether or not he is perceived to be a "cause" of his action, rather than a victim of environmental forces. Vidmar suggests that the existing theories of attribution processes, however, have omitted important variables that would allow us to predict when a defendant will be held responsible for his supposed crime. His study was concerned with the effect of the kind of decision that the jury has to make. He suggests that if the jury must choose between an extremely severe penalty and a verdict of not guilty, then the not guilty verdict will be more likely than in the situation in which a variety of penalties with differing degrees of leniency could be assigned. (This prediction is not based on any theory, but simply assumes, as do the Heider models as well as the Jones and Davis, that the human being is a relatively rational, reasonable organism.)

Vidmar also suggests that having chosen a not guilty verdict, the observer will rearrange his perception of the situation in a way that justifies his decision. This suggestion is similar to the one discussed in the Berscheid, Boye, and Walster (1968) article in this section. The individual arranges his perceptions so that the world appears to be a just and equitable place, even when it is not. This behavior protects the individual from a good deal of heartache, but also makes it difficult to induce people to recognize situations in which discrimination and injustice are present.

METHOD

The subjects, who were college undergraduates, were asked to read the summary of a murder trial, and to render a verdict "as if" they were the members of the jury at the trial. The subjects were given alternative decisions that they could make, varying in number and in severity of penalty required. They were then also asked to respond to 33 questions concerning their feelings about the defendant, the victim, and the persons giving testimony.

RESULTS

The predictions as to the verdict chosen were confirmed, as the reader can see in Table 1. To cite just one result, 54 percent of the subjects chose a not guilty verdict when the alternatives provided were "first degree murder" and "not guilty," while only 17 percent of the subjects chose a not guilty verdict when the alternatives provided were "second degree murder" and "not guilty." In addition, the predictions concerning the observer's perception of the situation received some support, but only for 6 of the 33 questions used.

DISCUSSION

Vidmar provides an interesting discussion on the possibility of applying his result to real-life situations, and the necessity for further research and modifications in the existing attribution theories.

With regard to real-life applications, Landy and Aronson (1969) have also shown that what might seem to be an irrelevant factor affects the decisions of "as if" jurors. Landy and Aronson found that criminal defendants were assigned greater penalties when the victim of the crime (who died as a result of an automobile accident) was described as "attractive" rather than "unattractive." This study has implications for the choice of a jury and the presentation of testimony, if one can assume that "as if" jurors are affected by the same factors as "real" jurors.

References

Bem, D. *Beliefs, attitudes and human affairs.* Belmont, California: Brooks/Cole, 1970.

Berscheid, E., Boye, D., & Walster, E. Retaliation as a means of restoring equity. *Journal of Personality and Social Psychology,* 1968, *10,* 370–376.

deCharms, R. *Personal causation.* New York: Academic Press, 1968.

Heider, F. Social perception and phenomenal causality. *Psychological Review,* 1944, *51,* 358–374.

Jones, E. E., & Davis, K. E. From acts to dispositions. In L. Berkowitz (ed.), *Advances in experimental social psychology.* Vol 2. New York: Academic Press, 1965.

Landy, D., & Aronson, E. The influence of the character of the criminal and his victim on the decisions of simulated jurors. *Journal of Experimental Social Psychology,* 1969, *5,* 141–152.

4.2 Effects of Decision Alternatives on the Verdicts and Social Perceptions of Simulated Jurors[1]

Neil Vidmar

Simulated jurors were asked to read a description of an attempted robbery and consequent killing of a store proprietor. They were asked to return a verdict on the defendant's guilt under one of seven conditions (plus a no-decision control group) which varied the number and severity of the decision alternatives. A postdecision questionnaire assessed their perceptions of the defendant and the trial testimony. Although jurors having at least a "moderate" penalty option seldom chose a verdict of "not guilty" (on average of 6% in six conditions), over half (54%) of the jurors faced with only a "severe" penalty option chose "not guilty." Implications for theories on attribution of responsibility are discussed.

Psychological theory and research dealing with attribution of responsibility in person perception have tended to ignore the potential impact on the process of decision making of (a) the perceiver's decision alternatives and (b) the magnitude of consequences of his decisions for the target person (see Jones & Davis, 1965; Maselli & Altrocchi, 1969, for literature reviews). The model of the attribution process proposed by Jones and Davis (1965), which is based on the theory proposed by Heider (1958), is essentially an inference model that sees responsibility attribution as a process based on the logical processing of cues about the target's acts, his ability to commit those acts, and his knowledge about the consequences of those acts. The "personal knowledge" model of deCharms (1968) implies that the attribution process is basically a projection by the perceiver to the target of his own intentions if he were to commit similar behaviors. Both models, however, do not deal with the many instances in which the perceiver is forced to make a decision about a target person knowing in advance that the decision will result in certain outcomes for the target. Consider some examples. A factory foreman may be put in the position of filing a "violation" report on a subordinate. Will he be more inclined to make a judgment of "willful" intent if the subordinate will only receive several days of suspension as opposed to the instance where the subordinate's employment will

Journal of Personality and Social Psychology, 1972, Vol. 22, No. 2, 211–218.

[1] This research was supported by Canada Council Grant No. S69-1602 and by a University of Western Ontario Faculty of Social Science Grant. The author is indebted to Michael S. Goodstadt for his advice throughout the study and to Linda Crinklaw, who offered criticisms of earlier drafts of this paper.

be terminated? Consider another example. Will a student's Ph.D. committee be more inclined to vote to pass him on comprehensive exams if they know a fail will result in termination of doctoral study than if they know a fail will merely result in the student having to rewrite all, or portions, of the exam? How will these decision makers then rationalize their judgments? A final example, which originally gave rise to speculation on these issues, is concerned with the decision alternatives made available to jurors by either the law or the judge's discretion in his instructions to the jury.

During the Detroit riots of 1967, three young black men were killed in the now infamous Algiers Motel incident (see Hersey, 1968). In the summer of 1969, a white policeman involved in that incident was brought to trial for the murder of one of the men. After both prosecution and defense had presented their cases, the judge in charge of the trial gave the jury only two choices in returning their verdict: guilty of first-degree murder or not guilty. The former alternative carried a mandatory sentence of life imprisonment. "Middle ground" verdicts of second-degree murder or manslaughter were not allowed, although their omission from consideration is "unusual" (but legal) in Michigan murder trials. A number of legal sources were reputed to feel that because of conflicting testimony on the part of the defense, the defendant would likely have been found guilty if the less severe alternatives had been available. Other legal sources disagreed and felt the proper charge had been given to the jury (see Lundy, 1969).

Disregarding the particulars in the Algiers Motel trial, discussions of the jury system indicate that such controversy is not unusual. Many sources indicate that the judge has considerable influence on jury outcome (see Winick, 1961, for a review). Even though some states allow the judge neither comment nor summary on a trial, there is no way of knowing how much informal influence a judge can exert (Kalven & Zeisel, 1966). The impact of the severity of the threatened penalty has also been studied. Punishment may dominate jury deliberation despite instructions to disregard it (Kalven & Zeisel, 1966, Ch. 21). At the same time, a study of instances where the jury was also allowed to set the penalty as well as deciding guilt failed to show differences from instances where juries were not allowed to set the penalty (Kalven & Zeisel, 1966, Ch. 21).

The broader psychological problem arising from the above discussion, then, may be summarized as follows: given instances in which a perceiver must make an overt judgment, or decision, about a target person, what effect does the number of decision alternatives and consequences arising from the decision alternatives have on the type of decision that is reached? An examination of the literature suggests that no attention has been given directly to this question. A second question asks, how does the perceiver rationalize his decision once it is made? There is some previous work dealing with the processes of the perceiver *after* he has made a decision about, or has performed some behavior having consequences for, a target person (Berscheid & Walster, 1967; Lerner, 1965; Lerner & Matthews, 1967; Lerner & Simmons, 1966; Rothbart, 1968; Walster & Prestholdt, 1966). Basically, this research supports the notions derived from dissonance theory (e.g., Festinger, 1957) that subjects will rationalize their perceptions of the target in such a way as to make it consistent with their decision. In a jury trial, for example, choice of a verdict with severe consequences should result in greater attribution of responsibility to the target person than when a less severe or "not guilty" verdict is chosen. Similarly, jurors should give greater weight to evidence supporting their decision.

The present research limits itself to simulated juror decisions in an analogue of the Algiers Motel trial. Suppose the evidence is such that given no restrictions a defendant would generally be perceived to be guilty of manslaughter or second-degree murder. If jurors are restricted to a limited number of guilt alternatives, will the number of acquittals increase as the severity of the consequences associated with the guilt alternative increases? One might hypothesize that in the instance of a choice between a guilty verdict which carries a too severe penalty or a not guilty verdict, jurors will say "the penalty is too severe even though the defendant is guilty, and hence I will judge him to be not guilty." On the other hand a juror might decide: "the penalty is too severe, but that is none of my business because the defendant is guilty, and I must indicate his guilt."

METHOD

General Strategy and Design

An abridged transcript of a murder trial was used as the task. It consisted of a neutral introduction to the facts of the case followed by the testimony of four witnesses. Because order of testimony might have a bearing on decision outcomes, all possible orders of evidence (hence, 24 orders of testimony) were used within each decision-alternative cell of the design. After reading the facts and testimony, the subjects were told to assume that they were members of a jury and to indicate their verdicts about the defendant. Following this decision they were asked a number of questions about the defendant, the testimony of the witnesses, and so forth. The experimental design had eight conditions regarding the number and kind of decision alternatives available to the simulated juror: (1) guilty of first-degree murder or not guilty; (2) guilty of second-degree murder or not guilty; (3) guilty of manslaughter or not guilty; (4) guilty of first-degree murder, second-degree murder, or not guilty; (5) guilty of first-degree murder, manslaughter, or not guilty; (6) guilty of second-degree murder, manslaughter, or not guilty; (7) guilty of first-degree murder, second-degree murder, manslaughter, or not guilty; (8) control condition where no verdict was requested.

Subjects

The subjects were 227 students taking an introductory course in social psychology at the University of Western Ontario. The questionnaires were administered during class time as a demonstration experiment in social psychology. The questionnaires were ordered so that the necessary 192 cells (8 decision-alternative conditions × 24 orders of testimony) would be filled. In order to keep the number of subjects and testimony orders equal in each cell, the responses of the additional 35 subjects were discarded from the analysis. Sex of subjects was not well controlled in the design and was to some extent influenced by class seating patterns. There were 74 males and 118 females in the final analysis. Cell frequencies for males ranged from only 2 males in Conditions 1 and 3 to 17 in Condition 4. An analysis of variance considering sex as a variable could still be attempted although not under ideal circumstances since the F ratio would be based on un-weighted means and hence would be only approximate.

Task

The criminal case was modified from an abbreviated description of a murder trial that actually took place in Canada. The evidence of the four witnesses was modified to range from testimony indicating first-degree murder, through "middle ground" guilt of second-degree murder or manslaughter, to not guilty. A pilot study (as well as the results of the final experiment) indicated that given no restrictions, the overwhelming majority of judges would choose between manslaughter or, second-degree murder. Middle-ground guilt was necessary to test the effects of giving only an alternative with a perceived "too severe" punishment. Subjects were given the following introductory instructions:

> We are interested in studying the manner in which people judge various criminal offenses. The following pages give an account of a criminal offense. Please read the case carefully because when you have finished reading the case account, you will be asked to give your personal opinions concerning the case.

The general introductory facts and testimony in the case were presented in a summary brief as follows:

> *Case of Charles Young,* accused of murder in the death of Yoshyuki Ono. On December 10, 1966, the defendant, Charles Young, entered the shop kept by the father of the victim at 502 West 4th Ave., Vancouver, for the purpose of robbery. The victim, 24 years old, Yoshyuki Ono, lived in the rear of the shop with his father and mother and 22-year-old brother. The living area consisted of a sitting room, kitchen, and bedrooms. The sitting room was separated from the rest of the shop by what is called a half-door with curtains on the store side extending to the floor. A bell would ring in the living area when the street door of the shop was opened.
>   On the occasion of the incident, Mr. and Mrs. Ono were sitting in the sitting room with the deceased son and his brother. The store bell having rung, the father left the room for some reason and the mother entered the shop. She saw that Young was carrying a revolver and uttered some expres-

sion which gave a warning to the others in the sitting room that a holdup was in progress. They had formerly gone through a similar experience, and the expression was understood. At about this point, a customer, Steve Wilson, entered the store. He quickly saw that a robbery was in progress and dove for a counter on the opposite side of the store. From this point on, the events and sequence of events are unclear. A struggle ensued between Young and the victim, Yoshyuki Ono. Three shots were fired from Young's revolver. One bullet entered Yoshyuki's hand, another entered his arm, and the third entered his head, causing a fatal wound. Young fled the shop but was apprehended a short time later.

In the murder trial the question of the attempted robbery is undisputed. However, the trial testimonies of Young, Mrs. Ono, Yoshyuki's brother, and the customer, Steve Wilson, differ.

The testimony of the witnesses, ordered in decreasing degree of guilt, was as follows:

Testimony of victim's brother. The brother states that he and Yoshyuki were sitting in the sitting room when they heard their mother's warning. Both men immediately jumped up and started toward the door to the shop. Yoshyuki was nearer to the door when two shots rang out, wounding him in the hand and arm. Yoshyuki continued his rush into the store and began to struggle with Young in order to get the gun away from him. In the struggle, Yoshyuki "had Young's wrist, raising it up in the air." Young managed to break away from Yoshyuki and rushed toward the street door. Just as he was opening the door, "he turned toward my brother who was just standing there. He aimed the gun and shot my brother in the head." Young then rushed out into the street.

Testimony of victim's mother. Mrs. Ono says that as soon as she signaled her family about the robbery, Young went immediately toward the curtains of the door leading into the sitting room, and, as he approached, he fired a shot which passed through the wooden partition at the side of the doorway. When he got to the curtains, he fired another shot through the curtains. The first shot wounded Yoshyuki in the hand and the second in the arm. Yoshyuki immediately came into the store and grappled with Young in an effort to disarm him. Mrs. Ono says that in the struggle Yoshyuki was attempting to take the pistol from Young "but could not reach because he was quite high [tall]." She added: "Young was holding the gun, and my son grabbed his wrist." Defense question: "Does she mean that Young was holding the gun in his hand?" Answer: "Yes, and my son was doing his best, and trying to bring it down, but he quite weak because he injured already." She continues that while they were struggling, she heard a shot and afterwards did not hear anything. After the shot, her son fell down, and Young ran off.

Testimony of Steve Wilson, customer. Wilson testified that just as soon as he had gotten inside the store, Mrs. Ono cried out, and he then saw the robber's gun. Since he had not been noticed by the gunman, Wilson quickly decided to take cover. While he was scrambling to hide behind a wooden counter, he heard two shots but did not see anything. When he looked out from the side of the counter, Young and Yoshyuki "were struggling." Question: "What were the positions of the two men relative to the door?" Answer: "Mr. Ono (Yoshyuki) was between Young and the door." Question: "Would you say that Ono was attempting to stop Young's escape?" Answer: "I don't know." Wilson said that the struggling men moved out of his field of vision. He heard a third shot. After "a few moments," he looked up and saw Yoshyuki on the floor.

   Testimony of Defendant Young. Young maintains that when he entered the store the revolver was in his pocket. Mrs. Ono entered the shop from the rear area and asked if she could help him. When he pulled the revolver from his pocket "the old lady started screaming." Young asserts that the commotion unnerved him, he hesitated, and then decided to run. But before he could make his move, Yoshyuki appeared from nowhere and began to struggle with him. Young managed to push Yoshyuki away from him but in the process was off balance, and, as he fell against a counter, a combination of the impact and the panic caused him to fire the revolver twice. Yoshyuki then reengaged in the struggle, grabbing at Young's wrist when the gun went off accidentally, inflicting the fatal wound. Young then ran off. Under defense cross-examination, the arresting officer corroborated the fact that this was what Young told him when first arrested: "He told me he was in a jam." Question: "What kind of a jam?" "He told me he took some store and said that 'the Jap came for me, and the gun went off.' "

Decision-Alternative Conditions

After reading the testimony, the subjects were given the following instructions:

> Assume you are a member of the jury. We are interested in your individual decision about the defendant, Charles Young. The judge gives the following instructions to the jury before sending it to the jury room to make its decision: There are four options (or three options or two options, depending on the condition) in bringing forth your verdict about the defendant. (*a*) He is guilty of first-degree murder (sentence required by law is 25 years to life imprisonment). (*b*) He is guilty of second-degree murder (sentence required by law is 5–20 years imprisonment). (*c*) He is guilty of manslaughter (sentence required by law is 1–5 years imprisonment). (*d*) He is not guilty.

Postdecision Questions

Following their verdict, the subjects were to indicate their feelings about the case on a series of 7-point semantic-differential-type scales. Question 1: Young is guilty (7), not guilty (1). Question 2: Young should be treated harshly (7), leniently (1). Question 3. Describe Young on each of the following scales: (*a*) violent–not violent; (*b*) good–bad; (*c*) unlucky–lucky; (*d*) reckless–cautious; (*e*) not responsible–responsible; (*f*) likable–unlikable. Question 4 asked the subject to describe the victim on the following adjective scale pairs: (*a*) good–bad; (*b*) unlucky–lucky; (*c*) reckless–cautious; (*d*) not responsible–responsible; (*e*) likable–unlikable. Questions 5, 6, 7, and 8 asked the subjects to describe the testimony of the victim's mother, the defendant Young, the victim's brother, and customer Wilson's testimony, respectively, on each of the following scales: (*a*) probable–improbable; (*b*) bad–good; (*c*) irrational–rational; (*d*) accurate–inaccurate; (*e*) unbiased–biased. The favorable adjective was always anchored with the scale point of 7, while the unfavorable adjective was anchored with the 1 scale point.

RESULTS

A preliminary analysis indicated that there were no significant effects due to order of testimony. Preliminary analysis also showed only three marginally significant sex effects out of 34 tests. Since we would expect approximately 2 out of 34 tests to yield "significant" results by chance, and since those three sex effects did not contribute to the understanding of the data, the remainder of the analyses disregarded sex as a variable.

Decision Alternatives and Verdicts

Table 1 shows, by condition, the frequency with which each alternative was chosen. It is quickly apparent that far more (54%) not guilty verdicts were returned in Condition 1, which forced the subjects to choose between a first-degree murder verdict or not guilty, than in any other condition. To test the statistical significance of this finding, the frequencies were treated as either a not guilty or guilty "to some degree" (hence, Condition 7 had 22 guilty and 2 not guilty verdicts). To test the controversial idea suggested by the Algiers Motel trial, Condition 1 was compared to Condition 7, which had all four decision-alternative possibilities. The two conditions were significantly different at the .001 level ($\chi^2 = 11.7$, $df = 1$). Some critics might (appropriately) suggest that the differences between Conditions 1 and 7 may have been due to the greater number of decision alternatives, and thus the opportunity to choose some verdict other than not guilty in Condition 7 rather than the greater severity of the guilty option in Condition 1. To test this interpretation, Conditions 2 and 3 were combined and compared to Condition 1. The former conditions were like Condition 1 in that there were only two alternatives, but they differed in that a guilty verdict would result in a less severe penalty of the defendant. Condition 1 was again significantly different ($\chi^2 = 14.3$, $df = 1$, $p < .001$). Conditions 4, 5, and 6, which had two guilt options, yielded only one not guilty verdict out of 72 subjects. It may be concluded then, that under conditions of restricted decision alternatives, the more severe the degree of guilt associated with the least severe guilt alternative, the greater were the chances of obtaining a not guilty verdict.

Postverdict Social Perceptions

Once an individual has chosen a decision alternative, how does he rationalize his decision? Dissonance theory and other consistency formulations would predict that those individuals choosing a guilty alternative should report the defendant to be more guilty and indicate that he should be treated more harshly than subjects choosing a not guilty alternative. Subjects choos-

TABLE 1 *Decision Alternatives and Frequency of Verdicts*

ALTERNATIVE	CONDITION							
	1	2	3	4	5	6	7	8[a]
First degree	11 (46%)	—	—	2 (8%)	7 (29%)	—	2 (8%)	—
Second degree	—	20 (84%)	—	22 (92%)	—	11 (46%)	15 (63%)	—
Manslaughter	—	—	22 (92%)	—	16 (67%)	13 (54%)	5 (21%)	—
Not guilty	13 (54%)	14 (17%)	2 (8%)	0 (0%)	1 (4%)	0 (0%)	2 (8%)	—

Note.—Blank cells indicate that that decision alternative was not available in the condition. There were 24 subjects in each condition. The percentage of verdicts within each cell within conditions is indicated in parentheses.

[a] Condition 8 was a control for the social perception question; no verdicts were requested.

ing guilty should also downgrade testimony that is favorable to the defendant. Hence, the perceptions of the 11 subjects in Condition 1 who chose not guilty and those of the 13 who chose guilty were compared with the perceptions of the subjects in Condition 8. These latter subjects were not asked to pass a verdict on the defendant, and thus served as a control group whose social perceptions should fall between the guilty and not guilty decision makers in Condition 1.

A one-way analysis of variance with three decision levels (guilty, Condition 1; not guilty, Condition 1; no decision, Condition 8) was conducted on each of the 33 social perception scales. Although only 7 scales yielded statistically significant differences, the data for 6 of these scales yield fairly strong support for the hypothesis. Table 2 shows that subjects choosing not

TABLE 2 *Means and F Ratios of Social Perception Items Showing Significant Differences Between Condition 1 (Not Guilty), Condition 1 (Guilty), and Condition 8 (No-Decision) Subjects*

	CONDITION			
ITEMS/SUBJECTS	Not guilty	Guilty (1)	No decision (8)	F ratio[a]
1. Young is guilty (7)	3.69	5.82	5.83	12.85**
2. Young should be treated harshly (7)	4.00	5.45	4.79	5.08*
3. Young is good (7)	3.38	2.64	2.33	4.30
4. Young is likable (7)	3.25	1.82	3.08	4.99
5. Mother's testimony biased (1)	3.46	4.75	4.45	4.07*
6. Brother's testimony biased (1)	1.79	2.73	2.15	3.26*
7. Customer's testimony improbable (1)	5.31	5.64	6.17	3.36*

Note.—Only one adjective of the bipolar scales is listed; the parentheses indicate the number with which that adjective was anchored.

[a] $df = 2/45$.
* $p < .05$.
** $p < .01$.

guilty saw the defendant as being less guilty, as deserving less harsh treatment, and as being less bad and more likable than subjects choosing a guilty verdict. Not guilty subjects also saw the victim's mother's and brother's testimony as being more biased than subjects choosing a guilty verdict. The means for the last scale in Table 2 suggest the possibility that the testimony of Steve Wilson, the customer, may have been perceived as ambiguous. Both decision makers who choose guilty and those who choose not guilty saw his testimony as less probable than the "no decision" subjects, and, in fact, the not guilty choosers saw it as less probable than the guilty decision makers.

DISCUSSION

Discussion of the study first centers around the limitations of the specific experiment and then suggests some implications for the broader problem of attribution of responsibility when the perceiver's decision has direct consequences for the target person.

The present data indicate that restricting the decision alternatives available to jurors, especially when the guilty alternative has a consequence which is perceived to be too severe, may increase the likelihood of obtaining a not guilty verdict. We should note, however, that the usual qualification of laboratory experiments should be applied before generalizing to actual jury decisions as in the Algiers Motel trial. First, the subjects knew that the task and the consequences for the defendant were hypothetical. Subjects' decisions might have been quite different if they were faced with a "real world" situation. Second, the subjects were the overstudied "college sophomores," who are probably unlike the populations typically chosen for jury duty, for example, age, education, personality differences. It is worth citing, however, that three additional experiments containing the most essential cells of the present study (Conditions 1, 7, and 8) have been conducted as part of classroom demonstrations on populations composed largely of primary and secondary school teachers. The results replicated the findings of the present study. Third, only a single task was used. The experimental results may be due to some variables (or set of variables) associated with this specific task.[2] Finally, it should be noted that the kind of guilt and the severity of punishment were confounded in the experiment. Different results may have been obtained if the subjects had been asked to make verdicts on the degree of intent (first-degree murder, second-degree murder, manslaughter) without considering the "sentence required by law" or vice versa. Additional research is needed to clarify the relative impact of the variables of degree of intent and severity of punishment.

The data on the postverdict social perceptions are also subject to a qualified interpretation. Supporting a dissonance theory explanation, those Condition 1 subjects who chose not guilty tended to see the defendant in a

---

[2] In somewhat parallel research, Kalman J. Kaplan and Roger I. Simon (personal communication, June 1971) used a different task and varied the race of the victim as well. These data, obtained from college student subjects, also yielded different proportions of not guilty verdicts, depending on the number and severity of decision alternatives. Thus, there is some evidence that the present results are not due to a specific task.

better light and adverse testimony in a worse light than the subjects who chose a guilty verdict. But it is possible that instead of reflecting a post-decision rationalizing mechanism, the data reflect a predecision tendency to see guilt or no guilt. That is, after reading the facts and testimony, some subjects were inclined to judge more harshly and actually found little conflict in choosing a first-degree murder verdict. Conversely, the jurors choosing not guilty may have been inclined in that direction prior to their decision. The use of the no-decision control group (Condition 8) did not alleviate these problems of interpretation, in that the mean social perception scores of those 24 subjects may have reflected the mean of both "guilty of first-degree murder" and not guilty tendencies. In retrospect, Condition 8 subjects should have been asked to make verdicts *after* they had marked the social perception questions. We could then have correlated the responses to the questions with verdict outcomes and tested the possibility that social perceptions influence verdicts, instead of the opposing hypothesis that verdicts influence social perceptions. The author nevertheless prefers the latter interpretation on a priori theoretical grounds until future experiments control for the alternative interpretation in their designs.

As indicated in the introduction, the present research points out some variables that have been ignored in theories of responsibility attribution. In their classic paper on the effects of interaction goals in person perception, Jones and Thibaut (1958) suggested that there are three basic types of perceiver sets, depending on the goal of the perceiver-target interaction. With a *value-maintenance* set, the attribution to the target person's motives involves relevance to the personal goals of the perceiver. Perceivers with a *causal-genetic* set are interested in the underlying social, physical, and biological conditions that give rise to the behavior. With a *situation-matching* set, the causal locus of behavior is more or less irrelevant to the inference process, but rather involves comparing the target person's behavior with regard to generalized norms that are perceived as relevant to the situation. The role of juror is presumably one of the purest examples of this latter set (Jones & Thibaut, 1958). The perceiver, therefore, should

> behave as an agent of social control in dispensing social rewards and punishments or in "passing judgment" on the appropriateness of another's behavior. The actor's main goal is to establish whether or not the other person is behaving appropriately, whether the person's behavior "matches" the norms which apply in the situation [Jones & Thibaut, 1958, p. 167].

The present experiment suggests that the severity of consequences associated with available decision alternatives may be a potent factor in juror decisions. These are more likely related to the subject's personal standards of appropriate retribution than to legally prescribed standards. Hence, it seems useful to elaborate the situation-matching set to discriminate between the "legal" norms which are formally supposed to be applied in the setting and the "moral" norms which the perceiver may apply instead. Whether in the laboratory or in the "real world," it may be very difficult, or even impossible, to enforce a legal norm as the perceiver's sole basis of inference about a target person. The dynamics of the situation matching set are perhaps more complex than Jones and Thibaut had considered.[3]

The experiment also raises questions about the adequacy of models dealing with the process of attribution. Neither the Heider-based inference model of Jones and Davis (1965) nor the personal knowledge model of deCharms (1968) have considered the impact of the number and severity of decision alternatives on the decision processes of the perceiver. The present data suggest that these variables may have considerable impact on the way information is processed. Responsibility attribution is not solely a function of logical inference and/or projecting input from knowledge of what one's own intentions would have been in a similar situation.

Finally, this experiment dealt with a jury setting where the consequences of the perceiver's decision have a negative impact on the target. One can also conceive of instances in which the perceiver's decision would result only in positive outcomes for the target (e.g., award committees) or in positive outcomes for the target if one decision is made and negative outcomes if another decision is made. Are the dynamics behind responsibility attribution in these latter examples different from the instances where judgments can result only in negative consequences for the target person? In short, the present study implies some important and fruitful avenues of research. There are obviously a large number of real-world instances in which responsibility attribution judgments are made under conditions of restricted decision alternatives. Furthermore, some of these instances (e.g., juror conditions) are in areas with important social implications.

References

Berscheid, E., & Walster, E. When does a harmdoer compensate a victim? *Journal of Personality and Social Psychology*, 1967, *6*, 435–441.

deCharms, R. *Personal causation: The internal affective determinants of behavior*. New York: Academic Press, 1968.

Festinger, L. *A theory of cognitive dissonance*. Evanston, Ill.: Row, Peterson, 1957.

[3] In an experiment designed to test the impact of various inferential sets on person perception, Jones and deCharms (1958) hypothesized that instead of the norms that had been experimentally specified in the situation-matching set, the subjects may have had their own ideas about appropriate norms. Those authors, then, were also aware of the possibility of more than one set of norms and the consequent difficulty in experimentally manipulating a specific set of norms.

Heider, F. *The psychology of interpersonal relations.* New York: Wiley, 1958.

Hersey, J. R. *Algiers Motel incident.* New York: Knopf, 1968.

Jones, E. E., & Davis, K. E. From acts to dispositions. In L. Berkowitz (Ed.), *Advances in experimental social psychology.* Vol. 2. New York: Academic Press, 1965.

Jones, E. E., & deCharms, R. The organizing function of interaction roles in person perception. *Journal of Abnormal and Social Psychology,* 1958, *57,* 155–164.

Jones, E. E., & Thibaut, J. W. Interaction goals as bases of inference in interpersonal perception. In R. Taguiri & L. Petrullo (Eds.), *Person perception and interpersonal behavior.* Stanford University Press, 1958.

Kalven, H., Jr., & Zeisel, H. *The American jury.* Boston: Little, Brown, 1966.

Lerner, M. J. Evaluation of performance as a function of performer's reward and attractiveness. *Journal of Personality and Social Psychology,* 1965, *1,* 355–360.

Lerner, M. J., & Matthews, G. Reactions to the suffering of others under conditions of indirect responsibility. *Journal of Personality and Social Psychology,* 1967, *5,* 319–325.

Lerner, M. J., & Simmons, C. H. Observer's reaction to the "innocent victim": Compassion or rejection? *Journal of Personality and Social Psychology,* 1966, *4,* 203–210.

Lundy, W. August is free, but the Algiers controversy goes on. Detroit Free Press, June 15, 1969, 2B.

Maselli, M. D., & Altrocchi, J. Attribution of intent. *Psychological Bulletin,* 1969, *71,* 445–454.

Rothbart, M. Effects of motivation, equity, and compliance on the use of reward and punishment. *Journal of Personality and Social Psychology,* 1968, *9,* 353–362.

Walster, E., & Prestholdt, P. The effect of misjudging another: Overcompensation or dissonance reduction? *Journal of Experimental Social Psychology,* 1966, *2,* 85–97.

Winick, C. The psychology of juries. In H. Toch (Ed.), *Legal and criminal psychology.* New York: Holt, Rinehart and Winston, 1961.

Foreword to Reading 4.3

INTRODUCTION

In recent years there has been increasing attention to subtle aspects of interaction behavior. For instance, research (Sommer, 1971) has indicated that people arrange themselves at a table or bench in a way that reflects their relationship with others in the room. As one example, two strangers would be likely to sit at either end of a three-person bench, while a late-arriving third person (if also a stranger) would be likely to stand rather than sit in the middle of the bench (thus indicating the absurdity of three-person benches in waiting rooms). The interest of Ellsworth and Carlsmith, however, lies not in showing when people use such nonverbal cues, but rather in how they react to the use of such cues by other people.

METHOD

Subjects were asked to participate in interviews concerning the issue of birth order (in other words, oldest in the family, second born, and so on) and its effect on personality. Two variables were manipulated: (a) extent of eye contact: The experimenter either met the interviewee's eyes frequently during the interview, or, when she looked up, she directed her gaze off into the distance (hitting on the interviewee's ears rather than her eyes most of the time); (b) favorability of content: The interviewee was asked to comment on the results of research relating to her own birth order. The research was either made to sound complimentary to people with that birth order or unpleasant and unflattering. Using all possible combinations of the two variables, it was necessary to have four conditions in the study.

While the eye-contact variable was carefully pretested, there was no prior check on the favorability-of-content variable. The authors assumed that hearing unfortunate experimental findings about one's birth order would be an unpleasant experience. Surprisingly, this appeared not to be the case.

153

Only female experimenters and female subjects were used in the study, largely because it has been found that females look at others they are with more than males do. Thus it was simpler to set up an eye contact situation for females than it would have been for males. This is an interesting sex difference, by the way. One wonders if it is related to what seems to be a greater social sensitivity and concern with social relationships in females than in males (see the commentary on Goldberg and Lewis, 1969, in this volume).

RESULTS AND DISCUSSION

The reader can see in Table 1 that the reaction to the look-no look variable depended on the content manipulation (i.e., the two variables interact). The reaction to favorable content was more positive when the experimenter gave frequent rather than infrequent looks; the reaction to unfavorable content was less positive when the experimenter gave frequent rather than infrequent looks. However, as mentioned above, if one compares the overall means of the favorable versus unfavorable conditions, they appear to be little different. Since these means represent responses to seven-point scales, it seems that both conditions were seen as relatively positive.

After studying their results, the authors discarded the "intensification" hypothesis, that eye contact intensifies the favorable or unfavorable reaction to pleasant or unpleasant interaction. Instead they suggest that lack of eye contact during favorable conversation reduces the normal positive reaction to such a conversation. (But why? Perhaps the other person seems disinterested?) This sounds similar to Rubin's (1970) finding that college dating couples who love each other a great deal (as measured by his romantic love scale) spend more time gazing into each other's eyes than couples who love each other to a lesser degree.

The authors also suggest that unfavorable content is not unpleasant when it gives one the opportunity to be open about oneself, perhaps admit things that one would not ordinarily say. However, in this situation, lack of eye contact is preferred to frequent eye contact (perhaps because it gives one privacy or makes the other person seem to be an uncritical listener). This last possibility may remind the reader of the "deindividuation" studies (e.g., Cannavale, Scarr and Pepitone, 1970, in this volume), in which it appears that a feeling of anonymity frees the group member to act in socially unacceptable ways. The efficacy of the confessional may well be due to somewhat the same principle.

The thought that eye contact can be aversive has been supported in studies more recent than this one. Ellsworth, Carlsmith, and Henson (1972) have reported that human beings avoid a staring stranger. In a series of field studies, they found, for instance, that cars cross an intersection faster if someone stands and stares at the driver when he or she stops for a red light. This seems similar to the strategy employed by teachers who stare at a talking student in order to obtain silence during a lecture.

References

Cannavale, F. J., Scarr, H. A., & Pepitone, A. Deindividuation in the small group: further evidence. *Journal of Personality and Social Psychology,* 1970, *16,* 141–147.

Ellsworth, P. C., Carlsmith, J. M., and Henson, A. The stare as a stimulus to flight in human subjects: a series of field experiments. *Journal of Personality and Social Psychology,* 1972, *21,* 302–311.

Goldberg, S., & Lewis, M. Play behavior in the year-old infant: early sex differences. *Child Development,* 1969, *40,* 21–31.

Rubin, Z. Measurement of romantic love. *Journal of Personality and Social Psychology,* 1970, *16,* 265–273.

Sommer, R. Spatial factors in face-to-face interaction. In E. P. Hollander & R. G. Hunt (eds.), *Current perspectives in social psychology* (3d ed.). New York: Oxford University Press, 1971.

4.3 Effects of Eye Contact and Verbal Content on Affective Response to a Dyadic Interaction[1]

Phoebe C. Ellsworth
J. Merrill Carlsmith

Effects of frequency of eye engagement and positiveness of verbal content were studied in a 2 × 2 factorial design. The results indicated that with positive verbal content, frequent eye contact produces more positive evaluations; with negative verbal content frequent eye contact produces negative evaluation. The pattern of obtained means was unexpected, and tentative hypotheses are offered as possible explanations.

A number of studies have indicated that the visual behavior of a dyad is related to the affective nature of the interaction between the members. Exline and Winters (1965a) found that subjects increase frequency of eye contacts with an interviewer evaluating them positively, and reduce eye contacts with a negatively evaluating interviewer. Their second experiment showed that after subjects had expressed a preference for one of two interviewers the difference between the frequency of eye engagement with the preferred over the nonpreferred interviewer (when both were present) increased significantly. It has also been found (Exline, Gray, & Schuette, 1965) that subjects look at an interviewer significantly less during a conversation consisting of personal and embarrassing questions than during a neutral conversation.

Other investigators (see Argyle & Dean, 1965; Kendon, 1967) have proposed that eye engagement, interaction distance, smiling, and the intimacy of the verbal content of an interaction summate on the dimension of general intimacy, and the relative amounts of these behaviors will be adjusted until an "equilibrium level" is attained. For example, Argyle and Dean (1965) have shown that as interaction proximity increases, resulting in "too much" intimacy, there is a decrease in the amount of eye contact.

Reprinted from the *Journal of Personality and Social Psychology,* 1968, *10,* 15–20. Copyright 1968 by the American Psychological Association and reprinted with permission.

[1] This study was supported in part by a National Science Foundation graduate fellowship to the first author and in part by National Science Foundation Grant 1115 to the second author. The authors would like to thank Taffy Ellsworth for her valuable assistance during the pilot phase of the research.

156

In all of these studies, the visual behavior of the subject has been the dependent variable. Taken together, their results show that during an interaction, the frequency and direction of a person's glances can be greatly altered by various other aspects of the situation. The authors' discussions, however, often go beyond the analysis of the factors which affect visual behavior, and attempt to define the function of the visual behavior itself (e.g., influencing the subject's affective reactions, regulating "intimacy," and so on). The fact that eye engagement increases and decreases in response to a variety of affective and other signals lends plausibility to the idea that the visual behavior may itself have a communicative function, but in order to make definitive statements about this function, it is also necessary to show that the visual behavior has an effect on other behaviors. It is necessary to show that something is actually communicated when one person seeks out or avoids another's gaze. Although it has been shown that a person can perceive with a high degree of accuracy whether or not another person is looking at him directly in the face (Gibson & Pick, 1963), there is no evidence that he actually does so in an ongoing interaction, or that his reaction to the situation is in any way influenced by the visual behavior of the other person.

The purpose of this study was to test the hypothesis that the amount of eye engagement in a dyadic interaction has a significant effect on the subject's reaction to both the situation and the other person, and that this effect depends on the verbal content of the interaction. Kendon (1967) suggested that "extended mutual gazes appear to be indicative of an intensifying of the direct relations between the participants [p. 48]." If these gazes are communicative as well as indicative, then increasing their frequency might cause a conversation with basically positive content to be perceived as more positive, and a conversation with basically negative content to be perceived as more negative. Specifically, it was hypothesized that when the verbal content of the interview was generally *favorable* to the subject, the subject's evaluation of the interviewer and the situation would be more positive with frequent than with infrequent eye contact, and that when the content was unfavorable or threatening, the subject's evaluation would be more negative under conditions of more frequent eye contact. A 2 × 2 factorial design was used in which favorable versus unfavorable interview content was varied with frequent versus infrequent eye engagements.

METHOD

Pretesting. Since it takes two people to produce eye contact, a major methodological problem to be solved was how to gain enough control over the frequency of eye contacts to create a stable independent variable which would be the same for all subjects. This has been a problem in studies using eye contact as a dependent variable, since in order to be sure that eye *contact* actually occurred the experimenters or confederates have had to maintain a rather unnatural fixed stare at the subject's eyes, so that whenever the subject looked up it could be scored as a "contact." Pretesting was carried out to develop a situation in which the experimenter shifted her gaze to the subject at points in the interview when the subject was most likely to be looking at the experimenter. In order to set up such a situation, a number of highly reliable naturalistic findings were drawn into service. On the basis of Exline et al.'s (1965) finding that females look at their partners more than males (71.9% of the time, in fact), especially when the other person is also female (Argyle & Dean, 1965), it was decided to run only female subjects with a female experimenter. It has also been found that Person A is much more likely to be looking at Person B when B is speaking than when A is speaking, and that this probability increases when Person B comes to the ends of phrases and utterances (Kendon, 1967). Taking these findings into account, the interview was constructed so that the experimenter's gazes always occurred at the ends of her own phrases and questions. During pretesting, an observer seated behind a one-way mirror noted the subject's glances at the experimenter's eyes, recording them on a copy of the experimenter's interview script. The observer also recorded the duration of each of the subject's glances. The structure of several sentences and the placement of the experimenter's gazes were revised during the pretesting, resulting in a final arrangement in which the subject was looking at the experimenter slightly over 95% of the total time that the experimenter was looking at the subject, and thus the independent variable could legitimately be called a manipulation of "eye contact," and not merely of "being looked at."

Subjects. Forty-three female Stanford University undergraduates served as subjects in individual sessions lasting from 30–45 minutes each. Of these, two were excluded from the data analysis because they were twins with no older or younger siblings. Forty-one percent of the remaining subjects were firstborns, and they were distributed fairly equally among the four conditions (three to five in each cell).

General overview. Subjects were brought into the experimental room and seated at a table across from the experimenter at a distance of 4 feet. The experimenter told the subjects that the interview was part of a large exploratory study of students' and parents' opinions about the effects of birth order on personality, and, more specifically, an attempt to get some idea of people's intuitive reactions to "recent experimental findings" in this area. The "experimental findings" on which the subjects were asked to comment were either consistently favorable to firstborns and highly derogatory of later-borns, or vice versa. Whether the subject was in a "favorable" or an "unfavorable" situation depended on her own birth order. During the interview, which lasted for 10–15 minutes, the experimenter either looked at the subject very frequently or hardly at all. Following the interview, subjects were given a questionnaire about the interview situation and the interviewer.

Favorability manipulation. The interview on birth order was identical in the two conditions, except that the terms "firstborn" and "later-born" were interchangeable. Nine of the experimenter's observations and questions were extremely one-sided, describing members of one of the original categories as dependent, unloved, generally incompetent, and so forth, and their counterparts in the other position as well-adjusted, intellectually superior, more spontaneous, etc. Two other questions were embedded in this context, and thus probably were also more or less "favorable" or "threatening," for example, "Do you think *you* are generally happy and well-adjusted?" following a remark that firstborns/later-borns had been shown to be happier and better adjusted. The first four questions were background questions unrelated to birth order.

Subjects were assigned at random to one of four interviews: look + negative to firstborns, look + negative to later-borns, no look + negative to firstborns, and no look + negative to later-borns. The experimenter instructed the subject not to say whether she was a firstborn or a later-born child, and thus did not know whether the subject was in a favorable or unfavorable condition. This precaution is particularly important in an experiment of this sort, since otherwise it would be impossible to distinguish among the effects of eye contact and those of other biasing nonverbal cues (see Rosenthal, 1964). The success of the attempt to keep the experimenter blind to the favorability condition is indicated by the fact that her guesses of the subjects' birth order, made (privately) during the interview, were no more accurate than would be expected by chance. The subject wrote down her birth order on a card immediately after the interview was over.

Eye engagement manipulation. In both conditions the experimenter's "looks" were between 5 and 8 seconds in duration and began within 5 seconds of the end of one of the experimenter's sentences. In the "look" condition, the experimenter looked the subject in the eyes 20 times—5 times during the introduction, 13 times during the actual questioning, and twice during the presentation of the questionnaire. Towards the end of each one of the 11 favorable or unfavorable questions, the experimenter looked at the subject. In the "no look" condition, the experimenter looked up at the exact same points in the interview, but at 16 of the 20 critical points she directed her gaze to one or the other of the subject's ears. Thus the stimulus properties of the two conditions were the same (in terms of the experimenter's head-raising and other orientation behaviors) except for a small difference in the direction of the experimenter's gaze. Gibson and Pick (1963) obtained accurate judgments of gaze deviations of this magnitude at a distance of 2 meters, so it seemed reasonable to assume that subjects were physically able to distinguish between the two fixation points. Aside from the desire to keep the experimenter's orientation constant, a major reason for selecting such a small gaze deviation was that during pretesting, whenever the experimenter directed her gaze much farther off center than the subject's ear, subjects tended to turn around to see what she was looking at. In the "no look" condition the experimenter looked the subject in the eyes only four times: once in the introduction, twice during the actual interview (at one of the neutral questions and at one of the two potentially favorable or unfavorable questions), and once during the presentation of the questionnaire.

Dependent variable. The dependent variable was a questionnaire which the subject was told was being filled out by *all* subjects who participated in social psychology experiments in which graduate students conducted interviews. The experimenter handed the subject an envelope containing the questionnaire, instructed her to place it in the mailbox of one of the social psychology faculty members when she was through filling it out, and left the room. She then met the subjects after they had deposited the questionnaire in the mailbox and took them back to the experimental room for debriefing.

On the cover sheet of the questionnaire was a paragraph addressed to "all undergraduate subjects in interviews conducted by graduate trainees" from the "social psychology faculty." It stated that one of the main problems of training graduate students to be good interviewers was providing individualized instruction geared to a student's particular strengths and weaknesses. In order to find out what these strengths and weaknesses were, it was "most important that we know how people react to the trainee in an interview situation." The subject's questionnaire answers would be "completely confidential," and, "along with those of other subjects interviewed by the trainee, [would] be used to guide us in deciding what sort of training the particular trainee needs most." The subject was reassured that his answers would be used only for training purposes, and would "have no influence whatsoever on [the interviewer's] academic standing," and the paragraph closed with a plea for careful, honest answers, since "carelessness or dishonest responses could result in the graduate student's receiving training in unnecessary areas at the expense of training he really needs."

The questionnaire itself consisted of five 7-point evaluative scales about the interview, and nine about the interviewer. These constituted the primary dependent variable of interest. In addition, there were three scales dealing with the cognitive complexity of the situation (see Exline & Winters, 1965b), three dealing with the interviewer's attentiveness and receptivity, one each on how "personal" the interview and the interviewer were, one on how tense the interviewer was, and a few on specific interviewing techniques (e.g., "recorded answer quickly—slowly") intended to lend plausibility to the rationale that the social psychology faculty was interested in training interviewers. The responses for this last category were not analyzed.

RESULTS

The five scales dealing with the interview and the nine scales dealing with the interviewer were all designed to elicit evaluative ("good—bad") responses, and a preliminary examination of the data revealed a consistency in the subjects' ratings across all of these scales which indicated that this purpose was achieved. Therefore the subjects' mean ratings for all evaluative scales were taken as a basis for analysis, the only separation retained being that between "interview" and "interviewer." Table 1 shows the mean evaluative ratings of the interviewer (nine scales) and the interview (five scales) in the four conditions. The correlation between ratings of the interview and ratings of the interviewer was .71.

Analyses of variance were carried out for the evaluations of the interview and the interviewer. The same pattern is apparent in the two analyses and strongly supports the hypothesis that the amount of eye contact in a dyadic interaction influences a subject's affective reaction to the situation and to the other person, and that the general direction of this influence depends on whether the verbal content is favorable or unfavorable to the sub-

TABLE 1 *Mean Evaluative Ratings of the Interviewer and the Interview*

	INTERVIEWER		INTERVIEW	
CONDITION	Unfavora-ble content	Favorable content	Unfavora-ble content	Favorable content
Look	5.16	6.05	5.05	5.80
No look	5.80	4.80	5.98	5.04

Note.—$n = 11$ in unfavorable/look cells and 10 in all others.

ject. For the rating of the interviewer the analysis of variance showed a highly significant interaction ($F = 35.50$, $df = 37$, $p < .001$), and the same was true for the ratings of the interview ($F = 20.20$, $df = 37$, $p < .001$). If the topic of conversation is neutral to generally positive, subjects like the interviewer significantly more when she looks them in the eyes ($t = 5.48$, $p < .001$), and they also react more positively to the interview itself ($t = 2.87$, $p < .01$). But in a conversation which is indirectly but persistently critical of the subject, this relationship is reversed: subjects like the interviewer *less* if she looks at them ($t = 2.87$, $p < .01$), and they react more negatively to the interview ($t = 3.60$, $p < .01$).

The same pattern of results occurs on most of the other variables tested, indicating that a general evaluative factor is present to a greater or lesser extent in all the ratings. In the favorable/look and unfavorable/no look conditions the interviewer is judged more attentive and receptive than in the other two conditions, as well as more relaxed, and the task is regarded as "easier." (There is also a significant main effect for "look" on this last dimension, which is a result complementary to Exline & Winters' [1965b] finding that subjects tend to reduce eye engagement when the cognitive complexity of a task is increased.) Finally, there is also a significant interaction in how personal the subjects thought the interviewer was, with the subjects in the favorable/look and unfavorable/no look conditions rating her as significantly more personal. There were no significant differences in subjects' ratings of how personal the interview itself was.

On none of the scales did the ratings made by firstborns differ significantly from those made by later-borns.

DISCUSSION

Although the data conform very well to the hypothesis that the effects of eye contact on subjects' affective reactions in a favorable situation are reversed in an unfavorable situation, this hypothesis no longer seems sufficient to explain the actual mean values obtained. In fact, it was originally expected that a main effect for favorability would also be present, such that the unfavorable/no look condition would be equal to or lower than the favorable/no look condition, and the unfavorable/look condition lowest of all; if this had been the obtained pattern of results, it would have been possible to speak with some confidence about eye contact as an intensifier of a general affective state induced by some other factor. Simply to state that the favorability manipulation was not as effective as it might have been is not to solve the problem, because the highly significant interaction is still left to be explained. (However, the fact that the "threat" was not perceived as very great in the unfavorable condition may have mediated against the intensifier hypothesis; further research with a more threatening manipulation is necessary to elucidate this question.)

Within the look condition there is no problem; the results are as expected. Within the no look condition, however, the data suggest that two additional phenomena are at work. First of all, in a positively toned interaction (favorable), talking to a person who almost never meets one's gaze may completely neutralize the effects of the positive content. The favorable/look condition, in this view, is not an intensification of anything, but is probably the normal state of affairs, from which not looking represents a negative deviation.

Second, the data in the unfavorable/no look condition suggest that there is something definitely rewarding about discussing oneself in negative terms with a person who is not looking. Ratings made by subjects in this cell were not significantly different from those made in the favorable/look condition, which was expected to be far more positive than any other. In rating the interview, the positive affect in the unfavorable/no look condition was actually higher than in the favorable/look condition. To say that looking "intensified" the negative affect is meaningless, since in the unfavorable/no look condition the affect expressed was as positive as in any other cell.

One possible explanation is that the subjects perceived the experimenter's not looking as a sign of discomfort at having to say potentially unpleasant things, and felt sorry for her. However, the ratings of the interviewer's tension show that subjects in this condition felt that the interviewer was more relaxed in the unfavorable/look condition. This evidence against the hypothesis must be taken as very tentative, since the subjects tended to approach the scales with a nonspecific evaluative set; it is, however, the only source of evidence available from the data.

A second hypothesis is that the interviewer was perceived as being tactful in a difficult situation. There are no data which bear on this hypothesis.

Finally, it is possible that there are times when people *like* to talk about themselves in negative terms. There is a widespread belief in our culture that it is not only good, but somehow satisfying to bring one's self-doubts out into the open. On the other hand, there is a danger in bringing them too far into the open, because there is always the possibility that the other person will react inappropriately. Eliciting a response like "Oh, I know just how it is—let me tell you about *my* neurosis" is unsatisfactory, because one's private problems are deprived of their noteworthy individuality. Equally frightening is the possible elicitation of expressions of contempt or pity which force one to backtrack in order not to seem too aberrant. A person who is attempting to establish frequent eye contact may be seen as threatening, whereas a person who looks away and signifies his interest merely by keeping quiet may be the ideal companion. Religious confessions and psychiatric sessions are analogous to the unfavorable/no look condition, in that the speaker is encouraged to say negative things about himself in the presence of someone who avoids all eye contact.

Some support for the notion that the unfavorable/no look condition involved an interaction in which a person made personal comments about herself in the presence of an ideal listener is provided by the finding that subjects in this condition rated the interviewer as more personal (as well as more positive) than those in the unfavorable/look condition. This could be a result of the fact that they themselves were making more personal responses in that condition. In order to investigate this hypothesis further, it was decided to look through the interview protocols for personal references to the subject's own family situations ("family situations" because the general interview topic was birth order).

Table 2 shows the total number of references to one's own family

TABLE 2 *Total Number of References to Own Family Situation*

CONDITION	CONTENT	
	Unfavorable	*Favorable*
Look	2 (2)	5 (5)
No look	8 (6)	4 (2)

Note.—$n = 11$ in unfavorable/look condition, 10 in all other conditions. Numbers in parentheses indicate number of subjects who made references to their own family situations; unparenthesized numbers indicate total number of references made.

situation made in each condition and the total number of subjects who made such responses (numbers in parentheses). Although very few personal references were made in any condition, it is apparent that they are more frequent in the unfavorable/no look condition than in any other.

The data for this condition are also somewhat in line with Argyle and Dean's (1965) hypothesis that different types of "intimacy" will substitute for each other until an equilibrium point is reached, but it is hard to see why this would not also result in more personal references in the favorable/no look condition. The results of the current experiment also definitely mediate against the assumption, frequent in the literature on visual behavior, that lack of eye contact automatically indicates a negative or uninterested reaction (e.g., Exline et al., 1965). Further research is in progress to study this phenomenon, and hopefully to begin to discriminate among the various possible explanations, in a setting where subjects make negative statements about themselves rather than having them provided by the interviewer.

References

Argyle, M., & Dean, J. Eye-contact, distance, and affiliation. *Sociometry*, 1965, *28*, 289–304.

Exline, R., Gray, D., & Schuette, D. Visual behavior in a dyad as affected by interview content and sex of respondent. *Journal of Personality and Social Psychology*, 1965, *1*, 201–210.

Exline, R., & Winters, L. C. Affective relations and mutual glances in dyads. In S. Tomkins & C. Izard (Eds.), *Affect, cognition, and personality*. New York: Springer, 1965. (a)

Exline, R., & Winters, L. C. The effects of cognitive difficulty and cognitive style upon eye-to-eye contact in interviews. Paper presented at the meeting of the American Psychological Association, Chicago, September 1965. (b)

Gibson, J. J., & Pick, A. D. Perception of another person's looking behavior. *American Journal of Psychology*, 1963, *76*, 386–394.

Kendon, A. Some functions of gaze direction in social interaction. *Acta Psychologica*, 1967, *26*, 22–63.

Rosenthal, R. The effect of the experimenter on the results of psychological research. In B. A. Maher (Ed.), *Progress in experimental personality research*. Vol. 1. New York: Academic Press, 1964.

Foreword to Reading 4.4

INTRODUCTION

This paper by Berscheid, Boye, and Walster fits into current research literature in two ways. For one, it could be related to studies on the attraction of one person for another. For the most part, these studies have concentrated either on the fact that people tend to like "similar" people (e.g., Byrne et al., 1970, in this volume), or on the fact that it is rewarding (reinforcing) to be liked (e.g., Aronson and Linder, 1965). In another way, this article is related to those studies which concern themselves with a seeking for justice (e.g., Lerner and Simmons, 1966; Lerner, 1971) or equity (e.g., Adams, 1965). Those studies are based on consistency or balance-type theories which assume that people are motivated to maintain consistency rather than inconsistency in their thoughts and behaviors. Lerner (Lerner and Simmons, 1966; Lerner, 1971) suggests that people have a need to believe in a "just" world in which people get what they deserve (and deserve what they get). His studies have demonstrated that an observer diminishes the attractiveness of a suffering person, and that this effect occurs even when the person is a "martyr," suffering in order to benefit others. In an article by Adams (1965), a general theoretical discussion of the notion of equity is presented. Adams suggests that people prefer that the amount that they put into an interaction be "fairly" matched with the amount that they get out of it. Thus, for instance, the man who feels that he has been overpaid may increase the amount or the quality of the work that he does. (Or, unfortunately for employers, he may decide that his high pay is balanced by poor employee washrooms or whatever.) It has never been clearly stated why people should (assuming that they do) seek for justice in this way. No doubt it has something to do with our culture and training. Perhaps the source lies in the ease of dealing with a world in which things are as one expects them to be, as should be the case in a just world.

Berscheid, Walster, and a number of others have concerned themselves with the restoration of equity or justice after harm-doing. In an interesting series of articles described in the introduction here, they have explored the conditions under which a victim will or will not receive compensation. The problem, from the victim's point of view, is that if one can convince himself that the victim deserved his suffering, then there is no inequity and therefore no need for compensation. Berscheid et al. suggest that in order to prevent such justification by the harm-doer, the victim could himself restore equity by retaliation against the harm-doer. In this way, the victim could at least escape the derogation of the harm-doer.

The experiment carried out to test this hypothesis had four conditions: varying both subjects' harm-doing and subjects' expectation of retaliation. The two variables were predicted to interact.

METHOD

In going over the procedure, the reader should, as always, note and evaluate the operational definitions of the dependent and independent variables. Harm-doing, for instance, consisted of shocking another "subject." Although the subject was acting under instructions, and for the sake of science (thereby perhaps reducing his guilt and his sense of inequity), it is also true that the particular schedule of shocks given was chosen by the subject. The dependent measure of attraction consisted of three questions, embedded in eight questions directed at the victim's response to stress (presumably the point of the experiment).

RESULTS AND DISCUSSION

For those students who do not profess statistical sophistication, the editors' advice is to concentrate on the table of means (Table 1), where the pattern of results is quite clear. As predicted, an interaction between retaliation and harm-doing was obtained.

The authors wanted to interpret their data as indicating that subjects did not need to justify their harm-doing by derogating the victim when the victim could retaliate for the harm. They present a careful assessment of alternative explanations, and conclude that they do not appear to be supported.

References

Adams, J. S. Injustice in social exchange. In L. Berkowitz (ed.), *Advances in experimental social psychology*. Vol. 2. New York: Academic Press, 1965.

Aronson, E., & Linder, D. Gain and loss of esteem as determinants of interpersonal attractiveness. *Journal of Experimental Social Psychology,* 1965, *1,* 156–171.

Byrne, D., Ervin, C. R., & Lamberth, J. Continuity between the experimental study of attraction and real-life computer dating. *Journal of Personality and Social Psychology,* 1970, *16,* 157–165.

Lerner, M. J. Observer's evaluation of a victim: justice, guilt, and veridical perception. *Journal of Personality and Social Psychology,* 1971, *20,* 127–135.

Lerner, M. J., & Simmons, C. M. Observer's reaction to the "innocent victim": compassion or rejection? *Journal of Personality and Social Psychology,* 1966, *4,* 203–210.

4.4 Retaliation as a Means of Restoring Equity[1]

Ellen Berscheid
David Boye
Elaine Walster

Previous research has shown that when a harm-doer is faced with the suffering of his victim he will attempt to eliminate the inequity he has created by compensating the victim. When this is not possble, he will restore psychological equity by justifying the victim's suffering. It was suggested that equity can be restored by still another method: the victim can "get even" with the harm-doer by retaliating against him. It was proposed that when compensation is impossible, a harm-doer will derogate a victim who is powerless to retaliate but will not derogate a victim from whom he anticipates retaliation. Ss who had not harmed the victim were not expected to respond in the same way. This hypothesis was confirmed.

Some recent interest in social psychology has focused on the reactions of a harm-doer to his deed. It is known that if a harm-doer is given the opportunity, he will often exert considerable effort to compensate his victim (i.e., Berkowitz, 1962; Berscheid & Walster, 1967; Berscheid, Walster, & Barclay, in preparation; Freedman, Wallington, & Bless, 1967; Walster & Prestholdt, 1966). Recent evidence, however, indicates that certain conditions may attenuate the harm-doer's tendency to compensate his victim. For example, if the perpetrator is publicly committed to the harmful act, he tends to avoid compensating his victim (Walster & Prestholdt, 1966). If available compensation cannot completely restore equity, the perpetrator will tend not to compensate (Berscheid & Walster, 1967). And, finally, if a delay is enforced before the perpetrator is allowed to compensate, his reluctance to make a less than totally adequate compensation increases (Berscheid et al., in preparation).

Laboratory experiments indicate that if the harm-doer doesn't compensate his victim, either because proper channels are not open (Davidson,

Reprinted from the *Journal of Personality and Social Psychology,* 1968, *10,* 370–76. Copyright 1968 by the American Psychological Association and reproduced with permission.

[1] This study was supported by National Science Foundation Grants GS-1577 and GS-1588 to Ellen Berscheid and Elaine Walster and by the Student Activities Bureau, University of Minnesota. The authors would also like to express their appreciation to Robert Fisher, who served as the experimental assistant.

1964; Davis & Jones, 1956; Glass, 1964) or because he chooses to withhold compensation (Walster & Prestholdt, 1966), he will then distort his perceptions in such a way as to justify his actions. Usually one justifies the harm he has done by derogating his victim, but one may also justify his behavior in other ways. He may minimize the harm he has done or he may deny responsibility for the harm (Brock & Buss, 1962, 1964; Sykes & Matza, 1957). It appears that the harm-doer will attempt to eliminate, at least in his own mind, the inequity that he has created, either by compensating his victim or by justifying his act.

Removal of inequity through justification rather than compensation is potentially dangerous. Not only does the harm-doer end up with a distorted and unreal assessment of his actions, but he may commit further acts based on these distortions (Berscheid, Boye, & Darley, 1967). When the harm-doer's response to his act is justification, the victim is likely to be left in sad straits. Not only has he been hurt, but as a result of justification of the harmful act the probability that the harm-doer will hurt him again has increased.

Obviously, from the victim's point of view, it is desirable to have equity restored before the perpetrator is forced to justify what he has done. Unfortunately for the victim, compensation—the most desirable and constructive means of equity restoration—is entirely under the control of the harm-doer. And, it is often the case that the harm-doer is either unwilling or unable to compensate. Under such circumstances, is there a means of restoring equity which is under the victim's control? The phrase "getting even" suggests that, in our culture at least, there may be. It is possible that the victim's immediate retaliation against the harm-doer may "even up" the inequity of the harm-doing situation and thus arrest the harm-doer's tendency to justify his harmful act.

The idea that retaliation restores equity to an inequitable relationship is a common one: retaliation far antedates compensation as a technique for establishing just relations between individuals. According to legal theorists (See Fry et al., 1959; Schafer, 1960), Hammurabi's Code (approximately 2250 B.C.) relied entirely on retaliation to establish justice. Not until Republican Roman Law (450–449 B.C.) was compensation conceived as a suitable means for restoring equitable relations between individuals.

At the present time, Negro militants often stress the importance of actual retaliation and the fear of anticipated retaliation, in producing equitable relationships between racial groups. Some militants have argued that widespread actual violence is necessary to restore the Negro to full citizenship. They talk of the "white devil," his guilt and subsequent denial of racial injustices, and the equity-establishing potential of actual violence. Other spokesmen for this position, for example James Baldwin, have argued that it is important for individuals to *anticipate* retaliation for their wrong doing. Baldwin (1963) stated:

Neither civilized reason nor Christian love would cause any of those people to treat you as they presumably wanted to be treated; only the *fear* of your power to retaliate would cause them to do that, or to seem to do it, which was (and is) good enough [p. 35].

The experiment reported in this paper was designed to investigate the effect that the *anticipation* of the victim's retaliation has on a harm-doer's tendency to justify his act through derogation of the victim. It was hypothesized that if the harm-doer believes that his victim will retaliate against him in kind, he will expect that his relationship with the victim will shortly be an equitable one and, thus, the harm-doer will have no need to restore psychological equity to the relationship by derogating the victim.

Overview

In order to test this hypothesis, it was necessary that half of the subjects harm another individual (by administering electric shock) and half simply observe the harm-doing. Secondly, it was necessary to lead half of the harm-doers and half of the observers to expect that the victim would be able to shock them at the conclusion of the experiment, and to lead the remainder to believe that he would be shocking someone else.

In accord with previous studies, harm-doers who did not expect retaliation were expected to derogate the victim. Harm-doers who expected retaliation were not expected to derogate the victim. Subjects who did not themselves harm the victim served as a control group. It was not anticipated that control subjects would feel more positively toward someone who would soon shock them than toward someone who would not. In brief, subjects' responsibility for harm-doing and subjects' expectations of being punished by the victim were expected to interact in affecting the subjects' liking for the victim.

METHOD

Forty-eight male students from nine Minnesota high schools participated in the experiment. Subjects were paid $4 for their participation.

When the five boys (four subjects and one confederate) who were scheduled for each session arrived, the experimenter provided a rationale for the experiment. At length he explained the three "purposes" of the research: (a) to study the effects of stress on verbal performance; (b) to try out the new research technique, designed to remove experimental bias, of having subjects run the experiment themselves; (c) to compare physiological and observational measures of stress. (Machines were said to provide the physiological measures; subjects were asked to provide the observational evaluations.) The experimenter elaborated on the importance of his research until he felt the subjects were interested and engrossed in it.

The experimenter then suggested that a "reader" (the victim) be chosen. Though selection of a reader was said to be random, in actuality the confederate was always chosen to read experimental material while being subjected to stress.

While the subjects watched and listened, the confederate was given his instructions. He was told that his task was to read, as clearly and distinctly as possible, 10 paragraphs from an article. He was instructed to pause at the beginning of each paragraph so that one of the subjects (the "trainer") could induce stress by administering one of five levels of electric shock to him. The others would observe him through a one-way mirror and would evaluate his reading performance. The confederate was told that he would never know which of the four boys was administering the electric shock.

All subjects, with the exception of the confederate, were then led into an adjoining room. This room contained a four-cubicle conformity apparatus with opaque screens between each cubicle. This arrangement made it impossible for the boys to know what the other boys were doing. The apparatus faced a one-way mirror, through which one could look into the room where the confederate was seated. Since the subjects' room was dimly lit, it was clear that although the subjects could clearly see the confederate, he could not see them.

Each cubicle was equipped with a five-choice response panel. The five levers were labeled "moderate," "somewhat strong," "strong," "very strong," and "severe." With this equipment it was possible for any of the harm-doers to choose any of five shock levels, for the experimenter to monitor these choices from a control room to make sure the subjects were administering the chosen shock levels, and for the experimenter to give feedback to control subjects as to the choice the harm-doer had made. Subjects were also provided with headphones over which they could hear either the experimenter or the victim.

The subjects then observed the confederate being seated in the adjoining room. The victim's room contained an array of electrical devices, including an Esterline Ampmeter, a large GSR indicator, several shock generators, timers, and so on. As soon as the victim was seated, an experimental assistant dressed in a white coat strapped some "physiological measuring devices" to the victim's head and arms. A microphone was put around his neck. A headpiece with a number of wires and electrodes dangling from it and with a small light bulb protruding from the front was attached to his head. (The light bulb lit up when the victim was receiving electric shock.) After the equipment was attached, the experimental assistant checked the victim's heart rate and pulse, and obtained other physiological information.

The experimenter told the subjects that *one* of them would be randomly chosen as the "trainer" (the harm-doer). The trainer's task was to map out a schedule of 10 shock intensities and then to deliver these shocks to the reader. While the victim was receiving shock, the subjects were to observe the level of shock the reader received (this level would be indicated on their control panels) and to observe its effect on his performance. No one (including the confederate) would know who had been the trainer and who had been observers.

Actually, *two* subjects, one on either end of the apparatus, were led to believe that they had been randomly chosen as the sole trainer. The two subjects in the center of the apparatus were led to believe that they were one of three observers. (Thus, one subject was run in each of the four experimental conditions during each experimental session.)

At this point, the experimenter went into an adjoining room where he remained for the rest of the experiment. Through their headphones, subjects then heard the experimenter instruct the harm-doer to map out a schedule of shocks. The experimenter emphasized that unless a wide variety of shocks was used it would be difficult to see much change in the reader's performance. Harm-doers were asked to write down the shocks that they would deliver and the order in which they would deliver them on a piece of paper.

After the harm-doers had devised their shock schedules, subjects were told that there would be a second session.[2] They were informed that in the second session the current reader would devise and administer the shock schedule, and one of the current subjects would be the reader. The reader during the second session was presumably also to be chosen by random processes. In actuality, one harm-doer and one observer were led to believe that they would be the second reader (and the second victim). The experimenter then indicated that the first session could begin.

It will be recalled that two subjects believed that they, and they alone, were administering shock to the reader. This posed some problems. It was inevitable that the harm-doers would administer their shocks at slightly different times, even though they were both administering them "when the victim paused for a paragraph." To forestall the suspicion that would have arisen had the victim responded at an inappropriate time to the harm-doer's shock, an explanation for any possible delay in response was provided. The experimenter explained that because of the electrical wiring it would take a moment for the shock to get to the reader. Everyone would know when the reader was being shocked, however, because the light bulb attached to the band on the reader's head would light up. During the shock trials, then, the experimenter would simply wait until both harm-doers had administered shock to the reader before lighting the bulb on the reader's head which indicated that the shock had finally arrived. The light also served a second purpose in that it gave the confederate the clue to respond as if he had received electric shock. When the bulb was lit, the confederate breathed heavily, moved around in an agitated way in his chair, and his reading appeared markedly disrupted.

Subjects could check on how much shock was being administered by looking at a light on their panel board which indicated the amount the victim was currently receiving. The particular shock magnitude indicated on a subject's panel was determined in the following way: Each observer was assigned as a partner to the harm-doer next to him. Whatever shock level the harm-doer administered to the confederate was flashed on the harm-doer's and the yoked observer's board immediately before the confederate's headlight flashed on. The stress procedure continued for 10 trials.

---

[2] The reader will note that at this point each subject knew whether he was the harm-doer or simply an observer. Subjects did not yet know, however, that there was a possibility that the victim would be able to shock them. The authors wanted all harm-doers to decide which shock levels to administer *before* they were exposed to the retaliation information, so that their choice of shock levels would not be affected by the retaliation manipulation.

At the end of the first session the experimenter reminded the subjects that one of them, the subject who had been randomly chosen previously, would be the second reader. Before that second session began, however, all subjects were asked to rate the first reader's performance. This rating questionnaire included eight questions, ostensibly designed to give the experimenter some idea of how the victim had responded to stress. Actually three of these questions constituted the dependent measure and were designed to determine how much subjects in various conditions liked the reader. Subjects were asked: "Was your impression of the speaker favorable or unfavorable?" Did the speaker have a likable personality?" From what you have seen of him so far, how much do you like the speaker personally?" Subjects could respond on an 18-point scale which varied from 0, indicating that the subject liked the confederate very much, to 17, indicating that the subject disliked him very much.

As is typically done in experiments dealing with the psychology of justification, the authors tried to block off all modes of justification save one—derogation (cf. Berscheid et al., in press). They also attempted to make it easy for subjects to utilize the derogation mode of justification. The victim was made to appear overweight and unattractive; unlike the other boys, he was not at all friendly with the others while they waited together before the experiment; he appeared to be somewhat unintelligent when reading the paragraphs.

Despite these efforts, it was possible, of course, for subjects to use justifications other than derogation. To assess whether or not subjects were in fact engaging in other types of justification, several additional items were included on the questionnaire: (a) "How much discomfort did shock cause the speaker?" It is possible that subjects could restore equity by minimizing the victim's suffering. The authors attempted to make this type of distortion difficult by labeling the degree of the victim's discomfort and having subjects actually observe his reactions. (b) "How important was the experiment?" It is probably easier to defend hurting another in the interest of an important scientific experiment than in connection with a trivial one. The authors attempted to make this type of distortion difficult by having the experimenter emphasize the experiment's importance in his introduction. (c) "Do you feel there is anything wrong with participating in experiments in which people are shocked?" Harm-doers could deny that they had done anything to feel guilty about. The authors attempted to make this type of distortion difficult by stressing in the preliminary instructions the subject's sole responsibility for his decision to harm the other and for his choice of the magnitude of shocks to be delivered, and by giving him repeated opportunities to leave during the experiment.[3]

Filler questions asked if the experiment had been conducted in a manner fair to the subject himself and how intelligent the speaker appeared to be. Immediately after all subjects had completed their questionnaires, the experimenter asked who was to be shocked next. All subjects in the re-

---

[3] One group of four subjects was discarded from the analysis because one subject refused to continue shocking the speaker. (This group yielded results similar to the other 11 groups.)

taliation conditions anticipated being the next reader. At this point subjects were debriefed.

RESULTS AND DISCUSSION

It was predicted that the subject's responsibility for harming the victim and his anticipation of being punished would interact in affecting liking for the victim: it was expected that a harm-doer would derogate his victim more when the victim was powerless to retaliate than when retaliation was likely; and that control subjects, who had done no harm, would not react to the anticipation of retaliation in the same way.

Since all four conditions were run in each of 11 different groups, analysis of the data required that each group be treated as one observation and the responses of each member of the group as a separate dependent variable. Thus, the design for the analysis is one cell with 11 observations and four dependent measures on each observation. To test whether various linear combinations of the four dependent measures were equal to 0, a multivariate analysis of variance was conducted. The particular linear combinations chosen for analysis were identical to those which would test hypotheses conventionally tested by main effects or interactions in univariate analysis of variance.[4]

Looking at the data (See Table 1), it can be seen that the hypothesis appears to be confirmed. When one has himself harmed the victim, he likes the victim more (or derogates him less) when he expects retaliation than when he does not. The relationship between retaliation and liking is reversed for control subjects: those who expect to be hurt by the victim in the future like him less than those who do not expect to be hurt. The predicted interaction is significant at the .05 level of confidence ($F = 5.19$, $df = 1/10$).

The reader will recall the authors attempted to maximize the probability that all subjects would use only the derogation mode of justification. It is possible, however, that subjects used other justification techniques despite efforts to block these other modes and to enhance the probability that the derogation mode be used. If the data revealed between-conditions differences in the use of justification techniques other than derogation, an alternative explanation of the results would be possible. It could be argued that retaliation, instead of eliminating the harm-doer's need to restore equity to his relationship through the use of a justification technique, may have had (for some unspecified reason) a different effect: anticipated retaliation may have made the harm-doer less likely to derogate the victim but more likely to restore equity by utilizing some other justification technique.

---

[4] The authors would like to thank G. William Walster for his help in analyzing the data.

TABLE 1 *Liking for the Confederate and Other Justification Measures for Subjects in the Various Conditions*

CONDITION	DEROGATION OF VICTIM[a]	ADDITIONAL JUSTIFICATIONS[b]			FAIRNESS OF THIS EXPERIMENT TO YOU[c]
		Minimization of suffering	Aggrandizement of project	Denial of wrongdoing	
Harm-doer—Retaliation expected	6.1	2.1	11.8	11.2	13.09
Harm-doer—No retaliation expected	6.8	1.3	8.9	6.9	14.68
Observer—Retaliation expected	7.3	2.1	11.9	10.6	8.73
Observer—No retaliation expected	6.1	3.6	11.4	8.9	13.82
F tests					
Harm-doer vs. observer	.79	1.59	3.24	.24	2.68
Retaliation vs. no retaliation	.26	.38	3.04	4.59	9.22*
Interaction	5.19*	4.39	.70	.45	1.67

[a] The higher the number, the less the subject likes the victim.
[b] The higher the number the more the subject is justifying having harmed the victim (minimizing his suffering, aggrandizing the importance of the project, and denying that there is anything wrong with administering shock in an experiment).
[c] The higher the number, the fairer the subject feels the experiment was.
* $p < .05$, $df = 1/10$.

The data, however, provide little support for such an alternative. If the correct explanation for this data is that harm-doers who expect retaliation (H-R subjects) still experience dissonance but reduce it by use of some mode of justification other than derogation, one would expect H-R subjects to be especially predisposed to score high on these alternative modes when compared to control subjects. There is no evidence for this. In no case is a significant interaction secured for alternative measures of justification ($Fs = 4.39, .70$, and $.45, df = 1/10$).[5]

The additional justification data are puzzling in one respect: Presumably harm-doers who do not anticipate retaliation (H-NR subjects) should have a more inequitable relationship with the victim (and have more dissonance to reduce) than do other subjects. Since the authors attempted to make it easy for subjects to reduce dissonance by derogating the victim and difficult for them to justify their behavior by utilizing other distortions, one would expect H-NR subjects to derogate the victim more than do O-NR subjects (which they do) and to score at least as high on the additional justification measures as do O-NR subjects (which they do not). On all three of the additional justification measures H-NR subjects receive lower justification scores than do other subjects. However, H-NR subjects do not score significantly lower than do other subjects. The interaction Fs for the three additional justification measures are nonsignificant, regardless of whether they are examined singly or combined into a total index. However, the fact that H-NR subjects consistently tend to secure lower scores on these three measures is puzzling and decreases the confidence that all of the variance to be accounted for in this experiment can be explained.

Main Effects

The authors' hypothesis concerned the possible interaction of two variables: (a) whether or not the subject shocked the victim, and (b) whether or not the subject expected to be shocked by the victim. In the previous section the data and the interaction Fs which could confirm or disconfirm the hypothesis were considered. In addition to interacting with each other it is also possible that the two independent variables, in and of themselves, might have had a strong impact on the dependent variable. For example, one might expect that Anticipation of Punishment would have a strong impact on an individual's ratings. The subject who anticipates being shocked is

---

5 In the case of "Minimization of harm," which almost reaches significance, the interaction is not produced by the propensity of H-R subjects to justify the victim's suffering by minimizing it; H-R subjects estimate his suffering exactly as do the comparable observers (O-R subjects). The obtained interaction is due to the fact that, more than any other group, O-NR subjects estimate that the victim has suffered little.

probably frightened. (Since the victim does not know who shocked him, both the observer and the harm-doer who anticipated shock have equal reason to be afraid, and so their possible reactions will be considered jointly.) Fear, regardless of whether or not the anticipated punishment will restore equity, might affect a subject's ratings.

Two different types of reactions sound possible:

1. *Self-deceptive reactions.* The subject who anticipates being shocked might wish to assure himself (at least until the shock comes) that he has little to fear. Several distortions would help to maintain an optimistic outlook: He could convince himself that the victim is a good person, who has no reason to be angry, and who will shock him only mildly. Such a desire to perceive coming events as pleasant could produce main effects of the following type: H-R and O-R subjects may rate the victim more highly, his suffering as less intense, the project as more important, and deny that they have done anything wrong, to a greater extent than do H-NR and O-NR subjects.

2. *Angry, resentful reactions.* One might make a plausible argument for predicting a main effect in the opposite direction. The frightening discovery that they are going to be shocked might make subjects angry and resentful. H-R and O-R subjects thus may react aggressively to everyone and everything they are asked to rate. If anger does breed aggressive reactions, one might expect the following main effects: H-R and O-R subjects might dislike the victim for what he is about to do to them and might express hostility toward the experiment by rating it as worthless and unfair. In addition, once they realize that they will be shocked, the victim's experiences might become more salient, and the amount of discomfort caused by the shocks might thus be magnified.

Examining the data on main effects: In no case did harm-doing have a significant effect on the subjects' ratings. Anticipation of punishment had one effect that approached significance and one significant effect on subjects' ratings: (*a*) Subjects who anticipated punishment tended to deny that they had done wrong to a greater extent than did subjects who did not expect shock. The difference was not significant, however; (*b*) subjects who were about to be punished felt the experimental procedure which had singled them out for shock was more unfair to them than did subjects who had escaped punishment. From an examination of the means, it appears that it is the O-R subjects who felt the experiment was most unjust. The O-R subjects rate the experiment as much less fair than do O-NR subjects ($D_M = 5.09$). H-R subjects rate the procedure as only slightly less fair than do H-NR subjects. ($D_M = 1.59$.) The O-R subjects are not significantly more critical of the experiment than are other subjects, however. The interaction F is definitely nonsignificant.

References

Baldwin, J. *The fire next time.* New York: Dial, 1963.

Berkowitz, L. *Aggression: A social psychological analysis.* New York: McGraw-Hill, 1962.

Berscheid, E., Boye, D., & Darley, J. M. Effects of forced association on voluntary choice to associate. *Journal of Personality and Social Psychology,* 1968, *7,* 13–19.

Berscheid, E., & Walster, E. When does a harmdoer compensate a victim? *Journal of Personality and Social Psychology,* 1967, *6,* 435–441.

Brock, T. C., & Buss, A. H. Dissonance, aggression, and evaluation of pain. *Journal of Abnormal and Social Psychology,* 1962, *65,* 192–202.

Brock, T. C., & Buss, A. H. Effects of justification for aggression in communication with the victim on postaggression dissonance. *Journal of Abnormal and Social Psychology,* 1964, *68,* 403–412.

Davidson, J. Cognitive familiarity and dissonance reduction. In L. Festinger (Ed.), *Conflict, decision, and dissonance.* Stanford, Calif.: Stanford University Press, 1964.

Davis, K. E., & Jones, E. E. Changes in interpersonal perception as a means of reducing cognitive dissonance. *Journal of Abnormal and Social Psychology,* 1960, *61,* 402–410.

Freedman, J. L., Wallington, S. A., & Bless, E. Compliance without pressure: The effect of guilt. *Journal of Personality and Social Psychology,* 1967, *7,* 117–124.

Fry, M. et al. Compensation for victims of criminal violence: A round table. *Journal of Public Law,* 1959, *8,* 155–253.

Glass, D. C. Changes in liking as a means of reducing cognitive discrepancies between self-esteem and aggression. *Journal of Personality,* 1964, *32,* 520–549.

Schafer, S. *Restitution to victims of crime.* London: Stevens, 1960.

Sykes, G. M., & Matza, D. Techniques of neutralization: A theory of delinquency. *American Sociological Review,* 1957, *22,* 664–670.

Walster, E., & Prestholdt, P. The effect of misjudging another: Over-compensation or dissonance reduction? *Journal of Experimental Social Psychology,* 1966, *2,* 85–97.

Foreword to Reading 4.5

INTRODUCTION

This article reminds the reader of the psychologist's conflict in deciding between field and laboratory studies or a combination of both. As a psychologist, you are interested in conclusions that apply to real life and real people. Why then should you conduct experiments in the artificial atmosphere of the laboratory (rather than in real situations or the "field")? The major reason is one of control. In the laboratory, it is possible to manipulate one variable and to hold all other variables relatively constant. Any differences in response, then, should be due to the experimenter-caused differences in the variable of interest. For instance, suppose that all of your subjects are female, all white, all juniors in college; all have volunteered to be in your experiment; all are to be paid one dollar and fifty cents for their participation. One-half of these subjects are told that they are to interact with a female, college-student partner who has many attitudes similar to their own; one-half are told that they are to interact with a female, college-student partner who has many attitudes different from their own. Now both groups of subjects are asked to indicate their pleasure or displeasure at the forthcoming interaction, and it appears that the first group is much more pleased than the second. To what may the differences in dependent (response) variable be attributed? Such variables as sex, race, and occupation were held constant. However, presumed similarity of partner was manipulated or varied and appears to have caused variations in response. In real life, though, things are never so clear. If differences in variable A are related to differences in B, one can never be sure whether A led to B, or B to A, or C to both of them.

Byrne explains the differences between the laboratory and field study of attraction. The reader may find his description of the laboratory model somewhat confusing. The idea is that the experimenter varies certain stimuli, and then measures the effect of these variations on attraction. It is hypothesized that people like people who reward rather than punish them. The experimenter can then predict the effect of a stimulus on attraction by considering it, in some degree, to be either a positive reinforcer (reward) or a negative reinforcer (punishment). These predictions have, in general, been confirmed. Also, experimenters have been able to increase the exactness of the predictions by arithmetic "weighting" of the stimulus variables. For instance, it seems to be the case that similarity with another person is rewarding. Similar people are easy to talk to; they understand you and can be expected to like you. Also, if they think as you do, they confirm that your attitudes are good and right. A person who is very similar would be more reinforcing than one who is somewhat similar. A person who thinks as you do on an important or controversial issue would be more positively reinforcing than one who confirms the obvious fact that the sky is blue. In making predictions, then, similarity on important items is given more of an arithmetic weight than similarity on unimportant items, and attraction should turn out to be positively correlated (or directly related) to the appropriately weighted proportion of similar, rather than dissimilar characteristics (positive reinforcement) possessed by the stimulus person.

The authors' aim here was to take this model from the laboratory and test it in a setting more closely related to real life.

METHOD

In order to allow for actual matching of the couple to be introduced, each subject was given a 50-item questionnaire. Ten items were chosen from each of five personality scales. The curious reader will be interested to know that EPPS refers to Edward's Personality Preference Schedule: a measure that assesses the extent to which particular needs or traits (e.g., affiliation, aggression etc.) make up one's personality.

Byrne et al. used both laboratory and field techniques in this experiment. In the field condition, each subject was introduced to another subject (of the opposite sex), who had actually responded to either some or many of the attitude-personality items in a manner similar to himself. Subjects were then either reminded of the original questionnaire, and informed of the degree of their similarity, or asked to suppose that they had been matched by such a questionnaire. (As the reader will note in the results section, this "salience" variable had no effects. Perhaps some of the subjects in the "no-salience" group recalled the earlier questionnaire and suspected its purpose. Byrne does not tell us if a good deal of time elapsed between the two sections of the study.) All of the subjects were then given fifty cents and asked to spend half an hour together at the local Student Union. (The editors in New York City were envious of the ability of fifty cents to "buy whatever you want.")

In both the laboratory and field sections of the study, several measures of attraction were taken. One measure (the Interpersonal Judgment Scale) had been used in previous research. The other measures were developed for this study. In addition, in the field condition of the study, each pair of subjects was rated as to how closely together they were standing when talking to the experimenter. This unobtrusive measure of attraction had the advantage that subjects did not know that they were being observed, and so couldn't "fake it" (intentionally or otherwise). Finally, again only in the field conditions, subjects were contacted several months later, and asked about further interaction with their experimental date.

RESULTS AND CONCLUSIONS

As can be seen in Table 1, subjects were more favorable toward a simulated stranger the more similar he was to them (means of 11.06 and 9.84). When the field study results were considered, again the variable of similarity was directly related to attraction (Table 2). This indicates the feasibility of applying the laboratory model to real life situations.

Finally, the reader should note that the two measures of proximity of the couple when talking to the experimenter, and further interactions after the arranged date, also seemed to bear out the validity of the laboratory study and measure of attraction.

The reader may be wondering at this point if we should drop altogether the maxim that "opposites attract." There seems to be little evidence to support it. However, one investigator, Robert Winch (e.g., Winch et al., 1954) has suggested that selection of a marriage partner is based on "complementary" rather than similar needs. Thus, Winch suggests that a sadist would be more satisfied if married to a masochist than to a fellow sadist! Similarly, a leader should team up with a follower, and so on. It is possible that complementary needs are indeed important in relationships in which the two persons expect to play different, rather than similar roles.

Reference

Winch, R. F., Ktsanes, T., & Ktsanes, V. The theory of complementary needs in mate selection: an analytic and descriptive study. *American Sociological Review*, 1954, *19*, 241–249.

4.5 Continuity Between the Experimental Study of Attraction and Real-Life Computer Dating[1]

Donn Byrne
Charles R. Ervin
John Lamberth

As a test of the nonlaboratory generalizability of attraction research, a computer dating field study was conducted. A 50-item questionnaire of attitudes and personality was administered to a 420-student pool, and 44 male-female pairs were selected on the basis of maximal or minimal similarity of responses. Each couple was introduced, given differential information about the basis for their matching, and asked to spend 30 minutes together at the Student Union on a "coke date." Afterward, they returned to the experimenter and were independently assessed on a series of measures. It was found that attraction was significantly related to similarity and to physical attractiveness. Physical attractiveness was also significantly related to ratings of desirability as a date, as a spouse, and to sexual attractiveness. Both similarity and attractiveness were related to the physical proximity of the two individuals while they were talking to the experimenter after the date. In a follow-up investigation at the end of the semester, similarity and physical attractiveness were found to predict accurate memory of the date's name, incidence of talking to one another in the interim since the coke date, and desire to date the other person in the future.

A familiar but never totally resolved problem with any experimental findings is the extent to which they may be generalized to the nonlaboratory situation. At least three viewpoints about the problem may be discerned. First, and perhaps most familiar, is instant generalization from the specific and often limited conditions of an experiment to any and all settings which are even remotely related. This tendency is most frequently seen at cocktail parties after the third martini and on television talk shows featuring those who popularize psychology. Second, and almost as familiar, is the notion that the laboratory is a necessary evil. It is seen as an adequate substitute for the real world, only to the extent that it reproduces the world. For ex-

Reprinted from the *Journal of Personality and Social Psychology,* 1970, *16,* 157–65. Copyright 1970 by the American Psychological Association and reproduced with permission.

[1] This research was supported in part by Research Grant MH-11178-04 from the National Institute of Mental Health and in part by Research Grant GS-2752 from the National Science Foundation. The authors wish to thank James Hilgren, Royal Masset, and Herman Mitchell for their help in conducting this experiment.

ample, Aronson and Carlsmith (1968) ask, "Why, then, do we bother with these pallid and contrived imitations of human interaction when there exist rather sophisticated techniques for studying the real thing [p. 4]?" They enumerate the advantages of experiments over field study, but emphasize that good experiments must be realistic in order to involve the subject and have an "impact" on him. Concern with experimental realism often is expressed in the context of positing qualitative differences between the laboratory and the outside world; it is assumed that in moving from simplicity to complexity, new and different principles are emergent. Third, and least familiar in personality and social psychology, is a view which is quite common in other fields. Laboratory research is seen not as a necessary evil but as an essential procedure which enables us to attain isolation and control of variables and thus makes possible the formulation of basic principles in a setting of reduced complexity. If experiments realistically reproduce the nonlaboratory complexities, they provide little advantage over the field study. Continuity is assumed between the laboratory and the outside world, and complexity is seen as quantitative and not qualitative. To move from a simple situation to a complex one requires detailed knowledge about the relevant variables and their interaction. Application and the attainment of a technology depend upon such an approach.

With respect to a specific psychological phenomenon, the problem of nonlaboratory generalization and application may be examined more concretely. The laboratory investigation of interpersonal attraction within a reinforcement paradigm (Byrne, 1969) has followed a strategy in which the effect of a variety of stimulus variables on a single response variable was the primary focus of interest. A model has evolved which treats all relevant stimuli as positive or negative reinforcers of differential magnitude. Attraction toward any stimulus object (including another person) is then found to be a positive linear function of the proportion of weighted positive reinforcements associated with that object. Attitude statements have been the most frequently employed reinforcing stimuli, but other stimulus elements have included personality variables (e.g., Griffitt, 1966), physical attractiveness (e.g., Byrne, London, & Reeves, 1968), economic variables (Byrne, Clore, & Worchel, 1966), race (e.g., Byrne & Ervin, 1969), behavioral preferences (Huffman, 1969), personal evaluations (e.g., Byrne & Rhamey, 1965), room temperature (Griffitt, 1970a), and sexual arousal (Picher, 1966).

Considering just one of those variables, attitude similarity-dissimilarity, why is it not reasonable to propose an immediate and direct parallel between laboratory and nonlaboratory responses? One reason is simple and quite obvious, but it seems often to be overlooked. Laboratory research is based on the isolation of variables so that one or a limited number of independent variables may be manipulated, while, if possible, all other stimulus variables are controlled. In the outside world, multiple uncontrolled stimuli are present. Thus, if all an experimental subject knows about a stranger is that he holds opinions similar to his own on six out of six political issues, the stranger will be liked (Byrne, Bond, & Diamond, 1969). We cannot, however, assume that any two interacting individuals who agree on these six issues will become fast friends because (*a*) they may never get around to discussing those six topics at all, and (*b*) even if these topics are discussed, six positive reinforcements may simply become an insignificant portion of a host of other positive and negative reinforcing elements in the interaction. A second barrier to immediate applicability of a laboratory finding lies in the nature of the response. It is good research strategy to limit the dependent variable (in this instance, the sum of two 7-point rating scales), but nonlaboratory responses may be as varied and uncontrolled as the stimuli. The relationship between that paper-and-pencil measure of attraction and other interpersonal responses is only beginning to be explored (e.g., Byrne, Baskett, & Hodges, 1969; Efran, 1969). The third barrier lies in the nature of the relationship investigated. For a number of quite practical reasons, the laboratory study of attraction is limited in its time span and hence might legitimately be labeled the study of first impressions. Whether the determinants of first impressions are precisely the same as the determinants of a prolonged friendship, of love, or of marital happiness is an empirical question and one requiring a great deal of research.

In view of these barriers to extralaboratory application of experimental findings, how may one begin the engineering enterprise? The present research suggests one attempt to seek a solution. Specifically, a limited dating situation is created in which the barriers to application are minimized. Independent variables identified in the laboratory (attitude similarity, personality similarity, and physical attractiveness) are varied in a real-life situation, and an attempt is made to make the variables salient and to minimize the occurrence of other stimulus events. Even though similarity has been the focus of much of the experimental work on attraction, the findings with respect to physical attractiveness have consistently demonstrated the powerful influence of appearance on responses to those of the opposite sex and even of the same sex. Both field studies (Megargee, 1956; Perrin, 1921; Taylor, 1956; Walster, Aronson, Abrahams, & Rottmann, 1966) and laboratory investigations (Byrne et al., 1968; McWhirter, 1969; Moss, 1969) have shown that those who are physically attractive elicit more positive responses than do those who are unattractive. The laboratory response measure was retained so that a common reference point was available, but additional response variables were also used in order to extend the generality and meaning of the attraction construct. Finally, in this experiment, the interaction was deliberately limited in time so that it remained close to a first-impression relationship. Given these deliberately limited conditions, it was proposed that the positive relationship between the proportion of weighted positive reinforcements and attraction is directly applicable to a nonlaboratory interaction. Specifically, it was hypothesized that in a computer dating situation (*a*) attraction is a joint function of similarity and physical attractiveness, and (*b*) the greater the extent to which the specific elements of similarity are made salient, the greater is the relationship between similarity and attraction.

The variety of ways in which similarity and attraction could be investigated in a field situation raises an interesting question of strategy. It should be kept in mind that there is no magic about the similarity effect. Similarity does not exude from the pores; rather, specific attitudes and other characteristics must be expressed overtly. It would be relatively simple to design a computer dating experiment in which no similarity effects would be found. For example, one could lie about the degree of similarity, and in a brief interaction, the subjects would not be likely to discover the deception. Another alternative would be to provide no information about similarity and then to forbid the subjects to talk during their date. Negative results in such studies would be of no importance as a test since they are beyond the boundary conditions of the theory. Another possible study would give no initial similarity information and then require an extended interaction period, but that has already been done. That is, people in the real world do this every day, and numerous correlational studies indicate that under such conditions, similarity is associated with attraction. The strategy of the present research was frankly to maximize the possibility of securing a precise similarity attraction effect in a real-life setting; in subsequent research, the limiting conditions of the effect may be determined.

METHOD

Attitude-Personality Questionnaire

In order to provide a relatively broad base on which to match couples for the dating process, a 50-item questionnaire was constructed utilizing five variables. In previous research, a significant similarity effect has been found for authoritarianism (Sheffield & Byrne, 1967), repression-sensitization (Byrne & Griffitt, 1969; Byrne, Griffitt, & Stefaniak, 1967), attitudes (Byrne, 1961, 1969), EPPS items,[2] and self-concept (Griffitt, 1966, 1970b). Each variable was represented by 10 items which were chosen to represent the least possible intercorrelations within dimensions; the rationale here was the desire to maximize the number of *independent* scale responses on which matching could be based.

[2] Unpublished data collected by Donn Byrne and John Lamberth.

Simulated Stranger Condition

In order to provide a base line for the similarity effect under controlled conditions, a simulated stranger condition was run in which the other person was represented only by his or her purported responses to the attitude-personality questionnaire. The study was described as an investigation of the effectiveness of the matching procedures of computer dating organizations. Subjects were told, "Instead of arranging an actual date, we are providing couples with information about one another and asking for their reactions." The simulated scales were prepared to provide either a .33 or .67 proportion of similar responses between stranger and subject. The subject was asked to read the responses of an opposite-sex stranger and then to make a series of evaluations on an expanded version of the Interpersonal Judgment Scale. This scale consists of ten 7-point scales. The measure of attraction within this experimental paradigm (Byrne, 1969) consists of the sum of two scales: liking and desirability as a work partner. This attraction index ranges from 2 to 14 and has a split-half reliability of .85. In addition, four buffer scales deal with evaluations of the other person's intelligence, knowledge of current events, morality, and adjustment. These variables are found to correlate positively with attraction, but they have somewhat different antecedents and are included in the analysis simply as supplemental information. Three new scales, added for the present study in order to explore various responses to the opposite sex, asked the subject to react to the other person as a potential date, as a marriage partner, and as to sexual attractiveness. Finally, a tenth scale was added in order to assess a stimulus variable, the physical attractiveness of the other person. In addition, the physical attractiveness of each subject was rated by the experimenter on the same 7-point scale on which the subjects rated one another.

Computer Dating Condition

Selection of dating couples. The attitude-personality questionnaire was administered to a group of 420 introductory psychology students at the University of Texas, and each item was scored in a binary fashion. By means of a specially prepared program, the responses of each male were compared with those of each female; for any given couple, the number of possible matching responses could theoretically range from 0 to 50. The actual range was from 12 to 37. From these distributions of matches, male-female pairs were selected to represent either the greatest or the least number of matching responses. There was a further restriction that the male be as tall as or taller than the female. Of the resulting pairs, a few were eliminated because (a) one of the individuals was married, (b) the resulting pair was racially mixed, or (c) because of a failure to keep the experimental appointment. The remaining 88 subjects formed 24 high-similar pairs, whose proportion of similar responses ranged from .66 to .74, and 20 low-similar pairs, whose proportion of similar responses ranged from .24 to .40.

Levels of information saliency. The experiment was run with one of the selected couples at a time. In the experimental room, they were introduced to one another and told:

In recent years, there has been a considerable amount of interest in the phenomenon of computer dating as a means for college students to meet one another. At the present time, we are attempting to learn as much as possible about the variables which influence the reactions of one individual to another.

In order to create differential levels of saliency with respect to the matching elements, subjects in the salient condition were told:

> Earlier this semester, one of the test forms you filled out was very much like those used by some of the computer dating organizations. In order to refresh your memory about this test and the answers you gave, we are going to ask you to spend a few minutes looking over the questions and your answers to them.
>
> The answers of several hundred students were placed on IBM cards and run through the computer to determine the number of matching answers among the 50 questions for all possible pairs of male and female students. According to the computer, the two of you gave the same answers on approximately 67% (33%) of those questions.

In the nonsalient condition, they were told:

> Imagine for the purposes of the experiment that you had applied to one of the computer dating organizations and filled out some of their information forms. Then, imagine that the two of you had been notified that, according to the computer, you match on approximately 67% (33%) of the factors considered important.

All subjects were then told:

> For our experiment, we would like to create a situation somewhat like that of a computer date. That is, you answered a series of questions, the computer indicated that you two gave the same responses on some of the questions, and now we would like for you to spend a short time together getting acquainted. Specifically, we are asking you to spend the next 30 minutes together on a "coke date" at the Student Union. Here is 50¢ to spend on whatever you would like. We hope that you will learn as much as possible about each other in the next half hour because we will be asking you a number of questions about one another when you return.

Measures of attraction. When they returned from the date to receive their final instructions, an unobtrusive measure of attraction was obtained: the physical distance between the two subjects while standing together in front of the experimenter's desk. The distance was noted on a simple ordinal scale ranging from 0 (touching one another) to 5 (standing at opposite corners of the desk). The subjects were then separated and asked to evaluate their date on the Interpersonal Judgment Scale.

Follow-up measures. At the end of the semester (2–3 months after the date), it was possible to locate 74 of the 88 original subjects who were willing to answer five additional questions. Each was asked to write the name of his or her computer date and to indicate whether or not they had talked to one another since the experiment, dated since the experiment, and whether a date was desired or planned in the future. Finally, each was asked whether the evaluation of the date was influenced more by physical attractiveness or by attitudes.

RESULTS

Simulated Stranger Condition

The mean attraction responses of two simulated stranger conditions[3] which were run separately from the computer dating experiment are shown in Table 1. Analysis of variance indicated that the similarity variable yielded

TABLE 1 *Mean Attraction Responses toward Similar and Dissimilar Simulated Strangers with Two Different Titles for Experiment*

TITLE OF EXPERIMENT	PROPORTION OF SIMILAR RESPONSES	
	.33	.67
Evaluational processes	9.47	10.78
Computer dating	10.21	11.33
M	9.84	11.06

Note.—The mean attraction responses were 10.12 and 10.77 for the evaluational processes and computer dating experiments, respectively.

the only significant effect ($F = 4.00$, $df = 1/46$, $p =$ approximately .05).

On the remaining items of the Interpersonal Judgment Scale, the only other significant similarity effect was on the intelligence rating ($F = 7.30$, $df = 1/46$, $p < .01$). Interestingly enough, there were several differences between the differently labeled experiments on the other Interpersonal Judgment Scale items. More positive responses were given in the "computer dating" experiment than in the "evaluational processes" experiment with respect to knowledge of current events ($F = 8.07$, $df = 1/46$, $p < .01$), adjustment ($F = 6.10$, $df = 1/46$, $p < .02$), and desirability as a marriage partner ($F = 6.57$, $df = 1/46$, $p < .02$). The sexual attractiveness item yielded a significant interaction effect ($F = 4.93$, $df = 1/46$, $p < .03$), with the dissimilar stranger rated as more sexually attractive in the computer dating experiment and the similar stranger as more sexually attractive in the

[3] Originally, the plan was to run the simulated stranger groups just after the computer dating groups. An unexpected finding was that almost all of the responses were positive and that the subjects were attired more attractively than is usual among undergraduates reporting for experimental sessions. From anecdotal olfactory evidence, even the perfume and shaving lotion level was noticeably elevated. In retrospect, it seemed clear that because the computer dating study was widely discussed and because this experiment was so labeled, the overwhelming majority of the 34 subjects were expecting to go on a date as part of their task. It then became necessary to rerun the simulated stranger groups at the end of the semester when the expectations of dates had diminished. The two levels of similarity were run under two different experimental titles, "Computer Dating" and "Evaluational Processes." The data reported in this paper are from these latter two experiments.

evaluational processes experiment. While these latter findings are gratuitous, they suggest the importance of minor variations in the stimulus context and the sensitivity of the Interpersonal Judgment Scale items to such variations.

Predicting Attraction in the Computer Dating Condition

The mean attraction responses for male and female subjects at two levels of information saliency and two levels of response similarity are shown in Table 2. Analysis of variance indicated the only significant effect to be that

TABLE 2 *Mean Attraction Responses of Males and Females with Similar and Dissimilar Dates at Two Levels of Saliency Concerning Matching Information*

LEVEL	PROPORTION OF SIMILAR RESPONSES	
	Low	High
Male Ss Information		
Salient	10.00	11.91
Nonsalient	10.56	11.38
Female Ss Information		
Salient	10.73	11.82
Nonsalient	10.33	12.15

of proportion of similar responses ($F = 13.67$, $df = 1/40$, $p < .001$). The attempt to make the matching stimuli differentially salient did not affect attraction, and there were no sex differences.

The other variable which was expected to influence attraction was the physical attractiveness of the date. It is interesting to note in the simulated stranger condition that while the manipulation of similarity influenced attraction, it had no effect on guesses as to the other person's physical attractiveness ($F < 1$). Thus, data in the computer dating condition indicating a relationship between attractiveness and attraction would seem to result from the effect of the former on the latter. Two measures of attractiveness were available: ratings by the experimenter when the subjects first arrived and by each subject of his or her own date following their interaction. The correlation between these two measures was significant; the correlation between the experimenter's ratings of male subjects and the females' ratings of their dates was .59 ($p < .01$) and between the experimenter's ratings of female subjects and the males' ratings of their dates was .39 ($p < .01$). As might be expected, the subject's own ratings proved to be better predictors than did the experimenter's ratings. In Table 3 are shown those correlations between physical attractiveness ratings and Interpersonal Judgment Scale responses which were consistent across sexes.

TABLE 3 *Correlations between Ratings of Physical Attractiveness of Date and Evaluations of Date*

| | ATTRACTIVENESS OF DATE | | ATTRACTIVENESS OF DATE | |
| VARIABLE | RATED BY Ss | | RATED BY E | |
	Male Ss	Female Ss	Male Ss	Female Ss
Attraction	.39**	.60**	.07	.32*
Dating	.66**	.57**	.21	.33*
Marriage	.56**	.55**	.18	.34*
Sex	.77**	.70**	.53**	.44**

$* p < .05.$
$** p < .01.$

Thus, the first hypothesis was clearly confirmed, but there was no support for the second hypothesis.

With respect to the prediction of attraction, it seems likely that a combination of the similarity and attractiveness variables would provide the optimal information. In Table 4 are shown the mean attraction responses

TABLE 4 *Mean Attraction Responses of Males and Females with Similar and Dissimilar Dates Who Are Relatively Attractive and Unattractive*

| PHYSICAL ATTRACTIVENESS OF DATE | PROPORTION OF SIMILAR RESPONSES | |
	Low	High
Male Ss		
Attractive	10.55	12.00
Unattractive	9.89	10.43
Female Ss		
Attractive	11.25	12.71
Unattractive	9.50	11.00

toward attractive (ratings of 5–7) and unattractive (ratings of 1–4) dates at two levels of response similarity. For both sexes, each of the two independent variables was found to affect attraction.[4] The physical attractive-

---

[4] The use of the term "independent variable" for physical attractiveness may be a source of confusion. In this experiment, there was obviously no manipulation of physical appearance, but attractiveness was conceptualized as one of the stimuli determining attraction. In other experiments, attractiveness has been successfully manipulated as an independent variable (e.g., Byrne et al., 1968; McWhirter, 1969; Moss, 1969). In the absence of any evidence that attraction determines perception of physical attractiveness (and some evidence to the contrary), it seems reasonable to consider attractiveness as an antecedent variable in studies such as the present one and that of Walster et al. (1966).

ness variable was significant for both males ($F = 3.85$, $df = 1/39$, $p < .05$) and for females ($F = 10.44$, $df = 1/40$, $p < .01$). The most positive response in each instance was toward similar attractive dates, and the least positive response was toward dissimilar unattractive dates. An additional analysis indicated no relationship between an individual's own physical attractiveness (as rated by the date) and response to the other person's physical attractiveness.

Other Effects of Similarity and Attractiveness

On the additional items of the Interpersonal Judgment Scale, similarity was found to have a significant positive effect on ratings of the date's intelligence ($F = 4.37$, $df = 1/40$, $p < .05$), desirability as a date ($F = 8.92$, $df = 1/40$, $p < .01$), and desirability as a marriage partner ($F = 4.76$, $df = 1/40$, $p < .05$).

The simplest and least obtrusive measure of attraction was the proximity of the two individuals after the date, while receiving their final instructions from the experimenter. If physical distance can be considered as an alternative index of attraction, these two dependent variables should be correlated. For females, the correlation was $-.36$ ($p < .01$) and for males, $-.48$, ($p < .01$); in each instance the greater the liking for the partner, the closer together they stood. Another way of evaluating the proximity variable is to determine whether it is influenced by the same independent variables as is the paper-and-pencil measure. For both sexes, physical separation was found to correlate $-.49$ ($p < .01$) with similarity. Thus, the more similar the couples, the closer they stood. Because similarity and proximity are necessarily identical for each member of a pair, it is not possible to determine whether the males, the females, or both are responsible for the similarity-proximity relationship. When the physical attractiveness measure was examined, however, there was indirect evidence that proximity in this situation was controlled more by the males than by the females. For females, there was no relationship between ratings of the male's appearance and physical separation ($r = -.06$). For males, the correlation was $-.34$ ($p < .05$).

In the follow-up investigation at the end of the semester, 74 of the 88 original subjects were available and willing to participate. For this analysis, each subject was placed in one of three categories with respect to the two stimulus variables of similarity and attractiveness. On the basis of the same divisions as were used in the analysis in Table 4, subjects were either in a high-similarity condition with a physically attractive date, a low-similarity condition with a physically unattractive date, or in a mixed condition of high-low or low-high. To maximize the possible effect, frequency analysis was used in comparing the two homogeneous groups ($N = 40$).[5] In response to the question about the date's name, the more positive the stimulus conditions at the time of the date, the more likely was the subject to remember correctly the date's name ($\chi^2 = 8.47$, $df = 1$, $p < .01$). With respect to talking to the other individual during the period since the experiment, the relationship was again significant ($\chi^2 = 4.95$, $df = 1$, $p < .05$). The same effect was found with regard to whether the individual would like or not like to date the other person in the future ($\chi^2 = 5.38$, $df = 1$, $p < .05$). The only follow-up question which failed to show a significant effect for the experimental manipulation was that dealing with actual dating; even here, it might be noted that the only dates reported were by subjects in the high-similarity, high-attractiveness condition.

The only other question in the follow-up survey represented an attempt to find out whether the subjects could accurately verbalize the stimuli to which they had been found to respond. Of the 74 respondents, about one-third indicated that both attitudes and physical attractiveness determined their response to the partner, while about one-sixth of the subjects felt they had responded to neither variable. With the remaining half of the sample, an interesting sex difference emerged. Physical attractiveness was identified as the most important stimulus by 14 of the 18 males, while attitudes were seen as the most important stimulus by 16 of the 19 females ($\chi^2 = 14.30$, $df = 1$, $p < .001$). The present subjects seemed to have accepted Bertrand Russell's observation that "On the whole, women tend to love men for their character, while men tend to love women for their appearance." In contrast to these verbal sentiments, it might be noted that the date's physical attractiveness correlated .60 with attraction responses of female subjects and only .39 among male subjects. A further analysis compared the similarity-attraction effect and the attractiveness-attraction effect for those subjects who indicated one or the other stimulus variable as the more important. The similarity-attraction effect did not differ between the two groups ($z < 1$). It has been reported previously that awareness of similarity is not a necessary component of the similarity effect (Byrne & Griffitt, 1969). There was, however, a difference in the attractiveness effect. For the subjects identifying attractiveness as the major determinant, physical attractiveness correlated .63 ($p < .01$) with attraction responses; for the subjects identifying similarity as the major determinant, attractiveness correlated $-.04$ (ns) with attraction. The difference was a significant one ($z = 2.16$, $p < .05$).

---

[5] When the 33 individuals who were heterogeneous with respect to similarity and attractiveness were included in the analysis, they fell midway between the similar-attractive and dissimilar-unattractive groups on each item. The probability levels were consequently reduced to the .02 level on remembering the date's name and to the .10 level on the talking and desire to date items.

CONCLUSIONS

Perhaps the most important aspect of the present findings is the evidence indicating the continuity between the laboratory study of attraction and its manifestation under field conditions. At least as operationalized in the present investigation, variables such as physical attractiveness and similarity of attitudes and personality characteristics are found to influence attraction in a highly predictable manner.

The findings with respect to the physical distance measure are important in two respects. First, they provide further evidence that voluntary proximity is a useful and unobtrusive measure of interpersonal attraction. Second, the construct validity and generality of the paper-and-pencil measure of attraction provided by the Interpersonal Judgment Scale is greatly enhanced. The significant relationship between two such different response measures is comforting to users of either one. In addition, the follow-up procedure provided evidence of the lasting effect of the experimental manipulations and of the relation of the attraction measures to such diverse responses as remembering the other person's name and engaging in conversation in the weeks after the termination of the experiment.

The failure to confirm the second hypothesis is somewhat puzzling. It is possible that present procedures, designed to vary the saliency of the elements of similarity, were inadequate and ineffective, that the actual behavioral cues to similarity and dissimilarity were sufficiently powerful to negate the effects of the experimental manipulation, or that the hypothesis was simply incorrect. There is no basis within the present experiment on which to decide among these alternatives.

In conclusion, it must be emphasized that striking continuity has been demonstrated across experiments using paper-and-pencil materials to simulate a stranger and to measure attraction (Byrne, 1961), more realistic audio and audiovisual presentations of the stimulus person (Byrne & Clore, 1966), elaborate dramatic confrontations in which a confederate portrays the stimulus person (Byrne & Griffitt, 1966), and a quasi-realistic experiment such as the present one, in which two genuine strangers interact and in which response measures include nonverbal behaviors. Such findings suggest that attempts to move back and forth between the controlled artificiality of the laboratory and the uncontrolled natural setting are both feasible and indicative of the potential applications of basic attraction research to a variety of interpersonal problems.

References

Aronson, E., & Carlsmith, J. M. Experimentation in social psychology. In G. Lindzey & E. Aronson (Eds.), *The handbook of social psychology*. Vol. 2. (2nd ed.) Reading, Mass.: Addison-Wesley, 1968.

Byrne, D. Interpersonal attraction and attitude similarity. *Journal of Abnormal and Social Psychology*, 1961, *62*, 713–715.

Byrne, D. Attitudes and attraction. In L. Berkowitz (Ed.), *Advances in experimental social psychology*. Vol. 4. New York: Academic Press, 1969.

Byrne, D., Baskett, G. D., & Hodges, L. Behavioral indicators of interpersonal attraction. Paper presented at meeting of the Psychonomic Society, St. Louis, November 1969.

Byrne, D., Bond, M. H., & Diamond, M. J. Response to political candidates as a function of attitude similarity-dissimilarity. *Human Relations*, 1969, *22*, 251–262.

Byrne, D., & Clore, G. L., Jr. Predicting interpersonal attraction toward strangers presented in three different stimulus modes. *Psychonomic Science*, 1966, *4*, 239–240.

Byrne, D., Clore, G. L., Jr., & Worchel, P. Effect of economic similarity-dissimilarity on interpersonal attraction. *Journal of Personality and Social Psychology*, 1966, *4*, 220–224.

Byrne, D., & Ervin, C. R. Attraction toward a Negro stranger as a function of prejudice, attitude similarity, and the stranger's evaluation of the subject. *Human Relations*, 1969, *22*, 397–404.

Byrne, D., & Griffitt, W. Similarity versus liking: A clarification. *Psychonomic Science*, 1966, *6*, 295–296.

Byrne, D., & Griffitt, W. Similarity and awareness of similarity of personality characteristics as determinants of attraction. *Journal of Experimental Research in Personality*, 1969, *3*, 179–186.

Byrne, D., Griffitt, W., & Stefaniak, D. Attraction and similarity of personality characteristics. *Journal of Personality and Social Psychology*, 1967, *5*, 82–90.

Byrne, D., London, O., & Reeves, K. The effects of physical attractiveness, sex, and attitude similarity on interpersonal attraction. *Journal of Personality*, 1968, *36*, 259–271.

Byrne, D., & Rhamey, R. Magnitude of positive and negative reinforcements as a determinant of attraction. *Journal of Personality and Social Psychology*, 1965, *2*, 884–889.

Efran, M. G. Visual interaction and interpersonal attraction. Unpublished doctoral dissertation, University of Texas, 1969.

Griffitt, W. B. Interpersonal attraction as a function of self-concept and personality similarity-dissimilarity. *Journal of Personality and Social Psychology*, 1966, *4*, 581–584.

Griffitt, W. B. Environmental effects of interpersonal affective behavior: Ambient effective temperature and attraction. *Journal of Personality and Social Psychology*, 1970, *15*, 240–244. (a)

Griffitt, W. B. Personality similarity and self-concept as determinants of interpersonal attraction. *Journal of Social Psychology*, 1970, in press. (b)

Huffman, D. M. Interpersonal attraction as a function of behavioral similarity. Unpublished doctoral dissertation, University of Texas, 1969.

McWhirter, R. M., Jr. Interpersonal attraction in a dyad as a function of the physical attractiveness of its members. Unpublished doctoral dissertation, Texas Tech University, 1969.

Megargee, E. I. A study of the subjective aspects of group membership at Amherst. Unpublished manuscript, Amherst College, 1956.

Moss, M. K. Social desirability, physical attractiveness, and social choice. Unpublished doctoral dissertation, Kansas State University, 1969.

Perrin, F. A. C. Physical attractiveness and repulsiveness. *Journal of Experimental Psychology,* 1921, *4,* 203–217.

Picher, O. L. Attraction toward Negroes as a function of prejudice, emotional arousal, and the sex of the Negro. Unpublished doctoral dissertation, University of Texas, 1966.

Sheffield, J., & Byrne, D. Attitude similarity-dissimilarity, authoritarianism, and interpersonal attraction. *Journal of Social Psychology,* 1967, *71,* 117–123.

Taylor, M. J. Some objective criteria of social class membership. Unpublished manuscript, Amherst College, 1956.

Walster, E., Aronson, V., Abrahams, D., & Rottmann, L. Importance of physical attractiveness in dating behavior. *Journal of Personality and Social Psychology,* 1966, *4,* 508–516.

Foreword to Reading 4.6

INTRODUCTION

Theories of the determinants of emotion have undergone something of a swing-back in the past few years. One of the earliest notable theories was that of James (1890), who suggested that we are afraid *because* we cry (and not vice versa). In other words, first we perceive a situation; next, we experience a physiological reaction to the situation; finally, we perceive our reaction, and this constitutes the emotion.

Cannon (1927) presented a number of objections to this theory. For instance, he pointed out that visceral (sympathetic nervous system) arousal presumably shows much the same pattern for different emotions. (Research since Cannon's time *has* found that different physiological states do differentiate such very different emotions as fear and anger.) Cannon's own theory, the "emergency theory," held that an external situation sets off activity in lower brain centers, which simultaneously triggers activity in the cerebral cortex (accounting for perception of emotion) and in body structures which change during emotion.

A more recent theory, which might be called "cognitive theory" (Morgan and King, 1966) incorporates some aspects of the James theory, while allowing for the validity of some of Cannon's objections. According to the cognitive theory, visceral arousal *is* relatively nonspecific; choice of emotion is determined by the context in which it occurs. Mandler (1962) likened this to a juke-box, suggesting that the visceral arousal is analogous to the insertion of the dime, the contextual situation to the selection of the record.

In the Schachter and Singer (1962) experiment described in the Nisbett and Schachter introduction, the subjects were injected with epinephrine (equivalent to insertion of the dime in Mandler's "juke-box"). This drug is a stimulant, and produces increased heart rate, and accelerated breathing and hand tremor. When some of these subjects were misinformed about the side-effects of the drug (for instance, told to expect numb feet and slight headache), they tended to follow the lead of an extremely emotional "stooge" (who was either euphoric, throwing paper balls around the room, etc., or angry). Other subjects who were led to expect the symptoms that they experienced tended to ignore the emotional carryings-on of the stooge. For those subjects, the description given by the experimenter matched their bodily state and provided the "record selection" or justification of their bodily state. The misinformed subjects needed a justification for their physiological symptoms, and "selected their own record" by ascribing to themselves an emotion similar to that portrayed by the stooge.

Nisbett and Schachter extended the reasoning of the earlier experiment to a situation in which a stimulus which would ordinarily produce definite emotional feelings (pain and fear) was presented. They hypothesized that, unless fear was extreme, the experienced pain would be less when it could be attributed to a non-fear evoking stimulus (a pill), than when it had to be attributed to the pain-producing stimulus (shock) itself.

RESULTS AND DISCUSSION

In looking at the result, the reader (and experimenter) must always ascertain the validity of the manipulation of the independent variable. (Did it "work"?) Mind you, it is a curious fact that traditionally, it need not be shown that say, high fear is really high, simply that it is higher than low fear (which may or may not be low by any absolute standard).

After noting the manipulation checks, the reader might look at Table 4 which indicates that the hypothesis was confirmed. Subjects in the low-fear condition who attributed their bodily changes to the pill (i.e., the non-fear evoking stimulus) were able to withstand more pain than subjects who correctly attributed their bodily changes to the shock. Table 5 adds other intriguing data. Subjects in the low-fear-pill-attribution condition reported their last shock to be less painful than did subjects in any of the other groups. The reader might consider if there is any practical significance of this for, say, hospital procedure. It might also be interesting to consider examples from real life that do or do not support the findings of this experiment.

References

Cannon, W. B. The James-Lange theory of emotions: a critical examination and an alternative theory. *American Journal of Psychology,* 1927, *39,* 106–124.
James, W. *Principles of psychology.* New York: Holt, Rinehart and Winston, 1890.

Mandler, G. Emotion. In R. Brown, E. Galanter, E. H. Hess, & G. Mandler (Eds.), *New directions in psychology.* New York: Holt, Rinehart and Winston, 1962.

Morgan, C. T., & King, R. H. *Introduction to psychology.* (3d ed.) New York: McGraw-Hill, 1966.

Schachter, S., & Singer, J. Cognitive, social and physiological determinants of emotional state. *Psychological Review,* 1962, *69,* 379–399.

Wolf, S., & Wolff, H. G. *Human gastric function.* (2d ed.) New York: Oxford University Press, 1947.

4.6   Cognitive Manipulation of Pain[1]

Richard E. Nisbett
Stanley Schachter

The experiment tests the notion that naturally occurring states of physiological arousal are manipulable in the same way that drug-induced arousal states have proven to be. The state of arousal studied is that produced by pain from electric shock. All subjects were given a placebo before the shock experience and half were told that the side effects would cause arousal symptoms such as palpitation, tremor, etc. The other half expected no such symptoms. Subjects believing themselves to be in an artificial state of arousal failed to attribute their shock-created arousal to the shock, and found the shock less painful and were willing to tolerate more of it. This "relabeling" of a naturally occurring state was shown to occur only for subjects in a relatively low state of fear.

In experiments conceived initially as studies of emotion, it has been repeatedly demonstrated that the "emotional labels" attached to aroused bodily states are, in good part, cognitively determined (Schachter, 1964; Schachter and Singer, 1962). These studies involved the manipulation of bodily state by the injection of epinephrine or placebo. In some conditions subjects were told the specific physiological symptoms, if any, to expect as a consequence of injection. In other conditions subjects did not expect that there would be such side effects. Where subjects experienced a state of arousal and were led to expect no such side effects, they proved readily manipulable into states of euphoria, anger, anxiety, and the like. Similar subjects, experimentally provided with an explanation for their aroused state, were almost completely nonmanipulable. This "plasticity" has been interpreted in terms of evaluative needs and labeling processes. Where an individual experiences a state of arousal for which he has no ready explanation, he labels this state in terms of cognitive and situational factors. It has been further demonstrated (Latané and Schachter, 1962; Schachter and Wheeler, 1962; Singer, 1963) that the intensity of the resulting emotion is a function of level of arousal.

Reprinted from the *Journal of Experimental Social Psychology*, 1966, *2*, 227–236, with permission of the senior author and the Academic Press. Copyright © 1966 by the Academic Press.

[1] The research described in this paper was supported by grant MH 05203 from the National Institute of Mental Health, United States Public Health Service, and by grant G 23758 from the National Science Foundation. The authors wish to express their warmest thanks to Harvey London for his assistance in the design and execution of the experiment.

These demonstrations of the plasticity of interpretation of bodily state have depended upon the experimental trick of simultaneously and independently manipulating physiological and cognitive factors. In nature, of course, cognitive or situational factors trigger physiological processes, and the triggering stimulus usually imposes the label we attach to our feelings. We see the threatening object; this perception-cognition initiates a state of sympathetic arousal, and this joint cognitive-physiological experience is labeled "fear."

Several considerations suggest that the line of reasoning guiding the experimental studies of emotion may be extended to these naturally occurring states and that the intensity of such states may be as modifiable as are experimentally induced states of arousal. As an example of this possibility, consider pain. Broadly, we can conceive of the intensity of experienced pain and of one's willingness to tolerate pain as a function of the intensity of stimulation of the pain receptors, of the autonomic correlates of such stimulation, and of a host of cognitive and situational factors. To the extent that we can convince a subject undergoing electric shock that his shock-produced symptoms and arousal state are due, not to shock, but to some outside agent such as a drug, he should, following the above considerations, experience less pain and be willing to tolerate more shock. Such an individual would, of course, regard his arousal as a drug-produced state rather than an indicator of pain or fear.

Since we would not expect that an individual undergoing *extreme* pain, fear, or rage could easily be persuaded to attribute the accompanying physiological arousal to an artificial source, there should be limits placed on the generality of these notions. We should be able to alter the labeling of a bodily state only within a range bounded at the lower end by the existence of at least some arousal, and at the upper end by experiences so extreme that no amount of manipulation of cognitions will persuade the individual to attribute his bodily state to an artificial source. Common sense would indicate that no amount of argument would persuade a man dodging machine-gun bullets that his physiological arousal was due to anything but the exigencies of his situation. The present experiment examines the extent to which relabeling processes affect pain thresholds under conditions of high and low fear.

PROCEDURE

Overview

The experimental test of these ideas required (a) administration of a placebo, (b) the "natural" production of an aroused bodily state by a painful stimulus, (c) manipulation of the extent to which this arousal could be attributed to the placebo, and (d) measurement of the extent to which the pain stimulus was tolerated and labeled as painful.

The experiment was described to subjects as one on skin sensitivity where the test of sensitivity would be electric shock. They were given a brief lecture on the importance of shock sensitivity research for the prevention of accidents and the control of shock dosage for patients undergoing electroshock therapy. This was followed by a description of the shock stimulus which the subject was to take. The shock was described to one group as being extremely painful, and to the other as being mild and easily tolerable.

Subjects were then told that the experimenters were interested in the effects on skin sensitivity of a drug called Suproxin. The drug was described as being a mild one that could do no harm, but which had certain transitory side effects which would last for 15 or 20 minutes. The description of the "side effects" of the placebo differed across conditions. In one set of conditions, the "side effects" were actually symptoms produced by the shock. In the other pair of conditions, the symptoms were irrelevant to shock. After taking the placebo tablet, subjects were told that they could expect the side effects to start within 2–4 minutes. They were then left to wait alone for a 10-minute period.

After the waiting period, subjects were taken into a room containing the shock apparatus. Electrodes were attached and subjects were given a series of shocks of gradually increasing intensity. Subjects reported when they could first feel the shock, when the shock first became painful, and when the shock was too painful to endure.

Manipulating Fear

High fear.   After describing the nature of the research, the experimenter concluded his patter with, "So what we'll ask you to do is very simple. We'd like to give you a series of electric shocks. Now I should be honest with you and tell you what you're in for. These shocks will hurt, they will be painful. If we're going to learn anything at all in this kind of research, it's necessary that the shocks be intense. What we'll do is hook some electrodes on your hand and give you a series of electric shocks. Again, I want to be honest with you and tell you that these shocks will be quite painful, but of course they won't do any permanent damage." The experimenter then continued with the instructions on Suproxin, the subjects took the pill and then waited alone for 10 minutes. At this point they were taken to the experimental room, the instructions about the painfulness of the shock repeated and the subjects given a sample "standardizing" shock which, to reinforce the manipulation, was a rather jarring and unpleasant 55 microamperes.

Low fear.   In introducing the experiment, the experimenter reassured the subject by saying "Before you get worried, let me tell you not to let the word 'shock' bother you. There's not going to be any discomfort and I'm sure you'll enjoy the experiment." He then continued his description of the research, concluding with, "So what we will ask you to do will be very simple. We would like to give you a series of very mild electric shocks. What you will feel will be more like a tickle or a tingle than anything unpleasant. So we will put some electrodes on your hand and give you a series of very mild shocks." The subjects then took the pill, waited 10 minutes, and were given a sample shock of a barely perceptible 22 microamperes.

Manipulating Attribution of Bodily State

The extent to which bodily state could be attributed to an external source was manipulated by creating a condition in which subjects expected, as "side effects" of the placebo, symptoms which would actually be caused by the shock (Pill Attrib condition). A condition was also created in which subjects expected symptoms which were irrelevant to the shock (Shock Attrib condition).

Pill Attrib subjects were told the following about the side effects of the placebo: "What will happen is that you may have some tremor, that is, your hand will start to shake, you will have some palpitation, that is, your heart will start to pound, and your rate of breathing may increase. Also, you will probably get a sinking feeling in the pit of your stomach, like butterflies." All of these are symptoms which were widely reported by pretest subjects who introspected about their physiological reactions to shock. To the extent that the manipulation is effective, subjects in this condition should attribute these shock-produced symptoms to the pill.

Shock Attrib subjects were told: "What will probably happen is that your feet will feel numb, you may have an itching sensation over parts of your body, and you may get a slight headache." None of these symptoms, of course, is produced either by the shock or the placebo. It seemed a distinct possibility that reeling off a list of symptoms, any symptoms, might make a subject more introspective and concerned with his bodily state. Therefore we employed this technique of "false" symptoms, rather than telling a subject that the pill would have no effects at all, as a means of making the two attribution conditions somewhat more comparable. Subjects in this condition, then, will experience the physiological symptoms produced by shock and anticipation of shock and, since no plausible alternative exists, will perforce attribute these symptoms to the shock experience.

After the 10-minute waiting period, subjects were reminded of the symptoms appropriate to their condition, and told that they were probably just starting. A second reminder immediately preceded the administration of the shock series.

In summary, there were four conditions; Hi Fear Pill Attrib, Hi Fear Shock Attrib, Lo Fear Pill Attrib, and Lo Fear Shock Attrib. There were 16 subjects in each of the Hi Fear groups and 12 in each of the Lo Fear groups. All were male volunteers from introductory psychology courses at Long Island University.

Measurement

Pain thresholds. After the 10-minute waiting period, the subject was ushered into the experimental room and introduced to a second experimenter who proceeded to apply the electrodes to the fingers of the subject's left hand, to administer the sample "standardizing" shock, and to explain the procedure to the subject. It was explained that a series of shocks would be administered and that they would progressively increase in intensity. Shocks were administered every 15 seconds and the shock proper had a duration of .10 second. Starting with a subthreshold 20 microamperes, each successive shock in the early part of the series was roughly 5–10 microamperes more intense than the preceding shock. This gap widened during the series to an average of about 100 microamperes. These intervals were determined on the basis of pretests to be subjectively equal increments. There were a total of 37 steps in the shock series, with the final step delivering 3000 microamperes of current.

Subjects were requested to report (1) when they first felt the shock (sensitivity threshold), (2) when the shock first became painful (pain threshold), and (3) when the shock was too painful to endure and they wanted it stopped (tolerance threshold).

The subjects were told that when they reached a point too painful to endure, the shocks would be terminated. If a subject endured the entire 37 steps of the series without so complaining, the experiment automatically ended after the thirty-seventh trial.

The experimenter who administered the shocks was aware of the fear condition of the subject, but was totally ignorant of his attribution condition.

Questionnaires.   In order to get measures of the effectiveness of the fear manipulation, subjects answered a questionnaire about "general physical and mental" state at the very end of the 10-minute waiting period. Embedded among a series of dummy items were two relevant scales dealing with how frightened they were about taking shock and how worried they were about the effects of the shock.

At the end of the shock series, the subjects answered a questionnaire concerned with the painfulness of the shocks, the extent to which the subject experienced the symptoms which had been described, when they occurred, and the extent to which they were attributed to the placebo.

A Note on the Noncomparability of Fear Conditions

As must be evident from the introduction to this paper, the primary interests of this study are the examination of (1) the effects of the symptom-attribution manipulation on pain, and (2) the interaction of the attribution and fear manipulations. In no sense were we directly concerned in this experiment with the effects of manipulated fear on pain. Because of these interests we deliberately sacrificed the elegance of a completely symmetrical experimental design in order to maximize the effects of the fear manipulation. For example, in the Hi Fear condition the sample shock was jolting and painful, while in the Lo Fear condition it was simply a tickly sensation. The language used in describing the various thresholds was slightly different in high and low fear conditions, e.g., for the sensitivity threshold, Lo Fear subjects were asked to note when they "first felt a tingle," while Hi Fear subjects noted when they first felt a "shock." Without question experimental touches such as these made Hi Fear subjects more fearful and Lo Fear subjects less fearful than they might otherwise have been. It is the case, however, that such variations in procedure make direct comparison of Hi and Lo Fear subjects dubious. Among other things, for example, the sample shock may have provided a different point of reference for the two groups of subjects in making judgments of pain. Similarly, describing thresholds somewhat differently to Hi and Lo Fear subjects obviously will affect threshold values. For reasons such as these direct comparison of Hi and Lo Fear conditions is meaningless, and we shall not discuss the effects of the fear manipulation on the dependent variable.

Within fear conditions, of course, the pairs of experimental conditions are identical in every respect other than the attribution manipulation.

RESULTS

The experimental test of the hypotheses requires first, the successful manipulation of fear; second, the actual production of symptoms described in the Pill Attrib condition; and, finally, the successful manipulation of attribution.

Effectiveness of fear manipulation. Evaluating first the effect of the fear manipulation, it can be seen in Table 1 that Ss in the Hi fear conditions

TABLE 1 *Mean Reported Fear and Worry Scores after Waiting Period*

CONDITION	FEAR	WORRY
Lo Fear Pill Attrib.	.46	.42
Lo Fear Shock Attrib.	.58	.31
Hi Fear Pill Attrib.	1.00	.70
Hi Fear Shock Attrib.	.92	.91
t Hi vs. Lo	2.50	2.78
p	<.02	<.01

report significantly more fear and worry after the waiting period than do subjects in the Lo Fear conditions. Means in Table 1 are for responses on four-point rating scales (0 = not at all, 3 = extremely) to the questions "How frightened are you about taking shock?" and "How worried are you about the effects of the shock?" The fear manipulation was clearly successful.

The level of physiological arousal. Table 2 presents the proportion

TABLE 2 *Proportion of Subjects Who Reported Arousal Symptoms*

CONDITION	N	% SUBJECTS REPORTING 'TRUE' SHOCK-PRODUCED SYMPTOMS
Lo Fear Pill Attrib.	12	75.0
Lo Fear Shock Attrib.	12	83.3
Hi Fear Pill Attrib.	16	75.0
Hi Fear Shock Attrib.	16	81.3
Total	56	78.6

of subjects in each condition who reported actually experiencing one or more of the symptoms (palpitation, tremor, breathing rate change, butterflies in the stomach) that we associate with receiving or anticipating shock. These data are simply tabulations of answers to the questions about each of these symptoms on the questionnaire administered at the end of the shock portion of the experimental session. There are no significant differences between conditions, and obviously the large majority of subjects in each of the conditions report experiencing one or more of the physiological symptoms associated with shock.

That subjects actually did experience these symptoms and are not simply being suggestible or accommodating is indicated by a comparison of these figures with the proportion of subjects reporting the irrelevant symptoms. While 78.6% of all subjects reported experiencing the true symptoms described in the Pill Attrib manipulation, only 21.2% of all subjects reported one or more of the "false" symptoms (itching skin, numb feet, headache) described in the Shock Attrib conditions.

Effectiveness of attribution manipulation. From their answers to the postexperimental questionnaire, most of the subjects who reported any arousal at all could be categorized as either attributing all of their symptoms to the pill or as attributing some or all of their symptoms to shock or fear. The frequencies in these categories are reported in Table 3. It can be seen

TABLE 3 *Attribution of Symptoms*

CONDITION	EXCLUSIVE ATTRIBUTION TO PLACEBO	SOME ATTRIBUTION TO SHOCK OR FEAR
Lo Fear Pill Attrib.	6	4
Lo Fear Shock Attrib.	1	7
Hi Fear Pill Attrib.	2	10
Hi Fear Shock Attrib.	1	9
COMPARISON	p [a]	
Lo PA vs. Hi PA	.05	
Lo PA vs. Hi SA	.03	
Lo PA vs. Lo SA	.05	
Lo PA vs. All Others	.01	

Note. Entries are the number of subjects with the designated attribution. The total for each condition is less than the number of subjects in the condition because some subjects reported no symptoms or could not be categorized as to attribution.

[a] p values are Fisher's exact p.

that in Lo Fear conditions the manipulation has worked. Some 60% of the Pill Attrib subjects attribute their symptoms to the pill, while only one of eight Shock Attrib subjects do so. Where the shock is presumed to be mild and harmless, the subjects accept the immediately provided explanation and attribute the shock-induced symptoms to the pill rather than the shock. In marked contrast, the overwhelming majority of Hi Fear subjects, regardless of attribution condition, attribute their symptoms to the shock. This, of course, is precisely what was anticipated, for the Hi Fear conditions were deliberately made as frightening as possible in order to provide subjects with a plausible alternative explanation for their bodily state. Obviously the intensity of the Hi Fear manipulation has made it more plausible for subjects in these conditions to attribute their arousal to shock or fear than to the pill.

Clearly, the experimental conditions necessary to test the hypotheses have been established. The subjects actually experienced symptoms of physiological arousal, the manipulation of fear was successful, and the attribution of symptoms conforms to the manipulations in the Lo Fear and not in the Hi Fear condition.

Effect of the manipulation on tolerance of shock. Our formulation of the pain experience as, in part, a function of the intensity of arousal symptoms and of the attribution of these symptoms leads us to expect, first, that the attribution manipulation will have effects only in the Lo Fear conditions, and second, that these effects will be manifested only when arousal symptoms are prominent. In Lo Fear conditions, then, we should anticipate marked differences in Tolerance Threshold, for at this point of "unbearableness" the arousal symptoms produced by shock and anticipation are undoubtedly at a maximum. In contrast, the attribution manipulation should have no effect on Sensitivity Threshold, for this is the point at which subjects first report that they are aware of some (nonpainful) sensation, and shock-produced arousal symptoms are nil. The effects on Pain Threshold should depend on the extent to which this "first sign of pain" is arousing. A low intensity pain is considerably less autonomically arousing (Valins, 1965) than is an intense pain. We should, then, expect the attribution manipulation to have relatively small effects on Pain Threshold. In Hi Fear, on the other hand, there should be no difference between the attribution conditions on any of the thresholds.

The extent to which the data support these expectations can be evaluated in Table 4, which presents the means for each of these thresholds. The figures in this table represent the average step in the series of 37 increasingly intense shocks at which subjects reported that they had reached a particular threshold. It can be seen that in the Lo Fear conditions, as anticipated, there is no difference in Sensitivity Threshold, a small difference in Pain Threshold, and a marked and extremely large difference in Tolerance Threshold. Translating these steps into amperage, the average Pill Attribution subject was able to tolerate 1450 microamperes while the Shock Attribution subjects found 350 microamperes, on the average, intolerable.

TABLE 4 *Mean Shock Thresholds*

CONDITIONS	SENSITIVITY THRESHOLD	PAIN THRESHOLD	TOLERANCE THRESHOLD
Lo Fear Pill Attrib.	4.58	11.58	25.75
Lo Fear Shock Attrib.	4.58	8.00	15.75
t	0	1.55	2.90
p	n.s.	n.s.	$<.01$
Hi Fear Pill Attrib.	5.44	15.06	26.31
Hi Fear Shock Attrib.	5.13	19.31	28.19
t	.63	1.47	0.59
p	n.s.	n.s.	n.s.

Obviously, the attribution of shock-produced symptoms to the pill has had a profound effect on the subject's ability or willingness to withstand pain.

In Hi Fear conditions pill and shock attribution subjects are similar on all three thresholds. As shown previously, the Hi Fear manipulation was successful enough to compel almost all of these subjects to attribute their symptoms to being shocked, and they behaved accordingly.

Testing the Fear × Attribution interaction, on the Pain Threshold an interaction t test yields $t = 2.01$ with $p = .05$. For the Tolerance Threshold, the interaction $t = 2.52$ with $p < .02$. The attribution manipulation affects the willingness to withstand pain only in the Lo Fear conditions.

In addition to these differences in tolerance of pain, there is evidence that the Lo Fear Pill Attrib subjects consciously experienced less pain than subjects in other conditions. On the post-experiment questionnaire, subjects were asked how painful they found the last shock they were willing to endure. The means for these responses are presented in Table 5. It can be seen

TABLE 5 *Mean Reported Pain of Last Shock*

CONDITION	PAIN
Lo Fear Pill Attrib.	1.37
Lo Fear Shock Attrib.	1.79
Hi Fear Pill Attrib.	2.16
Hi Fear Shock Attrib.	1.86

	t	p
Lo PA vs. All others	2.34	$<.05$

that the Lo Fear Pill Attrib subjects reported less pain than any of the other groups, despite the fact that they actually tolerated as much shock as subjects in any other group. A comparison of the mean for the Lo Fear Pill Attrib group vs. all other groups yields a t of 2.34 that is significant beyond the .05 level.

Finally, the categorization of subjects, in Table 3, into those who attributed their symptoms to the shock or fear vs. those who attributed their symptoms exclusively to the drug, suggests another means of analyzing the data. To the extent that subjects in any condition attributed their symptoms to the drug, they should have behaved like subjects in the Lo Fear Pill Attrib condition. If the tolerance threshold scores of the ten subjects in Table 2 who attributed their symptoms to the pill are contrasted with those of the thirty subjects who attributed their symptoms mainly to fear or the shock, it is found that four of the ten subjects in the former category were willing to take more shock than the shock apparatus could deliver, while this was true of none of the thirty subjects in the latter category. This difference is significant at the .003 level by Fisher's exact test. Further, the mean reported pain of the last shock for the pill-attributers is 1.53 and that for the shock-or-fear-attributers is 2.16. This difference yields a t of 2.83, which is significant beyond the .01 level.

The gist of the data is clear. Where subjects attribute shock-produced autonomic symptoms to the pill, they tolerate far more shock and report considerably less pain than when they attribute these symptoms to the shock proper. Earlier studies have demonstrated the cognitive manipulability of bodily states produced by the injection of epinephrine. The present study demonstrates that, within the limits of plausibility, the labeling of naturally occurring bodily states is similarly manipulable.

References

Latané, B., and Schachter, S. Adrenalin and avoidance learning. *Journal of Comparative and Physiological Psychology,* 1962, *65,* 369–372.

Schachter, S. The interaction of cognitive and physiological determinants of emotional state. In P. H. Leiderman and D. Shapiro (Eds.), *Psychobiological approaches to social behavior.* Stanford, Calif.: Stanford Univer. Press, 1964. Pp. 138–173.

Schachter, S., and Singer, J. Cognitive, social and physiological determinants of emotional state. *Psychological Review,* 1962, *69,* 379–399.

Schachter, S., and Wheeler, L. Epinephrine, chlorpromazine and amusement. *Journal of Abnormal and Social Psychology,* 1962, *65,* 121–128.

Singer, J. E. Sympathetic activation, drugs and fright. *Journal of Comparative and Physiological Psychology,* 1963, *56,* 612–615.

Valins, S. Emotionality and autonomic reactivity. Unpublished doctoral dissertation, Columbia University, 1964.

PART 5
Pro-and
Antisocial Behavior

The articles in this section deal with three related issues: antisocial or harmful behavior, pro-social or helpful behavior, and prejudice.

Social scientists have long been concerned with the questions of aggression and competition, perhaps because the world wars fostered a horror of war, and have suggested that future wars might have to be prevented by psychology, rather than by political maneuvering.

One approach to this research has been to provide subjects with the opportunity to be aggressive toward another person and to examine the conditions that increase or decrease this aggression. Two of the articles reprinted here illustrate the findings in this area. Milgram (1963) found that, when ordered to act in an aggressive manner, many subjects would do as they were told to do. Epstein (1966) found that the race of the model and the subject's personality characteristics are both important variables in determining imitation of an aggressive model.

A second approach to this research has been to ask subjects to play "games" in the laboratory, and to observe the conditions under which they are cooperative rather than competitive. However, one conclusion that has generally been reached is that American subjects do tend to be competitive, even when the situation of the game is such that they decrease their winnings by this strategy. Also, research has indicated that a cooperative strategy by a partner does not necessarily produce reciprocal cooperation but on the other hand, that subjects who are instructed to win as much for both themselves *and* their partners as possible are more cooperative than subjects who are instructed to win as much for themselves as possible. (The reader will find a summary and critique of this research in an article by Nemeth, 1972.)

On the other side of the coin, in the 1960s and 1970s, social scientists have broadened their rather one-sided concern with antisocial behavior, and have begun to look at the determinants of altruistic behavior. Two important types of situations have been examined and an example of each of these is provided here. Berkowitz (1969) has been concerned with the situation in which one person, often at little cost to himself, can help an-

209

other person who needs help. Latané and Darley (1968) have investigated the emergency situation and the reasons for the frequently noted failure to help in such situations. While the above studies are laboratory studies, two books on field studies in this area are recommended to the reader: Bickman and Henchy (1972), and Macaulay and Berkowitz (1970).

The third area of research included in this section, that relating to prejudice and intergroup hostility, might have turned up as well in the social perception section or in the section on the individual in the group. However, it has been included here since prejudice could be termed harmful behavior, and since many of the variables operating to determine aggression, such as personality and the presence of a model, no doubt also determine stereotyping and discrimination. The articles reprinted here, Sigall and Page (1971), and Sherif (1958), discuss the existence of stereotypes today, and a possible means for the reduction of intergroup hostility. Together with articles in other parts of this book (for instance, Hraba and Grant, 1970), they provoke interesting thoughts on where we are in black-white relations today and where we should or may be going.

References

Berkowitz, L. Resistance to improper dependency relationships. *Journal of Experimental Social Psychology*, 1969, *5*, 283–294.

Bickman, L., & Henchy, T. (Eds.) *Beyond the laboratory: field research in social psychology*. New York: McGraw-Hill, 1972.

Epstein, R. Aggression toward outgroups as a function of authoritarianism and imitation of aggressive models. *Journal of Personality and Social Psychology*, 1963, *67*, 371–378.

Hraba, J., & Grant, G. Black is beautiful: a reexamination of racial preference and identification. *Journal of Personality and Social Psychology*, 1970, *16*, 398–402.

Latané, B., & Darley, J. M. Group inhibition of bystander intervention in emergencies. *Journal of Personality and Social Psychology*, 1968, *10*, 215–221.

Macaulay, J., & Berkowitz, L. *Altruism and helping behavior*. New York: Academic Press, 1970.

Milgram, S. Behavioral study of obedience. *Journal of Abnormal and Social Psychology*, 1963, *67*, 371–378.

Nemeth, C. A critical analysis of research utilizing the prisoner's dilemma paradigm for the study of bargaining. In Berkowitz, L. (Ed.) *Advances in experimental social psychology*. Vol. 6. New York: Academic Press, 1972.

Sherif, M. Superordinate goals in the reduction of intergroup conflicts. *American Journal of Sociology*, 1958, *63*, 349–356.

Sigall, H., & Page, R. Current stereotypes: a little fading, a little faking. *Journal of Personality and Social Psychology*, 1971, *18*, 247–255.

Foreword to Reading 5.1

INTRODUCTION

The research conducted by Milgram is relevant to two questions in social psychology. One is the question of social influence. Milgram's studies have investigated the conditions under which a person will obey an order from another. The other is the question of aggression or harmful behavior. In Milgram's studies, the subjects have been ordered to deliver electric shocks to a person who has done them no harm.

You will note that Milgram compares his obedience situation to the one in Nazi Germany during World War II. Later authors (Baumrind, 1964) objected to this analogy. You might keep in mind that an experimental *analogy* is only that, never intended or expected to be an exact replica. Also, while the results here may not be relevant to all situations, they may be applicable to settings like the experiment (e.g., military, job, and even school settings), in which one tends to do as one is told.

METHOD

Since the method is described both in the introduction, and, in more detail, in the procedure, it is likely to be clear to the reader. Very briefly, the subjects were told that they were to act as "teachers" in a study of how people learn, and would have to administer electric shock to a "learner" whenever he made an error in a learning task.

Several points of interest, other than those noted by Milgram (in the introduction and discussion), may be observed. First, the subjects represented a wide spectrum of ages and occupations, thereby making this experiment more readily generalizable to various populations than the usual social psychological study. On the other hand, the volunteer nature of the subjects' participation could indicate that as a group they were unusually compliant, or hung-up, or socially responsible, or whatever.

The reader is advised to read the procedure carefully, and to consider for himself the various sources of what proved to be extreme pressure toward obedience (for instance, note the prods of the experimenter).

RESULTS AND DISCUSSION

Twenty-six out of 45 subjects (approximately 60 percent) were fully obedient and administered the most severe shock to the learner. Many subjects displayed extreme emotional tension, and yet proceeded with the experiment, even though Yale seniors and others had predicted that very little obedience would occur.

As pointed out by Milgram, there are a number of features in this experiment which tended to promote obedience. Some of these were investigated in later research (Milgram, 1965). For instance, in one variation, the experiment was carried out in an office building in Bridgeport, Connecticut, rather than a laboratory at Yale University. The firm conducting the research was said to be the Bridgeport Research Associates, "a private firm conducting research for industry." In all, the authority demanding obedience was presumably (there was no direct check on this) less legitimate than in the 1963 experiment. However, although there was some decrease in obedience (obedience level was 48 percent), the difference between the two experiments was not statistically significant.

In a second variation, "closeness of authority" was manipulated. There were three conditions. In one, the experimenter was present during the experiment (as in the reprinted article); in a second, the experimenter left the laboratory after giving initial instructions, but kept in touch by telephone; in a third, all instructions were provided by means of a tape recording. It was found that obedience dropped approximately two-thirds (from 60 percent) when the experimenter was present only by virtue of the telephone. Moreover, when the experimenter was not present during the experiment, many of the subjects repeatedly used the lowest shock on the board, while assuring the experimenter that they were following instructions to escalate the shocks.

In a third variation, "proximity of the victim" was manipulated. In one condition, much like that of the study reported here, the victim could not be seen or heard by the subject, until at 300 volts, he pounded on the wall in protest. He then gave no further answers after that point. In this condition, approximately 66 percent of the subjects were fully obedient. In a second condition, the learner's distress signals were more elaborate. At 75, 90, and 105 volts, he moaned and groaned. At 120 volts he shouted that the shocks were becoming painful, and continued to groan pitifully at 135 volts. At 150 volts, the learner cried to the experimenter to be let out. At 180 volts, he shouted that the pain was unbearable. At 270, he uttered an inarticulate, agonized scream. At 300 and 315 volts, he shouted that he would give no further answers, and from that point on, the subjects received no response other than an occasional shriek of pain. In this condition, approximately 62 percent of the subjects were fully obedient. In yet another condition, the victim was in the same room as the subject, and, at a predetermined time, removed his hand from the shockplate; the experimenter then ordered the subject to replace it. Under these circumstances, obedience was markedly decreased, but even here, one-third of the subjects obeyed the experimenter all the way and gave the highest shock.

Psychologists other than Milgram have now concerned themselves with problems related to that of obedience. Kaufmann (1968) has conducted research on the probability that a bystander (a third person asked to perform tasks other than shocking the victim) would intervene and stop the experiment. Few of the bystanders persisted in protesting the experiment. One might wonder what personal qualities or experiences made these few individuals so unusual. Larsen, Coleman, Forbes, and Johnson (1972) have found little relationship between a number of personality variables and willingness to administer shock.

Actually, the extent of further research on the shock and learning situation has been curtailed by a rash of criticism of the procedure. As a prime example, Diana Baumrind suggested that not only is it ungeneralizable, but also unethical. Certainly, one might agree that some subjects were given new and unpleasant insights into themselves, as well as feeling some resentment at the deception. However, in the 1965 article, and in his reply to Baumrind (Milgram, 1964), Milgram deflects some of the criticism by describing his careful treatment of the subjects. After the experiment, each subject was carefully debriefed. Not only did the subject have an "extended" discussion with the experimenter, but also a "friendly reconciliation" with the victim. A questionnaire mailed to the subjects after the experimental series had been completed indicated that most of the subjects were happy to have participated, and felt that more such experiments should be carried out. Moreover, a university psychiatrist who interviewed a sample of the subjects reported no ill effects.

Also, apropos of criticism of Milgram, it is interesting to note that other psychologists (see e.g., Epstein, 1966, in this volume) using essentially the same procedure as Milgram, have not been criticized or even noticed to the same extent. As Milgram himself (1964) has suggested, perhaps his threatening and unexpected results had as much to do with the public reaction as the procedure employed.

References

Baumrind, D. Some thoughts on ethics of research: after reading Milgram's behavioral study of obedience. *American Psychologist,* 1964, *19,* 421–423.

Epstein, R. Aggression toward outgroups as a function of authoritarianism and imitation of aggressive models. *Journal of Personality and Social Psychology,* 1966, *3,* 574–579.

Kaufmann, H. The unconcerned bystander. In Proceedings of the Annual Convention of the American Psychological Association, 1968.

Larsen, K. S., Coleman, D., Forbes, J., & Johnson, R. Is the subject's personality or the experimental situation a better predictor of a subject's willingness to administer shock to a victim? *Journal of Personality and Social Psychology,* 1972, *22,* 287–295.

Milgram, S. Issues in the study of obedience. *American Psychologist,* 1964, *19,* 848–852.

Milgram, S. Some conditions of obedience and disobedience to authority. *Human Relations,* 1965, *18,* 57–76.

5.1 Behavioral Study of Obedience[1]

Stanley Milgram[2]

This article describes a procedure for the study of destructive obedience in the laboratory. It consists of ordering a naive S to administer increasingly more severe punishment to a victim in the context of a learning experiment. Punishment is administered by means of a shock generator with 30 graded switches ranging from Slight Shock to Danger: Severe Shock. The victim is a confederate of the E. The primary dependent variable is the maximum shock the S is willing to administer before he refuses to continue further. 26 Ss obeyed the experimental commands fully, and administered the highest shock on the generator. 14 Ss broke off the experiment at some point after the victim protested and refused to provide further answers. The procedure created extreme levels of nervous tension in some Ss. Profuse sweating, trembling, and stuttering were typical expressions of this emotional disturbance. One unexpected sign of tension—yet to be explained—was the regular occurrence of nervous laughter, which in some Ss developed into uncontrollable seizures. The variety of interesting behavioral dynamics observed in the experiment, the reality of the situation for the S, and the possibility of parametric variation within the framework of the procedure, point to the fruitfulness of further study.

Obedience is as basic an element in the structure of social life as one can point to. Some system of authority is a requirement of all communal living, and it is only the man dwelling in isolation who is not forced to respond, through defiance or submission, to the commands of others. Obedience, as a determinant of behavior, is of particular relevance to our time. It has been reliably established that from 1933–45 millions of innocent persons were systematically slaughtered on command. Gas chambers were built, death camps were guarded, daily quotas of corpses were produced with the same efficiency as the manufacture of appliances. These inhumane policies may have originated in the mind of a single person, but they could only be carried out on a massive scale if a very large number of persons obeyed orders.

Obedience is the psychological mechanism that links individual action to political purpose. It is the dispositional cement that binds men to sys-

Reprinted from the *Journal of Abnormal and Social Psychology*, 1963, *67*, 371–378. Copyright 1963 by the American Psychological Association and reproduced with permission.

[1] This research was supported by a grant (NSF G-17916) from the National Science Foundation. Exploratory studies conducted in 1960 were supported by a grant from the Higgins Fund at Yale University. The research assistance of Alan C. Elms and Jon Wayland is gratefully acknowledged.

tems of authority. Facts of recent history and observation in daily life suggest that for many persons obedience may be a deeply ingrained behavior tendency, indeed, a prepotent impulse overriding training in ethics, sympathy, and moral conduct. C. P. Snow (1961) points to its importance when he writes:

> When you think of the long and gloomy history of man, you will find more hideous crimes have been committed in the name of obedience than have ever been committed in the name of rebellion. If you doubt that, read William Shirer's "Rise and Fall of the Third Reich." The German Officer Corps were brought up in the most rigorous code of obedience . . . in the name of obedience they were party to, and assisted in, the most wicked large scale actions in the history of the world [p. 24].

While the particular form of obedience dealt with in the present study has its antecedents in these episodes, it must not be thought all obedience entails acts of aggression against others. Obedience serves numerous productive functions. Indeed, the very life of society is predicated on its existence. Obedience may be ennobling and educative and refer to acts of charity and kindness, as well as to destruction.

General Procedure

A procedure was devised which seems useful as a tool for studying obedience (Milgram, 1961). It consists of ordering a naive subject to administer electric shock to a victim. A simulated shock generator is used, with 30 clearly marked voltage levels that range from 15 to 450 volts. The instrument bears verbal designations that range from Slight Shock to Danger: Severe Shock. The responses of the victim, who is a trained confederate of the experimenter, are standardized. The orders to administer shocks are given to the naive subject in the context of a "learning experiment" ostensibly set up to study the effects of punishment on memory. As the experiment proceeds the naive subject is commanded to administer increasingly more intense shocks to the victim, even to the point of reaching the level marked Danger: Severe Shock. Internal resistances become stronger, and at a certain point the subject refuses to go on with the experiment. Behavior prior to this rupture is considered "obedience," in that the subject complies with the commands of the experimenter. The point of rupture is the act of disobedience. A quantitative value is assigned to the subject's performance based on the maximum intensity shock he is willing to administer before he refuses to participate further. Thus for any particular subject and for any particular experimental condition the degree of obedience may be specified with a numerical value. The crux of the study is to systematically vary the factors believed to alter the degree of obedience to the experimental commands.

The technique allows important variables to be manipulated at several points in the experiment. One may vary aspects of the source of command, content and form of command, instrumentalities for its execution, target object, general social setting, etc. The problem, therefore, is not one of designing increasingly more numerous experimental conditions, but of selecting those that best illuminate the *process* of obedience from the sociopsychological standpoint.

Related Studies

The inquiry bears an important relation to philosophic analyses of obedience and authority (Arendt, 1958; Friedrich, 1958; Weber, 1947), an early experimental study of obedience by Frank (1944), studies in "authoritarianism" (Adorno, Frenkel-Brunswik, Levinson, & Sanford, 1950; Rokeach, 1961), and a recent series of analytic and empirical studies in social power (Cartwright, 1959). It owes much to the long concern with *suggestion* in social psychology, both in its normal forms (e.g., Binet, 1900) and in its clinical manifestations (Charcot, 1881). But it derives, in the first instance, from direct observation of a social fact; the individual who is commanded by a legitimate authority ordinarily obeys. Obedience comes easily and often. It is a ubiquitous and indispensable feature of social life.

METHOD

Subjects

The subjects were 40 males between the ages of 20 and 50, drawn from New Haven and the surrounding communities. Subjects were obtained by a newspaper advertisement and direct mail solicitation. Those who responded to the appeal believed they were to participate in a study of memory and learning at Yale University. A wide range of occupations is represented in the sample. Typical subjects were postal clerks, high school teachers, salesmen, engineers, and laborers. Subjects ranged in educational level from one who had not finished elementary school, to those who had doctorate and other professional degrees. They were paid $4.50 for their participation in the experiment. However, subjects were told that payment was simply for coming to the laboratory, and that the money was theirs no matter what happened after they arrived. Table 1 shows the proportion of age and occupational types assigned to the experimental condition.

Personnel and Locale

The experiment was conducted on the grounds of Yale University in the elegant interaction laboratory. (This detail is relevant to the perceived legitimacy of the experiment. In further variations, the experiment was dis-

TABLE 1 *Distribution of Age and Occupational Types in the Experiment*

OCCUPATIONS	20–29 YEARS n	30–39 YEARS n	40–50 YEARS n	PERCENTAGE OF TOTAL (OCCUPATIONS)
Workers, skilled and unskilled	4	5	6	37.5
Sales, business, and white-collar	3	6	7	40.0
Professional	1	5	3	22.5
Percentage of total (Age)	20	40	40	

Note.—Total $N = 40$.

sociated from the university, with consequences for performance.) The role of experimenter was played by a 31-year-old high school teacher of biology. His manner was impassive, and his appearance somewhat stern throughout the experiment. He was dressed in a gray technician's coat. The victim was played by a 47-year-old accountant, trained for the role; he was of Irish-American stock, whom most observers found mild-mannered and likable.

Procedure

One naive subject and one victim (an accomplice) performed in each experiment. A pretext had to be devised that would justify the administration of electric shock by the naive subject. This was effectively accomplished by the cover story. After a general introduction on the presumed relation between punishment and learning, subjects were told:

But actually, we know *very little* about the effect of punishment on learning, because almost no truly scientific studies have been made of it in human beings.

For instance, we don't know how *much* punishment is best for learning— and we don't know how much difference it makes as to who is giving the punishment, whether an adult learns best from a younger or an older person than himself—or many things of that sort.

So in this study we are bringing together a number of adults of different occupations and ages. And we're asking some of them to be teachers and some of them to be learners.

We want to find out just what effect different people have on each other as teachers and learners, and also what effect *punishment* will have on learning in this situation.

Therefore, I'm going to ask one of you to be the teacher here tonight and the other one to be the learner.

Does either of you have a preference?

Subjects then drew slips of paper from a hat to determine who would be the teacher and who would be the learner in the experiment. The drawing was rigged so that the naive subject was always the teacher and the accomplice always the learner. (Both slips contained the word "Teacher.") Immediately after the drawing, the teacher and learner were taken to an adjacent room and the learner was strapped into an "electric chair" apparatus.

The experimenter explained that the straps were to prevent excessive movement while the learner was being shocked. The effect was to make it impossible for him to escape from the situation. An electrode was attached to the learner's wrist, and electrode paste was applied "to avoid blisters and burns." Subjects were told that the electrode was attached to the shock generator in the adjoining room.

In order to improve credibility the experimenter declared, in response to a question by the learner: "Although the shocks can be extremely painful, they cause no permanent tissue damage."

Learning task. The lesson administered by the subject was a paired-associate learning task. The subject read a series of word pairs to the learner, and then read the first word of the pair along with four terms. The learner was to indicate which of the four terms had originally been paired with the first word. He communicated his answer by pressing one of four switches in front of him, which in turn lit up one of four numbered quadrants in an answer-box located atop the shock generator.

Shock generator. The instrument panel consists of 30 lever switches set in a horizontal line. Each switch is clearly labeled with a voltage designation that ranges from 15 to 450 volts. There is a 15-volt increment from one switch to the next going from left to right. In addition, the following verbal designations are clearly indicated for groups of four switches going from left to right: Slight Shock, Moderate Shock, Strong Shock, Very Strong Shock, Intense Shock, Extreme Intensity Shock, Danger: Severe Shock. (Two switches after this last designation are simply marked XXX.)

Upon depressing a switch: a pilot light corresponding to each switch is illuminated in bright red; an electric buzzing is heard; an electric blue light, labeled "voltage energizer," flashes; the dial on the voltage meter swings to the right; various relay clicks are sounded.

The upper left-hand corner of the generator is labeled Shock Generator, Type ZLB, Dyson Instrument Company, Waltham, Mass. Output 15 Volts–450 Volts.

Details of the instrument were carefully handled to insure an appearance of authenticity. The panel was engraved by precision industrial engravers, and all components were of high quality. No subject in the experiment suspected that the instrument was merely a simulated shock generator.[2]

Sample shock. Each naive subject is given a sample shock on the shock generator, prior to beginning his run as teacher. This shock is always 45 volts, and is applied by pressing the third switch of the generator. The shock is applied to the wrist of the naive subject, and has its source in a 45-volt battery wired into the generator. This further convinces the subject of the authenticity of the generator.

[2] A related technique, making use of a shock generator, was reported by Buss (1961) for the study of aggression in the laboratory. Despite the considerable similarity of technical detail in the experimental procedures, both investigators proceeded in ignorance of the other's work. Milgram provided plans and photographs of his shock generator, experimental procedure, and first results in a report to the National Science Foundation in January 1961. This report received only limited circulation. Buss reported his procedure 6 months later, but to a wider audience. Subsequently, technical information and reports were exchanged. The present article was first received in the Editor's office on December 27, 1961; it was resubmitted with deletions on July 27, 1962.

Shock instructions. The subject is told to administer a shock to the learner each time he gives a wrong response. Moreover—and this is the key command—the subject is instructed to "move one level higher on the shock generator each time the learner flashes a wrong answer." He is also instructed to announce the voltage level before administering a shock. This serves to continually remind subjects of the increasing intensity of shocks administered to the learner.

Preliminary and regular run. Pretests revealed that the procedure of reading words and administering shocks requires some practice before it can be handled smoothly. Therefore, immediately preceding the regular run, the teacher is given a preliminary series of 10 words to read to the learner. There are 3 neutral words in the practice series (i.e., words that the learner answers correctly), so that shocks are administered for 7 of the words, with the maximum shock at 105 volts (moderate shock). Almost all subjects master the procedure by the time the preliminary run is over.

Subjects are then presented with a second list, and are told that the procedure is the same as for the first list; the experimenter adds, however:

> When you get to the bottom of the list, repeat it over again, and continue giving shocks, until the learner has learned all the pairs correctly.

The experimenter instructs the subject to,

> start from 15 volts and increase the shock level one step each time the learner gives a wrong answer.

Feedback from the victim. In all conditions the learner gives a predetermined set of responses to the word pair test, based on a schedule of approximately three wrong answers to one correct answer. In the present experimental condition no vocal response or other sign of protest is heard from the learner until Shock Level 300 is reached. When the 300-volt shock is administered, the learner pounds on the wall of the room in which he is bound to the electric chair. The pounding can be heard by the subject. From this point on, the learner's answers no longer appear on the four-way panel.

At this juncture, subjects ordinarily turn to the experimenter for guidance. The experimenter instructs the subject to treat the absence of a response as a wrong answer, and to shock the subject according to the usual schedule. He advises the subjects to allow 5–10 seconds before considering no response as a wrong answer, and to increase the shock level one step each time the learner fails to respond correctly. The learner's pounding is repeated after the 315-volt shock is administered; afterwards he is not heard from, nor do his answers reappear on the four-way signal box.

Experimenter feedback. At various points in the experiment the subject may turn to the experimenter for advice on whether he should continue to administer shocks. Or he may indicate that he does not wish to go on. It was important to standardize the experimenter's responses to these inquiries and reactions.

If the subject indicated his unwillingness to go on, the experimenter responded with a sequence of "prods," using as many as necessary to bring the subject into line.

Prod 1: Please continue. *or* Please go on.
Prod 2: The experiment requires that you continue.
Prod 3: It is absolutely essential that you continue.
Prod 4: You have no other choice, you *must* go on.

The prods were always made in sequence: Only if Prod 1 had been unsuccessful, could Prod 2 be used. If the subject refused to obey the experimenter after Prod 4, the experiment was terminated. The experimenter's tone of voice was at all times firm, but not impolite. The sequence was begun anew on each occasion that the subject balked or showed reluctance to follow orders.

Special prods. If the subject asked if the learner was liable to suffer permanent physical injury, the experimenter said:

Although the shocks may be painful, there is no permanent tissue damage, so please go on. [Followed by Prods 2, 3, and 4 if necessary.]

If the subject said that the learner did not want to go on, the experimenter replied:

Whether the learner likes it or not, you must go on until he has learned all the word pairs correctly. So please go on. [Followed by Prods 2, 3, and 4 if necessary.]

Dependent Measures

The primary dependent measure for any subject is the maximum shock he administers before he refuses to go any further. In principle this may vary from 0 (for a subject who refuses to administer even the first shock) to 30 (for a subject who administers the highest shock on the generator). A subject who breaks off the experiment at any point prior to administering the thirtieth shock level is termed a *defiant* subject. One who complies with experimental commands fully, and proceeds to administer all shock levels commanded, is termed an *obedient* subject.

Further records. With few exceptions, experimental sessions were recorded on magnetic tape. Occasional photographs were taken through one-way mirrors. Notes were kept on any unusual behavior occurring during the course of the experiments. On occasion, additional observers were directed to write objective descriptions of the subjects' behavior. The latency and duration of shocks were measured by accurate timing devices.

Interview and dehoax. Following the experiment, subjects were interviewed; open-ended questions, projective measures, and attitude scales were employed. After the interview, procedures were undertaken to assure that the subject would leave the laboratory in a state of well being. A friendly reconciliation was arranged between the subject and the victim, and an effort was made to reduce any tensions that arose as a result of the experiment.

RESULTS

Preliminary Notions

Before giving an account of the experimental results, it is instructive to consider how persons predict others will perform when commanded to administer powerful shocks to another person. Fourteen Yale seniors, all psychology majors, were provided with a detailed description of the experimental situation. They were asked to reflect carefully on it, and to predict the behavior of 100 hypothetical subjects. More specifically, they were instructed to plot the distribution of obedience of "100 Americans of diverse occupations, and ranging in age from 20 to 50 years," who were placed in the experimental situation.

There was considerable agreement among the respondents on the expected behavior of hypothetical subjects. All respondents predicted that only an insignificant minority would go through to the end of the shock series. (The estimates ranged from 0 to 3%; i.e., the most "pessimistic" member of the class predicted that of 100 persons, 3 would continue through to the most potent shock available on the shock generator—450 volts.) The class mean was 1.2%. The question was also posed informally to colleagues of the author, and the most general feeling was that few if any subjects would go beyond the designation Very Strong Shock.

Result of Experiment I

Subjects accept situation. With few exceptions subjects were convinced of the reality of the experimental situation, that they were administering shocks to another person, and the most potent shocks were extremely painful. In the post-experimental interview subjects were asked: "How painful to the learner were the last few shocks that you administered to him?" Subjects were instructed to indicate their answers on a printed 14-point scale ranging from "Not at all painful" to "Extremely painful." The modal response was 14 (Extremely painful) with the mean at 13.42.

Signs of extreme tension. Many subjects showed signs of nervousness in the experimental situation, and especially upon administering the more powerful shocks. In a large number of cases the degree of tension reached extremes that are rarely seen in sociopsychological laboratory studies. Subjects were observed to sweat, tremble, stutter, bite their lips, groan, and dig their fingernails into their flesh. These were characteristic rather than exceptional responses to the experiment.

One sign of tension was the regular occurrence of nervous laughing fits. Fourteen of the 40 subjects showed definite signs of nervous laughter and smiling. The laughter seemed entirely out of place, even bizarre. Full-blown, uncontrollable seizures were observed for 3 subjects. On one occasion we observed a seizure so violently convulsive that it was necessary to call a halt to the experiment. The subject, a 46-year-old encyclopedia salesman, was seriously embarrassed by his untoward and uncontrollable behavior. In the post-experimental interviews subjects took pains to point out that they were not sadistic types, and that the laughter did not mean they enjoyed shocking the victim.

Distribution of scores. It had been conjectured that persons would not, in general, agree to administer shocks beyond the level designated as

Very Strong Shock. The distribution of maximum shocks for this experiment is shown in Table 2. The obtained distribution of scores deviates radically from the prediction.

TABLE 2 *Distribution of Breakoff Points*

VERBAL DESIGNATION AND VOLTAGE INDICATION	NUMBER OF SUBJECTS FOR WHOM THIS WAS MAXIMUM SHOCK
Slight Shock	
15	0
30	0
45	0
60	0
Moderate Shock	
75	0
90	0
105	0
120	0
Strong Shock	
135	0
150	0
165	0
180	0
Very Strong Shock	
195	0
210	0
225	0
240	0
Intense Shock	
255	0
270	0
285	0
300	5
Extreme Intensity Shock	
315	4
330	2
345	1
360	1
Danger: Severe Shock	
375	1
390	0
405	0
420	0
XXX	
435	0
450	26

Upon command of the experimenter, each of the 40 subjects went beyond the expected breakoff point. No subject stopped prior to administering Shock Level 20. (At this level—300 volts—the victim kicks on the wall and no longer provides answers to the teacher's multiple-choice questions.)

Of the 40 subjects, 5 refused to obey the experimental commands beyond the 300-volt level. Four more subjects administered one further shock, and then refused to go on. Two broke off at the 330-volt level, and 1 each at 345, 360, and 375 volts. Thus a total of 14 subjects defied the experimenter. It is instructive to reprint their remarks at the point of defiance, as transcribed from the tape recordings:

[0124] I think he's trying to communicate, he's knocking. . . . Well it's not fair to shock the guy . . . these are terrific volts. I don't think this is very humane. . . . Oh, I can't go on with this; no, this isn't right. It's a hell of an experiment. The guy is suffering in there. No, I don't want to go on. This is crazy. [Subject refused to administer more shocks.]

[0123] He's banging in there. I'm gonna chicken out. I'd like to continue, but I can't do that to a man. . . . I'm sorry I can't do that to a man. I'll hurt his heart. You take your check. . . . No really, I couldn't do it.

These subjects were frequently in a highly agitated and even angered state. Sometimes, verbal protest was at a minimum, and the subject simply got up from his chair in front of the shock generator, and indicated that he wished to leave the laboratory.

Of the 40 subjects, 26 obeyed the orders of the experimenter to the end, proceeding to punish the victim until they reached the most potent shock available on the shock generator. At that point, the experimenter called a halt to the session. (The maximum shock is labeled 450 volts, and is two steps beyond the designation: Danger: Severe Shock.) Although obedient subjects continued to administer shocks, they often did so under extreme stress. Some expressed reluctance to administer shocks beyond the 300-volt level, and displayed fears similar to those who defied the experimenter; yet they obeyed.

After the maximum shocks had been delivered, and the experimenter called a halt to the proceedings, many obedient subjects heaved sighs of relief, mopped their brows, rubbed their fingers over their eyes, or nervously fumbled cigarettes. Some shook their heads, apparently in regret. Some subjects had remained calm throughout the experiment, and displayed only minimal signs of tension from beginning to end.

DISCUSSION

The experiment yielded two findings that were surprising. The first finding concerns the sheer strength of obedient tendencies manifested in this situation. Subjects have learned from childhood that it is a fundamental breach of moral conduct to hurt another person against his will. Yet, 26 subjects abandon this tenet in following the instructions of an authority who has no special powers to enforce his commands. To disobey would bring no material loss to the subject; no punishment would ensue. It is clear from the remarks and outward behavior of many participants that in punishing the victim they are often acting against their own values. Subjects often expressed deep disapproval of shocking a man in the face of his objections, and others denounced it as stupid and senseless. Yet the majority complied with the experimental commands. This outcome was surprising from two perspectives: first, from the standpoint of predictions made in the questionnaire described earlier. (Here, however, it is possible that the remoteness of the respondents from the actual situation, and the difficulty of conveying to them the concrete details of the experiment, could account for the serious underestimation of obedience.)

But the results were also unexpected to persons who observed the experiment in progress, through one-way mirrors. Observers often uttered expressions of disbelief upon seeing a subject administer more powerful shocks to the victim. These persons had a full acquaintance with the details of the situation, and yet systematically underestimated the amount of obedience that subjects would display.

The second unanticipated effect was the extraordinary tension generated by the procedures. One might suppose that a subject would simply break off or continue as his conscience dictated. Yet, this is very far from what happened. There were striking reactions of tension and emotional strain. One observer related:

> I observed a mature and initially poised businessman enter the laboratory smiling and confident. Within 20 minutes he was reduced to a twitching, stuttering wreck, who was rapidly approaching a point of nervous collapse. He constantly pulled on his earlobe, and twisted his hands. At one point he pushed his fist into his forehead and muttered: "Oh God, let's stop it." And yet he continued to respond to every word of the experimenter, and obeyed to the end.

Any understanding of the phenomenon of obedience must rest on an analysis of the particular conditions in which it occurs. The following features of the experiment go some distance in explaining the high amount of obedience observed in the situation.

1. The experiment is sponsored by and takes place on the grounds of an institution of unimpeachable reputation, Yale University. It may be reasonably presumed that the personnel are competent and reputable. The importance of this background authority is now being studied by conducting a series of experiments outside of New Haven, and without any visible ties to the university.

2. The experiment is, on the face of it, designed to attain a worthy

purpose—advancement of knowledge about learning and memory. Obedience occurs not as an end in itself, but as an instrumental element in a situation that the subject construes as significant, and meaningful. He may not be able to see its full significance, but he may properly assume that the experimenter does.

3. The subject perceives that the victim has voluntarily submitted to the authority system of the experimenter. He is not (at first) an unwilling captive impressed for involuntary service. He has taken the trouble to come to the laboratory presumably to aid the experimental research. That he later becomes an involuntary subject does not alter the fact that, initially, he consented to participate without qualification. Thus he has in some degree incurred an obligation toward the experimenter.

4. The subject, too, has entered the experiment voluntarily, and perceives himself under obligation to aid the experimenter. He has made a commitment, and to disrupt the experiment is a repudiation of this initial promise of aid.

5. Certain features of the procedure strengthen the subject's sense of obligation to the experimenter. For one, he has been paid for coming to the laboratory. In part this is canceled out by the experimenter's statement that:

> Of course, as in all experiments, the money is yours simply for coming to the laboratory. From this point on, no matter what happens, the money is yours.[3]

6. From the subject's standpoint, the fact that he is the teacher and the other man the learner is purely a chance consequence (it is determined by drawing lots) and he, the subject, ran the same risk as the other man in being assigned the role of learner. Since the assignment of positions in the experiment was achieved by fair means, the learner is deprived of any basis of complaint on this count. (A similar situation obtains in Army units, in which—in the absence of volunteers—a particularly dangerous mission may be assigned by drawing lots, and the unlucky soldier is expected to bear his misfortune with sportsmanship.)

7. There is, at best, ambiguity with regard to the prerogatives of a psychologist and the corresponding rights of his subject. There is a vagueness of expectation concerning what a psychologist may require of his subject, and when he is overstepping acceptable limits. Moreover, the experiment occurs in a closed setting, and thus provides no opportunity for the subject to remove these ambiguities by discussion with others. There are few standards that seem directly applicable to the situation, which is a novel one for most subjects.

---

[3] Forty-three subjects, undergraduates at Yale University, were run in the experiment without payment. The results are very similar to those obtained with paid subjects.

8. The subjects are assured that the shocks administered to the subject are "painful but not dangerous." Thus they assume that the discomfort caused the victim is momentary, while the scientific gains resulting from the experiment are enduring.

9. Through Shock Level 20 the victim continues to provide answers on the signal box. The subject may construe this as a sign that the victim is still willing to "play the game." It is only after Shock Level 20 that the victim repudiates the rules completely, refusing to answer further.

These features help to explain the high amount of obedience obtained in this experiment. Many of the arguments raised need not remain matters of speculation, but can be reduced to testable propositions to be confirmed or disproved by further experiments.[4]

The following features of the experiment concern the nature of the conflict which the subject faces.

10. The subject is placed in a position in which he must respond to the competing demands of two persons: the experimenter and the victim. The conflict must be resolved by meeting the demands of one or the other; satisfaction of the victim and the experimenter are mutually exclusive. Moreover, the resolution must take the form of a highly visible action, that of continuing to shock the victim or breaking off the experiment. Thus the subject is forced into a public conflict that does not permit any completely satisfactory solution.

11. While the demands of the experimenter carry the weight of scientific authority, the demands of the victim spring from his personal experience of pain and suffering. The two claims need not be regarded as equally pressing and legitimate. The experimenter seeks an abstract scientific datum; the victim cries out for relief from physical suffering caused by the subject's actions.

12. The experiment gives the subject little time for reflection. The conflict comes on rapidly. It is only minutes after the subject has been seated before the shock generator that the victim begins his protests. Moreover, the subject perceives that he has gone through but two-thirds of the shock levels at the time the subject's first protests are heard. Thus he understands that the conflict will have a persistent aspect to it, and may well become more intense as increasingly more powerful shocks are required. The rapidity with which the conflict descends on the subject, and his realization that it is predictably recurrent may well be sources of tension to him.

13. At a more general level, the conflict stems from the opposition of two deeply ingrained behavior dispositions: first, the disposition not to harm other people, and second, the tendency to obey those whom we perceive to be legitimate authorities.

---

[4] A series of recently completed experiments employing the obedience paradigm is reported in Milgram (1964).

References

Adorno, T., Frenkel-Brunswik, Else, Levinson, D. J., & Sanford, R. N. *The authoritarian personality*. New York: Harper & Row, 1950.

Arendt, H. What was authority? In C. J. Friedrich (Ed.), *Authority*. Cambridge: Harvard University Press, 1958. Pp. 81–112.

Binet, A. *La suggestibilité*. Paris: Schleicher, 1900.

Buss, A. H. *The psychology of aggression*. New York: Wiley, 1961.

Cartwright, S. (Ed.) *Studies in social power*. Ann Arbor: University of Michigan Institute for Social Research, 1959.

Charcot, J. M. *Oeuvres complètes*. Paris: Bureaux du Progrès Médical, 1881.

Frank, J. D. Experimental studies of personal pressure and resistance. *Journal of general psychology* 1944, *30*, 23–64.

Friedrich, C. J. (Ed.) *Authority*. Cambridge: Harvard University Press, 1958.

Milgram, S. Dynamics of obedience. Washington: National Science Foundation, 25, January 1961. (Mimeo)

Milgram, S. Some conditions of obedience and disobedience to authority. *Human Relations*, 1964, in press.

Rokeach, M. Authority, authoritarianism, and conformity. In I. A. Berg & B. M. Bass (Eds.), *Conformity and deviation*. New York: Harper & Row, 1961. Pp. 230–257.

Snow, C. P. Either-or. *Progressive*, 1961 (Feb.), 24.

Weber, M. *The theory of social and economic organization*. Oxford: Oxford University Press, 1947.

Foreword to Reading 5.2

INTRODUCTION

Two clues may be most important in predicting the occurrence of any behavior: one is the possibility of reward and punishment, the other the presence of a model. A child may learn a new behavior simply by observing it performed by others. An older child or an adult (knowing the behavior) may copy others, either because he wishes to conform and behave properly, or because behavior from which he might otherwise be inhibited (such as aggression) does not appear to be censured in a particular situation since the model was not punished for it (see Grusec, 1972, in this volume).

Epstein suggests that there are other factors important in the prediction of hostile behavior against "outgroups," for instance the characteristics of the model and the personality of the observer. As far as the model is concerned, Epstein investigated the effect of the race and socioeconomic status of the model. With regard to the observer, the personality trait that Epstein chose for study is known as "authoritarianism." The "F" scale or measure of authoritarianism was designed by Adorno et al. (1950) to test for the personality type underlying attitudes of anti-Semitism, ethnocentrism, and political conservatism. The F scale items were chosen to correlate with scores on the latter three attitude scales (supposedly indicators for "Fascist" traits). Roger Brown (1965) describes the F scale as a measure of a tendency to put one's faith in authority, rather than logic or science. And we all know people who tend to approach most issues in this way. Brown reports evidence that the parents of prejudiced and authoritarian people are status-oriented, and harsh and punitive toward their children. The originators of the F scale interpreted this as indicating that harsh parental treatment induces children to repress or deny their hostilities in order to protect themselves from punishment. These repressed hostilities then vent themselves in prejudice and ethnocentrism. A less psychoanalytic or Freudian interpretation would be that harsh parents are actually rewarding the child for conformity or obedience. As a conformist, the child falls in with what he sees as the prejudiced norm of his society.

METHOD

One hundred and forty-four white, male subjects were administered the F scale. Then, it seems that the group was divided into thirds on the basis of the scores, the highest and lowest third being employed in the study.

The method used is similar to that of Milgram (1963, in this volume). Subjects were told that the study was concerned with the effect of shock upon learning. Each subject played the part of a "teacher" and chose the level of shock to be given to a "learner" after the learner had made errors in a learning task. Before playing the part of the teacher, each subject also saw a "model," presumably another subject, act as the teacher and choose high levels of shock. In all cases, the victim was a black person; the model was either a white person or a black person, and described himself as being of either high status or low status.

RESULTS AND DISCUSSION

As the reader will see, all of the predictions, with the exception of the one concerning social class, received at least some level of confirmation. Epstein suggests that this research has implications for the relationship between prejudice and discrimination. For instance, low authoritarians, on the average, administered lower levels of shock than high authoritarians. This may support the hypothesis that high authoritarians are not only more hostile than low, but also more conforming. (Further study with a "no-model" control group would be necessary to confirm this hypothesis.) The results also indicated that a black model induced more aggression from the subjects than a white model. This finding is contrary to other research indicating that models similar to the subject are imitated more than models dissimilar to the subject (e.g., Hornstein, Fisch, and Holmes, 1968). Epstein suggests that the finding indicates that dissension within an out-group prompts aggression from those who are prejudiced against that group. Finally, the results of the study indicated that race of the model and personality of the subject interact; however, this result fell short of statistical significance, and so must be viewed as a tentative one.

More recently, a procedure similar to the one reported here has been used to show additional variables predicting hostility toward outgroups. Donnerstein et al. (1972) found that white subjects exhibited less "direct" aggression toward black victims when they had reason to fear retaliation either during the experiment or after it than when retaliation was not possible. Aggression against white victims was not affected by possible retaliation by the victim, indicating that white persons fear blacks and act accordingly. However, it also appeared that this might not act to inhibit discrimination. When there was little "direct" aggression against the black victims, there was "indirect" aggression instead, and "direct" aggression showed an increase after a racial incident on the campus.

In forming his own ideas on this subject, the reader might be wary of making over-generalizations. The subjects in both studies were college males; no females or older persons have been utilized as subjects, and, as far as the editors are aware, there has been no investigation of behavior of blacks toward whites or of whites toward other minority groups.

References

Adorno, T. W., Frenkel-Brunswik, E., Levinson, D., & Sanford, R. N. *The authoritarian personality*. New York: Harper & Row, 1950.

Brown, R. *Social psychology*. New York: Free Press, 1965.

Donnerstein, E., Donnerstein, M., Simon, S., & Ditrichs, R. Variables in interracial aggression: anonymity, expected retaliation, and a riot. *Journal of Personality and Social Psychology*, 1972, *22*, 236–245.

Grusec, J. E. Demand characteristics of the modeling experiment: altruism as a function of age and aggression. *Journal of Personality and Social Psychology*, 1972, *22*, 139–148.

Hornstein, H. A., Fisch, E., & Holmes, M. Influence of a model's feeling about his behavior and his relevance as a comparison on other observers' helping behavior. *Journal of Personality and Social Psychology*, 1968, *10*, 222–226.

Milgram, S. Behavioral study of obedience. *Journal of Abnormal and Social Psychology*, 1963, *67*, 371–378.

5.2 Aggression Toward Outgroups as a Function of Authoritarianism and Imitation of Aggressive Models

Ralph Epstein

This experiment investigated the imitation of aggression towards outgroups as a function of the observer's personality characteristics and the stimulus characteristics of the aggressive model. Ss were randomly assigned to 8 experimental conditions in a 2 × 2 × 2 factorial design which was based on the following independent variables: observer's personality structure (authoritarianism) and the racial, socioeconomic characteristics of the model. The dependent variable, imitative aggression, was defined in terms of shocks administered to a Negro victim during a serial learning task. The findings that different ethnic models elicited comparable aggressiveness from high Fs whereas the low Fs were more imitative of a Negro than a white model were interpreted in terms of the undifferentiated cognitive functioning of high authoritarians. The finding that ethnic similarity between the victim and the model facilitated imitative aggression was evaluated in relation to current theories regarding outgroup hostility.

Although an increasing body of correlational evidence points to the role of imitation of ingroup attitudes as a determinant of prejudicial attitudes (Epstein & Komorita, 1966; Mosher & Scodel, 1960), experimental studies of imitatively derived hostility towards outgroups are virtually nonexistent. The potential fruitfulness of such studies is suggested by research demonstrating the imitative basis of diverse behavioral systems, for example, aggression (Bandura, Ross, & Ross, 1961), moral judgments (Bandura & McDonald, 1963), and autism (Eisenberg, 1957). The current study attempts to extend the range of investigated behaviors by focusing on imitation of overt aggression as manifested by the administration of shock to a victim. Furthermore, whereas previous investigations of imitation have focused upon either the observer's personality characteristics, that is, self-esteem (deCharms & Rosenbaum, 1960) or the model's characteristics, that is, status (Bandura & Kupers, 1964), social approval (Gelfand, 1962), the current study assumed that maximal prediction may be obtained by investigating the interaction between the observer's personality structure and the model's stimulus characteristics upon aggression towards outgroups.

Thus, the goal of this exploratory study was to investigate the personality characteristics of the observer and the stimulus characteristics of

Reprinted from the *Journal of Personality and Social Psychology*, 1966, *3*, 574–579. Copyright 1966 by the American Psychological Association and reproduced with permission.

aggressive models, that is, race and social status, as determinants of imitative aggression towards a Negro victim. On the basis of theory derived from the *Authoritarian Personality* (Adorno, Frenkel-Brunswik, Levinson, & Sanford, 1950), as well as research by Hart (1957), it may be assumed that authoritarian attitudes are a function of parental punishment for independent, autonomous behavior and parental approval for conforming, imitative, and submissive behavior. Therefore, it was predicted that high authoritarians will be more imitative of an aggressive model relative to low authoritarians. Furthermore, insofar as authoritarian attitudes result from harsh and punitive discipline which lead to excessive sensitization to power relations of strong versus weak, superior versus inferior, as these dimensions are culturally defined by social status, it was predicted that whereas high authoritarians will be more imitative of a middle-class than a working-class model, the low authoritarian's aggressiveness will be relatively uninfluenced by the model's differential social status.

The final prediction related to the ethnic characteristics of the aggressive model. It was assumed that conflict may be aroused by the cognition that one is aggressing (administering shock) against an individual and justification for the aggression in terms of the victim's provocative behavior or the presence of negative cognitions regarding the victim is lacking. It may be assumed that college students' awareness of the Negro's underdog status in American society would contribute to their perception of a white model giving shocks to a Negro victim as an instance of unjustifiable aggression. On the other hand, it is plausible to assume that justification for aggressing towards a member of a minority group may be derived by the prior observation that his own group considers him to be a legitimate target for aggression. This reasoning leads to the prediction that aggression towards a Negro will be facilitated by the prior observation of a Negro rather than a white aggressive model. Furthermore, on the basis of previous research (Berkowitz & Holmes, 1959; Weatherley, 1961) regarding the generalized and undifferentiated nature of authoritarian hostility, it is predicted that high authoritarians will show less differentiation among ethnic models relative to nonauthoritarian subjects.

METHOD

Subjects

Authoritarianism was measured by the 30-item F Scale which was group administered to 144 white, male, undergraduate students enrolled in introductory psychology courses at Wayne State University. One-third of the highest and one-third of the lowest scorers were randomly assigned to eight experimental conditions ($N = 8$ per cell) with the remaining 32 subjects assigned to a control group in which subjects were not exposed to an aggressive model. These experimental groups reflected a 2 × 2 × 2 factorial design based on the following independent variables: authoritariansm, high versus low; socioeconomic status of the model, low versus middle; and race of the model, Negro versus white.

Behavioral Situation

Aggression was defined operationally as a response which delivers noxious stimuli to another person. A modified "aggression machine" (Buss, 1961) was employed so that five intensities of electric shock ranging from very low to very high could be administered to a victim.

In addition to the white, naive subject, other participants included two accomplices, a Negro who played the role of the victim, and a Negro or white accomplice who served as an aggressive model. Upon arriving at the experimental room, subjects were told that they were participating in a study to evaluate the effect of shock upon learning. Thus, one participant would play the role of a learner, whereas the other two would serve as experimenters. In order to determine who would play the victim or learner's role, the participants were asked to select a number from 1 to 10. Insofar as this procedure was rigged, the same Negro accomplice was selected as the learner for all subjects. The remaining participants, the subject and accomplice, were told that they would play the role of experimenters in a study on the effects of shock upon learning. This role would be played by shocking the learner for incorrectly anticipating stimulus words presented serially on a memory drum. It was emphasized that the experimenter could press any one of the five buttons clearly marked from very low to very high. At this point, the remaining accomplice (Negro or white) "spontaneously" requested to play the role of the experimenter first since his time was limited. In this manner, the accomplice always served as the aggressive model. The naive subject was requested to observe and record the accomplice's selection of shock so that level of shock could be related to rate of learning. In this manner, the subject was given an opportunity to observe the level of shock employed by the second accomplice, now serving as an aggressive model.

Depending on the appropriate condition, the model was either Negro or white, low or high status. In the low status condition, the model wore old, disheveled clothes and responded to an orally administered questionnaire so as to reveal the following information about himself within the hearing distance of the naive subject: family income, less than $3,000; parental occupation, unemployed. In the high status condition, the model appeared well dressed and responded in the following manner: family income, $15,000 per annum; parental occupation, executive in an advertising firm.

The Negro victim made a programmed series of responses such that 32 shocks were administered by the model, and subsequently, by the naive subject in a seven-trial learning series. Unknown to the subject, however, a locked switch precluded the actual administration of shock to the victim. Furthermore, after an initial warm-up period in which the model delivered only weak shocks to the victim for errors during the first serial presentation, he delivered the highest level of shock; namely, "very high" shock, for subsequent errors. After the victim had learned the correct order of serially presented words, the subject was given the opportunity to play the role of the experimenter. This time the victim was asked to learn a new set of words. Recordings of the shock intensities were made by observing a series of differentially colored lights located in the experimenter's room and wired to the aggression machine.

Several procedures were employed in order to convince the subject that the aggression machine was operative. Prior to the first trial, subjects were encouraged to touch the victim's electrodes and receive a sample shock. In addition, the subject observed the experimenter carefully place the electrodes on the victim's wrist and fingertips. Finally, the victim emitted appropriate groans subsequent to each shock.

Measure of the Dependent Variable

The dependent variable, aggression, was operationally defined in terms of the intensity of shock administered to the victim. In line with Buss' (1961) suggestion that the administration of weak or mild shock levels may be indicative of a motive to help the victim learn more effectively, whereas utilization of very strong shock intensities may be more directly indicative of aggression, it was decided to score each subject's protocol by counting only those shocks whose intensities were labeled as "very strong."

RESULTS

For the purpose of intergroup comparisons, Table 1 summarizes the means and standard deviations of the very strong shocks for the eight experimental groups.

An analysis of variance based on these scores indicated that whereas the effect of the model's differential social status upon imitative aggression was not significant, the subject's authoritarianism and the model's ethnic characteristics were important determinants of imitative aggression. Thus, the main effects for authoritarianism ($F = 16.72$, $df = 1/64$), and race ($F = 10.05$, $df = 1/64$), both significant at the .01 level, indicate that high authoritarians were more aggressive than lows and the Negro model elicited greater aggression relative to the white model.

The predicted interaction between authoritarianism and race barely misses significance at the .05 level ($F = 3.90$, $df = 1/64$). It is likely that significance would have been achieved were it not for a mild heterogeneity of variance ($F = 10.60$, $df = 9$). However, this interaction does suggest an interesting trend whereby the Negro and white model elicited comparable levels of aggression from high authoritarians, whereas the low authoritarians' aggressiveness was differentiated according to the ethnic characteristics of the model. More specifically, low authoritarians, although administering generally less shock relative to high authoritarians, were more imitative of a Negro than a white model ($t = 8.20$, $p < .01$). Also, the white model was more imitated by high than low authoritarians ($t = 9.72$, $p < .01$). Insofar as the difference in shocks between the experimental groups ($M = 27.85$) and the control group ($M = 10.63$) is highly significant ($t = 8.52$, $p < .001$), it may be concluded that the observation of an aggressive model had a profound effect on levels of shock administered by the subjects. Finally, Table 1 indicates no support for the predicted interaction between authoritarianism and social status.

TABLE 1 *Means and Standard Deviations of Shocks of Experimental Groups*

SOCIAL STATUS	HIGH AUTHORITARIAN		LOW AUTHORITARIAN		M
	Negro	White	Negro	White	
Middle class	36.11	32.78	32.22	15.00	29.03
	(11.28)[a]	(10.30)	(16.00)	(9.13)	
Working class	35.56	31.67	26.67	12.77	26.67
	(16.72)	(15.11)	(5.27)	(8.50)	

	MEAN SHOCK INTENSITY
High authoritarian	34.03
Low authoritarian	21.67
Negro	32.64
White	23.06

[a] Standard deviations are enclosed in parentheses.

DISCUSSION

A primary finding in this study is that the imitation of anti-Negro aggression is a function of an interaction between the subject's level of authoritarianism and the model's racial characteristics. More specifically, these results support the prediction that whereas ethnic models will elicit comparable aggressiveness from high authoritarians, the low authoritarian's aggression is influenced differentially by the model's ethnic characteristics, that is, greater imitation of a Negro than a white model. Although these results are compatible with previous research (Anisfeld, Munoz, & Lambert, 1963; Berkowitz, 1962; Epstein, 1965; Epstein & Komorita, 1966) which demonstrated that authoritarian hostility is a generalized phenomenon across situations, they also suggest that this generality may be across models as well as targets. Thus, it would appear that the frequently reported relationship between authoritarianism and ethnocentrism (Adorno et al., 1950; Pettigrew, 1959) may not only be a function of the authoritarian individual's vulnerability to frustration as manifested by scapegoating behavior, but also a tendency to be more imitative of hostile models.

Furthermore, the low authoritarian's tendency to be significantly more imitative of a Negro than a white model is congruent with recent research

(Berkowitz, 1962; Weatherley, 1961) which demonstrates greater perceptual and cognitive differentiation among tolerant persons. Unlike these previous findings, however, the current results suggest that the greater discriminability among tolerant subjects may occur under nonstressful conditions, and in relation to aggressive models, as well as targets of aggression. It is interesting to note that whereas previous investigators have reported the greater responsiveness of low authoritarians to environmental or situational changes, that is, less childhood ethnocentrism as a result of an interracial experience (Mussen, 1950), lowered estimates of United States' superiority subsequent to the appearance of the sputniks (Mischel & Schopler, 1959), the current findings also demonstrate similar modifiability in overt aggressiveness as a function of external conditions.

There has been increasing recognition that a major limitation of traditional social-psychological conceptualizations of hostility towards outgroups is the neglect of outgroup characteristics which facilitate their selection as targets (Zawadzki, 1948). For example, the predictive efficiency of a specific conceptualization, for example, the "scapegoat" hypothesis, has been enhanced by attention to such characteristics, that is, "prior dislike" (Berkowitz, 1962), visibility (Williams, 1947), and social status (Epstein, 1965; Epstein & Komorita, 1966). The current study indicates the potential utility of further exploring the hypothesis that the perception of intragroup hostility may serve to justify and thereby contribute to the selection of a group as a target for aggression. This effect may be pronounced even for those individuals, that is, low authoritarians, who would ordinarily refrain from imitating an aggressive model. More specifically, these findings suggest that the low authoritarian's anxiety or inhibition regarding the expression of hostility towards outgroups may dissipate when these groups are viewed as victimized by their own member. The high authoritarian's greater imitativeness of the white model relative to low authoritarians is suggestive of the high Fs greater identification with the ingroup. This identification may result in a lower threshold for aggressive behavior when exposed to a white model.

An important reservation which may be placed on the conclusion that intragroup hostility within a minority group increases the aggressiveness of the majority is that this experiment has provided no information regarding the potential modeling effects of minority group members other than those from the victim's ethnic group. For example, it is conceivable that the use of an Oriental model may have elicited a comparable degree of aggression relative to the Negro model. In this case, one would conclude that aggression among minority group members, regardless of the degree of similarity between the model and the victim, increases the aggressiveness of the majority. Further research will be undertaken in which the ethnic affiliation of the subjects and victims as well as the models' will be varied in order to clarify these relationships.

An important implication of these results is that the development of attitudes of self-rejection and self-derogation among outgroups (Clark, 1963; Lewin, 1935), as these attitudes may be manifested by intragroup hostility within a minority group, may serve to increase the vulnerability of the group to rejection and hostility on the part of the majority. This interpretation is consistent with the naturalistic observation (Arendt, 1963), that the Nazis' aggression towards the Jews during World War II was made justifiable by the majority's perception of some Jews participating directly and indirectly in the liquidation of their own ethnic group.

Furthermore, this study may have important implications for current theory regarding the antecedents of hostility towards outgroups. The most prevalent formulation, the "scapegoat" hypothesis (Berkowitz, 1962) suggests that the anticipation of punishment for frustration-induced aggression directed towards the ingroup results in displacement from the original sources of frustration to outgroups. However, this hypothesis is not clearly compatible with the naturalistic observation of a striking dissimilarity between the ingroup frustraters and the victims of displaced aggression (Buss, 1961). Attempts to clarify this inconsistency between theory and observation have focused on the ethnocentric individual's "prior dislike" for outgroups (Berkowitz, 1959), as well as his poor discrimination under stressful conditions (Berkowitz, 1962). The current results suggest that the direction of hostility may be determined by an interaction between personality characteristics of the aggressor and the stimulus characteristic of the aggressive model.

Whereas previous research (Epstein, 1965; Epstein & Komorita, 1966) demonstrated that the social status of the victim relates to his vulnerability to displaced aggression, the current study indicates that the model's social status had minimal effect on the imitation of aggression. It would appear that the salient effects attributable to the ethnic characteristics of the model and the victim overshadowed the social status variable. Insofar as the social status of the victim was relatively undefined and somewhat ambiguous, further research might involve the manipulation of the status variable for both the model and the victim.

References

Adorno, T. W., Frenkel-Brunswik, E., Levinson, D. J., & Sanford, R. N. *The authoritarian personality.* New York: Harper & Row, 1950.

Anisfeld, M., Munoz, S. R., & Lambert, W. E. The structure and dynamics of ethnic attitudes of Jewish adolescents. *Journal of Abnormal and Social Psychology,* 1963, 66, 31–36.

Arendt, H. *Eichmann in Jerusalem: A report on the banality of evil.* New York: Viking Press, 1963.

Bandura, A., & Kupers, C. J. Transmission of patterns of self-reinforcement through modeling. *Journal of Abnormal and Social Psychology*, 1964, *69*, 1–9.

Bandura, A., & McDonald, F. J. The influence of social reinforcement and the behavior of models in shaping children's moral judgments. *Journal of Abnormal and Social Psychology*, 1963, *67*, 274–281.

Bandura, A., Ross, D., & Ross, S. A. Transmission of aggression through imitation of aggressive models. *Journal of Abnormal and Social Psychology*, 1961, *63*, 575–582.

Berkowitz, L. *Aggression: A social psychological analysis.* New York: McGraw-Hill, 1962.

Berkowitz, L., & Holmes, D. S. The generalization of hostility to disliked objects. *Journal of Personality*, 1959, *27*, 565–577.

Buss, A. *The psychology of aggression.* New York: Wiley, 1961.

Clark, K. B. *Prejudice and your child.* Boston: Beacon Press, 1963.

deCharms, R., & Rosenbaum, M. E. Status variables and matching behavior. *Journal of Personality*, 1960, *28*, 492–502.

Eisenberg, L. The fathers of autistic children. *American Journal of Orthopsychiatry*, 1957, *27*, 715–724.

Epstein, R. Authoritarianism, displaced aggression, and social status of the target. *Journal of Personality and Social Psychology*, 1965, *2*, 585–589.

Epstein, R., & Komorita, S. S. Childhood prejudice as a function of parental ethnocentrism, punitiveness, and outgroup characteristics. *Journal of Personality and Social Psychology*, 1966, *3*, 259–264.

Gelfand, D. M. The influence of self-esteem on rate of verbal conditioning and social matching behavior. *Journal of Abnormal and Social Psychology*, 1962, *65*, 259–265.

Hart, I. Maternal child-rearing practices and authoritarian ideology. *Journal of Abnormal and Social Psychology*, 1957, *55*, 232–237.

Lewin, K. Psycho-sociological problems of minority groups. *Character and Personality*, 1935, *3*, 175–187.

Mischel, W., & Schopler, J. Authoritarianism and reactions to "sputniks." *Journal of Abnormal and Social Psychology*, 1959, *59*, 142–145.

Mosher, D. L., & Scodel, A. A study of the relationship between ethnocentrism in children and the ethnocentrism and authoritarian rearing practices of their mothers. *Child Development*, 1960, *31*, 369–376.

Mussen, P. H. Some personality and social factors related to changes in children's attitudes toward Negroes. *Journal of Abnormal and Social Psychology*, 1950, *45*, 423–446.

Pettigrew, T. F. Regional differences in anti-Negro prejudice. *Journal of Abnormal and Social Psychology*, 1959, *59*, 28–36.

Weatherley, D. Anti-Semitism and the expression of fantasy aggression. *Journal of Abnormal and Social Psychology*, 1961, *62*, 454–457.

Williams, R. M., Jr. The reduction of intergroup tensions: A survey of research on problems of ethnic, racial, and religious group relations. *Social Science Research Council Bulletin*, 1947, No. 57.

Zawadzki, B. Limitations of the scapegoat theory of prejudice. *Journal of Abnormal and Social Psychology*, 1948, *43*, 127–141.

Foreword to Reading 5.3

INTRODUCTION

An experiment by Berkowitz and Daniels (1963) compared subjects ("workers") who thought that their work production would influence whether or not their "supervisor" got a prize, with subjects who were told that their work production would not help the supervisor (or themselves) in any way.

Subjects with a "dependent" supervisor worked harder than subjects with an independent supervisor. Since there was no reward for the subject, regardless of his productivity, this result ran counter to the usual notions of the human being as a hedonist, seeking reward and avoiding cost. Berkowitz and Daniels accounted for the result by postulating the existence of a social responsibility norm. They suggested that, in North American society, there is a social rule that one should help those who are dependent on one. In other words, social responsibility may be a value that we learn in the course of socialization, an ideal widely accepted in our culture. Of course, no one is expected to abide by such norms at all times, but there may well be a feeling of self-satisfaction when we do, and guilt when we do not.

Berkowitz and his coworkers (e.g., Berkowitz and Connor, 1966; Goranson and Berkowitz, 1966) have suggested that any conditions increasing the salience of the norm (i.e., reminding the person of its existence) or increasing the motivation to conform to the norm, increase the probability that people will act in accordance with the norm.

As predicted, they found that subjects worked harder for a liked than for a disliked supervisor (a manipulation of motivation), and worked harder when they themselves had previously been helped (a manipulation of salience).

In the article presented here, Berkowitz uses a slightly more complex theoretical analysis. He suggests that demands for help elicit resentment.

Brehm (1966) has called this reaction "reactance." Brehm suggested that people resent any reduction in their "free behaviors" (i.e., the behaviors that they feel free to choose), and are motivated to re-establish threatened or lost freedom. Berkowitz here suggests that help demands (perhaps because a norm implies that one *should* help) are perceived as a loss of free behaviors and thus elicit reactance. This places the potential helper in a conflict between resentment and the guilt engendered by not acting up to an ideal. The presence of a suitable "excuse" should allow the individual to give in to his resentment. If the person needing help requires it through his own fault, the potential helper has a suitable excuse. This leads to the prediction that a dependent peer who is perceived as being dependent through his own fault will be helped less (and resented more) than one whose need arises from external circumstances. In addition to this prediction, the study was concerned with investigating the source of conflicting results in terms of sex differences. Schopler and Bateson (1965), unlike Berkowitz (at Wisconsin), did not find that *male* subjects helped a person who was highly dependent on them more than one who had less need for their help.

METHOD

Rosenthal (1966) has presented some evidence that sex of experimenter is an important variable. For instance, male experimenters tend to elicit more creative problem solutions than female experimenters, but they also elicit inferior intellectual performance from children. Also, male experimenters are more friendly to their subjects, and opposite-sex experimenter-subject combinations take more time to complete an experiment than same-sex dyads. Therefore, Berkowitz decided to use subjects and experimenter of the same sex on any given trial.

Every subject was, seemingly by chance, chosen as "supervisor" over the two workers, and could compare the behavior of the two workers, the one who did ask for help (for varying reasons), and the one who did not. Two variables were manipulated:

a. magnitude of dependency: i.e., the extent to which the worker needed help from the subject, and
b. locus of dependency: i.e., whether the worker needed help because of the experimenter's blunder (external locus) or because of the worker's own shortcomings (internal locus).

RESULTS AND DISCUSSION

The reader will notice that the dependency manipulation did not succeed, nor (unlike previous studies) was there any differential effect on helping of the magnitude of the worker's dependency (even in the external locus condition, see Table 2). This raises the possibility that the results of the previous experiments were in some way specific to the previous procedure (and thus not as generalizable as one might have hoped). Berkowitz' own suggestion might be recalled here. Did subjects in the previous experiments think that, as workers, they were *supposed* to help the dependent supervisors, while as supervisors (as in the present experiment) they were free not to help?

Further inspection of Table 2 indicates that Berkowitz obtained the expected effect of locus of dependency in the high dependency condition. Berkowitz suggests that "people faced by a more legitimate request for help evidently overcame (their) reactance because of the absence of suitable excuses." Since the data tell us nothing about suitable excuses, Berkowitz' explanation is somewhat speculative.

Regarding sex differences in helping, and in keeping with the stereotype of the female as nurturant and kind, women were more helpful than men. The reader might consider for him or herself the source of such differences, and whether they might be ascribed to physiological differences, or to social norms concerning sex-typing.

References

Berkowitz, L. & Connor, W. H. Success, failure and social responsibility. *Journal of Personality and Social Psychology,* 1966, *4,* 664–669.

Berkowitz, L. & Daniels, L. R. Responsibility and dependency. *Journal of Abnormal and Social Psychology,* 1963, *66,* 429–436.

Brehm, J. W. *A theory of psychological reactance.* New York: Academic Press, 1966.

Goranson, R. E. & Berkowitz, L. Reciprocity and responsibility reactions to prior help. *Journal of Personality and Social Psychology,* 1966, *3,* 227–232.

Rosenthal, R. *Experimenter effects in behavioral research.* New York: Appleton-Century-Crofts, 1966.

Schopler, J. & Bateson, N. The power of dependence. *Journal of Personality and Social Psychology,* 1965, *2,* 247–254.

5.3 Resistance to Improper Dependency Relationships[1]

Leonard Berkowitz

Two hundred and twenty-eight college men and women were individually assigned to supervise the work of two same-sex peers who were eligible for a cash
prize although no prize was available for the subject. One of the workers asked
for help, either because of the experimenter's mistake (external locus of dependency), or because of the person's own deficiency (internal locus of dependency), while other information indicated the worker was either highly dependent,
moderately dependent, or only slightly dependent upon the subject's help in
order to gain the prize. The person asking for assistance was more disliked than
the worker not requesting help, even when the former's dependency was externally created, presumably because the help request restricted the subject's
behavioral freedom. The greatest dislike for the worker seeking help arose,
however, when it was this person's own fault he needed help. In accord with
Brehm's reactance theory, there was the least effort for the worker asking for
help when this person was highly dependent upon the subject but needed assistance because of his own shortcomings; the illegitimate help request evidently
gave the subject a suitable excuse, permitting him to succumb to the resentment
(or reactance) arising from the great implied demand upon him. Although the
women generally gave the worker more help than did the men, both sexes displayed this resentment at the improper help request and both tended to dislike
the worker seeking assistance.

Experiments by Berkowitz and his co-workers (Berkowitz and Daniels,
1963, 1964, Daniels and Berkowitz, 1963; Berkowitz, Klanderman, and
Harris, 1964) have demonstrated that many middle-class university students feel obligated to help people who are dependent upon them for their
goal attainment. Berkowitz suggested the students were responding to a
widely shared ideal in their society maintaining that assistance should be
given to people in need. The existence of such a "social responsibility norm"
does not mean, of course, that everyone will adhere to it or, for that matter,
that any one person will always behave in a consistent fashion with regard
to this moral standard. Even when they have learned this ideal, people will
conform to it in any given situation only if they are aware of the moral rule
on that occasion, and are motivated to adhere to it.

Reprinted from the *Journal of Experimental Social Psychology*, 1969, *5*, 283–294,
with permission of author and publisher. Copyright © 1969 by Academic Press.
  [1] The research reported in this paper was supported by a grant from the National
Science Foundation to the writer. I am indebted to Edward Tronick who helped plan
this study, developed some of the procedure, and generally carried out the research
with considerable skill and conscientiousness. Karen Kopps ably served as his assistant.

243

Motivation to help a dependent person is greatly affected by situational conditions. There are any number of reasons why we might be reluctant to help someone in need. For example, the costs of doing so might be too great; we might anticipate physical harm, embarrassment, financial losses (cf., Schopler and Bateson, 1965), an unwanted expenditure of physical effort, and so on. But in addition, motivation to help might also be lessened by resentment produced by having one's behavioral freedom reduced. Upon reviewing findings from a variety of investigations, the writer has observed that people often resent demands to assist another person, whether these demands are made explicitly to them or are only felt by them (Berkowitz, 1969). In accord with Brehm's (1966) theory of psychological reactance, these demands imply an unwelcome limitation of the range of behavioral options open to them. Horowitz (1968) recently has provided evidence consistent with this analysis. Male undergraduates expressed greater willingness to help a graduate student after being given a choice of whether to assist him or not compared to when they were required to help him. The coercion evidently bred resentment, lowering the student's motivation to aid the other person.

Often acting in the opposite direction are the discomforts produced by deviations—real or anticipated—from the conjectured "social responsibility norm" (and/or from one's self-image of being a helpful person). Generally speaking, the clearer the rule that help-giving is morally necessary in the given situation, the stronger is the discomfort aroused by anticipated departures from the ideal, and the greater is the person's motivation to aid the dependent other. Observing someone give assistance to a person in need may increase subsequent help-giving partly by increasing the salience of the help-giving norm or by showing clearly what is proper behavior in that situation (Berkowitz and Daniels, 1964; Bryan and Test, 1967; Wheeler and Wagner, 1968).

Clear standards prescribing help-giving on a particular occasion thus lessen the extent to which the individual will succumb to his resentment and resist the felt demands. The clear-cut rules minimize the possibility of establishing suitable excuses for not aiding the dependent individual. Such excuses can be found, for example, in the belief that the other person's dependency is improper or "illegitimate." As an illustration, Schopler and Matthews (1965) demonstrated that subjects gave greater assistance to a partner requiring their help because of factors beyond his control (external locus of dependency) than to a person needing help because of his own shortcomings (internal locus of dependency). The internally caused dependency was presumably regarded as relatively illegitimate. Thinking the other person's demand was improper, the subjects apparently gave in to their resentment at being coerced into aiding the other person. Similarly, in the previously cited study by Horowitz (1968), the subjects were more willing to assist an internally dependent individual if they had a choice as to whether to help him or not, perhaps because the choice lowered reactance and made it unnecessary to find an excuse for not assisting the other person.

The present investigation will seek two kinds of additional information relevant to this analysis. For one thing, we will attempt to assess the comparative level of resentment in subjects confronted by a legitimately dependent partner (i.e., a person needing assistance because of conditions he could not control), as well as in people faced by an internally dependent other. While earlier research has obtained signs of such resentment in subjects required to aid an externally dependent partner (Berkowitz and Daniels, 1963), Horowitz's subjects felt *somewhat* more coerced in the internally dependent than in the externally dependent conditions. If this is a reliable finding, there might be less resentment in subjects asked to help a properly dependent peer than in people working for someone who was illegitimately dependent on them.

Then too, the study will also inquire into sex differences in reactions to another's dependency. The earlier experiments at Wisconsin had not found any significant differences between men and women in this matter. By contrast, Schopler and Bateson (1965) obtained significant sex differences, with women displaying greater assistance to a highly dependent peer. One possible explanation for this discrepancy between the Wisconsin and North Carolina research can be found in the differences in the experimental settings. Putting this simply, the help-giving may have been more legitimate, proper, or even required in the Wisconsin situation; the Wisconsin subjects were told they were workers operating under their partner's supervision, and therefore, they were supposed to work for this person. If this is indeed an important distinction, we might find no differences between men and women when facing the properly dependent, externally dependent partner, but greater help-giving by the women when working for the individual who needed assistance because of his own deficiencies.

METHOD

Subjects

The subjects were 114 men and a like number of women who had volunteered from the introductory psychology classes at the University of Wisconsin in order to earn credits counting toward their course grade. The experimenter was always the same sex as the subject in order to minimize effects due to the subject's desire to please an opposite-sex experimenter.[2]

[2] Findings in the experiment by Berkowitz, Klanderman, and Harris (1964) suggest the subjects in this type of setting work hardest when there is an opposite-sex experimenter who will see their productivity right away. Contrary to a simple "demand characteristics" notion, there were also indications in this study that the subjects displayed the lowest output when a same-sex experimenter would be immediately aware of their work.

Procedure

Three same-sex subjects were scheduled for each experimental period. When each person arrived at the laboratory he (or she) was placed in a separate booth and asked to wait until the others arrived.[3] When all were assembled, the subjects were told the study was concerned with the effects of motivation on a worker's performance. Since wages provided the usual incentive for work in the "real world," as an analogous financial incentive a five-dollar gift certificate would be awarded to the worker earning the best grade. Another aspect of real-life work situations, they were informed, was the worker's supervisor, and one of the three would be chosen randomly to be the supervisor. The supervisor would *not* be eligible for the prize, only the two workers. The experimenter went on to say the two workers would first individually be given the "Layton Manual Dexterity Test," while the supervisor would be shown the product the workers were to make in the second phase and wrote instructions for manufacturing the product.

At the completion of this introduction the booths were closed. Three minutes later the experimenter communicated with each person over an intercom network, informing each of the three that he had been selected as the supervisor by chance. The subject was reminded that only the workers were eligible for the prize and was told they had already been started on the manual dexterity test. The supervisor's first task was to provide written instructions for the workers as to how to make a certain kind of paper pad. He would also have to supply any extra paper and staples that the workers might require. The experimenter then assured the subject that his performance would not be evaluated; he was functioning as a supervisor only to make the situation more realistic for the workers. He wouldn't get any credit in any way. If he was asked for help by one of the workers, the experimenter went on, and was willing to render this assistance, his (i.e., the subject's) work would count toward the worker's score, but the worker would not find out how much work the supervisor had done.

Experimental manipulations. The supervisor was then informed what part of the workers' grades was based on the workers' productivity. This information was used to vary each worker's perceived dependency on the subject. After this, the subject was given a model pad together with extra materials for the workers and was told to write instructions for making the pad to each of the two workers. Approximately 8 minutes later the experimenter returned, picked up the notes the subjects had written to each worker, and left, ostensibly to deliver the instructions.

Dependency degree. The first experimental variation, as mentioned above, was established by telling the subject how the workers' grades would be calculated. One-third of the subjects were informed that 80% (one-third were told 50% and the remaining third 20%) of the worker's score would be based on his productivity. The remaining part of the grade would supposedly be based on the manual dexterity test. As a consequence of this information, when the subject was later asked for help, he presumably would think his help was either greatly, moderately, or only slightly needed.

Dependency locus. About 5 minutes after the supposed delivery of

---

[3] The subject was informed all three were present even if this was not the case.

the supervisor's instructions to the workers, the experimenter returned with messages from these people. The note from Worker No. 2 always read: "I am running out of paper. Would you please send me some." However, the message designated as coming from Worker No. 1 differed with the subject's experimental condition. Half of the people in each of the three dependency-level groups received this message (External Locus of Dependency):

"The exp. gave me the wrong paper and now I have fallen behind. It's his fault. Would you please make some pads for me. Remember 80 (or 50 or 20) % of my score depends upon the number of pads prod. It's okay."

For the remaining subjects, those in the Internal Locus of Dependency condition, Worker No. 1's message read:

"I took it sort of easy during the 1st period and now I've fallen behind. Would you please make some pads for me. Remember 80 (or 50 or 20) % of my score depends on the number of pads prod. It's okay."

Each note was in either a masculine or feminine handwriting, depending upon the subject's sex (and consequently, the sex of the workers). The experimenter made a few remarks generally corroborating Worker No. 1's story when he delivered this person's message.

To summarize, we have a $2 \times 3 \times 2$ factorial design: sex of subject (Male or Female), level of the worker's dependency on the subject (Great, Moderate, or Low), and locus of Worker No. 1's dependency (External or Internal to himself). For several items there was also a "repeated measures," within-subjects classification (Worker No. 1 and Worker No. 2). There are 19 cases in each of the 12 experimental conditions.

Measures

The subject was left alone for 10 minutes after he was given the two notes. At the end of this work period the experimenter returned, quickly swept the subject's production into a box so that it would later be added to Worker No. 1's score, and then asked the subject to complete a questionnaire ostensibly designed to assess the supervisor's evaluation of each worker. The items dealt with such matters as each worker's competence, how much the supervisor thought he had helped each worker, the supervisor's motivation in the situation, the strength of his wish to know each worker better, and his impression of each worker's personality. When the subject finished filling out the questionnaire it was collected and the experimenter explained the deceptions that had been practiced. The experiment was discussed and the subjects were dismissed with a request that they not talk about the study for the remainder of the semester.

RESULTS

Effectiveness of the Experimental Manipulations

Other experiments in the writer's research program have employed several questionnaire items as indicators of the success of the dependency manipulation. Two similar measures were inserted in the final questionnaire: "My workers were very dependent upon my production for obtaining a good grade" (*strongly yes* to *strongly no*), and "If either of your workers had asked you to help him (her), to what extent would most people have expected you to help this person?" (*definitely* to *not at all*). Neither of these items was significantly affected by the present dependency manipulation, perhaps because of the complexity and ambiguity of the dependency relationship in this study in comparison to the fairly clear-cut and readily grasped dependency relationship established in the other experiments.

Interestingly enough, these two measures did yield significant main effects for the Locus of Dependency variable. Thus, when Worker No. 1 was in need of the subject's assistance because of the experimenter's error (External Locus of Dependency), in comparison to when he needed help because of his own behavior (Internal Locus), the subjects said their workers were more dependent upon their production ($F = 4.28$, 1 and 216 df, $p < .001$), and believed more definitely that most people would have expected them to help the worker requesting assistance ($F = 4.28$, 1 and 216 df, $p < .05$). The subjects evidently were more willing to acknowledge their partners' dependency on them when Worker No. 1 asked for help because of factors beyond his control.

Responses to several items demonstrated that the subjects discriminated between Worker No. 1 and Worker No. 2 as well as between the externally and internally caused dependency. Table 1 lists the question-

TABLE 1 *Questionnaire Items Yielding Significant Interaction between Dependency Locus and Worker*

| | EXTERNAL LOCUS | | INTERNAL LOCUS | |
| | *Worker* | | *Worker* | |
	1	*2*	*1*	*2*
2 Valuable—Worthless	4.53$_c$	5.34$_b$	3.40$_d$	5.79$_a$
3 Passive—Active	4.71$_b$	5.45$_a$	3.18$_c$	5.79$_a$
4 Weak—Strong	3.99$_b$	5.06$_a$	3.38$_c$	5.17$_a$
5 Bad—Good	4.75$_b$	5.09$_a$	3.69$_c$	5.23$_a$
8 Unpleasant—Pleasant	4.71$_{b,c}$	4.82$_{a,b}$	4.51$_c$	5.04$_a$
9 Slow—Fast	4.06$_c$	5.40$_b$	2.40$_d$	5.80$_a$
10 Good worker	6.67$_b$	8.35$_a$	4.87$_c$	8.62$_a$
12 Helped worker	7.27$_a$	5.22$_c$	5.95$_b$	4.98$_c$
13 Would like to know	6.98$_b$	7.75$_a$	6.28$_c$	7.86$_a$

Note.—Each mean is based on 114 cases. Separate analyses of variance were conducted for each item. Cells not having a subscript in common are significantly different at the .05 level by Duncan Multiple Range Test. Subscript "a" always indicates the favorable end of the dimension.

naire measures giving rise to a significant Dependency Locus by Worker interaction, together with the cell means involved in each interaction. Two patterns are readily seen in this table. First, in almost every instance (with the exception of one comparison out of the 18) Worker 1 was evaluated reliably less favorably than Worker No. 2. The subjects apparently resented Worker No. 1's request for help even when he had fallen behind because of the experimenter's error, and thought less highly of him than of the other person not seeking assistance. Second, as we would expect, Worker 1 was given the least favorable ratings when his need for assistance was his own fault. Thus, the individual restricting the subjects' behavioral freedom was disliked even when his request for help was relatively proper. The dislike was strongest, however, when the demand upon them was comparatively improper.

Magnitude of Help-Giving

Two significant terms were revealed in the analysis of variance of the productivity data: Sex of Subject ($F = 4.38$, 1 and 216 df, $p < .05$) and Locus of Dependency ($F = 6.54$, 1 and 216 df, $p < .02$). Consistent with the attitude differences shown in Table 1, the subjects worked significantly harder for the externally dependent (mean $= 7.47$) than for the internally dependent Worker 1 (mean $= 5.35$). In addition, over all conditions the women exerted greater effort in behalf of their dependent peer (mean $= 7.28$) than did the men (mean $= 5.54$). The women seemed to be more highly motivated to give help than were the male students. Closer inspection of the results indicates, nevertheless, that the male and female students reacted in a similar manner to the dependency locus and dependency level variations; sex of subject did not interact significantly with these treatments. In comparison to the men, then, our female students may have been more willing to assist their dependent peer regardless of how much this person needed help in order to win the prize.

Because of the earlier findings by Schopler and Matthews (1965) and the conservatism of the Duncan Multiple Range Test,[4] the means involved in the Dependency Degree by Dependency Locus interaction were compared. The results summarized in Table 2 suggest that the subjects' response to Worker No. 1's degree of dependency upon them was partially governed by the reason for this dependency. There was something of a tendency (although nonsignificant) for the subject to work harder for Worker 1 the greater his dependency on them when this dependency was externally caused. By contrast, the subjects generally exerted *less* effort in behalf of

---

[4] According to D. A. Grant (citing Duncan and other sources), it is not necessary to have a significant F-ratio in order to perform the Duncan Multiple Range Test.

TABLE 2 *Mean Productivity for Worker Requesting Help in Each Experimental Condition (Men and Women Combined)*

DEPENDENCY	EXTERNAL LOCUS	INTERNAL LOCUS
High	8.45_b	4.00_a
Mod	$6.87_{a,b}$	$6.05_{a,b}$
Low	$7.10_{a,b}$	$6.00_{a,b}$

Note.—Each mean is based on 38 cases. Cells not having a subscript in common are significantly different at the .05 level by Duncan Multiple Range Test.

the worker the greater his need for help when the dependency was his own fault. Because of these opposing trends, there was a reliably greater productivity under High Dependency for the externally dependent than for the internally dependent Worker No. 1. These results are in accord with Brehm's reactance theory. The subjects confronted by the internally dependent worker's demands apparently reacted more strongly against this pressure on them the greater the person's dependency on them and, consequently, the stronger the implied improper demand. The people faced by a more legitimate request for help evidently overcame this reactance because of the absence of suitable excuses.

Sex Differences in Response to Dependency

To say a person accedes to the felt pressures arising from his moral standards obviously does not mean he submits ungrudgingly. The women in the present sample generally rendered greater assistance to their dependent peer than did the male subjects, as shown by the significantly greater productivity by the girls. The men, furthermore, were apparently less responsibility oriented in that they were more apt to want reciprocity or compensation for their work. Thus, the males were reliably more insistent on the final questionnaire that they as supervisor should also have been eligible for a reward ($F = 31.34$, 1 and 216 df, $p < .001$). The men did what they "ought" to have done, but still seemed to be more conscious than the women of the disparity between the worker's and supervisor's outcomes. This finding is consistent with Schopler's (1967) notion that men are more attentive than women to relative status considerations.

Nevertheless, the women may have resented having to assist the worker at least as strongly as did the men. Some evidence of this resentment can be found in Table 3. If we look at the semantic differential ratings of Worker No. 2 shown in this table, we see that the female subjects were reliably more favorable to the worker not requesting help than were the

TABLE 3 *Items Yielding a Significant Sex of Subject by Worker Interaction*

	MALES		FEMALES	
	Worker		Worker	
	1	*2*	*1*	*2*
4 Weak—Strong	3.79_c	4.90_b	3.58_c	5.32_a
5 Bad—Good	4.20_c	4.90_b	4.25_c	5.41_a
8 Unpleasant—Pleasant	4.62_b	4.71_b	4.60_b	5.15_a

Note.—Each mean is based on 114 cases. Cells not having a subscript in common are significantly different at the .05 level by Duncan Multiple Range Test.

men. The women were generally friendlier to a fellow subject. In rating Worker No. 1, however, the female subjects did not differ from the men in evaluating this demanding person less favorably than the worker not asking for help. The female subjects either did not differ from the male subjects in disliking a person who would restrict their freedom by seeking help, or— assuming they started off at a friendlier level—may actually have had a stronger negative reaction to the would-be help recipient.

If we think of women as being more nurturant and considerate than men, we might conclude that women will be readier to forgive help requests arising from some personal inadequacy. Contrary to such an assumption, however, the results summarized in Table 4 suggest that the female subjects were at least as harsh as the males toward the internally dependent Worker 1. Thus, both the women and men (Item 11) said they were less interested in getting to know Worker 1 than Worker 2, (Item 10) evaluated 1 as being a poorer worker than 2, and (Item 9) rated 1 as slower than 2, in the Internal Locus as well as in the External Locus conditions. More important, the female subjects evaluated the internally dependent Worker No. 1 reliably less favorably than the externally dependent Worker 1 on all three of these items, whereas this significant difference arose on only two of the times in the case of the male subjects (10 and 9). Indeed, the women were significantly harsher than the men in their judgment of how good a worker the internally dependent Worker No. 1 had been.

But again we must note that felt obligations to give help do not necessarily coincide with attitudes toward the person in need of assistance. The women reported feeling a greater pressure to do a good job for Worker 1 than for 2 regardless of the former person's reason for requesting help. They acknowledged the demand on them even when it was improper. For the men, on the other hand, this difference in admitted felt pressure came about only when Worker 1's dependency was due to factors beyond his control; when he needed help because of his own inadequacy, the men said

TABLE 4 *Items Having a Significant Interaction of Sex of Subject by Worker by Dependency Locus*

| | MALES | | | | FEMALES | | | |
| | External | | Internal | | External | | Internal | |
	1	2	1	2	1	2	1	2
10 Good worker	6.19_c	8.16_a	5.28_d	8.18_a	7.14_b	8.54_a	4.46_e	9.07_a
11 Felt pressure	7.37_a	5.10_d	$6.79_{a,b,c}$	$6.16_{b,c,d}$	$7.25_{a,b}$	$5.72_{c,d}$	7.42_a	5.18_d
[a]13 Would like to know	6.44_c	7.26_d	6.18_c	7.18_b	7.56_b	8.25_a	6.39_c	8.54_a
9 Slow—Fast	3.95_e	5.37_b	2.60_d	$5.61_{a,b}$	4.18_c	$5.42_{a,b}$	2.19_d	5.98_a

Note.—Each mean is based on 57 cases. Cells not having a subscript in common are significantly different at the .05 level by Duncan Multiple Range Test. Subscript "a" refers to the favorable or high end of the scale.
[a] The interaction obtained with this item was significant at less than the .10 level.

they felt only the same moderate pressure they felt to assist Worker 2. Thus, the men evidently were somewhat inclined to deny feeling obligated to assist the person whose implied demand on them was improper.

DISCUSSION

The present results indicate all of the subjects resented Worker No. 1's request for assistance even when his dependency was created by factors beyond his control. They generally expressed greater dislike for Worker No. 1 if his need for help was his own fault rather than being due to the experimenter's mistake, but nevertheless, had a stronger dislike for Worker 1 than for Worker 2 (who had not asked for help) even when the former's need for assistance had been imposed upon him. This resentment, of course, was not necessarily a consequence of reactance; Worker 1's plea for help could have highlighted the disparity in rewards: *he* might get a prize but there would definitely be no money for the subjects. However, the productivity data provide suggestive support for the reactance conception. The subjects receiving the improper help request exerted the least amount of effort in behalf of Worker No. 1 when his dependency on them was great. Following Brehm, we can say the relatively great pressure was reacted against, leading to this low productivity, when the illegitimate demand enabled the subjects to find a suitable excuse for not helping their partner.

Both the men and women in this experiment displayed this resistance toward the improper strong demand. The findings thus do not support our tentative attempt to reconcile the Wisconsin and North Carolina studies; the men in the Schopler-Bateson (1965) investigation evidently did not react against their partner's great dependency on them because of the presumed illegitimacy of his need for help. The present group of females worked harder for their peer than did the men over all conditions, however. As long as their peer was dependent upon them to some degree, the women were more responsive than the men. This sex difference may stem, in part, from the male subjects' greater sensitivity to relative status considerations, as Schopler suggested (1967). The men may not have worked as hard because they were more resentful that prizes were not available for them as well as for their partners. Other findings indicate, nevertheless, that the women may also have a stronger and more generalized "social responsibility" ideal. Thus, the female subjects reported feeling a greater pressure to help Worker 1 than Worker 2 regardless of why the former needed assistance. Evidently, the mere existence of this dependency was sufficient to arouse some feelings of obligation. Like the women, the men apparently perceived Worker 1's implied demand on them, and resented this request as much as the women did, but still admitted feeling obligated to help Worker

1 only when he was legitimately dependent upon them. For them, in contrast to the women, only more restricted (and proper) circumstances would make them acknowledge a felt pressure to help the person calling for help.

References

Berkowitz, L. Beyond exchange: Ideals and other factors affecting helping and altruism. In R. Wills and M. Greenberg (Eds.), *Social exchange: Theory and research*. New York: Wiley, 1969.

Berkowitz, L., and Daniels, L. R. Responsibility and dependency. *Journal of Abnormal and Social Psychology*, 1963, *66*, 429–437.

Berkowitz, L., and Daniels, L. R. Affecting the salience of the social responsibility norm: Effects of past help on the response to dependency relationships. *Journal of Abnormal and Social Psychology*, 1964, *68*, 275–281.

Berkowitz, L., Klanderman, S. B., and Harris, R. Effects of experimenter awareness and sex of subject and experimenter on reactions to dependency relationship. *Sociometry*, 1964, *27*, 327–337.

Brehm, J. W. *A theory of psychological reactance*. New York: Academic Press, 1966.

Bryan, J. H., and Test, M. Models and helping: Naturalistic studies in aiding behavior. *Journal of Personality and Social Psychology*, 1967, *6*, 400–407.

Daniels, L. R., and Berkowitz, L. Liking and response to dependency relationships. *Human Relations*, 1963, *16*, 141–148.

Horowitz, I. A. Effect of choice and locus of dependence on helping behavior. *Journal of Personality and Social Psychology*, 1968, *8*, 373–376.

Schopler, J. An investigation of sex differences on the influence of dependence. *Sociometry*, 1967, *30*, 50–63.

Schopler, J., and Bateson, N. The power of dependence. *Journal of Personality and Social Psychology*, 1965, *2*, 247–254.

Schopler, J., and Matthews, M. W. The influence of the perceived causal locus of partner's dependence on the use of interpersonal power. *Journal of Personality and Social Psychology*, 1965, *2*, 609–612.

Wheeler, L., and Wagner, C. M. The contagion of generosity. Paper delivered at the Eastern Psychological Association meetings, Washington, D.C., April 1968.

Foreword to Reading 5.4

INTRODUCTION

The authors of this study, Latané and Darley, have been concerned by reports such as these:

> Kitty Genovese was set upon by a maniac as she returned home from work at 3:00 A.M. Thirty-eight of her neighbors in Kew Gardens came to their windows when she cried out in terror; none came to her assistance even though her stalker took over half an hour to murder her. No one even so much as called the police. She died.

> Andrew Mormille was stabbed in the stomach as he rode the A train home to Manhattan. Eleven other riders watched the 17-year-old boy as he bled to death; none came to his assistance even though his attackers left the car. He died. (Darley and Latané, 1970, p. 3)

Such stories strike terror into the heart of the big-city dweller. On hearing them, he decides to put an extra lock on his apartment door, or to move to the suburbs, or never to venture out at night again. In "Readings in Social Psychology Today" (1970, p. 3), an editor asserts that "most of America lives in cities, and it is one of the major tragedies of these times that our cities are in deep trouble." How has this happened? Is it just that city people are hopelessly cold and cruel or are there other explanations?

Latané and Darley suggest that it is doubtful that we have been turned into stone-like beings by living in cities. They say that the 38 witnesses to Kitty Genovese's murder did not merely look at the scene once and then ignore it. "Instead they continued to stare out their windows at what was going on—caught, fascinated, [and] distressed, unwilling to act but unable to turn away," (Latané and Darley, 1969, p. 244). Also, Latané and Darley note that city people *do* help in nonemergency situations, such as providing change or directions when they are requested by a stranger.

Why, then, do emergencies inhibit action as they do? Probably be-

255

cause emergencies are rare, unforeseen, and unhappy occurrences. We have little to gain by aiding in an emergency; we have not had much practice for such a role, are given only a short time to consider how to play it, and have scant knowledge of how to do so successfully.

In an effort to determine the conditions under which people might notice an event, decide that it is an emergency, feel responsible, and choose to act, Latané and Darley have carried out a series of experiments. In the introduction to the article here, they describe an experiment in which subjects heard a person undergoing an epileptic fit in another room. Subjects who thought that they alone heard the noises were more likely to take some action than subjects who thought that there were other bystanders. The authors called this phenomenon "diffusion." In another study (Latané and Rodin, 1969), students came to the university to take part in a consumer opinions survey. After they entered the testing room, a young woman entered (through a curtain across one side of the testing room) and distributed questionnaires to be filled out by the students. After she had handed out the questionnaires, the young woman announced that she would "be in her office," and left the room through the same curtain at the side of the room. Several minutes later, the students heard sounds from next door of someone falling off a chair, with accompanying moans and crashes. The experimenters noted the number of students who either called out offering help, or came to offer help in person. They found that, of 26 students who were *alone* in the testing room while filling out the questionnaire, 70 percent offered help. Of 40 *groups* of students who filled out the questionnaire with one other student, 20 percent offered help. Why was the unfortunate victim of the fall less likely to get help when potential samaritans were in groups rather than alone? The authors' explanations included the following:

(a) Diffusion of responsibility: Students who were in a group felt less responsibility for helping than students who were alone, since responsibility in a group is shared with other persons. Thus, people in a group are inclined to "let George do it." Similarly, diffusion of blame might have taken place, since any blame for failure to act is shared in the group, lessening the amount of blame falling on any one pair of shoulders.

(b) Fear of appearing foolish to other persons.

(c) Interpretation of the situation: Emergency sounds are often ambiguous. If someone else is present, and he appears not to perceive the situation as an emergency, then perhaps it is not.

In the experiment reprinted here, an attempt was made to measure the effect of group influence in emergencies, and minimize the effect of diffusion of responsibility and diffusion of blame. Since all of the subjects (or subjects and confederates) were in danger from smoke in the room, presumably all were equally responsible. Surely one cannot diffuse responsibility for one's own life.

METHOD

The subjects' behavior was measured under three conditions. Some of the subjects were alone in the experimental room, and some of the subjects were together with other subjects. Finally, some of the subjects were together with "passive" confederates, who had been instructed not to react to the emergency.

RESULTS

The results are most clear when the incidence of reporting smoke is considered. The passive confederates markedly reduced the amount of action (75 percent in the alone condition as compared to 10% in the two passive confederates condition.) There were similar results in the three real subjects condition (out of 8 groups of 3, only 38% had at least one person reporting the smoke).

The reader will find that the analysis is complicated by the fact that, in the 3-subject groups (as compared to the one-subject groups), there was a greater probability that *someone* would report the smoke. The proper comparison for the 3-person group is not really the one-subject group, but the "hypothetical" 3-person group constructed by computing the "expected" score for three-person groups (assuming that a three-person group is a combination of three "alone" individuals). However, the results here are clear, even to the "naked" eye, and the statistical tests are necessary only for confirmation.

DISCUSSION

Latané and Darley suggest that the presence of a crowd is an important factor in determining the urban failure to intervene. Also, in later studies (cited in Latané and Darley, 1969, 1970), they found that bystanders are more likely to help when they are friends with the other bystanders or are acquainted with the victim. Thus, the fact that there are many strangers in a big city might be a further explanation for the lack of helping in emergencies.

In general, Latané and Darley reject the idea that city people are alienated and heartless, and they urge reappraisal of the psychological effects of city living. As one example of such effects, the editors would suggest that the city provides experience in discovering that potential emergency cues need not indicate an emergency. A personal example might help to explain. The superintendent of the apartment building of one of the editors (LZS) recently climbed out on the roof of the building to investigate the source of some problem. Thinking that a young woman in a top floor apartment might be nervous at the sounds that he made, he called out to her: "Hello. Don't worry. It's the superintendent." Apparently, she wasn't impressed by this introduction, and promptly called the police. Hearing some noises, and thinking that his wife had come to call him for dinner, the superintendent left the roof to find himself faced with three policemen and as many drawn revolvers. The reader may consider whether this embarrassed young woman will run to call the police on future occasions.

Milgram (1971) provides an interesting analysis of the effect of city living that applies to the whole question of bystander action. He suggests that cities "overload" people with stimuli—that there is too much happening, too many people doing too many things, for anyone to take it all in. So people adjust to this overload by ignoring part of the input, as for instance, by ignoring dubious emergency cues, or by responding only to the needs of friends and relatives, rather than strangers. Thus, in Kitty Genovese's case, she may have had friends who would have helped her, but they were scattered over the city, rather than living next door, and so she died.

References

Darley, J. M., & Latané, B. When will people help in a crisis? In *Readings in social psychology today*. Del Mar, Calif.: CRM Books, 1970.

Latané, B., & Darley, J. M. Bystander "apathy." *American Scientist*, 1969, *57*, 244–268.

Latané, B., & Darley, J. M. *The unresponsive bystander: why doesn't he help?* New York: Appleton-Century-Crofts, 1970.

Latané, B., & Rodin, J. A lady in distress: inhibiting effects of friends and strangers on bystander intervention. *Journal of Experimental Social Psychology*, 1969, *5*, 189–202.

Milgram, S. The experience of living in cities. In E. P. Hollander, & R. G. Hunt (Eds.), *Current perspectives in social psychology*. (3d ed.) New York: Oxford University Press, 1971.

5.4 Group Inhibition of Bystander Intervention in Emergencies[1]

Bibb Latané[2]

John M. Darley[3]

Male undergraduates found themselves in a smoke-filling room either alone, with 2 nonreacting others, or in groups of 3. As predicted, Ss were less likely to report the smoke when in the presence of passive others (10%) or in groups of 3 (38% of groups) than when alone (75%). This result seemed to have been mediated by the way Ss interpreted the ambiguous situation; seeing other people remain passive led Ss to decide the smoke was not dangerous.

Emergencies, fortunately, are uncommon events. Although the average person may read about them in newspapers or watch fictionalized versions on television, he probably will encounter fewer than half a dozen in his lifetime. Unfortunately, when he does encounter one, he will have had little direct personal experience in dealing with it. And he must deal with it under conditions of urgency, uncertainty, stress, and fear. About all the individual has to guide him is the secondhand wisdom of the late movie, which is often as useful as "Be brave" or as applicable as "Quick, get lots of hot water and towels!"

Under the circumstances, it may seem surprising that anybody ever intervenes in an emergency in which he is not directly involved. Yet there is a strongly held cultural norm that individuals should act to relieve the distress of others. As the Old Parson puts it, "In this life of froth and bubble, two things stand like stone—kindness in another's trouble, courage in your own." Given the conflict between the norm to act and an individual's fears and uncertainties about getting involved, what factors will determine whether a bystander to an emergency will intervene?

We have found (Darley & Latané, 1968) that the mere perception that other people are also witnessing the event will markedly decrease the likelihood that an individual will intervene in an emergency. Individuals heard a

Reprinted from the *Journal of Personality and Social Psychology,* 1968, *10,* 215–221. Copyright 1968 by the American Psychological Association and reproduced with permission.

[1] We thank Lee Ross and Keith Gerritz for their thoughtful efforts. This research was supported by National Science Foundation Grants GS 1238 and GS 1239. The experiment was conducted at Columbia University.

person undergoing a severe epileptic-like fit in another room. In one experimental condition, the subject thought that he was the only person who heard the emergency; in another condition, he thought four other persons were also aware of the seizure. Subjects alone with the victim were much more likely to intervene on his behalf, and, on the average, reacted in less than one-third the time required by subjects who thought there were other bystanders present.

"Diffusion of responsibility" seems the most likely explanation for this result. If an individual is alone when he notices an emergency, he is solely responsible for coping with it. If he believes others are also present, he may feel that his own responsibility for taking action is lessened, making him less likely to help.

To demonstrate that responsibility diffusion rather than any of a variety of social influence processes caused this result, the experiment was designed so that the onlookers to the seizure were isolated one from another and could not discuss how to deal with the emergency effectively. They knew the others could not see what they did, nor could they see whether somebody else had already started to help. Although this state of affairs is characteristic of many actual emergencies (such as the Kitty Genovese murder in which 38 people witnessed a killing from their individual apartments without acting), in many other emergencies several bystanders are in contact with and can influence each other. In these situations, processes other than responsibility diffusion will also operate.

Given the opportunity to interact, a group can talk over the situation and divide up the helping action in an efficient way. Also, since responding to emergencies is a socially prescribed norm, individuals might be expected to adhere to it more when in the presence of other people. These reasons suggest that interacting groups should be better at coping with emergencies than single individuals. We suspect, however, that the opposite is true. Even when allowed to communicate, groups may still be worse than individuals.

Most emergencies are, or at least begin as, ambiguous events. A quarrel in the street may erupt into violence, but it may be simply a family argument. A man staggering about may be suffering a coronary or an onset of diabetes; he may be simply drunk. Smoke pouring from a building may signal a fire; on the other hand, it may be simply steam or air-conditioning vapor. Before a bystander is likely to take action in such ambiguous situations, he must first define the event as an emergency and decide that intervention is the proper course of action.

In the course of making these decisions, it is likely that an individual bystander will be considerably influenced by the decisions he perceives other bystanders to be taking. If everyone else in a group of onlookers seems to regard an event as nonserious and the proper course of action as nonintervention, this consensus may strongly affect the perceptions of any single individual and inhibit his potential intervention.

The definitions that other people hold may be discovered by discussing the situation with them, but they may also be inferred from their facial expressions or their behavior. A whistling man with his hands in his pockets obviously does not believe he is in the midst of a crisis. A bystander who does not respond to smoke obviously does not attribute it to fire. An individual, seeing the inaction of others, will judge the situation as less serious than he would if he were alone.

In the present experiment, this line of thought will be tested by presenting an emergency situation to individuals either alone or in the presence of two passive others, confederates of the experimenter who have been instructed to notice the emergency but remain indifferent to it. It is our expectation that this passive behavior will signal the individual that the other bystanders do not consider the situation to be dangerous. We predict that an individual faced with the passive reactions of other people will be influenced by them, and will thus be less likely to take action than if he were alone.

This, however, is a prediction about individuals; it says nothing about the original question of the behavior of freely interacting groups. Most groups do not have preinstructed confederates among their members, and the kind of social influence process described above would, by itself, only lead to a convergence of attitudes within a group. Even if each member of the group is entirely guided by the reactions of others, then the group should still respond with a likelihood equal to the average of the individuals.

An additional factor is involved, however. Each member of a group may watch the others, but he is also aware that the others are watching him. They are an audience to his own reactions. Among American males it is considered desirable to appear poised and collected in times of stress. Being exposed to public view may constrain an individual's actions as he attempts to avoid possible ridicule and embarrassment.

The constraints involved with being in public might in themselves tend to inhibit action by individuals in a group, but in conjunction with the social influence process described above, they may be expected to have even more powerful effects. If each member of a group is, at the same time, trying to appear calm and also looking around at the other members to gauge their reactions, all members may be led (or misled) by each other to define the situation as less critical than they would if alone. Until someone acts, each person only sees other nonresponding bystanders, and, as with the passive confederates, is likely to be influenced not to act himself.

This leads to a second prediction. Compared to the performance of individuals, if we expose groups of naive subjects to an emergency, the constraints on behavior in public coupled with the social influence process will lessen the likelihood that the members of the group will act to cope with the emergency.

It has often been recognized (Brown, 1954, 1965) that a crowd can cause contagion of panic, leading each person in the crowd to overreact to an emergency to the detriment of everyone's welfare. What is implied here is that a crowd can also force inaction on its members. It can suggest, implicitly but strongly, by its passive behavior, that an event is not to be reacted to as an emergency, and it can make any individual uncomfortably aware of what a fool he will look for behaving as if it is.

METHOD

The subject, seated in a small waiting room, faced an ambiguous but potentially dangerous situation as a stream of smoke began to puff into the room through a wall vent. His response to this situation was observed through a one-way glass. The length of time the subject remained in the room before leaving to report the smoke was the main dependent variable of the study.

Recruitment of subjects. Male Columbia students living in campus residences were invited to an interview to discuss "some of the problems involved in life at an urban university." The subject sample included graduate and professional students as well as undergraduates. Individuals were contacted by telephone and most willingly volunteered and actually showed up for the interview. At this point, they were directed either by signs or by the secretary to a "waiting room" where a sign asked them to fill out a preliminary questionnaire.

Experimental manipulation. Some subjects filled out the questionnaire and were exposed to the potentially critical situation while alone. Others were part of three-person groups consisting of one subject and two confederates acting the part of naive subjects. The confederates attempted to avoid conversation as much as possible. Once the smoke had been introduced, they stared at it briefly, made no comment, but simply shrugged their shoulders, returned to the questionnaires and continued to fill them out, occasionally waving away the smoke to do so. If addressed, they attempted to be as uncommunicative as possible and to show apparent indifference to the smoke. "I dunno," they said, and no subject persisted in talking.

In a final condition, three naive subjects were tested together. In general, these subjects did not know each other, although in two groups, subjects reported a nodding acquaintanceship with another subject. Since subjects arrived at slightly different times and since they each had individual questionnaires to work on, they did not introduce themselves to each other, or attempt anything but the most rudimentary conversation.

Critical situation. As soon as the subjects had completed two pages of their questionnaires, the experimenter began to introduce the smoke through a small vent in the wall. The "smoke" was finely divided titanium dioxide produced in a stoppered bottle and delivered under slight air pressure through the vent.[2] It formed a moderately fine-textured but clearly visible stream of whitish smoke. For the entire experimental period, the smoke continued to jet into the room in irregular puffs. By the end of the experimental period, vision was obscured by the amount of smoke present.

All behavior and conversation was observed and coded from behind a one-way window (largely disguised on the subject's side by a large sign giving preliminary instructions). If the subject left the experimental room and reported the smoke, he was told that the situation "would be taken care of." If the subject had not reported the presence of smoke by 6 minutes from the time he first noticed it, the experiment was terminated.

RESULTS

Alone condition. The typical subject, when tested alone, behaved very reasonably. Usually, shortly after the smoke appeared, he would glance up from his questionnaire, notice the smoke, show a slight but distinct startle reaction, and then undergo a brief period of indecision, perhaps returning briefly to his questionnaire before again staring at the smoke. Soon, most subjects would get up from their chairs, walk over to the vent, and investigate it closely, sniffing the smoke, waving their hands in it, feeling its temperature, etc. The usual alone subject would hesitate again, but finally walk out of the room, look around outside, and, finding somebody there, calmly report the presence of the smoke. No subject showed any sign of panic; most simply said, "There's something strange going on in there, there seems to be some sort of smoke coming through the wall. . . ."

The median subject in the alone condition had reported the smoke within 2 minutes of first noticing it. Three-quarters of the 24 people who were run in this condition reported the smoke before the experimental period was terminated.

Two passive confederates condition. The behavior of subjects run with two passive confederates was dramatically different; of 10 people run in this condition, only 1 reported the smoke. The other 9 stayed in the waiting room as it filled up with smoke, doggedly working on their questionnaire and waving the fumes away from their faces. They coughed, rubbed their eyes, and opened the window—but they did not report the smoke. The difference between the response rate of 75% in the alone condition and 10% in the two passive confederates condition is highly significant ($p < .002$ by Fisher's exact test, two-tailed).

Three naive bystanders. Because there are three subjects present and

---

[2] Smoke was produced by passing moisturized air, under pressure, through a container of titanium tetrachloride, which, in reaction with the water vapor, creates a suspension of tantium dioxide in air.

available to report the smoke in the three naive bystander condition as compared to only one subject at a time in the alone condition, a simple comparison between the two conditions is not appropriate. On the other hand, we cannot compare speeds in the alone condition with the average speed of the three subjects in a group, since, once one subject in a group had reported the smoke, the pressures on the other two disappeared. They legitimately could (and did) feel that the emergency had been handled, and any action on their part would be redundant and potentially confusing. Therefore the speed of the *first* subject in a group to report the smoke was used as the dependent variable. However, since there were three times as many people available to respond in this condition as in the alone condition, we would expect an increased likelihood that *at least* one person would report the smoke even if the subjects had no influence whatsoever on each other. Therefore we mathematically created "groups" of three scores from the alone condition to serve as a base line.[4]

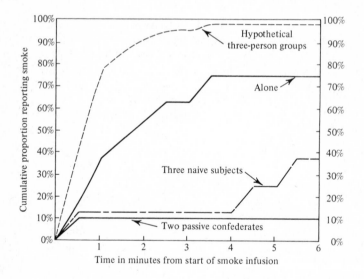

FIG. 1. Cumulative proportion of subjects reporting the smoke over time.

In contrast to the complexity of this procedure, the results were quite simple. Subjects in the three naive bystander condition were markedly in-

[4] The formula for calculating the expected proportion of groups in which at least one person will have acted by a given time is $1 - (1 - p)^n$ where p is the proportion of single individuals who act by that time and n is the number of persons in the group.

hibited from reporting the smoke. Since 75% of the alone subjects reported the smoke, we would expect over 98% of the three-person groups to contain at least one reporter. In fact, in only 38% of the eight groups in this condition did even 1 subject report ($p < .01$). Of the 24 people run in these eight groups, only 1 person reported the smoke within the first 4 minutes before the room got noticeably unpleasant. Only 3 people reported the smoke within the entire experimental period.

Cumulative distribution of report times.   Figure 1 presents the cumulative frequency distributions of report times for all three conditions. The figure shows the proportion of subjects in each condition who had reported the smoke by any point in the time following the introduction of the smoke. For example, 55% of the subjects in the alone condition had reported the smoke within 2 minutes, but the smoke had been reported in only 12% of the three-person groups by that time. After 4 minutes, 75% of the subjects in the alone condition had reported the smoke; no additional subjects in the group condition had done so. The curve in Figure 1 labeled "Hypothetical Three-Person Groups" is based upon the mathematical combination of scores obtained from subjects in the alone condition. It is the expected report times for groups in the three-person condition if the members of the groups had no influence upon each other.

It can be seen in Figure 1 that for every point in time following the introduction of the smoke, a considerably higher proportion of subjects in the alone condition had reported the smoke than had subjects in either the two passive confederates condition or in the three naive subjects condition. The curve for the latter condition, although considerably below the alone curve, is even more substantially inhibited with respect to its proper comparison, the curve of hypothetical three-person sets. Social inhibition of response was so great that the time elapsing before the smoke was reported was greater when there were more people available to report it (alone versus group $p < .05$ by Mann-Whitney U test).

Superficially, it appears that there is a somewhat higher likelihood of response from groups of three naive subjects than from subjects in the passive confederates condition. Again this comparison is not justified; there are three people free to act in one condition instead of just one. If we mathematically combine scores for subjects in the two passive confederates condition in a similar manner to that described above for the alone condition, we would obtain an expected likelihood of response of .27 as the hypothetical base line. This is not significantly different from the .37 obtained in the actual three-subject groups.

Noticing the smoke.   In observing the subject's reaction to the introduction of smoke, careful note was taken of the exact moment when he first saw the smoke (all report latencies were computed from this time). This was a relatively easy observation to make, for the subjects invariably showed a distinct, if slight, startle reaction. Unexpectedly, the presence of other persons delayed, slightly but very significantly, noticing the smoke. Sixty-three percent of subjects in the alone condition and only 26% of subjects in the combined together conditions noticed the smoke within the first 5 seconds after its introduction ($p < .01$ by chi-square). The median latency of noticing the smoke was under 5 seconds in the alone condition; the median time at which the first (or only) subject in each of the combined together conditions noticed the smoke was 20 seconds (this difference does not account for group-induced inhibition of reporting since the report latencies were computed from the time the smoke was first noticed).

This interesting finding can probably be explained in terms of the constraints which people feel in public places (Goffman, 1963). Unlike solitary subjects, who often glanced idly about the room while filling out their questionnaires, subjects in groups usually kept their eyes closely on their work, probably to avoid appearing rudely inquisitive.

Postexperimental interview. After 6 minutes, whether or not the subjects had reported the smoke, the interviewer stuck his head in the waiting room and asked the subject to come with him to the interview. After seating the subject in his office, the interviewer made some general apologies about keeping the subject waiting for so long, hoped the subject hadn't become too bored and asked if he "had experienced any difficulty while filling out the questionnaire." By this point most subjects mentioned the smoke. The interviewer expressed mild surprise and asked the subject to tell him what had happened. Thus each subject gave an account of what had gone through his mind during the smoke infusion.

Subjects who had reported the smoke were relatively consistent in later describing their reactions to it. They thought the smoke looked somewhat "strange," they were not sure exactly what it was or whether it was dangerous, but they felt it was unusual enough to justify some examination. "I wasn't sure whether it was a fire but it looked like something was wrong." "I thought it might be steam, but it seemed like a good idea to check it out."

Subjects who had not reported the smoke also were unsure about exactly what it was, but they uniformly said that they had rejected the idea that it was a fire. Instead, they hit upon an astonishing variety of alternative explanations, all sharing the common characteristic of interpreting the smoke as a nondangerous event. Many thought the smoke was either steam or air-conditioning vapors, several thought it was smog, purposely introduced to simulate an urban environment, and two (from different groups) actually suggested that the smoke was a "truth gas" filtered into the room to induce them to answer the questionnaire accurately. (Surprisingly, they were not disturbed by this conviction.) Predictably, some decided that "it must be some sort of experiment" and stoicly endured the discomfort of the room rather than overreact.

Despite the obvious and powerful report-inhibiting effect of other bystanders, subjects almost invariably claimed that they had paid little or no attention to the reactions of the other people in the room. Although the presence of other people actually had a strong and pervasive effect on the subjects' reactions, they were either unaware of this or unwilling to admit it.

DISCUSSION

Before an individual can decide to intervene in an emergency, he must, implicitly or explicitly, take several preliminary steps. If he is to intervene, he must first *notice* the event, he must then *interpret* it as an emergency, and he must decide that it is his personal *responsibility* to act. At each of these preliminary steps, the bystander to an emergency can remove himself from the decision process and thus fail to help. He can fail to notice the event, he can fail to interpret it as an emergency, or he can fail to assume the responsibility to take action.

In the present experiment we are primarily interested in the second step of this decision process, interpreting an ambiguous event. When faced with such an event, we suggest, the individual bystander is likely to look at the reactions of people around him and be powerfully influenced by them. It was predicted that the sight of other, nonresponsive bystanders would lead the individual to interpret the emergency as not serious, and consequently lead him not to act. Further, it was predicted that the dynamics of the interaction process would lead each of a group of naive onlookers to be misled by the apparent inaction of the others into adopting a nonemergency interpretation of the event and a passive role.

The results of this study clearly support our predictions. Individuals exposed to a room filling with smoke in the presence of passive others themselves remained passive, and groups of three naive subjects were less likely to report the smoke than solitary bystanders. Our predictions were confirmed—but this does not necessarily mean that our explanation for these results is the correct one. As a matter of fact, several alternatives are available.

Two of these alternative explanations stem from the fact that the smoke represented a possible danger to the subject himself as well as to others in the building. Subjects' behavior might have reflected their fear of fire, with subjects in groups feeling less threatened by the fire than single subjects and thus being less concerned to act. It has been demonstrated in studies with humans (Schachter, 1959) and with rats (Latané, 1968; Latané & Glass, 1968) that togetherness reduces fear, even in situations where it does not reduce danger. In addition, subjects may have felt that the presence of others increased their ability to cope with fire. For both of these reasons, subjects in groups may have been less afraid of fire and thus less likely to report the smoke than solitary subjects.

A similar explanation might emphasize not fearfulness, but the desire to hide fear. To the extent that bravery or stoicism in the face of danger or discomfort is a socially desirable trait (as it appears to be for American male undergraduates), one might expect individuals to attempt to appear more brave or more stoic when others are watching than when they are alone. It is possible that subjects in the group condition saw themselves as engaged in a game of "Chicken," and thus did not react.

Although both of these explanations are plausible, we do not think that they provide an accurate account of subjects' thinking. In the post-experimental interviews, subjects claimed, *not* that they were unworried by the fire or that they were unwilling to endure the danger; but rather that they decided that there was no fire at all and the smoke was caused by something else. They failed to act because they thought there was no reason to act. Their "apathetic" behavior was reasonable—given their interpretation of the circumstances.

The fact that smoke signals potential danger to the subject himself weakens another alternative explanation, "diffusion of responsibility." Regardless of social influence processes, an individual may feel less personal responsibility for helping if he shares the responsibility with others (Darley & Latané, 1968). But this diffusion explanation does not fit the present situation. It is hard to see how an individual's responsibility for saving himself is diffused by the presence of other people. The diffusion explanation does not account for the pattern of interpretations reported by the subjects or for their variety of nonemergency explanations.

On the other hand, the social influence processes which we believe account for the results of our present study obviously do not explain our previous experiment in which subjects could not see or be seen by each other. Taken together, these two studies suggest that the presence of bystanders may affect an individual in several ways; including both "social influence" and "diffusion of responsibility."

Both studies, however, find, for two quite different kinds of emergencies and under two quite different conditions of social contact, that individuals are less likely to engage in socially responsible action if they think other bystanders are present. This presents us with the paradoxical conclusion that a victim may be more likely to get help, or an emergency may be more likely to be reported, the fewer people there are available to take action. It also may help us begin to understand a number of frightening incidents where crowds have listened to but not answered a call for help. Newspapers have tagged these incidents with the label "apathy." We have become indifferent, they say, callous to the fate of suffering others. The results of our studies lead to a different conclusion. The failure to intervene may be better understood by knowing the relationship among bystanders rather than that between a bystander and the victim.

References

Brown, R. W. Mass phenomena. In G. Lindzey (Ed.), *Handbook of social psychology*. Vol. 2. Cambridge: Addison-Wesley, 1954.

Brown, R. *Social psychology*. New York: Free Press of Glencoe, 1965.

Darley, J. M., & Latané, B. Bystander intervention in emergencies: Diffusion of responsibility. *Journal of Personality and Social Psychology*, 1968, *8*, 377–383.

Goffman, E. *Behavior in public places*. New York: Free Press of Glencoe, 1963.

Latané, B. Gregariousness and fear in laboratory rats. *Journal of Experimental Social Psychology*, 1968.

Latané, B., & Glass, D. C. Social and nonsocial attraction in rats. *Journal of Personality and Social Psychology*, 1968, *9*, 142–146.

Schachter, S. *The psychology of affiliation*. Stanford: Stanford University Press, 1959.

Foreword to Reading 5.5

INTRODUCTION

The term "stereotype" was introduced by Walter Lippmann (1922), who suggested that stereotypes are "pictures in our heads" that are factually incorrect, produced through illogical reasoning, and rigidly held. Katz and Braly (1933) sought to determine the extent to which ethnic stereotypes were held by the Princeton undergraduates of the time. Their subjects were given an 84-adjective list and asked to select from it the traits that were typical of ten particular ethnic groups (Germans, Italians, Negroes, etc.). Then, they were also asked to select the five *most* typical adjectives for each group. Looking at this latter measure, it could be seen that the subjects had similar views of many of the groups. For instance, over one-half of the 100 subjects agreed that, most typically, Germans are scientifically minded and industrious, Italians artistic, English sportsmanlike, Jews shrewd, and Negroes superstitious and lazy. If a stereotype can be defined as agreement in the perception that one group has of another group (although this is not the same as Lippmann's definition), then Katz and Braly's subjects evidenced strong stereotypes. Katz and Braly's study has been repeated by other investigators (Gilbert, 1951; Karlins, Coffman, and Walters, 1969) who also used white Princeton undergraduates as subjects. Gilbert reported that stereotypes at Princeton had become less uniform by 1951, while in 1969 Karlins et al. found that, despite a return to high agreement concerning stereotypes, certain groups were viewed less positively or less negatively than before. For example, "Americans" (the term used in the study) were viewed less favorably, and "Negroes" more favorably.

Sigall and Page, in the article reprinted here, suggest that the results obtained by Karlins may have been affected by "social desirability" or "other demand-characteristic-related variables." The term "demand characteristic" has been encountered earlier in this volume (see the com-

270

mentary on Grusec, 1972). The "demand characteristics" of an experiment are the aspects of the situation that lead the subject to think that he "should" behave in a particular way if he is to be a "good subject." The assumption is that subjects, particularly those who volunteer for the job, are motivated to behave in a way that will please the experimenter, contribute to science, and confirm the hypothesis (Orne, 1962). The variable of "social desirability," on the other hand, is introduced through the subject's own desire to look as good as he can when he answers a questionnaire or responds in some way. This can be particularly biassing in personality questionnaires and must be controlled for in some way, as for instance, by having the subject choose between alternatives that are equally socially desirable, but which indicate different personality traits.

Since "putting down" America and being liberal toward minority groups does seem to be the vogue on college campuses today, it is conceivable that Karlins' results reflect either true changes in attitude since 1933, or the subjects' desire to sound fashionable or respectable or reasonable. In an effort to test the "true" attitudes of today's white college students, Sigall and Page carried out a stereotype study in which half of the subjects were told that a totally objective physiological measure of their "real" feelings was being taken. They were, however, also asked to indicate their attitudes themselves, since the experimenters wanted to "see if students today are in touch with their feelings." By comparing the responses of these subjects with subjects who were not told about a machine (the "bogus pipeline"), Sigall and Page were able to obtain an indication of the extent to which subjects might distort their responses in a stereotype study. The "pipeline" subjects were assumed to be trying to be as objective about themselves as possible in order not to be shown up as liars by the "magical" machine.

METHOD

Half of the subjects in each of the conditions (pipeline, and no pipeline) were asked to indicate their attitudes toward "Americans," and half were asked to indicate their attitudes toward "Negroes." The subjects were given a number of adjectives and asked to rate the extent to which each adjective was characteristic of the group designated.

RESULTS AND DISCUSSION

Sigall and Page did find that their subjects responded differently when they thought that a machine was revealing the truth about them. In that situation, they became less positive toward "Negroes" and more positive toward "Americans." This does not, however, invalidate Karlins' results; it simply indicates that social desirability might have been a factor in that study. The reader will find that Sigall and Page have provided an analysis of the differences between their study and that of Karlins, as well as a discussion of the possible demand characteristics in their own study.

The research on stereotypes has recently come under fire for failing to resolve the important issues. Brigham (1971) asserts that the Katz and Braly technique is biased in that the subject is asked to select the adjectives "typical" of a group, thus forcing him to overgeneralize about the group. (This could be considered as an example of a demand characteristic, by the way—the subject stereotyping to please the experimenter, who has suggested this way of thinking to him.) Also, since the subject is given a number of groups to describe, he inevitably compares one group to the other. The same group in a different context might be rated differently. Finally, Brigham suggests that the Katz and Braly technique has not been helpful in proving the existence of stereotypes as described by Lippmann, since it indicates nothing about rigidity of thinking, illogical reasoning, and so on.

Using Brigham's criteria, the Sigall and Page research would seem to be a significant step forward in the study of stereotypes. Each subject was asked to rate one group only, rather than a number of groups. And an attempt was made to discover the thought process behind the verbalization of stereotypes. The experiment is not the only situation in which the desire to say the right thing could lead the person to mouth the stereotypes of his group.

References

Brigham, J. C. Ethnic stereotypes. *Psychological Bulletin,* 1971, *76,* 15–38.

Gilbert, G. M. Stereotype persistence and change among college students. *Journal of Abnormal and Social Psychology,* 1951, *46,* 245–254.

Grusec, J. E. Demand characteristics of the modeling experiment: altruism as a function of age and aggression. *Journal of Personality and Social Psychology,* 1972, *22,* 139–148.

Karlins, M., Coffman, T. L., & Walters, G. On the fading of social stereotypes: studies in three generations of college students. *Journal of Personality and Social Psychology,* 1969, *13,* 1–16.

Katz, D., & Braly, K. Racial stereotypes of 100 college students. *Journal of Abnormal and Social Psychology,* 1933, *28,* 280–290.

Lippmann, W. *Public opinion.* New York: Harcourt Brace Jovanovich, 1922.

Orne, M. On the social psychology of the psychological experiment: with particular reference to demand characteristics and their implications. *American Psychologist,* 1962, *17,* 776–783.

5.5 Current Stereotypes: a Little Fading, a Little Faking[1]

Harold Sigall
Richard Page

The possibility that social-desirability-tainted responses emerge in the study of stereotypes is suggested and examined. Sixty white American subjects were randomly assigned to one of four experimental conditions. Subjects were asked to indicate how characteristic each of 22 adjective traits was of either "Americans" or "Negroes." This was cross-cut by a measurement variable: Half of the subjects responded in a rating situation in which they were presumably free to distort their responses. Remaining subjects responded under "bogus pipeline" conditions; that is, they were led to believe that the experimenter had an accurate, distortion-free physiological measure of their attitudes, and they were asked to predict that measure. The results supported our expectation that the stereotype ascribed to Negroes would be more favorable under rating than under bogus pipeline conditions. Americans were more favorably stereotyped under bogus pipeline than under rating conditions. A number of explanations for these results are discussed, and consideration is given to the relationship between verbally expressed attitudes and other, overt behavior.

Ethnic stereotypes have been subject to examination for quite some time. The first empirical investigation of such stereotypes was the now well-known study by Katz and Braly (1933). They looked at the stereotypes held by Princeton undergraduates toward 10 ethnic groups and thereby established a paradigm and a tradition. The tradition has been followed by Gilbert (1951) and more recently by Karlins, Coffman, and Walters (1969), who also examined the stereotypes held by Princeton students. The paradigm was a simple one: subjects were presented with a list of traits and asked to indicate which of them were necessary to adequately characterize each ethnic group. They also were asked to choose from among the assigned traits the five traits most typical of each group. Katz and Braly were then able to look at the qualitative descriptions ascribed to each group and to calculate the degree of uniformity associated with each stereotype.

From *Journal of Personality and Social Psychology*, 1971, Vol. 18, No. 2, 247–255. Copyright 1971 by the American Psychological Association and used with permission.

[1] This research was supported by Research Grant MH 17180-01 from the National Institute of Mental Health. The authors would like to thank Robert Strahan for helpful suggestions.

273

The smaller the number of traits needed to account for at least 50% of the ascriptions, the greater the uniformity of the stereotype.

Katz and Braly's (1933) results were quite striking. Their subjects manifested strong stereotyping, that is, high uniformity; they also demonstrated a powerful tendency to describe certain ethnic groups quite favorably, while viewing others rather unfavorably. Gilbert (1951) reported some fading of such stereotypes, finding that there was a considerable decrease in the uniformity of traits assigned to the groups. However, Karlins et al. (1969) reported a return to high uniformity in the stereotypes held by Princeton students. On the other hand, they did find "fading," but of another type. Certain groups who were viewed earlier as either extremely positive or extremely negative took on more moderate stereotypes. Perhaps most noteworthy for contemporary America was the sharp decrease in American chauvinism and the sharp increase in favorability ascribed to Negroes.

These latter findings represent the point of departure for the experiment reported here. While such findings may in fact reflect basic attitude change over time, it seems intuitively that social desirability (Crowne & Marlowe, 1964) or other demand-characteristic-related variables could affect responses in a study of stereotypes. For example, self-criticism by Americans and concern about Negroes currently are active phenomena on many college campuses. It certainly seems "modish" to be favorable when describing Negroes, and it may be fashionable to be less than favorable when describing Americans. The fact that many subjects in the research conducted by Karlins et al. and by Gilbert objected to participating in the studies documents the sensitive nature of the research situation.

In the present study we departed from the Katz and Braly paradigm and used a relatively new technique in an attempt to reduce socially desirable responses in the assessment of Negro and American stereotypes. The full rationale underlying this technique, a version of the "bogus pipeline," is described elsewhere (Jones & Sigall, in press). As used by Jones and Sigall, the term bogus pipeline refers to a paradigm in which an experimenter claims to have access (a pipeline) to his subject's covert reactions. Briefly, the procedure is designed to encourage the subject to respond honestly, by leading him to believe that the experimenter can assess precisely the direction and intensity of his attitudes, via a machine that provides a direct physiological measure of those attitudes. The subject is then asked to *predict* what the machine is saying about him. We assume that the subject will be motivated to predict the machine reading accurately—that he will not want to be second-guessed by it. Once the subject believes that the experimenter will know his real attitude anyway, distortion serves little purpose: at best, the experimenter would regard him as insensitive to his own feelings; at worst, he might be viewed as actively deceptive.

We expected that using this technique would lead subjects to present less socially desirable stereotypes than would result in a more typical rating-scale situation, where subjects are relatively free to distort. Half of our subjects responded under bogus pipeline conditions, while the remainder responded in a rating situation in which the experimenter did not claim to have independent evidence concerning attitudes.

METHOD

Subjects and Design

Sixty white male undergraduates were recruited from an introductory psychology course at the University of Rochester. Half of the subjects indicated how characteristic they felt each of a series of 22 traits was of "Americans." The other half did the same with respect to "Negroes." Within each of these groups, half of the subjects were led to believe that an independent and distortion-free physiological measure of their attitudes was being obtained. This design resulted in a 2 × 2 factorial, and subjects were randomly assigned to one of the four experimental conditions. Subjects were tested individually.

Apparatus

Subjects sat before a console. A semicircular 7-point scale ranging from −3 to +3 was drawn on the console, and a slot in which a label could be placed was located at each end of the scale. A steering wheel, mounted on a shaft which extended from the console, turned a pointer along the scale.

Alongside the console sat a hammertone gray metal box labeled "EMG." Dials, lights, and cable connections adorned the box. The box also contained a meter with a 7-point scale geometrically similar to one drawn on the console. This meter was labeled "EMG Output." Two skin electrodes were connected to the box by cable, and cables also extended from the box to an array of impressive-looking electrical junk, described as a small computer.

In an adjacent room a rheostat could be manipulated to control EMG-output meter readings.

Procedure

The subject reported to an experiment entitled "Perception." Upon arriving at a waiting room, the subject was greeted by the experimenter and presented with a five-item attitude inventory. The purpose of administering this inventory was to obtain information which later would be used to convince the subject that the EMG did provide an accurate measure of his attitudes. Since it was important that responses to these items would not be distorted, the attitude statements dealt with relatively innocuous issues. Subjects indicated agreement or disagreement, along a 7-point scale, with statements on movies, music, sports, automobiles, and record clubs. The experimenter left the waiting room, allowing the subject to fill out the questionnaire in private. A few minutes later the experimenter returned, escorted the subject to the experimental room, and seated the subject, such that he was facing the console with his back to the door of the room. The experimenter took the completed inventory and casually placed it on a table near the door, which was left slightly ajar so that an accomplice secretly could copy the responses from the corridor. The foregoing events took place in all conditions in order to maximize procedural similarity. Actually, they were necessitated only by the bogus pipeline or EMG conditions, which are described below.

EMG Conditions

The experimenter told the subject that using questionnaires in psychological research involved a variety of problems. He then informed him that the elaborate device before him was a recently developed "adapted electromyograph, or EMG," which made possible direct, accurate physiological measurement of attitudes, thereby eliminating some problems, including response distortion. The experimenter explained that EMG devices measured electrical potentials in muscle groups. He further explained that when a subject held the steering wheel, which was locked in place with its pointer at zero, and focused on the scale on the console, electrodes attached to his forearm would record his "first reaction tendency to turn the wheel— his undistorted response" to attitude statements read to him. The experimenter pointed out that the EMG recorded the potentials generated by implicit muscle movements, and that therefore no overt response was required for measurement. "In fact," the experimenter said, "the EMG is unaffected by gross muscle movements." The electrical junk was identified as a small computer which analyzed the electrophysiological input, and then presented the resultant information on the EMG output meter. Thus, the subject was led to believe that the EMG would indicate where he would turn the wheel, if the wheel was not locked, and if he was not distorting responses. The experimenter noted similarities between the EMG and the lie detector, and pointed out that the EMG had considerable advantages over the lie detector, the major one being that it was sensitive to both direction and intensity of responses, while the lie detector did not assess direction.

The experimenter placed the electrodes on the subject's forearms, and then "validated" the EMG. The validation was intended to convince the subject that the EMG did indeed possess its alleged powers. The experimenter explained that occasionally the EMG needed adjustment because of individual differences in base-line response levels. The experimenter told the subject that to check on whether much adjustment was necessary, EMG readings would be obtained on the same five sample items that the subject had responded to upon his arrival. "Agree" and "Disagree" labels were inserted in the slots on the console, and the subject was told to hold the wheel and concentrate on the scale. He was asked to remain silent. The experimenter read the first item and then threw a switch on the computer. The computer buzzed for a few moments, and then it seemingly turned itself off as the needle on the EMG output meter swung to a number. The second, third, and fifth items were handled in the same way. Prior to administering the fourth item, the subject was encouraged to try to "fool" the EMG. The experimenter, again emphasizing that the EMG was sensitive only to the implicit muscle movements generated by the first reaction tendency, suggested to the subject that he consciously think in opposition to his true feeling and that he exert pressure on the steering wheel in a similarly opposite direction. The experimenter pointed out that EMG readings should not be affected by either behavior. EMG readings were noted after each item. Actually, of course, both the buzzing by the computer and output meter readings were controlled from the adjacent room by the accomplice who had copied the subject's questionnaire answers. After the fifth item, the questionnaire was retrieved and compared with the EMG readings. Clearly, the EMG did not need adjustment; its readings were in perfect correspondence with the questionnaire for each item.

The subject was then told that the main purpose of the study was to assess perceptions of various groups. The labels "Characteristic" (+3) and "Uncharacteristic" (−3) were inserted in the console, and the subject was told that he would be presented with one group, Americans (Negroes), and that a series of traits would be read to him. The EMG would indicate how characteristic the subject felt each trait was of the group. The experimenter then informed the subject that he was also interested in seeing "to what extent people are in touch with their real feelings." He explained that in order to test how sensitive the subject was to his feelings, he would ask the subject to predict the EMG readings. The subject's view of the EMG meter was shielded, he was encouraged to present his undistorted reactions, and he was told that he would be permitted to see how well he had predicted upon completion of the list.

The experimenter proceeded to read 22 traits, 1 at a time. After each item he recorded the subject's prediction (the dependent measure) and also pretended to obtain and note the EMG reading.

Rating Conditions

In these conditions the electrodes were hidden, the computer was turned off, and the wheel was free to be turned. The apparatus was casually dismissed as a small computer used to analyze data. The experimenter informed the subject that there were certain problems inherent in paper-and-pencil measures, and that the steering wheel device was being employed because it produced greater attention and concentration from subjects than did questionnaires.[2] The subject was asked to turn the pointer to the appropriate place on the scale and to state the corresponding number aloud. The five-item questionnaire was used as illustration. The "purpose" of the experiment was described, and, as in the EMG conditions, the subject was asked to present his undistorted first reaction. The experimenter stressed the importance of honest responses. The experimenter read the 22 traits, 1 at a time, and recorded the subject's responses. All subjects were thoroughly debriefed.

---

[2] We do not view this rating situation as substantially different from other typical rating situations (e.g., those using paper-and-pencil measures). Support for this view comes from Byrne (1969), who has reported that responses indicated by simple physical manipulations do not differ from responses indicated with paper and pencil. We used the steering wheel as part of our attempt to keep the rating and EMG conditions as similar as possible.

RESULTS AND DISCUSSION

All subjects in the EMG conditions were successfully convinced that the EMG accurately measured attitudes. A few subjects, distributed throughout the four experimental conditions, did express some reluctance over attributing traits to groups. In these cases the experimenter acknowledged that he understood such reluctance and encouraged subjects to do their best anyway. Without exception, the subjects performed as requested.

Responses to specific traits could range from −3 (uncharacteristic) to +3 (characteristic). The mean trait assignments are presented in Table 1. The traits are listed in the order in which they were presented to the subjects. Table 1 also includes the F ratios resulting from the 22 separate analyses of variance, 1 for each trait. While we acknowledge that by performing so many analyses we run the risk of obtaining some statistically significant F ratios by chance, the large number of significant F ratios strongly suggests that on the whole we have tapped some very real differences. Let us consider the ethnic group's main effects first. Thirteen of the 22 traits were differentially assigned to Americans and Negroes at statistically significant levels. Americans were rated as characteristically more talkative, conventional, progressive, practical, intelligent, pleasure loving, industrious, ambitious, aggressive, and materialistic. Negroes were rated as more musical, ignorant, and physically dirty. Considering the data collected in the three previous Princeton studies, these main effects are not particularly surprising. In one or more of those studies, conventional, progressive, practical, intelligent, industrious, ambitious, aggressive, and materialistic were among the 10 most frequently selected traits for Americans, but not for Negroes; musical, ignorant, and physically dirty never were assigned to Americans with sufficient frequency to make the "top ten," but have been assigned with such sufficient frequency with respect to Negroes. "Pleasure loving" was assigned with approximately equal frequency to Americans and Negroes in the Karlins et al. (1969) study, and it is unclear why Americans were seen as significantly more pleasure loving than were Negroes in the present investigation. Our finding that Americans were rated as more talkative seems to run against earlier data: Karlins et al. reported that 13% of their subjects included that trait in their description of Negroes, while it was not among those frequently assigned to Americans. Our subjects suggested a possible explanation during the postexperimental interviews. They commented that the black students at the university seemed to "stay quietly to themselves." To the extent, then, that subject responses were influenced by exposure to black students on campus, it is understandable that Negroes received lower ratings on talkativeness.

It is appropriate at this point to comment on the relationship between

TABLE 1 *Mean Assignment of Traits and F Ratios*

| TRAIT | CONDITION | | | | F RATIOS | | |
| | Americans | | Negroes | | Ethnic group (A) | Measurement (B) | A × B |
	EMG	Rating	EMG	Rating			
Talkative	1.40	1.60	.67	.47	14.004****	<1	<1
Happy-go-lucky	.53	.53	.93	−.13	<1	2.841*	2.841*
Honest	.60	−.27	−.33	.67	<1	<1	14.866****
Musical	−.20	.53	1.53	2.00	31.683****	4.455**	<1
Conventional	.87	1.33	−.60	−.73	29.261****	<1	<1
Ostentatious	1.07	1.27	1.13	.33	1.627	<1	2.166
Progressive	1.47	1.33	.47	.40	12.991****	<1	<1
Ignorant	−.53	−.07	.60	.20	4.349**	<1	1.667
Practical	1.20	1.33	−.40	−.27	25.515****	<1	<1
Superstitious	−.40	−.13	.20	.00	<1	<1	<1
Intelligent	1.73	1.00	.00	.47	20.497****	<1	5.745**
Pleasure loving	1.93	2.07	1.80	1.07	4.267**	1.196	2.495
Imitative	.80	.33	.33	.20	<1	<1	<1
Stupid	−1.07	−.20	.13	−1.00	<1	<1	6.824**
Industrious	2.33	2.20	.07	.00	64.777****	<1	<1
Physically dirty	−1.67	−1.53	.20	−1.33	11.989****	5.501**	7.797***
Ambitious	2.07	2.13	−.07	.33	55.149****	<1	<1
Aggressive	1.73	1.60	1.20	.67	4.895**	1.012	<1
Unreliable	−.73	−.40	.27	−.67	1.244	<1	3.712*
Materialistic	2.42	2.20	.60	.87	33.892****	<1	<1
Sensitive	1.47	.07	.87	1.60	1.726	<1	9.016***
Lazy	−.80	−.40	.60	−.73	2.424	1.856	6.402**

* $p < .10.$ ** $p < .05.$ *** $p < .01.$ **** $p < .001.$

the present experiment and the Princeton studies. While major inconsistencies in the substance of results require attempts at explication, it must be stressed that vast differences in approach and procedure preclude placing extraordinary emphasis on direct comparisons. Beyond differences in time of testing, subject population, the introduction of a measurement variable, and a myriad of other minor variations, it is extremely important to note that subjects in the present study responded to only one ethnic group, whereas in the Katz and Braly paradigm subjects assigned traits to all ethnic groups considered. In addition, our subjects indicated *how* characteristic each trait was, while in the Katz and Braly procedure subjects simply indicated whether or not a trait applied. Thus, it is conceivable, though unlikely, that any particular trait could produce differences of great magnitude in the present study, say +2.80 for Negroes and +1.10 for Americans, but not show up as differentially assigned to the two groups in the Princeton studies. There are numerous other possible implications resulting from the difference in approaches: we just wish to caution against ignoring such differences and their implications. At the same time it is clear that we are interested in looking at the pattern and overall trends in our results in the context of the general findings and trends in the Princeton studies.

We will turn now to those traits which yielded Measurement × Ethnic Group interactions. It is these traits that illuminate most clearly the contrasting effects of using the bogus pipeline versus the more typical rating approach. Six traits yielded interactions, the statistical significance of which easily surpassed conventional standards: "honest," "intelligent," "stupid," "physically dirty," "sensitive," and "lazy." Two other traits, "happy-go-lucky" and "unreliable," produced F ratios significant at less than .10. Finally, directional interactions, with significance levels between .10 and .20, resulted from the analyses of "ostentatious," "ignorant," and "pleasure loving." The interaction F ratios for the remaining 11 traits were all less than one.

Is this pattern haphazard, or does it make sense? To answer this question, a variety of considerations must be entertained. Karlins et al. (1969) had their subjects rate the favorableness of all of the trait adjectives used by Katz and Braly. These ratings were made on a 5-point scale, ranging from +2 (very favorable) to −2 (very unfavorable). In our attempt to account for the present data, we made use of these ratings. Again, caution needs to be exercised. As Karlins et al. pointed out, ratings of adjectives out of context may not reflect the connotation of those adjectives when part of a stereotype. In addition the favorability assigned to a trait may change over time (Karlins et al. sampled in 1967, while our subjects were tested in 1969). Finally, it is possible that different subject populations value traits differentially. Nevertheless, it is useful to consider those trait-favorability values in attempting to conceptually organize the present results.

Table 2 presents the trait favorability according to Karlins et al. of the 22 traits employed here. We have organized the traits in the table so that one can easily see the favorability assigned to traits yielding interactions juxtaposed with traits that did not.

TABLE 2   *Trait Favorability of the 22 Adjectives*

TRAITS YIELDING A × B INTERACTION	FAVOR- ABILITY	TRAITS NOT YIELDING A × B INTERACTION	FAVOR- ABILITY
Intelligent	1.61	Industrious	1.32
Honest	1.56	Ambitious	1.06
Sensitive	.99	Progressive	.99
Pleasure loving	.46	Musical	.90
Happy-go-lucky	.45	Practical	.82
Ostentatious	−.89	Aggressive	.18
Lazy	−1.12	Talkative	−.13
Ignorant	−1.37	Conventional	−.30
Physically dirty	−1.45	Materialistic	−.45
Stupid	−1.59	Imitative	−.63
Unreliable	−1.64	Superstitious	−.84

One way to compare the two lists is in terms of the *absolute values* of trait favorability. The mean absolute value of traits yielding Ethnic Group × Measurement interactions was 1.19; the mean absolute value of the remaining traits was .69. Moreover, if we ignore those traits (ostentatious, ignorant, pleasure loving) which manifested the weakest interactions, the mean absolute value of interaction traits increases from 1.19 to 1.30. Unfortunately, due to the nature of these data—traits are not subjects and are not independent of one another—inferential statistics are not readily applicable. Therefore, we are left with the descriptive fact that the two means are quite different, and we are unable to assign probability values to the difference. Nevertheless, given the bogus pipeline concept, these data are very meaningful. Examining absolute values helps us to focus on the fact that interactions tended to result when a particular trait carried a relatively large amount of affective loading. If subjects' responses in stereotyping investigations are influenced by social desirability, then we would expect that such influences would be most marked when the adjectives were value laden. This, of course, is consistent with our procedure in which we deliberately used innocuous items when validating the EMG, precisely because we expected little distortion on items with bland content.

Further evidence for the notion that the EMG is affecting the social desirability of responses emerges when the direction of the interactions is examined. Looking at intelligent, honest, and sensitive, all highly favorable, it can be seen that in each instance the trait was reported as more characteristic of Americans in the EMG than in the rating condition, while these same adjectives were seen as more characteristic of Negroes in the rating than in the EMG condition. This effect was most pronounced in the case of honest, where the zero point was crossed. Taking the unfavorable traits, ostentatious, lazy, ignorant, physically dirty, stupid, and unreliable, we find a complementary pattern: these adjectives were reported as more characteristic of Americans in the rating than in the EMG condition, and more characteristic of Negroes in the EMG than in the rating condition. Pleasure loving and happy-go-lucky did not result in interactions consistent with the others. With both of these "favorable" traits, Americans were *not* more favorably viewed in the EMG condition, and Negroes were more favorably evaluated in the EMG condition. It is our feeling that the note of caution expressed previously, that traits rated out of stereotype contexts do not necessarily reflect their connotations in such contexts, is relevant here. While we may want our spouses and friends to be pleasure loving and happy-go-lucky, these traits can have negative connotations when they form part of a stereotype. The happy-go-lucky Negro dancing through his woe in Hollywood productions of the 1930s hardly represents a favorable image.

In analyzing our results we made one further use of the trait-favorability values reported by Karlins et al. (1969). We computed a "favorability" score for each subject by multiplying the trait value of each adjective by the score assigned by the subject to that adjective. For example, if the subject's response to stupid was +1, the favorability of that response was (-1.59) $(+1)$ or -1.59; if the subject indicated that stupid was uncharacteristic, say -2, the favorability score would be $+3.18$. We simply obtained a mean favorability score for each subject by averaging his 22 individual favorability scores. Given the trait values and the response range of -3 to $+3$, the possible range of mean favorability scores could extend from -2.83 (unfavorable) to $+2.83$ (favorable). Analyzing the data in this way allows an overview of the results to emerge, and also avoids some of the objections to conducting a large number of separate analyses. The mean favorability scores are presented in Table 3, and the analysis of

TABLE 3 *Mean Favorability of Assigned Stereotypes*

ETHNIC GROUP	EMG	RATING
Americans	.84	.53
Negroes	−.03	.49

variance for these scores appears in Table 4. It can be seen that Americans were assigned more favorable stereotypes than were Negroes. Moreover, the Ethnic Group × Measurement interaction again points to the utility of

TABLE 4 *Analysis of Variance of Favorability Scores*

SOURCE	df	MS	F
Ethnic group (A)	1	3.11	14.14**
Measurement (B)	1	.17	<1
A × B	1	2.56	11.64*
Within groups	56	.22	

$* p < .005.$
$** p < .001.$

the bogus pipeline. Americans received more favorable evaluations in the EMG than the rating condition, while Negroes were more favorably evaluated in the rating than in the EMG condition. If one were to examine only the EMG condition, a large difference in favorability would emerge. On the other hand, the difference in favorability within the rating condition was virtually nonexistent.

We would suggest that "demands" for social-desirability-related responses in the Katz and Braly paradigm fall somewhere in between the demands for such responses in our rating and EMG conditions. The EMG conditions clearly are designed to inhibit socially desirable responses. However, in the rating conditions social desirability may manifest itself at an especially high level. Despite the encouragement given to rating-condition subjects to emit undistorted responses, they responded in a one to one, face-to-face situation. In contrast, the subjects in the Katz and Braly paradigm, although free to distort, may have less need to do so by virtue of the fact that they were relatively anonymous, and were tested in large groups.

Earlier we pointed out that our data cannot be compared directly with the data collected in the Princeton studies. Similarly, the evidence we have gathered, which suggested that social desirability needs affected our rating-condition subjects, does not in any way prove that such demand characteristics were operative in any of the Princeton studies. Casual observation tells us that college students in the late 1960s were not as negative when talking about Negroes as they seem to have been 35 years earlier. In that respect the Karlins et al. study mirrors an intuitively ascertainable reality. The present experiment is not based on that research. That is, the present experiment would have been performed even if the Karlins et al. study had not been conducted. On the other hand, the existence of the work by Karlins et al. made our research easier in at least three direct ways. In the first place, as a well-conducted study of stereotyping, it provides hard data which strongly support casual observation and the latter is rarely, if ever, an adequate substitute for the former. One tends to stand on much sturdier ground when dealing with data than when dealing with intuition. Second, because of our approach, we had to select a relatively limited number of adjective traits. The Karlins et al. study was helpful in this regard because by examining their results, we were able to choose adjectives that would be likely to yield interesting response patterns. Finally, we are indebted to Karlins et al. (1969) for providing quantitative favorableness values for adjectives. As they noted: "the ratings are especially useful for present and future investigations, and they provide us with an overall index of the direction and intensity of stereotype composition [p. 11]."

In sum, we should state explicitly that we make no claims to have demonstrated the Karlins et al. findings to be artifactual. However, to the extent that our results indicate that subjects' responses in investigations of stereotypes are influenced by social-desirability needs, it does not seem unreasonable to speculate that while some of the neutralization found by Karlins et al. is real, some of it may reflect the social desirability needs of the respondents.

It will be obvious by this point that we have elected to interpret the results of the EMG condition as relatively distortion free, as more honest, and as "truer" than rating-condition responses. Thus, the EMG may be viewed as a lie detection device which facilitates truthful reporting. While we tend to *favor* this interpretation—indeed, it underlies the development of the bogus pipeline—it is not the only one possible. Rival, equally plausible, alternatives are available. They are more fully discussed by Jones and Sigall (in press). Here we will consider them briefly.

Perhaps the subjects in the EMG condition, uncertain about their ability to designate a number which describes precisely their feeling, prefer "negative" to "positive" errors. Aware of current norms and that they may be influenced by them in complex ways, subjects may decide to "predict" in a manner such that any errors in prediction would be on the negative side. As Jones and Sigall (in press) stated, "it may be better to admit being a bigot and have it shown that you are fairly liberal than to claim tolerance while being revealed as a bigot." The same could be said regarding chauvinism.

Another alternative involves the conceptualization of attitude as composed of an affective and a cognitive component. Perhaps the EMG, due to its purported sensitivity to physiological responses, places emphasis on the affective component. If EMG subjects are trying to report affective autonomic nervous system responses, while rating-condition subjects are reporting attitudinal or cognitive responses, we may well expect a difference between conditions. However, explaining the difference does not have to involve a consideration of distortion. Subjects in both conditions may be responding honestly. We may believe that most people, including ourselves, have hidden stereotyped negative feelings about certain ethnic groups—

feelings which we are unaware of. As Jones and Sigall (in press) pointed out: "When asked to estimate the affective component of their racial attitudes, therefore, it is not altogether surprising that they would accede to some extent to the implications of this stereotype."

Some Final Considerations

The enormous amount of work invested by students of attitudes and attitude change most likely reflects more than an interest in attitudes and attitude structure, per se. As other writers (e.g., Cohen, 1964; Wicker, 1969) have suggested, many investigators make the assumption that verbally expressed attitudes are indicators of other, overt, social behaviors. Certainly, many social psychologists interested in overt social behavior consider verbally stated attitudes as indicators of behavior, if for no other reason than because it is easy and economical to do so (cf. Aronson & Carlsmith, 1968).

Wicker (1969) has examined the relationship between verbally expressed attitudes and overt actions. After reviewing a sizable portion of the literature, he concluded that there is little evidence to support the assumption that verbally expressed attitudes correlate highly with the overt behaviors implied by those attitudes. One possible reason for this is that verbally expressed attitudes may frequently be distorted because the subject wants to appear socially desirable (see Wicker, 1969, for a discussion of many other considerations). One potentially fruitful line of research which hopefully will be stimulated by the bogus pipeline involves investigating the relationship between attitudes assessed with the bogus pipeline and overt behavior, and comparing that relationship with one between typical ratings and identical overt behavior.

At the same time we must remain cognizant of the fact that although laboratory behavior may differ in many respects from real-world behavior, the latter is not unaffected by those forces which influence the former. That is, real-world behavior is also susceptible to effects accruing from social desirability needs. Even if it turns out that we can safely assume that the EMG gives low-distortion responses, we will still have to be extremely careful to scrutinize any particular overt behavior before deciding which type of attitudinal measure would be most likely to correspond highly with it.

References

Aronson E., & Carlsmith, J. M. Experimentation in social psychology. In G. Lindzey & E. Aronson (Eds.), *Handbook of social psychology.* Vol. 2. (2nd ed.) Reading, Mass.: Addison-Wesley, 1969.

Byrne, D. *Attitudes and attraction*. In L. Berkowitz (Ed.), *Advances in experimental social psychology*. Vol. 4. New York: Academic Press, 1969.

Cohen, A. R. *Attitude change and social influence*. New York: Basic Books, 1964.

Crowne, D. P., & Marlowe, D. *The approval motive*. New York: Wiley, 1964.

Gilbert, G. M. Stereotype persistence and change among college students. *Journal of Abnormal and Social Psychology*, 1951, *46*, 245–254.

Jones, E. E., & Sigall, H. The bogus pipeline: A new paradigm for measuring affect and attitude. *Psychological Bulletin*, in press.

Karlins, M., Coffman, T. L., & Walters, G. On the fading of social stereotypes: Studies in three generations of college students. *Journal of Personality and Social Psychology*, 1969, *13*, 1–16.

Katz, D., & Braly, K. W. Racial stereotypes of one-hundred college students. *Journal of Abnormal and Social Psychology*, 1933, *28*, 282–290.

Wicker, A. W. Attitudes versus actions: The relationship of verbal and overt behavioral responses to attitude objects. *Journal of Social Issues*, 1969, *25*, 41–78.

Foreword to Reading 5.6

INTRODUCTION

The concern of Sherif's paper is the reduction of intergroup conflict. Theories of the reduction of conflict and prejudice are generally based on hypotheses concerning their causes. There are three major types of causation theories (Collins, 1970). The general description of each of these theories can be found in Sherif's introduction.

1. *Realistic group conflict.* Sherif speaks of the "functional relations" of the group. Conflict between groups may develop for a "realistic" reason; for instance, two groups may begin to behave and feel negatively toward one another because they are in competition or have incompatible goals. This could arise through status difference (the majority group justifying their favored status by derogating the minority group), or through scarcity of desired resources. For instance, restriction of unions to white workers is sometimes explained as protection from a threat of job loss.

2. *Symptom theories.* Sherif mentions "analysis of individuals who have endured unusual degrees of frustration or extensive authoritarian treatment." It is possible to consider hostility and prejudice as symptoms or indications of deeper conflict. For instance, according to the frustration-aggression theory proposed by Dollard et al. (1939), aggression is an inevitable result of frustration. Since it is not always possible or safe to aggress against the cause of the frustration, aggression may be "displaced" to a safer target. Such "scapegoating" might then be the explanation of prejudice. Somewhat along the same line is the notion of the development of the authoritarian personality. Authoritarianism presumably develops when harsh, rigid parents punish their children with severity. Although frustrated, the children are afraid to aggress against the punitive parents, and so displace the aggression, while also projecting their own hostility and negative attributes on others (i.e., attributing those characteristics to others rather than to themselves). (The Frustration-Aggression theory and its

derivations run into considerable conceptual difficulties, however, as outlined in Kaufmann, 1970, and others.)

3. Social learning. Sherif speaks of "internalization of group norms, and example of high status members." It is possible that prejudice is learned in the same way as any other attitude or behavior. Through differential reinforcement (reward or punishment), prejudiced parents may teach prejudice to their children. Both peers and parents may set examples of prejudiced behavior. With or without childhood training in prejudice, the individual may be affected by pressure to conform to a prejudiced group to which he belongs or wishes to belong. Research on conformity indicates the strong impact of social pressure on behavior and thought.

4. To this we might add another important source of group conflicts, namely differing subjective behavior-outcome contingencies. There are various ways in which another person's inferred purposes or intentions may be misunderstood: We may "read into" him the same-behavior outcome relationships that we profess. Our reasoning might be as follows, "When I engage in the type of behavior I have just observed, I do so in order to obtain a specific outcome. Therefore he, having engaged in that behavior, must be seeking to attain that same outcome." If the observed person has a different view of the state of the world and perceives his actions as likely to lead to another outcome than the one we perceive, then we shall have misunderstood and misinterpreted the purpose of the behavior we have observed. But we have misunderstood not only his motives but also the way he perceives his world.

Applying these theories to the question of reduction of prejudice, it follows that this might be accomplished through increase in scarce resources or introduction of compatible goals, reduction of frustration or punitivity of parents, or re-education campaigns in which new information, new norms, and new ways of empathizing are stressed.

In Sherif's study, a "realistic group conflict" was created and then reduced. The study was carried out in three stages:

Stage 1: Two groups of unacquainted 12-year-old boys were brought to separate parts of a campsite. The two groups were isolated from one another until each had developed some in-group feeling through working together on attractive goals (like fixing up the swimming hole).

Stage 2: The two groups were introduced to one another in a context of competition (for instance athletic contests), and a hostile conflict between the groups developed.

Stage 3: In the first attempt to reduce the conflict, the two groups were brought together in pleasurable activities. However, it seemed that these activities served only as opportunities for the expression of hostility (e.g., garbage fights in the dining hall). In the second attempt to reduce the conflict, the two groups were brought together in the context of superordinate goals, goals which could be attained only through the cooperation of the two groups. This procedure, as shown by various measures described by Sherif, accomplished the desired effect.

This research can be related to other studies dealing with the reduction of intergroup prejudice. Some of these studies have found that bringing the two groups together (as for instance in integrated housing, Deutsch and Collins, 1951, or in integrated army units, Stouffer et al., 1949) produces a reduction of prejudice. On the other hand, in other situations, intergroup contact has been known to aggravate a bad situation (Amir, 1969). For instance, when black housing begins to move closer to white housing, white fear and dislike of blacks seem to increase, rather than decrease. Both Amir (1969) and Ashmore (in Collins, 1970) suggest that a crucial factor may be having a common goal and cooperating to reach it. Ashmore analyzes the situation in which a "superordinate goal" is present and suggests that its success lies in the fact that it provides an opportunity for close contact, enabling the participants to learn that their stereotypes are incorrect, and that the members of the other group are not as different from them as they had supposed. Of course, once the two groups get together, there is always the danger that they will find that their stereotypes are basically correct, but this is less likely to happen when the two groups have equal status in the contact situation. An integrated work situation will have little impact if all of the black people are janitors and all of the white people executives. Then, a second problem is that the change in attitude is sometimes strictly limited to the intergroup situation. People in integrated work situations may decide that they are perfectly happy to work with the members of the other group, but that they still have no intention of letting them live in their neighborhood. Here the problem may be that the norms and atmosphere of the home community are working against the changes brought about at work. Finally, a shared goal situation will have little effect if the goal is not reached; in fact, one group may blame the other for the failure, and hostility may be increased. Nevertheless, Pettigrew (1969), after analyzing the difficulties and discomforts of integration, maintains that extensive racial integration in all realms of life must be attained. "To prescribe more separation," he says, "is like getting drunk again to cure a hangover."

References

Amir, Y. Contact hypothesis in ethnic relations. *Psychological Bulletin*, 1969, *71*, 319–342.

Collins, B. *Social psychology*. Reading, Mass.: Addison-Wesley, 1970.

Deutsch, M., & Collins, M. E. *Interracial housing: a psychological evaluation of a social experiment.* Minneapolis: University of Minnesota Press, 1951.

Dollard, J., Doob, L. W., Miller, N. E., Mowrer, O. H., Sears, R. R. *Frustration and aggression.* New Haven: Yale University Press, 1939.

Kaufmann, H. *Aggression and altruism.* New York: Holt, Rinehart and Winston, 1970.

Pettigrew, T. F. Racially separate or together? *Journal of Social Issues,* 1969, *25,* 43–60.

5.6 Superordinate Goals in the Reduction of Intergroup Conflicts

Muzafer Sherif

In the past, measures to combat the problems of intergroup conflicts, proposed by social scientists as well as by such people as administrators, policymakers, municipal officials, and educators, have included the following: introduction of legal sanctions; creation of opportunities for social and other contacts among members of conflicting groups; dissemination of correct information to break down false prejudices and unfavorable stereotypes; appeals to the moral ideals of fair play and brotherhood; and even the introduction of rigorous physical activity to produce catharsis by releasing pent-up frustrations and aggressive complexes in the unconscious. Other measures proposed include the encouragement of co-operative habits in one's own community, and bringing together in the cozy atmosphere of a meeting room the leaders of antagonistic groups.

Many of these measures may have some value in the reduction of intergroup conflicts, but, to date, very few generalizations have been established concerning the circumstances and kinds of intergroup conflict in which these measures are effective. Today measures are applied in a somewhat trial-and-error fashion. Finding measures that have wide validity in practice can come only through clarification of the nature of intergroup conflict and analysis of the factors conducive to harmony and conflict between groups under given conditions.

The task of defining and analyzing the nature of the problem was undertaken in a previous publication (Sherif and Sherif, 1953). One of our major statements was the effectiveness of superordinate goals for the reduction of intergroup conflict. "Superordinate goals" we defined as goals which are compelling and highly appealing to members of two or more groups in conflict but which cannot be attained by the resources and energies of the groups separately. In effect, they are goals attained only when groups pull together.

Reprinted from the *American Journal of Sociology*, 1958, *63*, 349–356, with permission of the author and the University of Chicago Press. Copyright 1958 by the University of Chicago.

INTERGROUP RELATIONS AND THE
BEHAVIOR OF GROUP MEMBERS

Not every friendly or unfriendly act toward another person is related to the group membership of the individuals involved. Accordingly, we must select those actions relevant to relations between groups.

Let us start by defining the main concepts involved. Obviously, we must begin with an adequate conception of the key term—"group." A group is a social unit (1) which consists of a number of individuals who, at a given time, stand in more or less definite interdependent status and role relationships with one another and (2) which explicitly or implicitly possesses a set of values or norms regulating the behavior of individual members, at least in matters of consequence to the group. Thus, shared attitudes, sentiments, aspirations, and goals are related to and implicit in the common values or norms of the group.

The term "intergroup relations" refers to the relations between two or more groups and their respective members. In the present context we are interested in the acts that occur when individuals belonging to one group interact, collectively or individually, with members of another in terms of their group identification. The appropriate frame of reference for studying such behavior includes the functional relations between the groups. Intergroup situations are not voids. Though not independent of relationships within the groups in question, *the characteristics of relations between groups cannot be deduced or extrapolated from the properties of in-group relations.*

Prevalent modes of behavior within a group, in the way of co-operativeness and solidarity or competitiveness and rivalry among members, need not be typical of actions involving members of an out-group. At times, hostility toward out-groups may be proportional to the degree of solidarity within the group. In this connection, results presented by the British statistician L. F. Richardson are instructive. His analysis of the number of wars conducted by the major nations of the world from 1850 to 1941 reveals that Great Britain heads the list with twenty wars—more than the Japanese (nine wars), the Germans (eight wars), or the United States (seven wars). We think that this significantly larger number of wars engaged in by a leading European democracy has more to do with the intergroup relations involved in perpetuating a far-flung empire than with dominant practices at home or with personal frustrations of individual Britishers who participated in these wars (Pear, 1950, p. 126).

In recent years relationships between groups have sometimes been explained through analysis of individuals who have endured unusual degrees of frustration or extensive authoritarian treatment in their life-histories. There is good reason to believe that some people growing up in unfortunate life-circumstances may become more intense in their prejudices and hostilities. But at best these cases explain the intensity of behavior in a given dimension (Hood and Sherif, 1955). In a conflict between two groups—a strike or a war—opinion within the groups is crystallized, slogans are formulated, and effective measures are organized by members recognized as the most responsible in their respective groups. The prejudice scale and the slogans are not usually imposed on the others by the deviate or neurotic members. Such individuals ordinarily exhibit their intense reactions within the reference scales of prejudice, hostility, or sacrifice established in their respective settings.

The behavior by members of any group toward another group is not primarily a problem of deviate behavior. If it were, intergroup behavior would not be the issue of vital consequence that it is today. The crux of the problem is the participation by group members in established practices and social-distance norms of their group and their response to new trends developing in relationships between their own group and other groups.

On the basis of his UNESCO studies in India, Gardner Murphy concludes that to be a good Hindu or a good Moslem implies belief in all the nasty qualities and practices attributed by one's own group—Hindu or Moslem—to the other. Good members remain deaf and dumb to favorable information concerning the adversary. Social contacts and avenues of communication serve, on the whole, as vehicles for further conflicts not merely for neurotic individuals but for the bulk of the membership (Murphy, 1953).

In the process of interaction among members, an in-group is endowed with positive qualities which tend to be praiseworthy, self-justifying, and even self-glorifying. Individual members tend to develop these qualities through internalizing group norms and through example by high-status members, verbal dicta, and a set of correctives standardized to deal with cases of deviation. Hence, possession of these qualities, which reflect their particular brand of ethnocentrism, is not essentially a problem of deviation or personal frustration. It is a question of participation in in-group values and trends by good members, who constitute the majority of membership as long as group solidarity and morale are maintained.

To out-groups and their respective members are attributed positive or negative qualities, depending on the nature of functional relations between the groups in question. The character of functional relations between groups may result from actual harmony and interdependence or from actual incompatibility between the aspirations and directions of the groups. A number of field studies and experiments indicate that, if the functional relations between groups are positive, favorable attitudes are formed toward the out-group. If the functional relations between groups are negative, they give rise to hostile attitudes and unfavorable stereotypes in relation to the out-group.

Of course, in large group units the picture of the out-group and relations with it depend very heavily on communication, particularly from the mass media.

Examples of these processes are recurrent in studies of small groups. For example, when a gang "appropriates" certain blocks in a city, it is considered "indecent" and a violation of its "rights" for another group to carry on its feats in that area. Intrusion by another group is conducive to conflict, at times with grim consequences, as Thrasher showed over three decades ago (1927).

When a workers' group declares a strike, existing group lines are drawn more sharply. Those who are not actually for the strike are regarded as against it. There is no creature more lowly than the man who works while the strike is on (Hiller, 1928). The same type of behavior is found in management groups under similar circumstances.

In time, the adjectives attributed to out-groups take their places in the repertory of group norms. The lasting, derogatory stereotypes attributed to groups low on the social-distance scale are particular cases of group norms pertaining to out-groups.

As studies by Bogardus show, the social-distance scale of a group, once established, continues over generations, despite changes of constituent individuals, who can hardly be said to have prejudices because of the same severe personal frustrations or authoritarian treatment (1947).

Literature on the formation of prejudice by growing children shows that it is not even necessary for the individual to have actual unfavorable experiences with out-groups to form attitudes of prejudice toward them. In the very process of becoming an in-group member, the intergroup delineations and corresponding norms prevailing in the group are internalized by the individual (Horowitz, 1944).

A RESEARCH PROGRAM

A program of research has been under way since 1948 to test experimentally some hypotheses derived from the literature of intergroup relations. The first large-scale intergroup experiment was carried out in 1949, the second in 1953, and the third in 1954.[1] The conclusions reported here

[1] The experimental work in 1949 was jointly supported by the Yale Attitude Change Project and the American Jewish Committee. It is summarized in Sherif and Sherif (1953, chaps. IX and X). Both the writing of that book and the experiments in 1953–54 were made possible by a grant from the Rockefeller Foundation. The 1953 research is summarized in Sherif, White, and Harvey (1955). The 1954 experiment was summarized in Sherif, Harvey, White, Hood, and Sherif (1954). For a summary of the three experiments see chaps. VI and IX in Sherif and Sherif (1956).

briefly are based on the 1949 and 1954 experiments and on a series of laboratory studies carried out as co-ordinate parts of the program.[2]

The methodology, techniques, and criteria for subject selection in the experiments must be summarized here very briefly. The experiments were carried out in successive stages: (1) groups were formed experimentally; (2) tension and conflict were produced between these groups by introducing conditions conducive to competitive and reciprocally frustrating relations between them; and (3) the attempt was made toward reduction of the inter-group conflict. This stage of reducing tension through introduction of super-ordinate goals was attempted in the 1954 study on the basis of lessons learned in the two previous studies.

At every stage the subjects interacted in activities which appeared natural to them at a specially arranged camp site completely under our experimental control. They were not aware of the fact that their behavior was under observation. No observation or recording was made in the subjects' presence in a way likely to arouse the suspicion that they were being observed. There is empirical and experimental evidence contrary to the contention that individuals cease to be mindful when they know they are being observed and that their words are being recorded.[3]

In order to insure validity of conclusions, results obtained through observational methods were cross-checked with results obtained through sociometric technique, stereotype ratings of in-groups and out-groups, and through data obtained by techniques adapted from the laboratory. Unfortunately, these procedures cannot be elaborated here. The conclusions summarized briefly are based on results cross-checked by two or more techniques.

The production of groups, the production of conflict between them, and the reduction of conflict in successive stages were brought about through the introduction of problem situations that were real and could not be ignored by individuals in the situation. Special "lecture methods" or "discussion methods" were not used. For example, the problem of getting a meal through their own initiative and planning was introduced when participating individuals were hungry.

Facing a problem situation which is immediate and compelling and which embodies a goal that cannot be ignored, group members *do* initiate discussion and *do* plan and carry through these plans until the objective is achieved. In this process the discussion becomes *their* discussion, the plan *their* plan, the action *their* action. In this process discussion, planning, and action have their place, and, when occasion arises, lecture or information

[2] For an overview of this program see Sherif (1954).
[3] E.g., see Miller (1954) and Wapner and Alper (1952).

has its place, too. The sequence of these related activities need not be the same in all cases.

The subjects were selected by rigorous criteria. They were healthy, normal boys around the age of eleven and twelve, socially well adjusted in school and neighborhood, and academically successful. They came from a homogeneous sociocultural background and from settled, well-adjusted families of middle or lower-middle class and Protestant affiliations. No subject came from a broken home. The mean I.Q. was above average. The subjects were not personally acquainted with one another prior to the experiment. Thus, explanation of results on the basis of background differences, social maladjustment, undue childhood frustrations, or previous interpersonal relations was ruled out at the beginning by the criteria for selecting subjects.

The first stage of the experiments was designed to produce groups with distinct structure (organization) and a set of norms which could be confronted with intergroup problems. The method for producing groups from unacquainted individuals with similar background was to introduce problem situations in which the attainment of the goal depended on the co-ordinated activity of all individuals. After a series of such activities, definite group structures or organizations developed.

The results warrant the following conclusions for the stage of group formation: When individuals interact in a series of situations toward goals which appeal to all and which require that they co-ordinate their activities, group structures arise having hierarchical status arrangements and a set of norms regulating behavior in matters of consequence to the activities of the group.

Once we had groups that satisfied our definition of "group," relations between groups could be studied. Specified conditions conducive to friction or conflict between groups were introduced. This negative aspect was deliberately undertaken because the major problem in intergroup relations today is the reduction of existing intergroup frictions. (Increasingly, friendly relations between groups is not nearly so great an issue.) The factors conducive to intergroup conflict give us realistic leads for reducing conflict.

A series of situations was introduced in which one group could achieve its goal only at the expense of the other group—through a tournament of competitive events with desirable prizes for the winning group. The results of the stage of intergroup conflict supported our main hypotheses. During interaction between groups in experimentally introduced activities which were competitive and mutually frustrating, members of each group developed hostile attitudes and highly unfavorable stereotypes toward the other group and its members. In fact, attitudes of social distance between the groups became so definite that they wanted to have nothing further to do with each other. This we take as a case of experimentally produced "social distance" in miniature. Conflict was manifested in derogatory name-calling and invectives, flare-ups of physical conflict, and raids on each other's cabins and territory. Over a period of time, negative stereotypes and unfavorable attitudes developed.

At the same time there was an increase in in-group solidarity and co-operativeness. This finding indicates that co-operation and democracy within groups do not necessarily lead to democracy and co-operation with out-groups, if the directions and interests of the groups are conflicting.

Increased solidarity forged in hostile encounters, in rallies from defeat, and in victories over the out-group is one instance of a more general finding: Intergroup relations, both conflicting and harmonious, *affected the nature of relations within the groups involved.* Altered relations between groups produced significant changes in the status arrangements *within* groups, in some instances resulting in shifts at the upper status levels or even a change in leadership. Always, consequential intergroup relations were reflected in new group values or norms which signified changes in practice, word, and deed within the group. Counterparts of this finding are not difficult to see in actual and consequential human relations. Probably many of our major preoccupations, anxieties, and activities in the past decade are incomprehensible without reference to the problems created by the prevailing "cold war" on an international scale.

REDUCTION OF INTERGROUP FRICTION

A number of the measures proposed today for reducing intergroup friction could have been tried in this third stage. A few will be mentioned here, with a brief explanation of why they were discarded or were included in our experimental design.

1. Disseminating favorable information in regard to the out-group was not included. Information that is not related to the goals currently in focus in the activities of groups is relatively ineffective, as many studies on attitude change have shown (Williams, 1947).
2. In small groups it is possible to devise sufficiently attractive rewards to make individual achievement supreme. This may reduce tension between groups by splitting the membership on an "every-man-for-himself" basis. However, this measure has little relevance for actual intergroup tensions, which are in terms of group membership and group alignments.
3. The resolution of conflict through leaders alone was not utilized. Even when group leaders meet apart from their groups around a conference table, they cannot be considered independent of the dominant trends and prevailing attitudes of their membership. If a leader is too much out of step in his negotiations and agreements with out-groups, he will cease to be followed. It seemed more realistic, therefore, to study the influence of leadership within the

framework of prevailing trends in the groups involved. Such results will give us leads concerning the conditions under which leadership can be effective in reducing intergroup tensions.

4. The "common-enemy" approach is effective in pulling two or more groups together against another group. This approach was utilized in the 1949 experiment as an expedient measure and yielded effective results. But bringing some groups together against others means larger and more devastating conflicts in the long run. For this reason, the measure was not used in the 1954 experiment.

5. Another measure, advanced both in theoretical and in practical work, centers around social contacts among members of antagonistic groups in activities which are pleasant in themselves. This measure was tried out in 1954 in the first phase of the integration stage.

6. As the second phase of the integration stage, we introduced a series of superordinate goals which necessitated cooperative interaction between groups.

The social contact situations consisted of activities which were satisfying in themselves—eating together in the same dining room, watching a movie in the same hall, or engaging in an entertainment in close physical proximity. These activities, which were satisfying to each group, but which did not involve a state of interdependence and co-operation for the attainment of goals, were not effective in reducing intergroup tension. On the contrary, such occasions of contact were utilized as opportunities to engage in name-calling and in abuse of each other to the point of physical manifestations of hostility.

The ineffective, even deleterious, results of intergroup contact without superordinate goals have implications for certain contemporary learning theories and for practice in intergroup relations. Contiguity in pleasant activities with members of an out-group does not necessarily lead to a pleasurable image of the out-group if relations between the groups are unfriendly. Intergroup contact without superordinate goals is not likely to produce lasting reduction of intergroup hostility. John Gunther, for instance, in his survey of contemporary Africa, concluded that, when the intergroup relationship is exploitation of one group by a "superior" group, intergroup contact inevitably breeds hostility and conflict (Gunther, 1955).

INTRODUCTION OF SUPERORDINATE GOALS

After establishing the ineffectiveness, even the harm, in intergroup contacts which did not involve superordinate goals, we introduced a series of superordinate goals. Since the characteristics of the problem situations used as superordinate goals are implicit in the two main hypotheses for this stage, we shall present these hypotheses:

1. When groups in a state of conflict are brought into contact under conditions embodying superordinate goals, which are compelling but cannot be achieved by the efforts of one group alone, they will tend to co-operate toward the common goals.
2. Co-operation between groups, necessitated by a series of situations embodying superordinate goals, will have a cumulative effect in the direction of reducing existing conflict between groups.

The problem situations were varied in nature, but all had an essential feature in common—they involved goals that could not be attained by the efforts and energies of one group alone and thus created a state of interdependence between groups: combating a water shortage that affected all and could not help being "compelling"; securing a much-desired film, which could not be obtained by either group alone but required putting their resources together; putting into working shape, when everyone was hungry and the food was some distance away, the only means of transportation available to carry food.

The introduction of a series of such superordinate goals was indeed effective in reducing intergroup conflict: (1) when the groups in a state of friction interacted in conditions involving superordinate goals, they did co-operate in activities leading toward the common goal and (2) a series of joint activities leading toward superordinate goals had the cumulative effect of reducing the prevailing friction between groups and unfavorable stereotypes toward the out-group.

These major conclusions were reached on the basis of observational data and were confirmed by sociometric choices and stereotype ratings administered first during intergroup conflict and again after the introduction of a series of superordinate goals. Comparison of the sociometric choices during intergroup conflict and following the series of superordinate goals shows clearly the changed attitudes toward members of the out-group. Friendship preferences shifted from almost exclusive preference for in-group members toward increased inclusion of members from the "antagonists." Since the groups were still intact following co-operative efforts to gain superordinate goals, friends were found largely within one's group. However, choices of out-group members grew, in one group, from practically none during intergroup conflict to 23 per cent. Using chi square, this difference is significant ($P < .05$). In the other group, choices of the out-group increased to 36 per cent, and the difference is significant ($P < .001$). The findings confirm observations that the series of superordinate goals produced increasingly friendly associations and attitudes pertaining to out-group members.

Observations made after several superordinate goals were introduced showed a sharp decrease in the name-calling and derogation of the out-group common during intergroup friction and in the contact situations without superordinate goals. At the same time the blatant glorification and bragging about the in-group, observed during the period of conflict, diminished. These observations were confirmed by comparison of ratings of stereotypes (adjectives) the subjects had actually used in referring to their own group and the out-group during conflict with ratings made after the series of superordinate goals. Ratings of the out-group changed significantly from largely unfavorable ratings to largely favorable ratings. The proportions of the most unfavorable ratings found appropriate for the out-group—that is, the categorical verdicts that "all of them are stinkers" or ". . . smart alecks" or ". . . sneaky"—fell, in one group, from 21 per cent at the end of the friction stage to 1.5 per cent after interaction oriented toward superordinate goals. The corresponding reduction in these highly unfavorable verdicts by the other group was from 36.5 to 6 per cent. The over-all differences between the frequencies of stereotype ratings made in relation to the out-group during intergroup conflict and following the series of superordinate goals are significant for both groups at the .001 level (using chi-square test).

Ratings of the in-group were not so exclusively favorable, in line with observed decreases in self-glorification. But the differences in ratings of the in-group were not statistically significant, as were the differences in ratings of the out-group.

Our findings demonstrate the effectiveness of a series of superordinate goals in the reduction of intergroup conflict, hostility, and their by-products. They also have implications for other measures proposed for reducing intergroup tensions.

It is true that lines of communication between groups must be opened before prevailing hostility can be reduced. But, if contact between hostile groups takes place without superordinate goals, the communication channels serve as media for further accusations and recriminations. When contact situations involve superordinate goals, communication is utilized in the direction of reducing conflict in order to attain the common goals.

Favorable information about a disliked out-group tends to be ignored, rejected, or reinterpreted to fit prevailing stereotypes. But, when groups are pulling together toward superordinate goals, true and even favorable information about the out-group is seen in a new light. The probability of information being effective in eliminating unfavorable stereotypes is enormously enhanced.

When groups co-operate in the attainment of superordinate goals, leaders are in a position to take bolder steps toward bringing about understanding and harmonious relations. When groups are directed toward incompatible goals, genuine moves by a leader to reduce intergroup tension may be seen by the membership as out of step and ill advised. The leader may be subjected to severe criticism and even loss of faith and status in his own group. When compelling superordinate goals are introduced, the leader can make moves to further co-operative efforts, and his decisions receive support from other group members.

In short, various measures suggested for the reduction of intergroup conflict—disseminating information, increasing social contact, conferences of leaders—acquire new significance and effectiveness when they become part and parcel of interaction processes between groups oriented toward superordinate goals which have real and compelling value for all groups concerned.

References

Bogardus, E. S. Changes in racial distances. *International Journal of Opinion and Attitude Research,* 1947, *1,* 55–62.

Gunther, J. *Inside Africa.* New York: Harper & Row, 1955.

Hiller, E. T. *The strike.* Chicago: Univer. of Chicago Press, 1928.

Hood, W. R., and Sherif, M. Personality oriented approaches to prejudice. *Sociology and Social Research,* 1955, *40,* 79–85.

Horowitz, E. L. Race attitudes. In Otto Klineberg (Ed.), *Characteristics of the American Negro,* part 4. New York: Harper & Row, 1944.

Miller, F. B. "Resistentialism" in applied social research. *Human Organization,* 1954, *12,* 5–8.

Murphy, G. *In the minds of men.* New York: Basic Books, 1953.

Pear, T. H. *Psychological factors of peace and war.* New York: Philosophical Library, 1950.

Sherif, M. Integrating field work and laboratory in small group research. *American Sociological Review,* 1954, *19,* 759–771.

Sherif, M., Harvey, O. J., White, B. J., Hood, W. R., and Sherif, Carolyn W. *Experimental study of positive and negative intergroup attitudes between experimentally produced groups: robbers cave study.* Norman, Okla.: Univer. of Oklahoma, 1954 (Multilithed).

Sherif, M., and Sherif, Carolyn W. *Groups in harmony and tension.* New York: Harper & Row, 1953.

Sherif, M., and Sherif, Carolyn W. *An outline of social psychology,* Rev. Ed. New York: Harper & Row, 1956.

Sherif, M., White, B. J., and Harvey, O. J. Status in experimentally produced groups. *American Journal of Sociology,* 1955, *60,* 370–379.

Thrasher, F. M. *The gang.* Chicago: Univer. of Chicago Press, 1927.

Wapner, S., and Alper, T. G. The effect of an audience on behavior in a choice situation. *Journal of Abnormal Social Psychology,* 1952, *47,* 222–229.

Williams, R. M. *The reduction of intergroup tensions. Social Science Research Council Bulletin,* 57. New York, 1947.

PART 6

The Individual
and His Group

The basic question in social psychology is the way in which the individual is affected by the people around him; therefore, any of the research reprinted in the previous chapters could have been in this section. Questions of socialization, attitude change, social perception, and pro- and anti-social behavior all involve the individual in relation to the group. But scientists and book publishers do put their work into categories, partly for the sake of convenience, so that traditionally, the study of group dynamics has been a particular area of investigation. Presently, this study includes work on the pressures to uniformity in groups; power and influence in groups; leadership in groups; performance in groups; cooperation in groups; and so on.

The work reprinted here represents a selection from the many possibilities in this area. Four diverse subjects of research are covered. In the Sarnoff and Zimbardo (1961) article, the question of when people seek to be with other people is discussed. While the cliché is that "man is a social animal," in fact, there are times when we want to be alone, and other times when we desperately need someone else around. This tendency to seek out other people is related, not only to circumstance, but also to the birth order of the person. In the Shomer and Centers (1970) article, the question of the effect of the group norm on attitude is discussed. Surprisingly, the authors found that feminist attitudes were affected by so subtle a manipulation as the number of males and females in the group filling out the attitude questionnaire. The Hollander (1960) article is considered a classic in the area of influence and leadership. Hollander suggests that a judicious combination of conformity and nonconformity can make a leader out of a follower. Cannavale, Scarr and Pepitone (1970) attempted to revive interest in a neglected issue in social psychology, the effect of feeling anonymous. In this era of big cities and masses of people this is a question of vital importance. There are times when the most important person is reduced to a number on an IBM card.

The reader should be aware that there are many other fascinating topics covered by readings not reprinted here. (For instance, why do people in groups make more risky decisions than do individuals? And how is the individual affected by the communication network in an organization?) However, it is thought that these readings will provide some insight into the group's effect on the individual as well as the individual's effect on the group.

References

Cannavale, F. J., Scarr, H. A., & Pepitone, A. Deindividuation in the small group: further evidence. *Journal of Personality and Social Psychology,* 1970, *16,* 141–147.

Hollander, Edwin P. Competence and conformity in the acceptance of influence. *Journal of Abnormal and Social Psychology,* 1960, *61,* 365–369.

Sarnoff, I., & Zimbardo, P. G. Anxiety, fear and social affiliation. *Journal of Abnormal and Social Psychology,* 1961, *62,* 356–363.

Shomer, R., & Centers, R. Differences in attitudinal responses under conditions of implicitly manipulated group salience. *Journal of Personality and Social Psychology,* 1970, *15,* 125–132.

Foreword to Reading 6.1

INTRODUCTION

In 1959, Stanley Schachter published a fascinating series of studies on affiliation. Why do people spend time together? Schachter suggested a number of reasons, including esteem, prestige, and goal attainment. Schachter also noted that isolated people (e.g., hermits and prisoners in solitary confinement) often go through a period of overwhelming anxiety. This led him to suspect that affiliation may have the opposite effect, in other words, reduction of anxiety. One motivation for affiliation, then, could be anxiety reduction.

In order to test this hypothesis, Schachter carried out an experiment in which subjects were in either one of two conditions: high anxiety or low anxiety. All subjects thought that they were participating in an experiment concerned with physiological reactions to electric shock. In the high-anxiety condition, the subjects were told that they were going to be given shocks that would be painful, but not permanently damaging. In the low-anxiety condition, the subjects were told that the shocks would be mild, little more than a tingle or tickle. After these instructions, all subjects (high and low anxiety) were told that there would now be a ten-minute delay during which it was necessary for them to leave the room so that the experimenter could set up the equipment. "To ensure their comfort," the subjects were given a choice of either waiting alone or waiting in the company of others who were also about to be in the experiment. As predicted, subjects in the high anxiety condition were more likely to choose to wait with others (i.e., to affiliate) than subjects in the low anxiety condition.

Schachter suggested a number of explanations for this result. For instance, he suggested that anxious subjects might have been looking for distraction from their worries. He then disproved this hypothesis in a subsequent experiment in which it appeared that anxious subjects wanted

305

only to be with those who were also about to be in the experiment. As Schachter put it, "Misery loves miserable company." After a number of other variations on his basic experiment, Schachter concluded that the two best explanations of the anxiety-affiliation relationship were: (a) direct anxiety reduction: When people are anxious, they derive comfort and support from one another, and (b) social comparison: According to Festinger's theory of social comparison (1954), people have a drive to evaluate themselves, their beliefs and their abilities. They want to know if they are right, good, or correct. In some cases, objective or physical reality may be available to validate a belief. (It is easy to see whether or not the table is hard or will support my weight.) In other cases, there is no physical reality, and so people turn to "social reality." They look for social support for their beliefs, whether about themselves or anything else. (For instance, think of the discussion and persuasion that goes on among voters just before an election.) Schachter proposed that people feel the same need to check on their emotions as they do their beliefs, and in new and strange situations, in which there is no other guide, they search for an emotional social reality (see the Nisbett and Schachter, 1966, article in this volume). Anxious people might prefer affiliation to isolation because they wish to compare their own emotional reactions with those of others in the same situation, in order to find out whether or not their feelings are the appropriate ones.

Sarnoff and Zimbardo propose a conceptual distinction not made by Schachter. They suggest that fear and anxiety are not the same thing. This distinction stems from Freud, who saw anxiety as arising from fear that the instincts (sex and aggression) will get out of control. In an attempt to defend themselves against anxiety, people tend to repress (or push into the unconscious) the sources of anxiety. Freud distinguished between realistic fear, specific to a particular threatening situation, and neurotic anxiety, which is diffuse (since the source is repressed), and unrealistic.

Sarnoff and Zimbardo suggest that, according to this distinction, Schachter was manipulating fear, not anxiety. They justify the hypothesis that fear leads to a desire for affiliation, while anxiety (since one cannot admit it) leads to a desire for isolation.

METHOD

Four conditions were included in the experiment: high fear, low fear, high anxiety, and low anxiety. When reading the procedure, the reader might note the operational definitions of fear and anxiety. It does seem, even if one rejects the Freudian notions, that there was a difference here. In one case (high fear), the subject was anticipating pain, in the other case (high anxiety), extreme embarrassment.

Sarnoff and Zimbardo "checked" their manipulation of fear and anxiety (i.e., the independent variable) in an unusual manner. Rather than asking the subjects to report their level of fear or anxiety, they asked them to describe a subject seen in some slides of the experiment. (As an aside, the editors wonder about the effect of the slides on the magnitude of desire for social comparison. In a sense, these subjects started out with more information about the emotional reactions of others than Schachter's subjects.) Sarnoff and Zimbardo present several cogent justifications for this procedure. Certainly, a manipulation check made before the dependent variable is measured could reveal the hypothesis to the subject. A manipulation check taken after the dependent variable is contaminated by the response on the dependent variable, and is not determined solely by the effect of the independent variable. It is also true that verbalized emotional reactions, for whatever reason, often do not mirror physiological reactions and therefore, are presumably inaccurate.

Sarnoff and Zimbardo assumed that subjects would "project" their anxiety or fear on to the person in the slides. In the concept "projection," we have another Freudian (or psychoanalytic) notion. Persons defending themselves against unacceptable impulses or thoughts may not only repress them, but attribute them to another person.

RESULTS

Inspection of Table 2 (as confirmed in the reported statistical tests), indicates that the predicted result was obtained. Note that each condition has a different number of subjects in it. Think of the 12 subjects in the low fear condition choosing "together" as twelve-fourteenths (80 percent) as compared to the nineteen-twentieths (95 percent) choosing together in the high fear condition. This difference is not as large as one might have expected from Schachter's results. However, there was a reversal in the anxiety conditions (thus indicating an interaction of fear and anxiety). In the low anxiety condition, eleven-fifteenths (73 percent) chose "together," while in the high anxiety condition, ten-twenty-seconds (45 percent) chose "together." Moreover, the reasons given for choosing to affiliate or be isolated gave some support for the theoretical analysis.

The final item of results deals with "ordinal position." Schachter suggested that the anxiety-affiliation relationship (Sarnoff and Zimbardo would say fear-affiliation) should be strongest for those who are first-born (or oldest) in their families. It is first or only children who experience the parents' undivided attention and concern and thus who are most likely to learn to perceive other people as anxiety-reducers. Later-born children, on the other hand, not only receive less concern from their busy parents, but also may find other siblings to be anxiety-provoking (the well-known consideration of sibling rivalry). Thus, they are less likely to learn that affiliation reduces anxiety (or fear). On the basis of this, Schachter predicted (and found) that a higher proportion of later-borns than first-borns become alcoholics (solitary drinkers), and a higher proportion of first-borns than later-borns accept and persist in free psychotherapy (a social situation) offered to disabled veterans.

As an aside, Schachter (1971) has continued to probe into fascinating areas of study. His most recent book *Emotion, Obesity and Crime* might well be of interest to fat and thin readers alike.

References

Festinger, L. A theory of social comparison processes. *Human Relations,* 1954, *7,* 117–140.

Nisbett, R. E., & Schachter, S. Cognitive manipulation of pain. *Journal of Experimental Social Psychology,* 1966, *2,* 227–236.

Schachter, S. *The psychology of affiliation.* Stanford, Calif.: Stanford University Press, 1959.

Schachter, S. *Emotion, obesity and crime.* New York: Academic Press, 1971.

6.1 Anxiety, Fear, and Social Affiliation

Irving Sarnoff
Philip G. Zimbardo[1]

In his recent monograph, Schachter (1959) reports that anticipated exposure to a painful external stimulus determines the degree to which persons wish to affiliate with each other: the greater the anticipated pain, the stronger the desire to await the onset of that pain in the company of others in the same predicament. In attempting to account theoretically for this finding, Schachter mentions such motivational forces as the subjects' needs for reassurance, distraction, escape, and information. However, among the various possible explanations, Schachter appears to favor one derived from Festinger's (1954) theory of social comparison processes. Adapting that theory to the phenomena under investigation, Schachter postulates that the arousal of any strong emotion evokes a need for comparison. Emotions are assumed to be quite unspecific states of affect. Hence, persons can only evaluate the quality, intensity, and appropriateness of their emotions properly by comparing their own reactions with those of others. Moreover, novel emotion producing stimuli should induce a greater tendency to affiliate than familiar stimuli. By definition, a novel stimulus is one that is more difficult to fit into a person's established frame of reference for emotive states. Accordingly, the individual is more obliged to seek out others in order to define the emotional effects of novel stimuli.

The explication of Schachter's (1959) results in terms of the theory of social comparison processes is appealingly parsimonious. However, it requires the assumption that *all* emotive states have the same effect on affiliative behavior. Thus, Schachter, like many contemporary psychologists, does not deal with the possible conceptual distinctions between fear and anxiety. Yet, it seems to us that, by adopting an alternative assumption about the psychological properties of emotions, to be presented briefly below, it is possible to formulate predictions concerning affiliative responses

Reprinted from *Journal of Abnormal and Social Psychology,* 1961, 62, 356–363. Copyright 1961 by the American Psychological Association and reproduced by permission.

[1] The authors are indebted to the Yale Communication Research Project, directed by C. I. Hovland, for its material support of this study, and to C. I. Hovland for his encouragement and helpful suggestions. Our thanks are extended to Jacob Rabbie and Harold Gerard for their contributions to the study. We also wish to acknowledge the expert and enthusiastic participation of our research assistants, Ted Sheldon, Sally Whitcher, and Ira Grushow.

that could not have been derived from the theory of social comparison processes. Indeed, by employing Freud's (1949a, 1949b) conceptual distinctions between fear and anxiety, we are led to predict a tendency toward social isolation—rather than affiliation—as a consequence of certain conditions of emotional arousal.

The present experiment was, thus, undertaken with two objectives: to assess the empirical validity of conceptual differentiation between fear and anxiety, and to evaluate the extent to which the theory of social comparison processes may be applied to the relationship between all emotions and affiliative behavior. In order to implement these objectives, we have conducted an experimental investigation of the differential effects of fear and anxiety upon social affiliation.

Functional Relationship between Emotions and Motives

The guiding assumption of our experiment holds that all emotions are consciously experienced epiphenomena of motives.[2] When our motives are aroused, we experience subjective reactions to which we learn, over time, to attach commonly agreed upon labels that signify the various emotions.

Motive, on the other hand, is defined as a tension producing stimulus that provokes behavior designed to reduce the tension. Each of our motives (innate or learned) requires the performance of a *different* response for the maximal reduction of its tension.

Fear and Anxiety Viewed as Motives

The motive of fear (which Freud called objective anxiety) is aroused whenever persons are confronted by an external object or event that is inherently dangerous and likely to produce pain. Only one type of overt[3] response can maximally reduce our fear: separation from the threatening aspects of the feared object, accomplished by flight from the object, at one extreme, and conquest, at the other. In the case of fear, then, one's energies are mobilized toward dealing with the external stimulus; to eliminate, through some mode of escape or attack, the threat that is clearly and objectively present in the stimulus.

---

2 The concept of motivation which we have chosen to employ has been elaborated elsewhere (Sarnoff, 1960a).

3 Space limitations do not permit a consideration of the two types of covert (ego defensive) responses, denial and identification with the aggressor, which persons may employ in their efforts to cope with external threat. A full discussion of these ego defenses is presented by Sarnoff (1960a).

If we examine the consequences of anxiety (which Freud termed neurotic anxiety), we see no such correspondence between the internal disturbance of the person and an objectively harmful environmental stimulus. Instead, anxiety is typically aroused by stimuli which, objectively considered, are *innocuous*.[4] For example, in the case of the classical phobias, harmless objects possess a special motivational significance for certain people. These objects activate some motive other than fear, and this other motive, in turn, arouses the consciously perceived motive of anxiety. Hence, the emotional reaction of the anxious person is inappropriate to the inherent characteristics of the external stimulus.

Regardless of their content, the motives whose arousal evokes anxiety share a common property: they are all *repressed*. These repressed motives continue unconsciously to press for the reduction of their tensions; and anxiety signals the threat of possible expression of these repressed motives. Consequently, the person develops a number of additional ego defenses that function to safeguard the initial effects of repression. If the ego defenses do their work effectively, the motives are kept under repression, the inner danger passes and the individual's anxiety is reduced.

Implications of the Motives of Anxiety and Fear for Affiliative Behavior

It follows from the foregoing discussion that, when their anxieties are aroused, people are more inclined to become preoccupied with the reassertion of inner self-control than with modes of dealing with the anxiety-evoking external object. Because the anxious person tends to be aware of the element of *inappropriateness* in his feelings, he is loath to communicate his anxieties to others. To avoid being ridiculed or censured, he conceals anxiety aroused by stimuli which he guesses do not have a similar effect upon others, and which, he feels, ought not so to upset him. Thus, when anxiety is aroused, a person should tend to seek isolation from others. On the other hand, when fear is aroused and he is unable to flee from the threatening object, he welcomes the opportunity to affiliate. Since the usual responses to fear, flight and fight, are restricted in the experimental situation, the sub-

---

[4] In fact, since anxiety arousing stimuli are often related to unconscious libidinal motives, they may be regarded by most people as intrinsically pleasurable, rather than in any way painful. For example, owing to the manner in which their heterosexual motives have been socialized, some men may tend severely to repress their sexual cravings for women. Hence, when such men are shown photographs of voluptuous nudes, stimuli which might be quite evocative of pleasurable fantasies among most of their fellows, they are likely to experience anxiety (Sarnoff & Corwin, 1959).

ject seeks other fear reducing responses. Therefore, the probability of affiliation increases because it mediates fear reduction through the potentiality for catharsis and distraction as well as the emotional comparison offered by interpersonal contact.

We are led, therefore, to the hypothesis that the motives of fear and anxiety should influence social affiliation behavior differently: the greater the fear aroused, the more the subjects should choose to be together with others while they await actual contact with the fear arousing object. Conversely, the greater the anxiety elicited, the more the subjects should choose to be alone while they await contact with the anxiety arousing object.

METHOD

The experiment was presented to the subjects as a physiological investigation of the cutaneous sensitivity of various parts of the body. A 2 × 2 design was used in which two levels of fear and of anxiety were experimentally aroused. The dependent variable of social affiliation was measured by having the subjects state whether they preferred to spend an anticipated waiting period alone or in the company of others.

Subjects

The subjects were 72 unpaid, male undergraduate volunteers from six introductory psychology classes in Yale University. An additional 36 subjects were used to pretest the manipulations and measuring devices, and an additional 13 subjects were excluded from the analyses because they did not qualify as acceptable subjects, that is, were friends, misunderstood the instructions, did not believe the rationale.

Procedure

Background information was collected by an accomplice alleged to be from the counseling program of the Student Health Department. A questionnaire was designed to obtain background information on the subjects and also their preferred mode of defense mechanism. The latter data were in response to four Blacky cards. As in a recent experiment by Sarnoff (1960b), each card was accompanied by three alternatives that were to be rank ordered according to the subjects' reaction to the theme of the card (sibling rivalry, achievement, and two of sucking). The alternatives reflected predominantly an acceptance of the motive, projection of the motive upon others, or a reaction formation against the motive.

About one month later, the experimenter was introduced to the psychology classes as a physiological psychologist studying physiological responses to sensory stimuli. The subjects were subsequently recruited individually, and randomly assigned to the four experimental treatments. The specious purpose of the experiment and of the conditions of waiting were further established by marking the experimental room "Sensory Physiology Laboratory" and two nearby rooms "Waiting Room A" and "Waiting Room T." Because of absentees, the size of the groups tested varied from three to five, and was usually composed of four subjects. In order to avoid the development of superficial friendships during the experiment, and eliminate the possibility that the subjects might react to cues from each other or from the experimenter, the subjects were isolated in adjacent cubicles, no communication was allowed, and the tape-recorded instructions were presented through earphones.

The experimental conditions and instructions common to all subjects will be presented first. After rolling up their sleeves, removing their watches from their wrists, and gum or cigarettes from their mouths ("They interfere with the recording electrodes"), the subjects were told:

> Our experiment falls in the general area of physiological psychology. As you may know, one branch of physiological psychology is concerned with the reactions of the sense organs to various kinds of stimulation. Our present experiment deals with the skin [or mouth] as an organ of sensation. We are interested in studying individual differences in response to particular stimuli applied to it.
>
> There has been a good deal of controversy about the relative sensitivity of the fingertips [lips] as compared to the palms [tongue], and upper surface of the hand [palate]. Our experiment will help to provide data upon which we may be able ultimately to draw a detailed map of the cutaneous sensitivity of the human hand [mouth].
>
> In order to measure your physiological reactions, we are now going to attach some instruments to your arm and finger [corner of your mouth]. These instruments are electrodes which are connected to a machine which records exactly the strength of your response to each stimulus. . . . Electrode jelly will be applied first to the area to insure that we get a good electrical contact. (The electrodes were then attached by a female laboratory assistant of middle age.)

In order to provide a reasonable basis for asking the subjects to wait in other rooms (and, thus, for making the choice of affiliation or isolation), the subjects were told that it was necessary to assess their basal rates of responding prior to the application of the actual stimuli. They were led to believe that their individual sensitivities were being recorded while they viewed a series of slides of a typical subject who had participated in the experiment. They anticipated that a waiting period would come after the slides, and then in the second—and purportedly major—part of the experiment their direct reactions to the actual stimuli would be measured. Accordingly, they were told:

> Now that your basal rates have been recorded on our polygraph recorder, it will take us about 10 minutes while we tally the data and reset our measuring instruments so that they will be geared to your individual basal rates as you are run one at a time through the rest of the experiment. While we are doing these things, we are going to ask you to wait in other rooms which are available to us. We will come to get you when it is your turn to

go through with the experiment. Incidentally, we have found that some of our subjects prefer to do their waiting alone, while others prefer to wait together with other subjects. Therefore, we are going to give you your choice of waiting alone or with others. In either case, you will be ushered to a comfortable room furnished with adequate reading material.

After indicating their preference of waiting alone or together with others, the subjects also indicated the intensity of this preference on an "open-ended" scale in which 0 represented a very weak preference and 100 a very strong preference. On this relatively unstructured scale there was as much as 175 points of difference between subjects (from "75-alone" to "100-together").

Presentation of the slides during the experiment served two purposes in addition to the one previously mentioned. The content of the slides (appropriate to each experimental treatment) served to reinforce the subjects' differential expectations of the nature and severity of the stimulus situation. Furthermore, the subject seen in the slides became a focal point for measuring the effectiveness of the experimental manipulations. It was assumed that a direct attempt (by means of a scaled question) to appraise the level of the subjects' fear or anxiety would be likely to: sensitize them to the true purpose of the experiment; yield unreliable results since the subjects might neither be consciously aware of, nor able to verbalize, their anxiety reaction; and evoke resistance since some subjects might not want to admit to being anxious or fearful, calling their masculinity into question.

Therefore, it was necessary to use an indirect, disguised measure to evaluate whether the experimental inductions had actually aroused two levels of both fear and anxiety. Immediately after the slides had been shown (but before the affiliation choices had been made), the subjects were told:

> As you may know, an individual shows his physiological reaction in a variety of behavioral forms. We are interested in seeing whether it is possible to estimate how ill-at-ease or upset individuals are at the prospect of receiving the stimulation in this experiment. Recalling the subject whom you just saw in the slides, how upset or ill-at-ease did he seem to you? Please assign a number anywhere from zero to 100 to indicate your feeling. (Zero = unconcerned, at ease; 100 = extremely concerned and ill-at-ease.)

Since the subject in the slides was a posed model instructed to remain poker faced throughout, it was assumed that there was no objective difference in his expression. Thus, any systematic difference in ratings between groups should reflect a projection of the subjects' own motives upon this screen.

However, because the content of the slides was not identical for every group but rather "tailored" to each specific treatment, it was possible that the model may have actually looked more fearful in the slides shown to the subjects in the High Fear than in the Low Fear condition. As a control check on this possibility, four additional introductory psychology classes ($N = 108$) served as judges. They were told that the slides were of a typical subject in a recently completed experiment, and their task was to estimate how ill-at-east and concerned he appeared (on the same scale used by the experimental subjects). Two of the classes saw only the face of the model (the rest of the slide was blacked out) and were told only that he was a subject in a physiological experiment in which stimuli were applied and responses measured. The other two classes saw the entire stimulus field of the slides and were given the same complete description that the experimental subjects received. Since each class of judges rated the slides for all four experimental treatments, the order of presentation was counterbalanced.

After the projective measure of motive arousal and the measure of affiliation, the electrodes were removed and a measure taken of the subjects' reasons for choosing to affiliate or be isolated. This was done with the rationale that a social psychologist had become interested in the fact that some of our subjects preferred to be together while others preferred to be alone, and he had asked us to get some information for him about the reasons underlying this preference.

The questionnaire, designed by Gerard and Rabbie (1960), contained both open-ended and structured questions asking for reasons for the affiliation choice. Finally, the subjects noted whether or not they wished to continue in the experiment. Only one subject (in the High Fear condition) refused to remain for the "stimulation" part of the experiment.

The true purpose, hypothesis, design, and reasons for the various deceptions (and, at a later time, the results) were explained fully to each subject.

High Fear

A high level of fear was induced by leading the subjects to anticipate a series of painful electrical shocks. Although they expected to endure each of the shocks for 2 minutes, the subjects were assured that the shocks would not cause damage or injury.

The female assistant (dressed in a white lab coat, as was the experimenter) then attached electrodes to each subject's arm and fingertip and strapped his arm onto a cotton-padded board. The leads from the electrodes appeared to go to a polygraph recorder, which also was seen in the series of slides of the typical subjects. Another slide showed an enormous electrical stimulator, and the implication was that it was behind a curtain in the experimental room. It was called to the subjects' attention that:

> The four dials shown in the upper right-hand corner of the stimulator enable us to regulate automatically the frequency, duration, delay, and intensity of the shock you will get.

The other slides portrayed the subject with earphones and electrodes attached (like the subjects themselves), "listening to the instructions," and then "about to receive his first painful shock," administered by the experimenter, who could be seen in the background manipulating the dials on the stimulator. A final situational factor that may have enhanced the effectiveness of the High Fear manipulation was that the experimental room housed electrical generators which made a continuous buzzing sound, a cue interpreted by the High Fear subjects as the electrical stimulator "warming up," but unnoticed or quickly adapted to by the other subjects. An unobtrusively posted sign reading "Danger/High Voltage," present only for the High Fear subjects, gave further credence to this notion.

Low Fear

In the Low Fear condition the word "shock" was never used, and all cues in the situation associated with shock, fear, or pain were removed; that is, no white lab coats, arms not strapped to boards, and so on. The expectations of these subjects were guided by instructions stating that our methodology was to apply a 10-second stimulus of very low intensity that would be just sufficient to elicit a measurable physiological response.

In the series of slides viewed by these subjects, the imposing electrical stimulator was replaced by a small innocuous looking apparatus (actually a voltmeter), and the experimenter was seen not in the active role as an agent of pain, but in the passive role of recording data from the polygraph recorder.

High Anxiety

Anxiety was manipulated by arousing a motive that was assumed to have been repressed by most of the subjects. In Freudian terminology, the motive might be called "oral libido," a desire to obtain pleasurable gratification by sucking on objects that are clearly related to infantile nursing experiences. The female breast is, of course, the prototype of such objects, but others include nipples, baby bottles, and pacifiers. Thus, to arouse this oral motive and, hence, the anxiety that should follow its arousal, subjects in the High Anxiety condition were led to believe that they would have to suck on a number of objects commonly associated with infantile oral behavior. They were told that their task would be to suck on these objects for 2 minutes while we recorded their physiological responses from the skin surfaces stimulated by the objects. In clear view in front of the subjects were the following items: numerous baby bottles, oversized nipples, pacifiers, breast shields (nipples women often wear over their breasts while nursing), and lollipops.

The same variety of stimulus objects was shown arrayed in front of the subject in the slides. He could be seen, tongue hanging out, lips puckered, about to suck his thumb (as one of the objects of stimulation) or one of the other objects. Subjects were told that the contact taped to the mouth recorded the direct reaction to the oral stimulation, while the arm contact recorded peripheral reactions.

Low Anxiety

The instructions to the Low Anxiety subjects did not mention "suck," nor any stimulation that they would receive from putting the objects in their mouths. Moreover, they were led to believe that they would keep each object in their mouths for only 10 seconds. The stimulus objects were not in immediate proximity to the subjects while their electrodes were being attached. The stimulus objects which they anticipated putting in their mouths were shown in the slides: whistles, balloons, "kazoos," and pipes. Since these objects do not require sucking (but rather, in general, blowing), the model's tongue was not seen as he prepared to use the stimuli in the slides.

RESULTS

Evidence of the Effectiveness
of the Experimental Manipulations

In using the subjects' estimates of the degree to which the model seen in the slides was upset by the prospect of receiving the stimulation in the experiment, it was assumed that the subjects would tend to project their induced level of fear and anxiety. Table 1, which presents the mean projection

TABLE 1 *Mean Projection Scores for Each Experimental Treatment*

| MOTIVE | LEVEL OF AROUSAL | | p VALUE |
	Low	High	
Fear	24	42	$<.01$ ($t = 3.05$)
Anxiety	14	31[a]	$<.01$ ($t = 2.95$)
	ns	ns	

Note.—The larger the score, the greater the degree of projection.

[a] Variance greater than in High Fear group, $p < .10$; SD for High Anxiety = 24, for High Fear = 16.

scores for each experimental treatment, offers evidence that this assumption was valid and the manipulations effective. The High Arousal subjects perceived the model to be significantly[5] more upset, concerned, and ill-at-ease than did the the Low Arousal subjects.

Our theoretical distinction between fear and anxiety, and the way these concepts were operationally defined in this experiment, lead to the prediction that, assuming similarity of past experience, persons facing the same clearly, objectively present threat should react in a relatively homogeneous fashion. This close correspondence between stimulus and response is not assumed to hold for anxiety. We have already noted that a stimulus that produces anxiety for some persons is not an anxiety producing cue for many others. Since the significance of the stimulus depends upon its symbolic and generally idiosyncratic associations, one would expect that a stimulus which elicited anxiety for persons with relevant predispositions (repressed motives) would have less effect on those who had more adequately resolved the conflict over the expression of the same motives. Thus, one way of determining whether our experimental manipulations produced two different motives, fear and anxiety (rather than only two levels of one motive), is to compare the variability in response between treatments.

[5] All p values reported throughout the paper are based on two-tailed tests of significance.

The heterogeneity of response in the High Anxiety group is, as predicted, greater than in the High Fear and the Low Arousal conditions. The same difference in response variability between the High Anxiety group and all other groups is manifested as well in the dependent variable of social affiliation. The questionnaire data to be presented in a later section offer further support to the distinction between fear and anxiety.

Before presenting the major results, it is necessary to account for two possible sources of artifact in the just reported data on projection. They are: by chance sampling, the High Arousal groups could have contained more subjects who characteristically used projection as a mechanism of defense than the Low Arousal groups; and the subject seen in the High Fear and High Anxiety slides was objectively more upset and concerned than he was in the Low Fear and Low Anxiety slides. If either of these alternatives were true, then the projection measure would not be a reflection of differences due to the experimental arousal of levels of fear and anxiety.

The pretest data of the subjects' mode of defense preference on the Blacky Projection test show no initial significant difference between any of the groups in their tendency to use projection.

Among the groups of neutral judges who evaluated all the slides shown in the study, from 68 percent to 98 percent reported perceiving either no difference in the degree to which the model appeared upset, or a difference opposite to that reported in Table 1. This result holds for both fear and anxiety, and regardless of the order of presentation or amount of the stimulus field seen (model's face only or entire slide). Thus, it appears that the projection measure can be used as an index of the efficacy of the experimental conditions and manipulations.

Effects of Fear and Anxiety on Social Affiliation

The results bearing upon the hypothesis of the study are presented in Table 2, where for each condition the mean intensity of desire to affiliate, as well as the number of subjects choosing to affiliate and to be alone, are presented. It is evident that there is a strong positive relationship between fear and the index of affiliative tendency, but a strong negative relationship between anxiety and affiliation, so that as fear increases affiliation also increases, while an increase in anxiety results in a decrease in affiliation. Thus, our prediction of an interaction between kind of motive and level of arousal is clearly supported by the data. While some 95 percent of the High Fear subjects chose the "together" alternative (with more than 0 intensity), only 46 percent of the High Anxiety subjects chose to wait together. The marked mean difference between these groups in intensity of choice (51.0–8.0) is significant well beyond the .01 level ($t = 3.63$). The large mean difference in affiliative tendency between the High and Low Fear groups

TABLE 2 *Relationship of Motive to Social Affiliation*

| | MEAN AFFILIATION STRENGTH[a] | NUMBER OF SUBJECTS CHOOSING | |
		Together	Alone or "0-Together"
Fear			
Low	34.0	12	3
High	51.0	19	1
Anxiety			
Low	27.0	11	12
High	8.0	10	12
Interaction: (Motive × Level) $p < .05$, $t = 2.30$, $df = 68$.			

[a] The larger the score, the greater the affiliation tendency; isolation intensity score subtracted from affiliation intensity score.

($p < .07$, $t = 1.96$) represents a replication of Schachter's (1959, p. 18) results. While the mean difference between High and Low Anxiety was even larger than that between the Fear conditions, it only approached significance ($p = .16$, $t = 1.46$) due to the marked heterogeneity of variance of the High Anxiety group.

Reasons Given for Affiliation Choice

The final measure taken was a questionnaire that explored the reasons the subjects gave for choosing to wait together with others or to wait alone. The 11 structured items on the questionnaire each presented a possible motive for affiliation; and each was accompanied by a 70-point scale on which the subject indicated how important he thought the motive was in determining his choice. The highly significant interaction between experimental treatment and questions ($p < .001$, $F = 3.74$, $df = 30.570$) on a repeated-measurement analysis of variance justified a search for those questions (motives for affiliation) that differentiated the groups.

Since there were too few subjects choosing the alone condition, the analysis is limited to those wanting to affiliate. The motives for affiliation that were most important for the High Fear subjects and most distinguished them from the Low Fear subjects were (the lower the mean, the greater the importance; 10 = extremely important):

1. I am not sure whether I am reacting in the same way as the others to the prospect of getting shocked and would like to compare my reactions to theirs. [Emotional comparison] High Fear $\bar{x} = 38$, Low Fear $\bar{x} = 54$, $p < .001$.
2. I feel worried about getting shocked and would like to know to what extent

the others are worried too. [Extent of comparison] High Fear $\bar{x} = 40$, Low Fear $\bar{x} = 61$, $p < .001$.
3. I want to be distracted in order to take my mind off the prospect of getting shocked. [Distraction] High Fear $\bar{x} = 44$, Low Fear $\bar{x} = 59$, $p < .01$.
4. I am worried about the prospect of getting shocked and felt that talking with someone about it would get it off my chest. [Catharsis] High Fear $\bar{x} = 50$, Low Fear $\bar{x} = 59$, $p < .05$.

The reasons for affiliation given spontaneously to a single open-ended question also reflect the importance of these same considerations. Among High Anxiety subjects choosing to be alone, the major reason given spontaneously and supported by the scaled questions is the desire "to be alone to think about personal affairs and school work."

Curiosity as to "what the others were like" was important, but equally so across all conditions. Of least importance among all subjects are the following motives for affiliation ("oral stimulation" substituted for "shock" for Anxiety groups):

"It would be clearer in my own mind as to how I feel about getting shocked if I could express my reactions to someone else." "I anticipated that the others would offer reassuring comments." "I want to be with others to reassure myself that I am not the only one who was singled out to be shocked." "I feel that perhaps together we could somehow figure out a way to avoid getting shocked."

There are several large differences between the High Fear and High Anxiety groups; with the former finding the following motives as significantly more important: emotional comparison, extent of comparison, distraction, catharsis, and the physical presence of others ($p < .05$ in each instance). Similarly, an internal analysis of the High Fear group reveals these same motives (especially catharsis and emotional comparison) to be more important for those subjects who chose to affiliate most strongly than for those below the group median in affiliation strength.

Ordinal Position and Its Relation to Affiliation

While the reasoning used in the planning of the present study did not include predictions of the effects of ordinal position upon affiliation, data relevant to this question were nevertheless obtained, to check on Schachter's (1959) finding that affiliation tendencies increased with emotional arousal only among first- and only-born children. This finding is duplicated in the present study. First-born children want to affiliate significantly more than later-borns under conditions of high fear, but not when the level of fear is low. While the mean affiliation intensity for the first-born High Fear subjects was 62, it was only 23 for the later-born High Fear subjects ($p = .05$, $t = 2.10$). This same general finding holds for the High Anxiety group, but again the within-group variability does not permit the large mean difference obtained (16 for first-borns and -3 for later-borns) to be statistically significant.

DISCUSSION

Since our basic hypothesis has been supported, our results lend credence to the previously drawn conceptual distinction between fear and anxiety. In view of the fact that our anxiety arousing stimulus was specifically designed to tap only one kind of repressed motive, it of course remains an empirical question whether or not the evocation of other types of presumably repressed motives also leads to social isolation.

In order to predict the consequences of the arousal of a motive, therefore, it is necessary to know which responses are required to reduce its tension. The probability of the social comparison response is, thus, a function of: the kind of motive aroused, the intensity of the motive, the degree of novelty of the emotional experience, the response hierarchy associated with the specific motive, and certain attributes of those with whom the person is to affiliate.

We do not question the assumption that the need for some kind of cognitive-emotional clarity and structure is a basic human motive. However, we feel that the need for self-evaluation is not the *most* salient motive aroused in the experimental situations that Schachter (1959) and we employed. We do not view the cognitive need to structure a vague emotional state as the primary motive in these experiments; we see social comparison not as an end in itself but merely as one of the several responses that are *instrumental* in reducing the tension associated with the situationally more salient motives of fear and anxiety.

Strict application of the theory of emotional comparison processes to the present experimental situation should lead one to predict greater affiliation tendencies for the High Anxiety subjects than the High Fear subjects, since the Anxiety situation was more unusual than that of Fear, and the emotion aroused was probably more novel and vague. The opposite prediction, supported by the results, demands an approach, such as the one followed here, that specifies the probability of the response alternatives evoked by the dominant motives aroused.

As the emotional experience becomes very novel and unusual, the need for comparison of one's reactions with others should increase, and, hence, intensify affiliation tendencies. The induction of esoteric states of consciousness by "anxiety producing drugs" (being studied presently by Schachter) may be the kind of situation in which emotional comparison theory offers the best explanations and predictions. Under such circumstances, it may be possible to create emotional states that are epiphenomena of motives whose neurophysiological bases had never previously been set into motion. A more natural counterpart of this novel emotional experience occurs the first time a person experiences the emotions associated with the death of a loved one.

The predictive importance of knowing the specific responses appropriate to the motive aroused is clearly illustrated by the following examples. If a person's guilt is aroused, his response to feelings of guilt should be to seek out others only if they could be expected to punish him and, thus, to expiate his guilt, but not to affiliate with individuals perceived as unable to fill this role. Similarly, if repressed homosexual anxieties are aroused, isolation should generally be preferred to affiliation, as with oral anxiety in the present study. However, affiliation tendencies should increase if the subject is allowed to wait with females, but not if he can wait only in the company of males.

While our questionnaire data offer support for the importance of emotional comparison, they also point up the role of other motives such as need for catharsis and distraction. The marked difference in the importance of the reasons given for affiliation between the High Fear and High Anxiety groups is perhaps the most substantial evidence that the experimental manipulations have indeed led to the arousal of two quite different motives.

A final point of interest concerns the data about ordinal position. The finding that firstborn children show greater affiliation tendencies than later-born children when either fear or anxiety is aroused supports Schachter's (1959) results. Theoretical and experimental attempts to uncover the dynamics underlying this "static" variable should prove interesting and fruitful.

SUMMARY

This experiment tests the utility of the psychoanalytic distinction between fear and anxiety for making differential predictions about social affiliation. It also assesses the breadth of generalization of Schachter's (1959) empirical finding of a positive relation between emotional arousal and affiliation. Seventy-two subjects were randomly assigned to four experimental treatments in which low and high levels of fear and anxiety were manipulated. The success of these inductions was established by a projective device and questionnaire data. The dependent variable of social affiliation was measured by having the subjects choose to await the anticipated exposure to the stimulus situation either alone or together with others.

The results show that, while the desire to affiliate increases as fear increases (a replication of Schachter's, 1959, results), the opposite is true for anxiety; as anxiety increases the desire to affiliate decreases. Thus, as predicted, our findings lend empirical support to the theoretical distinction between fear and anxiety. At the same time, our results suggest that the theory of social comparison processes may not be adequate to account for the general relationship between emotions and affiliative tendencies.

References

Festinger, L. A theory of social comparison processes. *Human Relations*, 1954, *7*, 117–140.
Freud, S. *Inhibitions, symptoms, and anxiety*. (Originally published 1936) London: Hogarth, 1949. (a)
Freud, S. *New introductory lectures on psychoanalysis*. (Originally published 1933) London: Hogarth, 1949. (b)
Gerard, H. B., & Rabbie, J. M. Fear and social comparison. Unpublished manuscript, Bell Telephone Research Laboratories, 1960.
Sarnoff, I. Psychoanalytic theory and social attitudes. *Public Opinion Quarterly*, 1960, *24*, 251–279. (a)
Sarnoff, I. Reaction formation and cynicism. *Journal of Personality*, 1960, *28*, 129–143. (b)
Sarnoff, I., & Corwin, S. M. Castration anxiety and the fear of death. *Journal of Personality*, 1959, *27*, 374–385.
Schachter, S. *The psychology of affiliation*. Stanford: Stanford University Press, 1959.

Foreword to Reading 6.2

INTRODUCTION

If you know all of the "groups" that a person belongs to or identifies with, you will have some basis for inferring many of his attitudes. For instance, this editor (LZS) suspects that the majority of college students favor student "power," and oppose the military drafting of college students. However, one person may belong to a number of groups which prescribe conflicting norms or attitudes. Charters and Newcomb (1952) suggest that the attitude expressed by an individual depends on the "potency" of his various membership groups. Among other factors, potency may vary depending on the salience (or the individual's awareness) of a group. The young college student in a group of his peers may find himself thinking about or expressing different attitudes than those he expresses at the family dinner table. The young American Jew who considers that he retains little of his Judaic background, may be surprised to find himself sounding very Jewish when anti-Semitic comments or threats to Israel are being discussed.

Shomer and Centers point to previous research demonstrating the importance of the effect of salience on various behaviors (voting, pain tolerance) as well as for experimental procedure in surveys and tests of attitude. They also point out that group salience is irrelevant when the group has no norms (or rules of acceptable behavior) that pertain to a particular issue.

METHOD

In this study, salience of male and female chauvinist norms was manipulated by having subjects complete questionnaires in groups with or without members of the opposite sex. The editors were surprised to note that a

324

Feminist Attitude questionnaire devised in 1936 still remains relevant to distinguish between male and female feminist attitudes.

As is often the case in psychological studies, responses were assigned weights, and each subject given a total score by summing his weighted responses.

RESULTS AND DISCUSSION

As expected, there were no variations in response to the child-rearing scale, a measure chosen because it was thought to be irrelevant to norms of female and male behavior.

As the reader will see, however, male responses to the feminist attitudes scale did vary according to salience condition, an interesting effect when you consider the extreme subtlety of the manipulation. These results, along with the authors' suggested interpretation, are further pictured for the reader in Figure 1. The authors propose that two conflicting norms, those of chivalry and male chauvinism, operate for the male population. This editor wonders if one could not also define conflicting norms for the female population, perhaps femininity versus feminism.

All of this postulation of norms has one strong flaw in terms of scientific reasoning. Given an unconfirmed prediction, one can always pull a new norm out of the hat, and thus end up with an endless number of norms. The answer, as pointed out by Shomer and Centers, is to obtain independent evidence of the existence of a norm that has been suggested by one particular piece of research.

Reference

Charters, W. W. Jr., & Newcomb, T. M. Some attitudinal effects of experimentally increased salience of a membership group. In E. Maccoby, T. M. Newcomb, E. L. Hartley (Eds.), *Readings in social psychology.* (3d ed.) New York: Holt, Rinehart and Winston, 1958.

6.2 Differences in Attitudinal Responses Under Conditions of Implicitly Manipulated Group Salience[1]

Robert W. Shomer
Richard Centers

It was hypothesized that the salience of group membership might be aroused implicitly by cues provided in the objective situation without the explicit reminders of group membershp used in previous research. Further, that by merely varying the number of persons of each sex, in an aggregate responding to a questionnaire which included material relevant to the sex group norms, the salience of the norms of the respective groups would be aroused, and these norms would influence responses to the relevant material. Subjects responded anonymously to a questionnaire dealing with attitudes toward feminism and toward child rearing, under three conditions of group composition, with either a male or female experimenter. The hypothesis was clearly supported for males but not for females. That is, males' responses on feminist items varied significantly over the conditions of group composition, but females' did not. Responses to the child-rearing items did not vary for either sex over conditions of group composition. The pattern of results for male subjects was accounted for as the result of the resolution of conflicting norms—chauvinism and chivalry. The relevance of this experiment to methodological procedures is indicated, it being stressed that in the administration of group questionnaires, even though anonymous, neither the characteristics of the individuals composing the aggregate nor those of the administrator could be ignored.

Man as a social being is a member of many groups. In discussing the implications of this fact in relation to the psychological consequences of minority group membership, Kurt Lewin (1935) pointed out that the characteristics of a social situation might so enhance the feeling of membership in a given group that such a feeling would be dominant in the determination of responses in the situation. In the more than a third of a century since Lewin's statement, remarkably little has been done in the way of research on its implications. Festinger (1947, 1950) was apparently the first to deliberately experimentally manipulate cues designed to focus attention on awareness of group membership. He highlighted its importance in the voting

Reprinted from the *Journal of Personality and Social Psychology*, 1970, *15*, 125–132. Copyright 1970 by the American Psychological Association and reproduced with permission.

[1] This research was supported by a faculty research grant at the University of California, Los Angeles.

behavior of Catholics and Jews. Members of both of these groups tended to vote predominantly for a person identified as a member of their own group in a situation where they were electing a club officer and the religious affiliation of the candidates was made known to them.

Later researchers (Charters & Newcomb, 1952; Kelley, 1955; Lambert, Libman, & Poser, 1960) have explicitly manipulated the salience of religious group membership in their respective studies by means of more or less vivid reminders of such membership. Charters and Newcomb demonstrated an effect of group membership salience on the attitudinal responses of Catholics on questions related to their religion. Kelley provided partial confirmation of the hypothesis that the resistance to change of group-anchored attitudes is directly related to the salience of the group membership feeling in Catholics. Lambert et al. demonstrated an increase in tolerance for pain when membership feelings of Christians and Jews were made salient. Charters and Newcomb (1952) concluded from their study that "an individual's expression of attitudes is a function of the relative-momentary potency of his relevant group memberships [p. 420]."

The expectation of the investigators in the preceding studies has been that heightening the awareness of membership in a group thereby makes salient the attitudinal, belief, and behavioral norms of that group. Kelley (1955) has explicitly called attention to the arousal of conformity motivation in such a case, saying,

We might expect that at any given moment conformity to a specific group's norms will depend upon the degree to which cues associated with [membership in] that group successfully compete with other cues in the individual's environment, capture his attention, and arouse his conformity motives [p. 275].

The norms of religious groups are relatively unambiguous and fairly well known to their members, and in each of the previously mentioned studies there has been a quite explicit manipulation of the salience of group membership. A distinctly more dramatic and powerful test of the effects of group salience might be found in a situation in which only an implicit manipulation was employed and in a case where the group norms involved might be more ambiguous to the members. Situations occur in everyday life in which information that could arouse the salience of group belongingness may be conveyed in an implicit manner. This may happen in a situation where sex, race, distinct dress, insignia, badges, or other cues such as length of hair, hair style, presence of beard, and style of beard may inform an individual of the composition of the aggregate of persons present. Casual observation leads us to the hypothesis that such cues can also arouse or make salient, consciously or unconsciously, group belongingness factors that may determine or mediate verbal and nonverbal responses. This would be most likely to the degree that stimuli were also present to point up or subtly remind the individual of difference, conflict, or controversy.

The present research sought to examine the implications of the foregoing thoughts and, simultaneously, by deliberate systematic variation of the composition of an aggregate of subjects, also to test a hypothesis of essentially methodological relevance. For at least half a century, it has been common procedure in psychological, educational, sociological, and other social science research to administer tests and questionnaires intended to measure values, motives, traits, attitudes, and beliefs in group settings such as classrooms, PTA meetings, union halls, fraternity houses, club and association meetings, etc. Aside from the experiments discused earlier which were designed explicitly to arouse the salience of group membership, there has been an apparent disregard of any implicit group salience effects— effects that might be caused by the composition of the group or the setting in which the measurements were obtained. The results of the innumerable studies employing group-administered questionnaire techniques have typically been interpreted as reflections of the personality dispositions of the respondents independently of the test situation. The present research will adduce evidence to indicate that this is at best a dubious conclusion. Hitherto, with the exception of studies in the context of door-to-door survey interviews (Blankenship, 1940; Katz, 1942), and experimental inquiry into "demand characteristics" (Rosenthal, 1963, 1966), there have been relatively few studies concerned with the possible effects created by the group membership attributes of the person administering a test or questionnaire. Recently it has been found (Bittner & Shinedling, 1968; Pedersen, Shinedling, & Johnson, 1968) that the sex of the examiner has a significant effect on children's performance in intellectual tasks. Other experimenter effects may, of course, be particularly important in situations where the subject matter of the questionnaire relates to racial or other minority groups, or to age, or to sex-group issues. In such situations, the characteristics of the tester may be more salient and thus interact with feelings of group belongingness aroused by other individuals present. For this reason, the present research was designed to take account of the possible effects of the characteristics of the experimenter as well as the effects of group composition.

The principal hypothesis of the present inquiry was that responses to a questionnaire involving issues relevant to the norms of the group members would be affected by the composition of the group in a direction conforming to, or congruent with, the norms of the group, whereas responses to a questionnaire lacking issues relevant to the norms of the group would not be so affected. More concretely, for example, in a situation in which males and females are represented in varying numbers and where two types of questionnaire items are used, some relevant to being either male or female and the others unrelated to sex group, we would expect cues provided by the aggregate composition to make sex-group membership salient. This, in turn, would evoke and make salient the attitudinal norms of the respective sexes toward the sex-related issues and elicit motivation to conform to the norms in the respective cases. On the basis of previous research (Centers, 1961), it was assumed that an attitudinal norm of male chauvinism repressive toward females would mediate the responses of male subjects, whereas females' responses would be activated (or mediated) by chauvinistic attitudes assertive and supportive for their sex group. On the other hand, although they may exist, no specific norms were known which might mediate differential responses by the two sexes to the questions on child rearing. A second hypothesis was that questionnaire responses of group members would be affected by the sex of the experimenter (or administrator), such that the bias in the direction of the group norm would be reinforced for males with a male experimenter and for females with a female experimenter.

METHOD

In order to have group membership distinguishable on the basis of appearance alone and thus produce what might be considered a minimal manipulation of the group salience factor, it was decided to vary the number of males and females comprising sizable groups responding anonymously to a questionnaire composed of items of related but different content. Kirkpatrick (1936a, 1936b, 1936c) and Centers (1961) have indicated substantial and consistent sex differences in the responses of males and females to questionnaires measuring attitudes toward women; hence it was considered appropriate that the Kirkpatrick Feminist Attitude Scale (FA—Kirkpatrick, 1936a) be employed as an instrument likely to involve sex group norms. For the related topic, items were selected from the Parental Attitude Research Instrument (PARI—Schaeffer & Bell, 1955) to comprise a measure of degree of leniency or strictness with regard to child-rearing practices. There was no expectation that responses to the PARI items would be appreciably or systematically related to the sex of the respondent. The FA scale is composed of 80 economic, domestic, political-legal, and conduct status items. Each item is related to women's rights, duties, and obligations in one of the four areas. In half the items, a profeminist position is indicated by agreement, and in the other half by disagreement, with the item. Items from the PARI consisted of questions on aspects of child rearing such as encouraging verbalization, breaking the will, strictness, and equalitarianism. For both the PARI and the FA items, weights of $+2$, $+1$, 0, -1, and -2 were assigned to response categories of strongly agree, agree, undecided, disagree, and strongly disagree, in that order. Item scores were combined so as to yield a total score for each instrument.

Subjects were requested not to identify themselves by name, but to indicate their age, sex, and marital status by checking an appropriate box in a list following the brief introductory directions. Age and marital status indicators were included, not because of any interest we had in the influence of these variables per se, but simply in an attempt to prevent the identification of the subject as male or female itself from possibly functioning to arouse group membership salience, as we feared it might if standing entirely alone.

Subjects were 214 "volunteers"[2] from introductory psychology classes at UCLA. They were recruited by means of a standardized departmental sign-up sheet which simply indicated that the study was concerned with marriage and family life, and that they would receive 1 hour's credit toward completion of their laboratory requirement.

Three conditions of group composition were used: (a) all subjects of the same sex; (b) half the subjects from each sex; (c) all subjects of the same sex, except for one. In the first condition, maximum salience arousal was expected, since members of a sex group were the subject of the questionnaire. The second condition was one wherein the expectation was for minimal or no salience arousal. A half-and-half sex mixture is common and usual in everyday life, both on campus and off. If any feelings of group salience are aroused, these might be as vague as feelings of being all "fellow students" or just "people." The third condition was included because, after a discussion of the kind of cues that might evoke salience, we were led to wonder if these might not be far more complex than was initially supposed. We wondered whether the presence of a lone member of the opposite sex in an aggregate of people might arouse even more salience of group membership norms in the remaining members than would be the case in a group composed of individuals who were all of the same sex.

In the first and third conditions two groups were run, one with males predominant and one with females predominant. In the second condition only one group was run. In order to examine the possible effects of the sex of the experimenter, the entire group design was run twice, once with a male experimenter and once with a female.[3] The resulting pattern yields a $2 \times 2 \times 3$ design with two levels for sex of subject, two for sex of experimenter, and three for type of group composition.[4] The original plan was to have a total of 25 subjects in each group, but because of the failure of some subjects to keep their appointment, group size varied from 17 to 25.

Subjects were seated in a large room at several tables with enough space between them to make observation of the content of each other's papers at least difficult, if not impossible. They were requested not to discuss the material or to otherwise converse with each other during the session, and, if they had any questions to come to the experimenter with them so

2 "Volunteers" at least in the sense that they could choose to participate in the study from among numerous other alternatives to fulfill their laboratory requirement.

3 Grateful acknowledgment is hereby made to Alice Davis Friedman who served as the female experimenter.

4 Since four groups were run in Condition 3 the four "solitary sex" subjects may be thought of as responding in another condition of group composition: one in which the subject is the only one of his or her sex in the aggregate. Because of the small number of such subjects (two of each sex) for this condition, however, their scores were not made a part of the analysis.

that they might be dealt with in private. Subjects were told that the purpose of the study was to collect anonymous attitudinal data for some questionnaires to be used in a larger study. Nothing was done or said by the experimenter that might call attention to the composition of the group, and no behavior of any of the subjects that might do so was observed.

RESULTS

The predictions relative to the particular groups and attitude instruments employed were that first, subjects' responses to the Feminist scale would show a large sex difference (with females more pro-feminist than males), but responses to the Child-Rearing scale would not. Second, responses to the Feminist scale would vary over the three conditions of group composition, but responses to the Child-Rearing scale would not. More specifically, for reasons explained above, males' attitudes in all-male groups with one female present would display the greatest degree of antifeminism, males' attitudes in all-male groups somewhat less antifeminism, and males' attitudes in groups composed of half of each sex should display the least antifeminism. Females' attitudes should show corresponding degrees of profeminism in analogous conditions. Third, subjects' responses to the Feminist scale would vary under all conditions of group composition in accordance with the sex of the experimenter, but responses to the Child-Rearing scale would not.

Group averages for both the Feminist and the Child-Rearing scales over the three conditions of group composition appear in Table 1. The means for the Feminist scale for both sexes for the three conditions of group composition obtained under experimenters of different sex are shown in Table 2.

In order to obtain proportional numbers of subjects for analysis, following the method of Lindquist (1953), additional scores based on the cell means were added to certain cells and scores were randomly eliminated from other cells. Two hundred of the original 210 scores remained after this procedure. Separate three-way analyses of variance were carried out on the Feminist scores and on the Child-Rearing scores. The results in Table 3 indicate that for the feminist items there was a large sex difference ($F = 13.43$, $df = 1/188$, $p < .001$). Not surprisingly, females' average pro-feminist scores were higher than those for males. For the Child-Rearing scores (Table 4), on the other hand, as expected, the effect of sex of subject was nonsignificant ($F < 1$). Thus, in support of the first prediction, responses to the feminist items were systematically related to the sex of the subject but responses to the Child-Rearing scale were not.

With respect to the second prediction, the effect of group composition,

TABLE 1 *Mean Profeminist and Child-Rearing Scores for Three Conditions of Group Composition*

SEX OF S	PROFEMINIST SCORES				CHILD-REARING SCORES			
	$LMOS^a$	Equal	All	M	$LMOS^a$	Equal	All	M
Male	23.0	18.0	5.5	15.1	4.3	5.7	2.1	3.7
n	38	21	38	97	38	21	38	97
Female	27.4	27.3	29.8	28.3	3.6	5.6	3.9	4.1
n	47	21	45	113	47	21	45	113

[a] Lone member of the opposite sex.

TABLE 2 *Mean Profeminist Scores for Three Conditions of Group Composition and Male and Female Experimenter*

SEX OF S	MALE E				FEMALE E			
	$LMOS^a$	Equal	All	M	$LMOS^a$	Equal	All	M
Male	32.1	16.0	1.8	15.8	14.8	20.2	10.1	14.3
n	18	11	21	50	20	10	17	47
Female	23.9	30.4	28.5	26.9	30.8	24.9	31.4	29.8
n	23	9	24	56	24	12	21	57

[a] Lone member of the opposite sex.

TABLE 3 *Analysis of Variance of Profeminist Scores*

SOURCE	SS	df	MS	F
Sex of S (A)	8,911.1	1	8,911.1	13.43**
Group composition (B)	2,768.6	2	1,384.3	2.09
Sex of E (C)	13.0	1	13.0	<1
A × B	4,503.6	2	2,251.8	3.39*
A × C	602.0	1	602.0	<1
B × C	2,583.4	2	1,291.7	1.95
A × B × C	1,763.5	2	881.8	1.33
Error variance	124,774.0	188	663.7	

* $p < .05$.
** $p < .001$.

TABLE 4 *Analysis of Variance on Child-Rearing Scores*

SOURCE	SS	df	MS	F
Sex of S (A)	8.8	1	8.8	<1
Group composition (B)	203.8	2	101.9	1.46
Sex of E (C)	15.7	1	15.7	<1
A × B	69.6	2	34.8	<1
A × C	33.3	1	33.3	<1
B × C	130.0	2	65.0	<1
A × B × C	214.3	2	107.1	1.53
Error variance	13,134.1	188	70.0	

the results indicate that as expected, for the Child-Rearing scale, the effect of group composition was not significant ($F < 1$) nor were any of the interactions. Also, contrary to the prediction, for feminist items the group composition effect failed to reach an acceptable level of significance ($F = 2.09$, $df = 2/188$, $p < .10$). However, a significant Sex of Subject × Group Composition interaction was obtained ($F = 3.39$, $df = 2/188$, $p < .05$). Therefore, an analysis of the simple effect of group composition was carried out. The results of this analysis, shown in Table 5, indicate that the effect

TABLE 5 *Analysis of Variance for Simple Effect of Group Composition*

SOURCE	SS	df	MS	F
B (males)	7,135.6	2	3,567.8	5.58*
B (females)	108.5	2	54.3	<1
Error variance	124,744.0	195	639.9	

* $p < .01$.

of group composition was significant for males ($F = 5.58$, $df = 2/195$, $p <$ .01), but not for females ($F < 1$). Evidently, when responding to a questionnaire involving women's rights, duties, and responsibilities, males are influenced by the number of each sex present, but females are not.

As indicated in Tables 3 and 4, the third prediction was only partially confirmed. As expected, the sex of the experimenter had no effect on responses to the Child-Rearing scale. However, contrary to expectation, the influence of sex of experimenter on feminist attitudes also failed to reach significance. Although it has no significant overall effect (see Table 2), the sex of the experimenter does seem to relate in a complex way to specific conditions of group composition. The nature of this relationship will be discussed in the section to follow.

DISCUSSION

As was indicated earlier, it was assumed that attitudes of sex group chauvinism were the mediating determinants of the differing responses of the respective sex groups. Although the data for females fail to show such an effect, those for males appear to bear out the assumption quite well. Yet there remain some quite puzzling questions when one examines Table 2, in which the mean scores for males are seen to vary quite markedly over the conditions of group composition as well as sex of experimenter. Attention is called especially to the mean scores obtained when there is a lone member of the female sex present in an otherwise all male group with a male experimenter. This score of 32.1 represents the highest mean profeminist score of any group, *male or female*, and contrasts sharply with the mean score of 1.8 obtained when the group is composed of males only with a male experimenter. The presence of a lone female in an otherwise all male group produces an almost astounding effect. It was initially supposed that the presence of a lone female would possibly make membership salience in the males of such a group even stronger than it would have been had no female been present. Obviously, the supposition was wrong, for the results do not sustain the assumption, at least not in terms of arousal of male chauvinistic norms.

But the hypothesis that the presence of a lone female would produce high group-membership salience in an otherwise all male aggregate is plausible if we suppose that the presence of the lone female arouses a conflicting male norm, that of *chivalry toward females*. This may appear lacking in credibility, however, when we look for a corresponding effect in the other condition where a lone female subject was present, for there, with a female experimenter, the profeminist score drops to only 14.8. It would be hasty to be thus convinced, however, for this drop becomes quite sensible if we assume conflicting male norms to be operating in this whole array of condi-

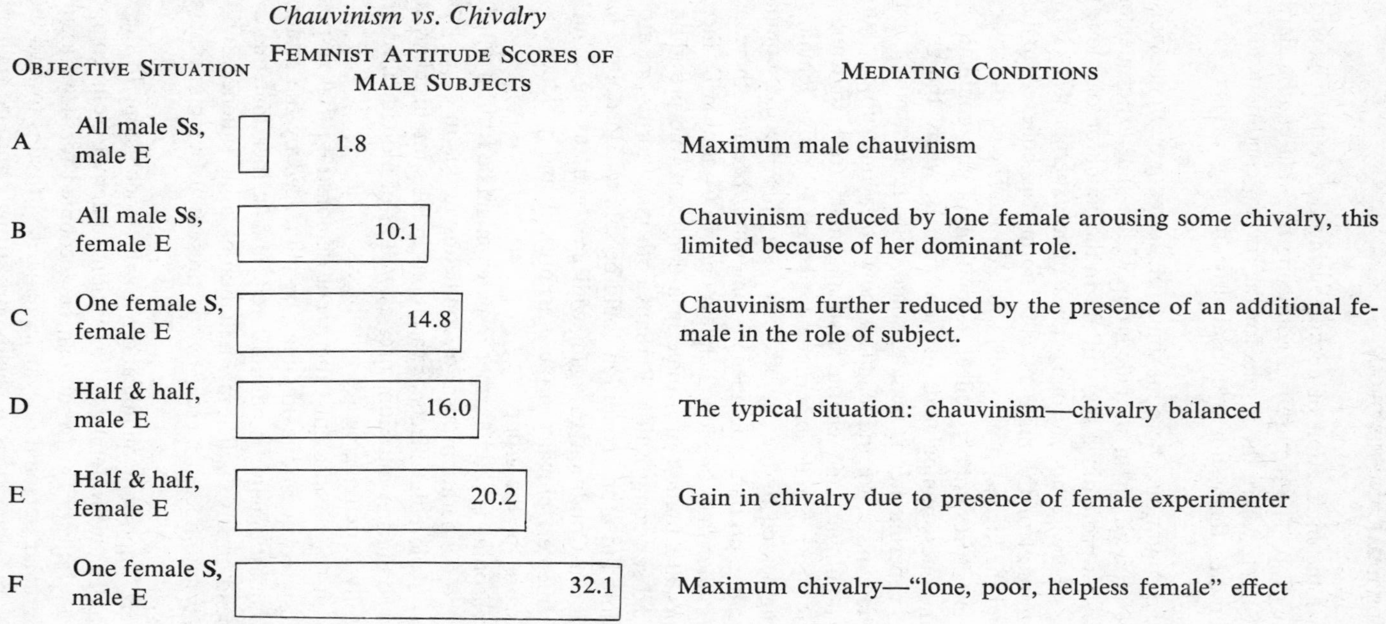

Chauvinism vs. Chivalry

Objective Situation	Feminist Attitude Scores of Male Subjects	Mediating Conditions
A All male Ss, male E	1.8	Maximum male chauvinism
B All male Ss, female E	10.1	Chauvinism reduced by lone female arousing some chivalry, this limited because of her dominant role.
C One female S, female E	14.8	Chauvinism further reduced by the presence of an additional female in the role of subject.
D Half & half, male E	16.0	The typical situation: chauvinism—chivalry balanced
E Half & half, female E	20.2	Gain in chivalry due to presence of female experimenter
F One female S, male E	32.1	Maximum chivalry—"lone, poor, helpless female" effect

Fig. 1. Chauvinism versus chivalry.

tions, and that the interaction of cues arousing the conflicting norms accounts for the drop. The picture is a confusing one, but can be clarified by the aid of Figure 1, where the results for the several conditions are arrayed in a way ordered by the assumed arousal of conflicting norms of chauvinism versus chivalry.

Under the condition where maximum male sex-group chauvinism was believed to be aroused, in an all male group with a male experimenter (A), we find the lowest profeminist score of all. In the condition of a lone female subject in an otherwise male group with a male experimenter (F), where the greatest arousal of the male chivalry norm was believed to have occurred, we find the highest profeminist score of all. The conditions between these polar ones presumably reflect resolution of the conflicting norms aroused by the cues manipulated. In Condition B, where the group is all male but the experimenter is female, some chivalry is aroused, but so is some male chauvinism, for the female is now not a lone subject, but a lone female in a dominant, and characteristically male role. In Condition C, where there is also a female experimenter as well as a lone female subject, chivalry is augmented by the subject, increasing the effect as compared to Condition B, but probably dampened somewhat, because there are now two females, rather than one lone helpless one. In Condition D, there is the normal and usual situation of a male in a dominant role presiding over a group of mixed sex composition. Perhaps both male norms are aroused in such a situation, but if any condition could be said to constitute a base-line one, this is it. In Condition E, again with an equal sex mix, but with a female experimenter, chivalry arousal is present and produces a higher profeminist score for the group.

If this reasoning is valid, further research might be fruitful which would (a) involve the deliberate arousal of conflicting norms in other group settings, and (b) explore the effects of variations in the stimulus characteristics of those who administer questionnaires as well as of individual respondents in systematically varied aggregates of subjects.

The results of the present experiment demonstrate that responses on group-administered questionnaires may be influenced by the group setting in which the questionnaire is administered, and further that this influence does not depend on any explicit manipulation of group salience. Individuals' responses may be affected merely by the presence of certain others in the group setting.

There are important qualifications to this conclusion. In the case of females' attitudes toward feminist propositions, different group compositions had little if any effect. This result can be accounted for if we assume that due to their greater personal relevance, females' attitudes toward their own rights, duties, and obligations are held more strongly and are anchored more deeply than those of males toward these issues.

History itself attests to the emotionality and intensity of women in fighting for their rights, their militancy and determination in the face of the uncomprehending and often amused males, secure in their strength and established dominance (who gave in, incidentally, mostly out of feelings of chivalry). We must suppose socialization into the female culture of our society to be the principal agent for so deeply anchoring women's attitudes on these matters which are so vital to them. Kelley (1955) has shown that strongly anchored attitudes are highly resistant to change or influence, and Kirkpatrick (1936b), using his own feminist scale as the measuring instrument in an experiment, wherein the attempt was made to modify attitudes by male-female discussion, found his female subjects showed considerably more resistance to such social influence than did males.

If this interpretation is a valid one, it should follow that males, although their situations are not strictly comparable in various ways, would be less labile in situations of varying group composition than females if the attitudes being elicited had to do with masculine rights, privileges, and obligations. This hypothesis will be examined in future research.

Another qualification has to do with the availability or existence of group norms relevant to the attitudinal responses being elicited in group settings. The present findings seem to indicate that our groups lacked norms of attitudes relevant to child-rearing practices; hence, the arousal of group membership salience had little if any effect. Stated in more general terms, in situations in which the membership or reference group either does not have norms relevant to the issue or attitude-object under concern, or where the individual does not perceive such relevance, differing group compositions will have no effect, even when group membership salience is aroused. It would, of course, be desirable if assumptions concerning the existence of norms and the perceptions or conceptions of them by group members could be replaced by empirical data. This might be accomplished by using questionnaires designed to elicit estimates of the responses of members of designated groups, for example, those of one's own sex, race, or class as well as those of a different sex, race, or class. Research is currently being carried out along these lines.

A possible extension of our findings may be to those situations where there is no explicit arousal of group salience and where there is no distinct dress, badge, or appearance to mark members from nonmembers. If attitudes are elicited in a group setting in some relatively restricted area, then location alone may be sufficient to inform individuals that all those present belong to the same group. Possible examples are union halls, club houses, and classrooms of professional schools.

With the above qualifications in mind, we conclude that individuals' responses on attitude questionnaires may be influenced by factors merely present in the group setting without any explicit arousal of the salience of group membership. The factor of group composition may therefore heighten the influence of group norms on attitudinal responses and possibly other forms of behavior in a wide variety of social situations.

From a methodological standpoint, finally, attitude studies based on data collected from established or readily identifiable group members, or in settings institutionally or otherwise normally restricted to persons of given membership character, may not reflect the attitudes of such individuals which might have been revealed had they responded in a different context.

References

Bittner, A. C., & Shinedling, M. M. A methodological investigation of Piaget's concept of conservation of substance. *Genetic Psychology Monographs*, 1968, *77*, 135–165.

Blankenship, A. The effect of interviewer bias upon the response in a public opinion poll. *Journal of Consulting Psychology*, 1940, *4*, 134–136.

Centers, R. Authoritarianism and mysogymy. *Journal of Social Psychology*, 1961, *61*, 81–85.

Charters, W. W., Jr., & Newcomb, T. M. Some attitudinal effects of experimentally increased salience of a membership group. In G. E. Swanson, T. M. Newcomb, & E. L. Hartley (Eds.), *Readings in social psychology*. (rev. ed.) New York: Holt, Rinehart and Winston, 1952.

Festinger, L. The role of group belongingness in a voting situation. *Human Relations*, 1947, *1*, 154–180.

Festinger, L. Laboratory experiments: The role of group belongingness. In J. G. Miller (Ed.), *Experiments in social process*. New York: McGraw-Hill, 1950.

Katz, D. Do interviewers bias poll results? *Public Opinion Quarterly*, 1942, *6*, 248–268.

Kelley, H. H. Salience of membership and resistance to change of group-anchored attitudes. *Human Relations*, 1955, *8*, 275–289.

Kirkpatrick, C. The construction of a belief-pattern scale for measuring attitudes toward feminism. *Journal of Social Psychology*, 1936, *7*, 421–437. (a)

Kirkpatrick, C. An experimental study of the modification of social attitudes. *American Journal of Sociology*, 1936, *41*, 649–656. (b)

Kirkpatrick, C. A comparison of generations in regard to attitudes toward feminism. *Journal of Genetic Psychology*, 1936, *49*, 343–359. (c)

Lambert, W. E., Libman, E., & Poser, E. G. The effect of increased salience of a membership group on pain tolerance. *Journal of Personality*, 1960, *28*, 350–357.

Lewin, K. Psycho-sociological problems of a minority group. *Character and Personality*, 1935, *3*, 175–187.

Linquist, F. F. *Design and analysis of experiments in psychology and education.* Boston: Houghton Mifflin, 1953.

Pedersen, D. M., Shinedling, M. M., & Johnson, D. L. Effects of sex of examiner and subject on children's quantitative test performance. *Journal of Personality and Social Psychology*, 1968, *10*, 251–254.

Rosenthal, R. On the social psychology of the psychological experiment: The experimenter's hypothesis as unintended determinant of the experimental results. *American Scientist,* 1963, *51,* 268–283.

Rosenthal, R. *Experimenter effects in behavioral research.* New York: Appleton-Century-Crofts, 1966.

Schaeffer, E. S., & Bell, R. Q. Parental Attitude Research Instrument (PARI): Normative data. Unpublished manuscript, Library, National Institute of Mental Health, Bethesda, Maryland, 1955.

INTRODUCTION

Hollander's notion of competence is that it may be exhibited by "further(ing) the attainment of group goals," being an "expediter," "advocate," or "task specialist." The context, then, is one of groups which have a task or goal, competence being related to that task or goal. "Conformity," in Hollander's view, involves "perceived adherence to the normative behaviors and attitudes of (the) group." Hollander does not define normative for his reader. The term norm usually refers to the accepted standards of action and values for a group. By definition, the majority of group persons pay at least lip service to the norm, even though they may not behave in accordance with it. "Influence" is another undefined term here; however, the general usage of the word is to persuade or change.

Hollander's theory is that the status of a person emerges through interaction in a group. As the person gains the approval of others by conformity and competence, he also gains the freedom to act unlike the other group members. Hollander predicts, then, that the optimal way for a group member to attain influence is early conformity to group standards (in conjunction with competence) and later nonconformity to group standards. (This theory forms an interesting contrast to the usual notions that conformity "buys" acceptance in a group, and that the deviate is rejected.)

METHOD

There are a number of ways that Hollander could have tested his prediction. He could have made observations on real, existent groups; he could have conducted interviews; he could have formed groups in the laboratory and observed the emergence of status and influence, or, finally, he could have formed groups in the laboratory and instructed a confederate to behave in specified conforming and nonconforming ways. This last method was the one that he chose. In this way, he was able to hold all conditions constant with the exception of one variable (conformity of the confederate). He was then able to attribute changes in behavior to that one cause.

One point of importance in assessing a procedure is to relate it to the theory that it attempts to test. For instance, in this experiment, consider whether Hollander manipulated or operationalized competence and conformity in a way that fulfilled the definitional requirements. Certainly, the stooge did further the group in its effort to solve a "problem," and did act in accordance with a group-set rule. However, there may be doubts as to whether or not such temporary rules constitute norms. Also, since conformity is defined as *perceived* adherence, it is unfortunate that this perception on the part of the other group members was assumed, rather than proven (say, by means of a questionnaire).

RESULTS AND DISCUSSION

Hollander's prediction concerning past and present nonconformity can be stated as an interaction between past and present nonconformity; the sequence of past conformity-present nonconformity was expected to differ from the other possible sequences in terms of its ability to produce conformity.

While Hollander did obtain an interaction of past and present non-conformity, you can see by looking at the table of means that the expected pattern was obtained in Zone II (trials 6–10) only. In Zone III, the means are all very close to another; it is unfortunate that Hollander did not discuss this further.

Hollander concludes that he has supported his theory. What do you think? Can you think of other ways to test his prediction or other predictions from his theory? Also, does Hollander's theory "fit" your observation of groups with which you are familiar, starting perhaps with your classroom group?

6.3 Competence and Conformity in the Acceptance of Influence[1]

Edwin P. Hollander

When one member influences others in his group it is often because he is competent in a focal group activity. A member may show such competence by individual actions that further the attainment of group goals (cf. Carter, 1954); more specific situational demands may variously favor the ascent of the expediter, advocate, or what Bales and Slater (1955) have termed the task specialist. An additional condition for the acceptance of influence involves the member's perceived adherence to the normative behaviors and attitudes of his group. His record of conformity to these expectancies serves to sustain eligibility of the sort Brown (1936) calls "membership character."

A person who exhibits both competence and conformity should eventually reach a threshold at which it becomes appropriate in the eyes of others for him to assert influence; and insofar as these assertions are accepted he emerges as a leader. But it is still necessary to account for the "nonconformity" that leaders display as they innovate and alter group norms. Certain shifts must therefore occur in the expectancies applicable to an individual as he proceeds from gaining status to maintaining it.

This process has been considered recently in a theoretical model of status emergence (Hollander, 1958). It features the prospect that behavior perceived to be nonconformity for one member may not be so perceived for another. Such differentiations are seen to be made as a function of status, conceived as an accumulation of positively disposed impressions termed "idiosyncrasy credits." A person gains credits, i.e., rises in status, by showing competence and by conforming to the expectancies applicable to him at the time. Eventually his credits allow him to nonconform with greater

Reprinted from the Journal of Abnormal and Social Psychology, 1960, *61*, 365–369. Copyright 1960 by the American Psychological Association and reproduced with permission.

[1] This paper is based upon a study completed under ONR Contract 1849(00), while the author was at the Carnegie Institute of Technology. The views expressed here are those of the author and do not necessarily reflect those of the Department of the Navy. The considerable assistance of H. Edwin Titus in this study is gratefully acknowledged.

Parts of the paper were reported at the symposium on "Recent Conceptions in Influence and Authority Process," held under the auspices of Division 8 at the 1959 APA Convention.

impunity.[2] Moreover, he is then subject to a new set of expectancies which direct the assertion of influence. Thus, whether for lack of motivation or misperception, his failure to take innovative action may cause him to lose status.[3]

It is readily predictable that in task oriented groups a member giving evidence of competence on the group task should with time gain in influence. If he simply nonconforms to the procedures agreed upon, the opposite effect should be observed. But the sequential relationship of nonconformity to competence is especially critical.

From the model, it should follow that, with a relatively constant level of manifest competence, the influence of a person who nonconforms *early* in the course of group interaction should be more drastically curtailed than in the case of a person who nonconforms *later*. Indeed, a reversal of effect would be predicted in the latter instance. Once a member has accumulated credits, his nonconformity to general procedure should serve as a confirming or signalizing feature of his status, thereby enhancing his influence. Accordingly, it may be hypothesized that given equivalent degrees of task competence, a member should achieve greater acceptance of his influence when he has conformed in the past and is now nonconforming than he should when nonconformity precedes conformity.

METHOD

Design

Twelve groups, each composed of four male subjects, were engaged in a task involving a sequence of 15 trials. A group choice was required for each trial from among the row alternatives in a 7×7 payoff matrix (see Figure 1). In every group, a fifth member was a confederate whose prearranged response was contrived to be correct on all but four trials, i.e., 2, 3, 6, and 12, thus reflecting considerable competence on the task. All interactions among participants took place through a system of microphones and headsets from partitioned booths. Subjects were assigned numbers from 1 to 5 for communicating with one another. The central manipulation was the confederate's nonconformity to procedures agreed upon by each group in a pretrial discussion. In terms of a division of the 15 trials into three zones—early, middle, and late—of 5 trials each, six treatments were applied: nonconformity throughout, nonconformity for the first two zones, for the first zone alone, for the last two zones, for the last zone alone, and a control with no nonconformity. In one set of treatments the confederate

[2] This is a newer formulation of an observation long since made regarding the latitude provided leaders (e.g., Homans, 1950, p. 416). It is further elaborated in Hollander (1959).

[3] This proposition is consistent with various findings suggestive of the greater social perceptiveness of leaders (e.g., Chowdhry & Newcomb, 1952).

	Green	Red	Blue	Yellow	Brown	Orange	Black
Able	−1	−12	+5	−1	−2	+15	−4
Baker	+10	−1	−2	−7	+4	−3	−1
Charlie	−5	+5	−3	+3	−11	−1	+12
Dog	+5	−7	+10	−2	−5	+1	−2
Easy	−4	−1	−1	+1	+13	−10	+2
Fox	−6	+15	−5	−1	−3	−1	+1
George	−1	−1	−2	+10	+4	−2	−8

FIG. 1. Matrix used in group task.

was designated number 5, and in the other number 4, to test possible position effects. Acceptance of the confederate's influence was measured by the number of trials by zone in which his recommended response was accepted as the group's. This was supplemented by post-interaction assessments.

Subjects

The 48 subjects were all juniors in the College of Engineering and Science at the Carnegie Institute of Technology. All had volunteered from introductory psychology sections after being told only that they would be taking part in a study of problem solving in groups. Care was taken in composing the 12 groups so as to avoid either placing acquaintances together or having membership known in advance. Thus, no two subjects from the same class section were used in the same group, and subjects reported at staggered times to different rooms. By the time a subject reached the laboratory room where the experiment was actually conducted, he had been kept apart from the others and was not aware of their identity. The subjects never saw one another during the entire procedure, nor were their names ever used among them.

Instructions and Set

Once seated and assigned a number, every subject was given a sheet of instructions and the matrix used for the task. These instructions fell into two parts, both of which were reviewed aloud with each subject individually, and then with the entire group over the communication network. The first part cautioned the subjects to always identify themselves by number (e.g., "This is Station 3 . . .") before speaking and not to use names or other self-identifying references. The second part acquainted them with the procedures to be used, emphasized the aspect of competition against a "system," and established the basis for evident procedural norms. It read as follows:

> 1. You will be working with others on a problem involving a matrix of plus and minus values. Everyone has the same matrix before him. The goal is to amass as many plus units as possible, and to avoid minus units. Units are are worth 1 cent each to the group; the group begins with a credit of 200 units. You cannot lose you own money, therefore. There will be fifteen trials in all.

2. In any one trial, the task involved is for the group to agree on just *one* row—identified by Able, Baker, Charlie, etc.—which seems to have strategic value. Once the group has determined a row, the experimenter will announce the column color which comes up on that trial. The intersecting cells indicate the payoff. Following this announcement, there will be thirty seconds of silence during which group members can think individually about the best strategy for the next trial, in terms of their notion about the system; note please that there are several approximations to the system, although the equation underlying it is quite complex. But work at it.

3. At the beginning of each trial the group members must report, one at a time, in some order, as to what they think would be the best row choice on the upcoming trial. Members may "pass" until the third time around, but must announce a choice then. Following this, groups will have three minutes on each trial to discuss choices and reach some agreement; this can be a simple majority, or unanimous decision; it is up to the group to decide. If a decision is not reached in three minutes, the group loses 5 units.

4. Before beginning the trials, the group will have five minutes to discuss these points: (*a*) The order of reporting; (*b*) How to determine the group choice for a given trial; (*c*) How to divide up the money at the end. These decisions are always subject to change, if the group has time and can agree. After the 15th trial, group members may have as much as five minutes to settle any outstanding decisions. Then headsets are to be removed, but group members remain seated for further instructions, and the individual payment of funds.

Instruments and Procedure

The matrix was specially constructed for this study to present an ambiguous but plausible task in which alternatives were only marginally discrete from one another.[4] The number of columns and rows was selected to enlarge the range of possibilities beyond the number of group members, while still retaining comprehensibility. The fact that the rows are unequal in algebraic sum appears to be less important as a feature in choice than the number and magnitude of positive and negative values in each; there is moreover the complicating feature of processing the outcome of the last trials in evaluating the choice for the next. All considered, the matrix was admirably suited to the requirements for ambiguity, challenge, conflict, immediate reinforcement, and ready manipulation by the experimenter.

The confederate, operating either as 4 or 5 in the groups, suggested a choice that differed trial by trial from those offered by other members; this was prearranged but subject to modification as required. Since subjects rather typically perceived alternatives differently, his behavior was not unusual, especially during the early trials. For the 11 trials in which the confederate's row choice was "correct," the color that "came up" was contrived to yield a high plus value without at the same time providing a similar value for intersection with another person's row choice. Had his recommendation been followed by the group on these trials, high payoffs would have accrued.

The device of a 5-minute pretrial discussion had special utility for es-

---

[4] The matrix is an adaptation, at least in spirit, of a smaller one used with success by Moore and Berkowitz (1956).

tablishing common group expectancies, in the form of procedures, from which the confederate could deviate when called for in the design. Predictable decisions on these matters were reached unfailingly. But their importance lay in having a *public affirmation* of member intent. Thus, on order of reporting, it was quickly agreed to follow the order of the numbers assigned members. Each group, despite minor variants suggested, decided on simple majority rule. Regarding division of funds, equal sharing prevailed, sometimes with the proviso that the issue be taken up again at the end.

In the zones calling for nonconformity, the confederate violated these procedures by speaking out of prescribed turn, by questioning the utility of majority rule, and by unsupported—but not harsh—challenges to the recommendations made by others. He manifested such behaviors on an approximate frequency of at least one of these per trial with a mean of two per trial considered optimum. Thus, he would break in with his choice immediately after an earlier respondent had spoken and before the next in sequence could do so; when there were periods of silence during a trial he would observe aloud that maybe majority rule did not work so well; and he would show a lack of enthusiasm for the choice offered by various others on the matter of basis. Lest he lose credibility and becomes a caricature, in all instances he chose his moments with care and retained an evident spontaneity of expression.[5]

RESULTS AND DISCUSSION

The task gave quite satisfactory signs of engrossing the subjects. There was much talk about the "system" and a good deal of delving into its basis, possibly made the more so by the subjects' academic background; the returned matrices were littered with diagrams, notations, and calculations. Though quite meaningless in fact, the confederate's tentative accounts of his "reasoning" were evidently treated with seriousness, perhaps as much because of the contrived time constraint, which prevented probing, as of his jargon regarding "rotations" and "block shifts." In any case, the confederate at no time claimed to have the system completely in hand. He delayed his response from the sixth trial onward to suggest calculation of an optimum choice in the face of conflicting alternatives; and the four trials on which he was "wrong" were spaced to signify progressive improvement, but not total perfection.

Most pertinent, however, is the fact that there were no manifestations of suspicion concerning the confederate's authenticity. The others seemed to believe that he was one of them and that he was "cracking" the system; the post-interaction data were in full agreement.

Since all of the interactions were available on tape, it was possible to derive a number of indices of acceptance of influence. The most broadly

[5] The same person, H. E. Titus, was the confederate throughout.

revealing of these appeared to be the frequency of trials on which the confederate's recommended solution was followed.

In Table 1 this index is employed to discern the effects of three major variables. The analysis is arranged by zones (Z) of trials, and in terms of the confederate's nonconformity (NC) in the *current* zone and immediate *past* zone.[6] The means given in each cell indicate the number of trials, out of five per zone, on which the confederate's choice was also the group's. In a chi square test, the effect of position upon this measure was found to be nonsignificant, and is therefore omitted as a distinction in the analysis of variance.

The significant F secured from Zones is in accord with prediction. It reveals the ongoing effect of task competence in increasing the acceptance of the confederate's choice, to be seen in the rising means across zones. While current nonconformity does not yield a significant effect, past nonconformity does. Viewing the table horizontally, one finds that the means for "without" *past* NC exceed the means for "with" *past* NC in all instances but one. Regarding the significant interaction of *current* and *past* NC, the combination "without-without" has a sequence (2.00, 3.75, 4.75) of persistently higher value than has "with-with" (1.67, 3.25, 4.00); this, too, is in line with prediction. Finally, the maximum value of 5.00 in Zone II for the combination "without" *past* NC but "with" *current* NC confirms the key prediction from the model, at least within the context of the relative magnitudes there; the same value is also seen in Zone III for the identical combination; still another reading of 5.00 holds there, however, for the inverse combination, but in a tight range of values quite beyond separation of effects for interpretation.

Considerable consistency was found too in the post-interaction data. On the item "overall contribution to the group activity," 44 of the 48 subjects ranked the confederate first; on the item "influence over the group's decisions," 45 of the 48 ranked him first. Two things bear emphasis in this regard: subjects had to individually write in the numbers of group members next to rank, hence demanding recall; and their polarity of response cut across all six treatments, despite significant differences among these in the actual *acceptance of influence*. That the confederate therefore made an impact is clear; but that it had selective consequences depending upon the timing of his nonconformity is equally clear.

In detail, then, the findings are in keeping with the predictions made from the model. The operational variable for measuring acceptance of in-

---

[6] For Zone I, the "past zone" refers to the discussion period. If he was to nonconform there, the confederate would question majority rule and suggest that the division of funds be left until the end rather than agree then on equal shares.

TABLE 1 *Mean Number of Trials on Which a Group Accepts Confederate's Recommended Solution*

CONFEDERATE'S PREVIOUS CONFORMITY	ZONE I (TRIALS 1–5)		ZONE II (TRIALS 6–10)		ZONE III (TRIALS 11–15)	
	Nonconforming[a]	Conforming	Nonconforming	Conforming	Nonconforming	Conforming
With Procedural nonconformity in immediate *past* zone	1.67 6[b]	—	3.25 4	3.00 2	4.00 4	5.00 2
Without Procedural nonconformity in immediate *past* zone	—	2.00 6	5.00 2	3.75 4	5.00 2	4.75 4

ANALYSIS OF VARIANCE

SOURCE	SS	df	MS	F
Current Nonconformity	.20	1	.200	—
Zones	47.05	2	23.525	35.01**
Past Nonconformity	3.36	1	3.360	5.00*
Int: Current NC × Z	1.22	2	.610	—
Int: Current NC × Past NC	13.52	1	13.520	20.12**
Int: Z × Past NC	.72	2	.360	—
Int: Current NC × Z × Past NC	4.11	2	2.055	3.06
Residual	16.12	24	.672	
Total	86.30	35		

[a] Confederate showed procedural nonconformity on the trials in this zone.
[b] Indicates number of groups upon which cell is based.
* $p < .05$.
** $p < .001$.

fluence was confined to the task itself, but nontask elements are touched as well. In that respect, the findings corroborate the subtle development of differential impressions as a function of even limited interpersonal behavior.

Some unquantified but clearly suggestive data are worth mentioning in this regard. Where, for example, the confederate began nonconforming *after* the first zone, his behavior was accepted with minimal challenge; by the third zone, his suggestion that majority rule was faulty yielded a rubber stamping of his choice. Again, if he had already accrued credit, his pattern of interrupting people out of turn not only went unhindered but was taken up by some others. Quite different effects were elicited if the confederate exhibited nonconformity from *the outset,* notably such comments of censure as "That's not the way we agreed to do it, five."

The findings are especially indicative of the stochastic element of social interaction and its consequence for changing perception. Especially interesting is the fact that these effects are produced even in a relatively brief span of time.

SUMMARY

A study was conducted to test the relationship between competence on a group task and conformity or nonconformity to procedural norms in determining a person's ability to influence other group members. Data were gathered from 12 groups engaged in a problem solving task under controlled conditions. Each was made up of five members one of whom was a confederate who evidenced a high degree of competence during the 15 trials. His nonconformity to the procedural norms agreed upon by the group was introduced at various times, early, middle, or late, in the sequence of trials. Influence was measured by the number of trials (per segment of the entire sequence) in which the confederate's recommended solution was accepted as the group's choice. As a broad effect, it was found that a significant increase in his influence occurred as the trials progressed, presumably as a function of the successive evidences of competence. Past conformity by the confederate was also found to be positively and significantly related to the acceptance of his influence; finally, there was a statistically significant interaction between past and current nonconformity reflected in high influence in the groups in which the confederate had conformed earlier in the sequence of trials but was presently nonconforming. These results were all thoroughly consistent with predictions made from the "idiosyncrasy credit" model of conformity and status.

References

Bales, R. F., & Slater, P. E. Role differentiation in small decision-making groups. In T. Parsons, R. F. Bales, et al. (Eds.), *Family, socialization, and interaction process.* Glencoe, Ill.: Free Press, 1955.

Brown, J. F. *Psychology and the social order.* New York: McGraw-Hill, 1936.

Carter, L. F. Recording and evaluating the performance of individuals as members of small groups. *Personnel Psychology,* 1954, *7,* 477–484.

Chowdhry, Kamla, & Newcomb, T. M. The relative abilities of leaders and nonleaders to estimate opinions of their own groups. *Journal of Abnormal Social Psychology,* 1952, *47,* 51–57.

Hollander, E. P. Conformity, status, and idiosyncrasy credit. *Psychological Review,* 1958, *65,* 117–127.

Hollander, E. P. Some points of reinterpretation regarding social conformity. *Social Review,* 1959, *7,* 159–168.

Homans, G. C. *The human group.* New York: Harcourt Brace Jovanovich, 1950.

Moore, O. K., & Berkowitz, M. I. Problem solving and social interaction. *ONR tech. Rep.,* 1956, No. 1. (Contract Nonr-609(16), Yale University Department of Sociology)

Foreword to Reading 6.4

INTRODUCTION

The early social psychologists, LeBon and Tarde, were fascinated with the question of mob behavior. They felt that there must be something like a "group mind" impelling, say, a lynch mob. Otherwise, they could not imagine how a large group could act so closely together in such an extreme fashion. Festinger, Pepitone, and Newcomb (1952) suggested that, in any group, not only a crowd, there may be freedom from inhibition. They hypothesized that this happens to the extent that the person in the group is "deindividuated," or feels anonymous. This suggestion may be compared to that of Latané and Darley (1968), in this volume, who proposed that persons in a group feel less "responsibility" than persons who are by themselves. In addition to the Festinger, Pepitone, and Newcomb study, two other studies have reported on the relationship of deindividuation to unrestrained behavior (Zimbardo, 1969; Singer, Brush, and Lublin, 1965). In the Zimbardo study, girls who wore white lab coats and were not readily identifiable gave longer electric shocks than girls who were greeted by name and wore name tags. In the Singer, Brush, and Lublin study, one-half of the subjects were asked to wear a suit or dress when appearing for the experiment. The other half were asked to wear old clothes, and were given an oversized white lab coat to put on when they arrived to participate. When asked to discuss some pornographic literature, the "high-identifiable" group used fewer obscene words than the "low-identifiable" group. In addition, the high-identifiable group indicated less enjoyment of the discussion. Presumably, then, the less identifiable (or more deindividuated) a group member feels, the less constrained he is by the usual social niceties.

The present study was an attempt both to replicate the earlier Festinger, Pepitone, and Newcomb study, and to stimulate further research on this topic.

METHOD

The reader will note that in this research, as compared to most other studies in this text, the independent variable (deindividuation) was not manipulated by the experimenter. The deindividuation that occurred in each group was measured and then related to the reduction in restraint (or freedom from inhibition) that occurred. This was not an experiment, then, but rather a "correlational" study. The disadvantage of this type of study is that one is left with the possibility that groups varying in deindividuation varied in other unmeasured ways as well.

In each group, subjects were asked to discuss a statement that persons unwilling to express hostility toward their parents are actually the most hostile toward their parents. Subjects were thus encouraged to express negative feelings toward their own parents. Without elaborating all of the complications, the subsequent deindividuation in each group was indicated by subjects' errors in identifying who had made statements that had appeared in the group discussion; reduction in restraint was operationalized as relative number of negative statements made about parents.

RESULTS AND DISCUSSION

As predicted, deindividuation was positively related to reduction in restraint. This relationship appeared both when "general memory errors" (thinking a statement had been made when it had not, or vice versa) were subtracted from "identification" errors, and when general memory errors were controlled through "partial correlation." A partial correlation refers to the correlation of factor A with factor B, with factor C held constant. As you know, any correlation indicates the relationship of two measures (say A and B). However, suppose that factor B is correlated with factor C. Part of the correlation of A and B, then, might really be AC. One way to correct for this is to hold C constant, not allow it to vary (as it does when B varies, since they are correlated). This is done using statistical formuli.

Contrary to prediction, the relationship of deindividuation to restraint reduction at first appeared to hold only for all-male groups. However, when anxiety level was held constant, a partial correlation of the two factors under study was statistically significant for all-female and mixed groups as well.

Finally, unlike the Festinger, Pepitone, and Newcomb study, this study did not find a strong positive relationship between restraint reduction and attraction to the group. Cannavale, Scarr, and Pepitone suggest that strong confirmation of the prediction was not to be expected, since the expression of hostility arouses guilt and anxiety, and this should lessen the attraction to the group.

The reader who is intrigued by the notion of deindividuation might want to look at the discussion of Zimbardo (1969). Zimbardo suggests reasons for being attracted to a condition of deindividuation with its accompanying freedom, and cites such real life examples as the Mardi Gras, Ku Klux Klan, and Hallowe'en. He also extends the anonymity notion to include "dehumanization," the state of being of people who are treated as objects or numbers, rather than as human beings. People who deal with "dehumanized" others find it disturbingly easy to act in an antisocial manner toward them (as witness inhuman acts in concentration camps). Zimbardo (1972) demonstrated this in a simulated prison in a college laboratory using preselected, mentally healthy boys as both prisoners and guards. The experiment had such strong effects on both prisoners and guards, some of the former being totally demoralized and some of the latter being totally brutal, that Zimbardo was compelled to end the study soon after it began.

References

Festinger, L., Pepitone, A., & Newcomb, T. Some consequences of deindividuation in a group. *Journal of Abnormal and Social Psychology*, 1952, *47*, Supplement, 282–289.

Latané, B., & Darley, J. M. Group inhibition of bystander intervention in emergencies. *Journal of Personality and Social Psychology*, 1968, *10*, 215–221.

Singer, R. P., Brush, C., & Lublin, S. D. Some aspects of deindividuation: identifiability and conformity. *Journal of Experimental Social Psychology*, 1965, *1*, 356–378.

Zimbardo, P. G. The human choice: individuation, reason and order versus deindividuation, impulse and chaos. Nebraska Symposium on Motivation, 1969, *18*, 237–307.

Zimbardo, P. G. Pathology of imprisonment. *Society*, 1972, *9*, 4–8.

6.4 Deindividuation in the Small Group: Further Evidence

F. J. Cannavale
H. A. Scarr
A. Pepitone

The present study was designed to replicate and extend the 1952 Festinger, Pepitone, and Newcomb study of deindividuation in small discussion groups, which showed that groups whose members were relatively unable to identify who had made certain statements in the discussion (deindividuation) were those in which a relatively large amount of hostile feelings and sentiments were expressed (reduction in restraint), and that those groups which overcame most restraint were found to be most attractive to the members. A third finding of relevance to the hoary concept of the group mind was that the correlation between deindividuation and the reduction in restraint held only when the group was used as the unit of analysis. The present experiment confirmed the positive correlation between deindividuation and restraint reduction, which is significant only when the group is used as the unit of analysis. The failure of reduction in restraint to be correlated with group attraction and the role of preexisting discussion apprehension in "not-all-male groups" are discussed, along with a general theoretical analysis of the deindividuation phenomenon.

Crowd behavior has long been of interest to sociology and social psychology, and the mass violence that is commonplace today stimulates an even greater interest. LeBon's (1896) analysis can probably still be regarded as the most important attempt to analyze the behavior of crowds and other collectives. LeBon attributed the violent excesses of the street throng in the French Revolution to the group mind. It is the emergence of the group mind that accounts for the fact that the different individuals who comprise a collective lose their distinct personalities and become a homogeneous and highly emotional mass. There are two related processes involved in the group mind: (*a*) the intellectual and rational parts of the self, which normally would restrain persons from extreme behavior, disappear and thus allow primordial instincts and emotions to be given full expression. In other words, the group mind leads to a primitivation or regression; and (*b*) the uncontrolled emotion spreads across the crowd, stimulating and provoking it into mindless savagery. Unfortunately, LeBon's analysis of the dynamics that underlie the group mind does not penetrate much beyond description. The basic process is that through "suggestion," the individual enters a trance-like state, in which he loses his sense of responsibility and adopts the unitary consciousness of the crowd. But as many have pointed out, including Freud (1910), suggestion is a statement of the phenomenon rather than the explanation of it. The idea that being submerged mentally in the crowd disinhibits people through weakening their sense of responsibility is a plausible one, but it begs the question of what is meant by submergence. One concrete possibility implied by LeBon is that members of a collective who feel that they are unseen and cannot be personally identified are free to express primitive feelings and impulses. This line of thinking led Festinger, Pepitone, and Newcomb (1952) to attempt a relatively precise conceptualization of such a state of "deindividuation," that being "a state of affairs" in which "individuals are not seen or paid attention to as individuals . . . and do not feel that they stand out as individuals [p. 382]." These authors hypothesized that when a state of deindividuation occurs in a group (a) normally inhibited behavior is expressed, and (b) people are attracted to the group which enabled them to overcome such restraints. The experiment presented evidence consistent with both hypotheses. In the ensuing years there have been only a few scattered experimental contributions to the area.[1] Since presumably deindividuation is a universal phenomenon with manifestly important consequences, it would seem desirable to obtain further confirmation of the Festinger et al. hypotheses and to elaborate a theory which will stimulate additional research. That was the purpose of the present study.

The general plan of the experiment was exactly the same as the original study: a small ad hoc group was presented with the results of a survey, and the subjects were asked to express their own attitudes and feelings about the topic of the survey. The measure of lowered restraint was the frequency of negative sentiments expressed in the discussion. The measure of deindividuation was the inability of the subjects to identify who had made statements in the discussion. There are three variables relevant to the hypotheses: (a) the ability to identify who said what, (b) the degree to which restraints are overcome, and (c) the postdiscussion attraction to the group.

---

[1] Zimbardo (1969) has shown that subjects who were masked administered shocks of greater duration to another subject (in the context of making "empathic judgments" of her) than subjects who are not hidden from each other. In the same vein Singer, Brush, and Lublin (1965) found that subjects who donned nondistinguishable lab coats upon request by the experimenter vocalized more obscene expressions in analyzing pornographic passages than those who were "dressed up" for the occasion.

METHOD

Procedure

Subjects were undergraduate and graduate students enrolled in sociology courses at the University of Pennsylvania and Villanova University. The sample consisted of nine groups of males, two groups of females, and three groups of males and females. The size of the groups ranged between four and seven.

As the subjects arrived, they were seated around a conference table and identified by a name and number tag. The results of a brief questionnaire disclosed that the subjects did not know each other beyond the level of recognition. The findings of an alleged survey were then read to the group by the experimenter. (See Festinger et al., 1952, for the full statement.)

A highly representative sample of 2,364 students (1,133 female and 1,231 male) on 14 campuses, from all socioeconomic classes and several nationality backgrounds, was subjected to an intensive 3-week psychiatric analysis, consisting of repeated depth interviews and a battery of sensitive diagnostic tests. The results showed unequivocally that 87% of the sample possessed a strong, deep-seated hatred of one or both parents, ranging from generalized feelings of hostility to consistent fantasies of violence and murder. A finding of further significance was that those individuals who at first vehemently denied having such hostile impulses or who were unwilling to discuss their personal feelings in the matter were subsequently diagnosed as possessing the most violent forms of hostility. In other words, conscious denial, silence, or embarrassment were found to be almost sure signs of the strongest kind of hatred. Of the 13% in whom no trace of hostility was found, the great majority thought they probably hated their parents and were willing to discuss every aspect of their feelings with the investigator.

Subjects were told that they had 40 minutes in which to discuss the topic. The discussion was to focus upon the subjects' own relations with their parents. During the 40-minute period, the experimenter continuously recorded the discussion in 4-minute intervals. He recorded all sentiments regarding parent-child relations and all remarks related to group process. The positive and negative statements the subjects made about their own parents formed the basis of the reduction in restraint measure.[2]

The experimenter also recorded verbatim 10 statements made during the discussion. These formed the basis of the deindividuation measure. They were selected according to the same criteria used by Festinger et al.[3] Five

[2] The percentage of agreement between this tabulation of the interaction in the four categories and the "true" tabulation based on a tape recording of the discussion was 91%. Two of the 14 sessions were run by Peter Buffum. The investigators appreciate his time and help.

[3] Thus, the content of each statement should be clear and distinct from other statements, the statement should be about one sentence in length, the statement should be grammatically coherent, as many persons as possible should contribute to the 10 selected statements, and the statements should be distributed as evenly as possible over time.

statements composed in advance by the experimenter were added to the list of 10 to form the basis of a test of general memory.

After the discussion, the experimenter read off to the group the statements that he had recorded and the five "standard" statements that had not been made in the discussion. Each subject was then asked to indicate on a form (a) whether or not he remembered the statement as having been made and, if so, (b) who had made it (name or number). After the forms were collected, a questionnaire was administered in order to measure the subjects' attraction to the group. Finally, the group was given a full explanation of the purposes and procedures of the experiment.

Operational Measures of the Variables

There are two kinds of memory errors measured by the test of recall: identification errors (i errors) and memory errors (m errors). An i error means that the subject correctly identified a statement as having been made, but could not attribute it to any particular person in his group or attributed it to the wrong person. An m error means that the statement had not actually been made, but the subject thought it had been made, or that the statement had been made, but the subject thought it had not. Inevitably, in most groups there were statements which were ambiguous or otherwise inadequate for the two tests of memory. The elimination of these was based on the same objective criteria employed by Festinger et al.[4] The elimination of statements meant, of course, that the calculation of identification and memory errors had to be corrected so that the base number of statements was the same across groups. The *corrected* measure, that is, I errors, was based on the number of statements recorded (10) divided by the number remaining after elimination. This quantity was then multiplied by the number of i errors made by each subject. Similarly, M errors equaled the number of m statements recorded (the 10 provided by the group members plus 5 standard statements added by the experimenter) divided by the number of m statements actually retained. This quantity was then multiplied by the number of m errors made by each subject.

Deindividuation was now defined as the average number of I errors minus M errors (I − M). The number of memory errors was subtracted from identification errors to control for general memory.

The measurement of lowered restraint for each individual group member was simply the number of negative (N) statements a subject made about his own parents minus the number of positive (P) statements he made about them. The average N − P in the group was assumed to reflect the reduction in restraint that occurred in that group. The use of the net frequency of negative expressions controls for the absolute number of evaluative sentiments about parents.

---

[4] In groups of five persons or more, a statement was eliminated if (a) all or all but one subject made errors on it, or (b) all but two made errors, and the subject who made the statement erred himself. In groups of four subjects, a statement was eliminated if all, or all but one, including the subject who made the statement, made errors on it.

The present study also included a measure of the subjects' feelings of apprehension prior to the discussion. On the basis of informal observations, it was felt that preexisting anxiety level was a variable which might affect the lowering of restraint. The measure of apprehension was a question asked just before the discussion: "On the following scale indicate with a check the position that best represents the degree of apprehension you feel about participating in this experiment." A 6-point scale ranging from "very apprehensive" to "no apprehension" was used.

Finally, the measure of attraction was based on the same postdiscussion question as Festinger et al. used: "Frankly, how much would you like to return for further discussions of similar topics with this same group?" A 6-point scale ranging from "definitely want to return" to "definitely do not want to return" was used.

RESULTS

The major theoretical question concerns the relationship between deindividuation and lowered restraint. To facilitate comparison of these results with the findings of the earlier study, both sets of results are presented in Table 1. In addition to the correlations based on all-male groups (as in the Fest-

TABLE 1 *Correlations between Deindividuation and Lowered Restraint and between Lowered Restraint and Group Attraction*

VARIABLE	FESTINGER ET AL. (1952) DATA ($n = 22$)	PRESENT (1968) DATA	
		Male ($n = 9$)	Mixed + female ($n = 5$)
I − M × N − P	.57**	.56[a]	.00
N − P × Attraction	.36*	.20	−.60

[a] A correlation of .58 is necessary for a t significant at the .10 level.
* $p \leq .12$.
** $p \leq .01$.

inger et al. study), the correlations based on groups including females (two all-female groups and three mixed groups) are presented. The earlier experiment gave reason to believe that all-female groups would show the same trends as all-male groups, although not as strongly. Since only two all-female groups could be run in the present study, however, all-male groups were compared with "not-all-male" groups.

As can be seen in Table 1, the correlation between deindividuation (I − M) and lowered restraint (N − P) is .56. This compares with a coefficient of .57 obtained by Festinger et al. The reliability of a correlation of .56 is estimated by a t transformation to be at about the .10 level of significance. Thus, it would appear that the original hypothesis predicting a positive relationship between deindividuation and lowered restraint tends to be supported, although at a lower level of confidence. It can also be seen in Table 1 that the correlation between lowered restraint and group attraction is .20. Although consistent in direction with the marginally significant coefficient of .36 obtained by Festinger et al., this coefficient cannot be considered significantly different from zero. Thus, the second hypothesis linking disinhibition with attraction was not reconfirmed.

TABLE 2 *Relationships among M Errors, I Errors, and Negative Minus Positive Statements (N − P)*

VARIABLES	FESTINGER ET AL. (1952) DATA (N = 22)	PRESENT (1968) DATA	
		Male (n = 9)	*Mixed (n = 5)*
I errors × M errors	.24	−.33	.31
I errors × N − P	.31	.55[a]	.47
M errors × N − P	−.39*	−.28	.45
I errors × N − P × M errors	.45*	.51	.39

[a] A correlation of .58 is necessary for a *t* significant at the .10 level.
*$p \leq .10$.

Consider separately the relations between the measure of restraint reduction (N − P) and the measures of the two kinds of memory errors. We would expect the I and N − P relationship to be positive, although, because of confounding of I errors with general memory ability, it should not be as high as the I − M and N − P relationship. However, as can be seen in Table 2, the correlation *is* about as high as the correlation involving I − M. In other words, the measure of the inability to identify who said what is apparently not affected by the uncontrolled general memory factor.

Perhaps a logically more defensible way of controlling for general memory error is to partial out of the I and N − P relationship the effects of M errors. As shown in Table 2, the partial correlation of I and N − P holding M errors constant is equal to .51. Thus, inability to identify who said what is substantially correlated with the reduction in restraint, even when the effects of general memory errors are partialed out.

The correlation between the average number of M errors and the average reduction in restraint was $r = -.28$, which was not significant. This compares with a correlation coefficient of −.39 obtained by Festinger et al. In the original study, a negative coefficient was interpreted to mean that the fewer the hostile sentiments, that is, the more restrained subjects were, the less distinctive were the statements recorded by the observer. Alternatively, the more the negative contributions, the better the subjects could recall what was said. When they expressed negative feelings, the more attentive and interested they became, and the better their memory. Although neither correlation was significant, the consistency in direction suggests that an increase in the expression of negative attitudes toward parents is accompanied by an increase in the inability to identify who said what, *in spite of* a general improvement in memory.

Is Deindividuation an Individual or Group Phenomenon?

A fundamental question is whether deindividuation can properly be regarded as an emergent group phenomenon in the sense that LeBon conceived it. That is, does deindividuation involve a reciprocal withdrawal of attention from each other? Or, is the $I - M$ and $N - P$ relationship strictly intraindividual and independent of the social environment? The Festinger et al. approach to this question was to examine the $I - M$ and $N - P$ relationship in individuals, irrespective of the particular discussion group in which they participated. If the deindividuation effect is reducible to an individual phenomenon, the positive correlation between $I - M$ and $N - P$ should obtain when the individual is used as the unit of analysis. If, on the other hand, the correlation within individuals is not significant, it would tend to support the view that the deindividuation-disinhibition effect is a group phenomenon. To investigate this important theoretical question, Festinger et al. grouped individual subjects according to the absolute level of their $N - P$ score. Three absolute levels of $N - P$ were established: greater than zero, zero, or less than zero. They found no significant differences in $I - M$ across these categories. In the present experiment the data were categorized in exactly the same way. Again, the differences in $I - M$ among the three categories were not significant. The overall correlation between the $I - M$ and $N - P$ scores based on 72 individuals in the sample was only .21, not significantly different from zero. Although this coefficient was not significantly lower than that based on groups, the strong suggestion is that deindividuation is more likely to be a phenomenon that occurs among individuals than within individuals.

Group Composition

Festinger et al. found that in female groups, the ability to identify who said what was considerably poorer than it was in male groups, thus precluding any sizable correlation between deindividuation and restraint reduction. The present data show no difference in the level of identification or memory errors between the male and the not-all-male groups. However, among these latter five groups, a significant positive correlation was found (.86) between the prediscussion average group level of apprehension and the average number of I − M errors. On the other hand, the correlation between apprehension and I − M for the male groups was zero (.04). In the not-all-male groups, a zero coefficient representing the deindividuation-disinhibition relation was found, in contrast to the .56 in the all-male groups. It is not clear why apprehension should be associated with deindividuation in groups composed of all females and mixed sexes, while it is not associated at all in all-male groups. Perhaps it is the relatively greater uncertainty and fear about the kinds of opinions and feelings that were expected to be expressed by female and mixed groups. Perhaps it was easier for these groups to reduce such anxiety by not paying attention to who was speaking. In any event, the authors are led to suppose that when identification errors are affected by anxiety concerning the discussions, they do not reflect deindividuation or that anxiety prevents deindividuation from reducing restraint. The full implications of this view are discussed below.

DISCUSSION AND CONCLUSIONS

The results clearly confirm the Festinger et al. finding on the association between deindividuation and the reduction in restraint. The results also show that this effect is primarily a group phenomenon. However, the predicted significant association between the degree of disinhibition and attraction to the group was not observed in the present experiment.

In any correlational study the question arises as to the causal direction of the obtained relationship. The present authors (and Festinger et al.) have argued that it is the state of deindividuation that permits the group members to overcome their inhibitions against the expression of hostile sentiments and feelings toward their parents. Could the causal relation be the other way around? That is, could a relatively large production of hostile material affect negatively the ability to identify the source of such sentiments? There is a plausible hypothesis that could account indirectly for such an effect of disinhibition: abundant aggressive content makes people pay close attention and remember such material better. The more people pay attention to and remember the content of what was said, the less well they can remember who said it. The negative correlation between I errors and M errors (−.33) is consistent with this interpretation, but the coefficient failed to approach statistical significance. Nevertheless, the present authors strongly suspect that when the effect of "danger" on group behavior through time is considered, there are several circular causal processes underlying the correlation between deindividuation and the reduction of restraint. The following theoretical propositions[5] summarize some observations in this regard.

1. Individuals in groups including crowds often have a need to overcome restraints against the expression of hostile feelings or the taking of aggressive actions. In the present groups, this need was created by the discussion task that was set for the group.

2. The common need to overcome restraint, or the common danger entailed in overcoming restraint, tends to strengthen emotional bonds of the members. This feeling of "we-ness" allows group members to express hostile feelings and take aggressive actions.

3. However, hostile expressions and actions increase both inner and outer threats. Thus, individuals who openly state negative sentiments may experience guilt inasmuch as hostility violates their conscience. Moreover, people who express hostility or undertake violent actions toward others may become suspicious and distrustful of each other. They have "exposed" themselves, and may even be threatened by the aggressive tendencies they have witnessed in their colleagues. Following aggression, in other words, they may begin to suffer "aggression anxiety" (Berkowitz, 1958). Thus, aggressive acts and hostile expressions place group members in a conflict.

4. Considering that strong emotional bonds allow the group to act out and express hostility in the first place, one would predict that developing an even stronger feeling of closeness and warmness would allow the conflict to be resolved. However, there is probably a limit to the feeling of we-ness that can be induced by the perception of common danger. There is an additional consideration already alluded to. Expressions and acts of hostility by group members result in greater knowledge about each other. Exposure of the person involves the danger of attack and rejection. Even if stronger emotional ties were possible, the greater "cognitive" ties would make matters worse.

5. Given a conflict that is maintained if not strengthened by increasing familiarization, group members reach the point where they seek to reduce the input of knowledge about each other, while retaining emotional support. This circumstance, in essence, is the basis of deindividuation. In the present and the Festinger et al. studies, to resolve the conflict over the expression of hostile feelings, the subjects ceased paying attention to each other. When they have achieved a critical level of "submergence" in the group, they are able to "break" the conflict.

It should be emphasized that there is no explanation in the above for

---

[5] This set of propositions is part of a more detailed theoretical analysis of collective and group behavior in dangerous situations being prepared for publication by Albert Pepitone.

why any particular group needs and obtains deindividuation more than any other.

There are several points in the "process" theory relevant to group attraction. For one thing, it was proposed that a group facing a common danger will show an increase in cohesiveness. Evidence for this proposition already exists (Pepitone & Kleiner, 1957). Second, it was proposed that cohesiveness affects the volume of expressed hostility. Experimental evidence does indeed show that experimentally manipulated cohesiveness enables groups to express hostile fellings (Pepitone & Reichling, 1955). However, it was also proposed that the expression of hostility arouses guilt and aggression anxiety, which in turn are exacerbated by the increased knowledge about each other. It is not surprising, therefore, that in both the Festinger et al. and present experiments, the correlation between disinhibition and attraction, although positive, was of marginal significance. On the other hand, since theoretically the state of deindividuation should resolve the conflict based on the fear generated by increased personal knowledge of each other, group members should be satisfied with such a state. In the present experiment, the correlation between deindividuation and the attractiveness of the group was consistent with this derivation ($r = .62$, $p < .10$).

In the light of the foregoing theoretical propositions, what may be concluded from the behavior of the not-all-male groups? Despite the small number of groups, the striking contrast in the correlation patterns leads us to some speculations. The first point to take note of is that the deindividuation-disinhibition effect simply did not occur. The correlation between $I - M$ and $N - P$ was literally zero. One possible explanation for the failure is that in all-female and mixed groups, the $I - M$ measure reflects not deindividuation, but general level of anxiety. Thus, we found a highly positive correlation ($r = .86$, $p < .10$) between average level of prediscussion apprehension and $I - M$. In other words, in groups including females, level of anxiety rather than deindividuation determines the number of identification errors. Accordingly, the deindividuation effect could not occur. The negative correlation of $-.60$ between $N - P$ and attraction to the group is thus not surprising, since a positive correlation is only predictable when $N - P$ is controlled by deindividuation. If, analytically, we could eliminate the effect of prediscussion apprehension, we should expect the deindividuation-disinhibition effect to appear. A partial correlation between $I - M$ and $N - P$, with average apprehension level held constant, showed this to be the case (.72). The Festinger et al. reference to the fact that females produced an inordinate number of identification errors may thus imply that there was a higher level of anxiety in their female subjects. It may be concluded that if general apprehension does not interfere with the attainment of deindividuation, the deindividuation-disinhibition phenomenon is quite general.

References

Berkowitz, L. The expression and reduction of hostility. *Psychological Bulletin,* 1958, *55,* 257–283.

Festinger, L., Pepitone, A., & Newcomb, T. Some consequences of de-individuation in a group. *Journal of Abnormal and Social Psychology,* 1952, *47,* 382–389.

Freud, S. *Group psychology as the analysis of the ego.* London: Hogarth Press, 1910.

LeBon, G. *The crowd.* London: Ernest Benn, 1896.

Pepitone, A., & Kleiner, R. The effects of threat and frustration on group cohesiveness. *Journal of Abnormal and Social Psychology,* 1957, *54,* 192–199.

Pepitone, A., & Reichling, G. Group cohesiveness and the expression of aggression. *Human Relations,* 1955, *8,* 327–339.

Singer, J., Brush, C., & Lublin, S. Some aspects of deindividuation: Identification and conformity. *Journal of Experimental Social Psychology,* 1965, *1,* 356–378.

Zimbardo, P. The human choice: Individuation, reason and order, vs. deindividuation, impulse, and chaos. *Nebraska Symposium on Motivation,* 1969, *17,* 237–307.

Author Index

Subject Index

CORRELATION OF CHAPTERS IN OTHER TEXTS ON SOCIAL PSYCHOLOGY WITH SPECIFIC READINGS IN THIS BOOK

CHAPTERS IN LISTED TEXTS	FREEDMAN, CARLSMITH & SEARS (12 CHAPTERS)	HOLLANDER (15 CHAPTERS)	COLLINS (10 CHAPTERS)
	(READINGS NUMBERS IN THIS BOOK)		
1	6.1, 4.6	——	2.4, 3.2, 5.1, 4.4
2	4.2, 5.5	——	4.5, 6.3
3	4.3, 4.4, 4.5, 5.6	——	4.1, 5.5
4	2.4, 5.2	——	3.1, 3.3
5	6.3	2.3, 2.4, 4.1, 5.4, 6.2	——
6	6.4	3.1, 3.2, 3.3	5.3, 6.4
7	6.2	4.2, 4.3, 4.4, 4.5, 5.3	——
8	——	2.4	——
9	3.1, 3.2, 3.3	——	2.1, 5.2
10	——	5.2	5.6
11	4.4, 5.1, 5.3, 5.4	2.1, 2.2	——
12	Part 1	6.4	——
13	——	5.5, 5.6, 6.1	——
14	——	5.1, 6.3	——

Freedman, J. L., Carlsmith, J. M., & Sears, D. O. *Social psychology*. Englewood Cliffs, N.J.: Prentice-Hall, 1970.

Hollander, Edwin P. *Principles and methods of social psychology*. 2d ed. New York: Oxford University Press, 1971.

Collins, B. *Social psychology*. Reading, Mass.: Addison-Wesley, 1970.

CHAPTERS	KAUFMANN (15 CHAPTERS)	ELMS (10 CHAPTERS)	WRIGHTSMAN (20 CHAPTERS)
1	—	—	—
2	1.2	—	—
3	2.3	5.2	4.4, 5.3, 5.4
4	2.2	5.1, 6.3	4.1
5	2.1, 2.2, 2.3, 2.4	3.1, 3.2, 3.3	—
6	2.1, 2.2	—	2.4, 5.2
7	3.1, 3.2	2.2, 4.4, 5.3, 5.4	2.1, 2.2
8	3.1, 3.2, 3.3	4.6, 6.1	—
9	4.1, 4.2, 4.3, 4.4	5.6	5.5
10	4.6	—	3.1, 3.2, 3.3
11	4.3, 4.5	—	5.6
12	2.1, 2.2, 5.2, 5.5	—	6.2
13	5.1, 5.2, 5.3, 5.4, 5.6	—	5.1
14	6.1, 6.2, 6.3, 6.4	—	4.3, 4.5, 6.1, 6.4
15	6.1, 6.2, 6.3, 6.4	—	4.2
16	—	—	—
17	—	—	6.3
18	—	—	—
19	—	—	2.3
20	—	—	—

Kaufmann, H. *Social psychology: The study of human interaction.* New York: Holt, Rinehart and Winston, 1973.

Elms, A. C. *Social psychology and social relevance.* Boston: Little, Brown, 1972.

Wrightsman, L. S. *Social psychology in the seventies.* Monterey, Calif.: Brooks/Cole, 1972.